THE PATH OF THE 50TH

Lieut.-Colonel Derek Seagrim, V.C.
Green Howards

C.S.M. S. E. Hollis, V.C.
Green Howards

Pte. Adam Wakenshaw, V.C.
Durham Light Infantry

Pte. Eric Anderson, V.C.
East Yorkshire Regiment

THE PATH OF THE 50TH

THE STORY OF THE 50TH (NORTHUMBRIAN) DIVISION
IN THE SECOND WORLD WAR

1939-1945

BY

MAJOR EWART W. CLAY, M.B.E.

The Naval & Military Press Ltd

Published by

The Naval & Military Press Ltd
Unit 5 Riverside, Brambleside
Bellbrook Industrial Estate
Uckfield, East Sussex
TN22 1QQ England

Tel: +44 (0)1825 749494

www.naval-military-press.com
www.nmarchive.com

In reprinting in facsimile from the original, any imperfections are inevitably reproduced and the quality may fall short of modern type and cartographic standards.

CONTENTS

	Page
FOREWORD	xiii
INTRODUCTION	1

PART ONE

CHAPTER I 5
Territorial Background—Training at Home—France—Battle of Arras and the First Round with Rommel.

CHAPTER II 22
The Withdrawal to the Coast—Perimeter Defence—The Last Division to leave Dunkirk.

CHAPTER III 27
Lessons of the Campaign and some Reflections on Morale—50th Division mans the Dorset Coast—The Desert looms ahead.

APPENDIX TO PART ONE 32
Order of Battle as on 10th May, 1940.

PART TWO

CHAPTER IV 39
Orders for Overseas—To Egypt via the Cape—The Division split up, then reunited in Cyprus—Another Separation—Into Iraq—50th Division enters the Desert.

CHAPTER V 46
The Desert—Adventures of 150th Brigade—In the Line—Operation "Full-size"—Last Preparations before the Storm, and some Misgivings.

CHAPTER VI 56
The Afrika Korps strikes—The Cauldron—Tragedy of 150th Brigade.

CHAPTER VII 63
The Battle lost—50th Division breaks out—Withdrawal to the Frontier—Rearguard Action to Matruh, and another Break-out—The Struggle on Ruweisat Ridge—The Germans stopped.

APPENDIX TO PART TWO . . . 81
Order of Battle as in June, 1941.

CONTENTS

PART THREE

Page

CHAPTER VIII 85
  Reorganizing in the Delta—Back to the Ruweisat Area—Adventures of 69th Brigade—50th Division on Guard in the Delta.

CHAPTER IX 92
  151st Brigade in the New Zealand "Box"—50th Division in the Line again—Preparations for the Battle of El Alamein—The Battle—151st Brigade in "Supercharge"—Break-through and Pursuit.

CHAPTER X 109
  50th Division's Fate in the Balance—A Period of Training—Forward to Mareth.

CHAPTER XI 124
  A Brief Rest, and a sudden Call to Action—The Battle of the Wadi Akarit—Two V.Cs.

APPENDIX TO PART THREE . 131
  Order of Battle as in October, 1942.

PART FOUR

CHAPTER XII 137
  Closing Stages in Tunisia—The 2,000-mile Trek back to Egypt.

CHAPTER XIII 141
  Planning for the Invasion—151st Brigade selected to Assault—Training at Kabrit and a Rehearsal at Akaba—Embarkation at Suez.

CHAPTER XIV 148
  The Target in Sicily, and the Plan—Order of Battle of 50th Division—The Assault goes in—Landings in the wrong place—Into the Fortress of Europe.

CHAPTER XV 164
  The Thrust North—69th Brigade's struggle to reach Lentini—First stage of the Battle of Primosole Bridge—Over the River Simeto, and 168th Brigade's first Battle.

CHAPTER XVI 202
  Static Warfare at Primosole Bridge—The Enemy Withdraws—An Exacting Pursuit and a Seaborne Landing—Capture of Messina and the end of the Campaign.

CHAPTER XVII 217
  Out of Action—The Balance Sheet—Homeward Bound.

APPENDIX TO PART FOUR . 222
  Order of Battle as in July, 1943.

CONTENTS

PART FIVE

Page

CHAPTER XVIII 227
A quiet Homecoming—50th Division cast for a Leading Role in the Invasion of Normandy—A Bustle of Training—Planning in London—The Enemy's Defensive Layout—Allied Military, Naval and Air Plans, and 50th Division's part in them—Composition of the Division for the Assault.

CHAPTER XIX 237
D Day—First glimpses of Normandy—The Battles of 69th and 231st Brigades—Six miles inland—The capture of Port-en-Bessin.

CHAPTER XX 250
The Enemy's Problem—50th Division's next task—D.L.I. and Dorsets in an Armoured Thrust—The First Battle for Villers Bocage.

CHAPTER XXI 260
Static Battles in the Bocage—Towards Hottot—Fall of the Village—Casualties to the end of July.

CHAPTER XXII 266
On the threshold of the Break-through—Fall of Villers Bocage—Fighting advance to Conde—The trap closed, and the destruction of an Army—On to Antwerp, and adventures on the way.

CHAPTER XXIII 285
50th Division's last Battles in Europe—60th Brigade Force the Albert Canal—151st Brigade's bitter struggle at Gheel—The operation that culminated at Arnhem—First Infantry into Holland—Endurance at Nijmegen—"The Island"—Home.

APPENDIX I TO PART FIVE 307
Order of Battle and list of Commanders and Staff, 22nd May, 1944.

APPENDIX II TO PART FIVE 313
Casualties in France, Belgium and Holland, 1944.

EPILOGUE 315

INDEX 317

ILLUSTRATIONS

Facing page

Four Winners of the Victoria Cross	*Frontispiece*
50th Division arrives in France	8
The scene as the last Troops embarked at Dunkirk	25
50th Division Concert Party	46
Troops of 151st Brigade reach the Frontier—and safety	72
A picture taken during "Supercharge"	102
Men of the D.L.I. "reconstruct" their human pyramid technique in the Mareth anti-tank ditch	117
Landing craft off shore near Avola	159
Troops with a suspect civilian in a beautiful Sicilian grove	162
Troops storm ashore near La Riviere	239
"A murderous fire was directed upon the craft and the troops fighting their way ashore . . ."	242
A typical scene in the Normandy bocage	252

MAPS

	Page
MAP SHOWING APPROXIMATE GERMAN ADVANCE BY THE 21ST OF MAY, 1940	15
ARRAS OPERATIONS	21
EL GAZALA	to face 80
BATTLE OF ALAMEIN	107
MARETH	to face 122
AKARIT	129
NORTH AFRICA	to face 140
SICILY	215
THE BEACH-HEAD	to face 248
VILLERS-BOCAGE	to face 264
CONDE	to face 284
GHEEL	288
ARNHEM—NIJMEGEN	to face 306
NORTH-WEST EUROPE	to face 306

FOREWORD

As an old friend of the 50th Division, I am not only glad but honoured to write a Foreword to this History of a great fighting formation.

My first introduction to them was at the beginning of the war in France, where they were amongst the last to leave the beaches of Dunkirk.

In the late summer of 1942 they again came under my command, this time in the Western Desert, when, as one of the divisions of the Eighth Army, they took an active part in that great campaign which ended in the Battle of Tunis and the surrender of a quarter of a million enemy soldiers.

Two months after the freeing of the North African shores the Division was amongst the first in the assault landing on the island of Sicily.

At the conclusion of the short but successful campaign this famous Division, which had seen as much active service as any in the British Army, formed part of a select group of divisions which was chosen to proceed to England to train for the coming invasion in the West.

In October, 1943, they left the Mediterranean and passed out of my command, to my loss and the regret of all their friends in the Eighth Army. But they went to write another glorious page in the history of the British Army and to add fresh lustre to their already great name.

This book will tell the reader of fine deeds performed by grand men under great leaders, and it is unique because each of the five divisional commanders has sketched the basis of the account of the period of his command.

I wish this record of a famous fighting division every success.

Alexander of Tunis.
F.M.

OTTAWA, CANADA.
25th September, 1947.

INTRODUCTION

This book about the 50th (Northumbrian) Division is the work of many hands. The real authors are the thousands of ordinary soldiers who served in its ranks during the Second World War. They wrote it on the battlefields of the Near East and of Europe.

Their deeds have now been translated into words by several former members of the Division. The broad theme of the book was outlined by the Divisional Commanders concerned; it was developed by scores of men who served under them, from senior staff officers to private soldiers. Notebooks, old maps, letters home, war diaries and personal diaries have gone to its making. One expert has written one section, another has drafted a second. Here an intelligence officer has described an action; there a platoon runner has given his version of an attack.

Thanks are due to all these contributors, and they are offered now. But no attempt is made to thank individuals by name; for to thank in this way all who have helped would be well-nigh impossible, and to thank a selected few would be invidious.

It should be said that this book has no literary aspirations. It is intended to be a plain and accurate account of the war record of the 50th Division. It is written primarily for the members of the Division; for their relatives; for the North Country from which it springs; and for members of the public who are interested in a formation which was described by a famous general in 1944 as "the most experienced battle-fighting division in the British Army."

Even so, the book falls short of what is desired. There are pages missing from the story, particularly in the early sections. If the book runs to a second edition it may be possible to close the gaps.

E. W. C.

PANNAL (YORKS) *and*
KING'S LANGLEY (HERTS).
 28th January, 1947.

PART ONE

CHAPTER I

Territorial Background—Training at Home—France—Battle of Arras and the First Round with Rommel

1939 TO MAY, 1940

Between the wars the 50th (Northumbrian) Division, a Territorial formation drawing its men from Northumberland, Durham and Yorkshire, had remained practically at full strength.

And when, at a late hour, in 1938, Britain turned to try to put her military forces in order, the 50th Division required less attention than many other comparable formations.

The Territorial infantry units included East Yorkshires (drawn mainly from Hull and the East Riding), Green Howards (North Yorkshire and the Yorkshire coast) and Durham Light Infantry (three battalions all from that county); the artillery regiments were drawn in the main from Tynecastle, and the R.A.S.C. from Hull.

From Northumberland came the 4th Royal Northumberland Fusiliers (reconnaissance unit).[1]

These territorial "roots" gave point to the new divisional badge (evolved in 1939 as a result of a proposal from Major Freeman Attwood, who was G.S.O.2 at Divisional Headquarters). The two superimposed T's, red on a black background, stood for Tyne and Tees. It was then noticed that when the badge was looked at sideways the two T's formed an H; so that the three main rivers which flowed through the Northumbrian Division's area—Tyne, Tees and Humber —were thus represented in the sign.

This, then, was the origin of one of the most famous signs in the British Army—the "TT sign"—which was to mark the path of the 50th through nearly a score of countries and through most of the places where there was hard fighting in the years ahead.

Towards the end of 1938 it had been decided that the 50th Division was to become one of the new motorized formations, with its own transport for dismounted personnel so that it should be highly mobile and capable of acting in close support to armoured forces.

---

[1] Units and formations in the Division in the early part of 1940 are shown in Appendix I to Part I. They are substantially the same as at the outbreak of war, except for the 25th Infantry Brigade, added to the Division in the spring of 1940.

In order that the Division should be a "handy" size, it was decided that it should contain only two infantry brigades, two regiments of artillery, two field companies and two field ambulances. On the other hand, the Division was to have two mechanical transport companies, each of three sections, and each company was to transport all the dismounted personnel of an infantry brigade.

For reconnaissance there was a motor-cycle battalion, which included a platoon of eleven scout cars.

At the end of February, 1939, Major-General Sir G. le Q. Martel was sent to take over the Division from Major-General Herbert, who had finished his tenure of appointment. The Division now had to apply itself to its new role. Discussions and tactical exercises without troops were held to study movement problems.

The usual summer camps were followed by the event they were designed to meet.

Tension mounted during the summer; the 3rd of September brought the formal declaration of war, and in October the 50th Division moved to the Cotswold country in Oxfordshire to complete training and mobilization.

Technique for movement and acting in co-operation with armoured forces was studied and practised in every detail. The Division had visions of forming part of a great mechanized striking force in France, driving deep into the enemy positions, cutting his communications and carrying out the type of mobile armoured warfare which many of those in the Division had cherished for a long time.

The training was handicapped by lack of equipment. To a large extent this was inevitable, but it was increased by the peace-time system of indenting on which the Ordnance insisted and which caused great difficulty and delay. Many units received large issues of equipment which were delivered at their billets after they had left for France, which caused further trouble and correspondence later.

In spite of these difficulties the Division had become a happy and united family before they left for France. Before the end of 1939 they were well trained and ready for war.

His Majesty The King inspected the Division in January, 1940. A picturesque feature of this royal *Ave atque Vale* was staged at Broadway, in Worcestershire. Mine host of "The Lygon Arms" said that according to local tradition they had never had a King of England there since Charles I, and he begged the Division to arrange if possible for King George VI to pass through the village.

It seemed fitting that three hundred years later, at another crisis in English history, the Monarch should appear again in this world-renowned spot, and so it happened that the King and Queen delighted everybody by walking down the broad village street between lines of khaki-clad soldiers and cheering villagers, and under the immemorial Cotswold slopes.

The 50th Division marched out to war a few days later. The broad accents of Yorkshire and Northumberland and the strange oaths of Durham had embedded themselves firmly in the affections of their Southern hosts, and the Northerners carried with them memories of a warm-hearted countryside "at peace under an English heaven" to take them through years of fighting under alien skies. The Division sent out a *pour prendre congé* card to their many befrienders:

> "To say farewell, and to thank you for all your kindness and assistance to the 50th (Northumbrian) Division during their stay in the Cotswold country, October, 1939, to January, 1940."

They got a "rocket" afterwards for a breach of security. Apparently it was thought that the dull-witted rustics of this part would not otherwise have noticed that the Division had departed.

The Division left for France on the 19th of January. It was intensely cold in the Cotswolds, and great difficulty was experienced over the frozen roads and also with many of the new vehicles which had been received only a few days before the departure. The disembarkation was at Cherbourg, and the Division then moved to the Le Mans area, with Divisional Headquarters at Evron. On the 22nd of January the G.O.C. went ahead and reported to Headquarters, II Corps, at Phalempin (near Lens). The plan was for the Division to work on the defences which were being constructed along the frontier, but there was difficulty over arranging the billeting areas.

The advance parties from the Division arrived at Lens on the 27th of January, but the main move could not take place, as the roads were closed owing to the alternate frost and thaw conditions.

On the 4th of February Divisional Headquarters opened at Billy Montigny, three miles south-east of Lens. The Division was to work in the II Corps reserve line, known as "The Fromelles Switch," but nothing could be done until they arrived. On the 14th of February orders were received that the 50th Division was to go to a training area near Amiens instead of working on the defences, and the advance party left Billy Montigny to plan accommodation in the Amiens area. On the 19th, Divisional Headquarters was established at Que-vau-Villiers, fifteen miles south-west of Amiens. During the following week the thaw restrictions were lifted and the whole Division was able at last to assemble and start intensive training.

A very useful month was spent in the Amiens area, and then orders were received that the Division was to move up to the area round Loos (two miles west of Lille) in G.H.Q. reserve, and to work on the II Corps reserve line. Divisional Headquarters opened at Loos on the 28th of March. The sector of the line which the Division was to construct ran from Loos south-east for eight miles through Seclin to Wavrin. The 150th Infantry Brigade was working on the north half and the 151st on the south. Weapon training was continued in detachments on ranges near the coast.

The order of battle of the Division at this period and before operations had started is given in the Appendix on page 32. It is shown with the inclusion of the 25th Infantry Brigade, who joined the Division on the 11th of May. Brigadier Kreyer had unfortunately fallen sick, and this was a great loss to the Division, but his brigade was taken over by Brigadier Haydon, who proved to be a tower of strength.

On Divisional Headquarters, Colonel Sir Donald Banks as A.A. and Q.M.G. had steered the Division through all its troubles with remarkable success. Although he had great experience in the First World War as a regimental commander, the administrative side was new to him, and it was remarkable how quickly he grasped all the intricacies. The Division owed much to him. On the 26th April he was taken to work in a higher sphere at G.H.Q., and Lieutenant-Colonel Benoy replaced him. On the General Staff side Major Freeman Attwood, who had been the senior general staff officer in peace time and had been largely responsible for the training, was taken to be G.S.O.1 of a division at home. Colonel M. Everett became G.S.O.1, 50th Division, and did valuable work.

Mention must be made of the work of the padres. The North Countryman in his quiet way is often deeply religious, and the G.O.C. had taken endless trouble to help his senior chaplain, the Reverend R. T. Newcombe, in collecting a team of padres who would understand these men. The results were remarkable.

The senior chaplain started a system of hostels, and with the help of the A.A. and Q.M.G. the idea spread throughout the Division. Whenever a unit reached the village in which they would be billeted the best house was nearly always chosen as the hostel. This was the Padre's House. The men could come in and write their letters, etc. No alcoholic drink was sold, and a room at the top of the house was set aside as a chapel. It was always spotlessly clean, with a cross on a table. The North Countrymen would come in, and many of them would go quietly to "the chapel" to talk to the Padre or to pray. Each hostel had its own Crusader Shield to mark the house. With such a backing it is no wonder that the Division was able with ease to meet the scourge of disease and drink that was rampant in France at that time.

British Official Photograph] [*Crown Copyright Reserved*

50th Division arrives in France. Sergt. Gregson (4th Green Howards) calls the roll on disembarkation.

The construction of the defences was a very congenial task for a North Country division. The work consisted mainly of the excavation of a wide and deep anti-tank obstacle and of the construction of concrete pill-boxes at intervals along the line. If the Division asked for mechanical excavators the reply came that they were making the anti-tank ditch much faster without these machines than any other division could complete such work even with the excavators. The North Country miners had not used picks and shovels for a year, and they revelled in stripping to the waist and wiping the eye of all competitors in this excavation work. The field companies were equally successful in constructing the concrete pill-boxes. The defences were soon completed.

While the B.E.F. was preparing defences and holding a sector in front of Lille, plans were being made for action in the event of the Germans advancing. A scheme, known as "Plan 'D,' " was adopted. The Allies were to advance sixty miles into Belgium and hold the line of the River Dyle. The Belgians were reported to have prepared defences in this line. The northern portion could be flooded, and the line of the Dyle in front of Brussels provided a strong defensive position, but farther south the position which would be held by the First French Army seemed weak from a defensive point of view.

The plan for the advance of the B.E.F. from their area round Lille to the Dyle position beyond Brussels was prepared in great detail. The I Corps was to move on the right and the II Corps on the left. Traffic control was to be highly organized on the routes, and the 4th Royal Northumberland Fusiliers was to be employed for this purpose while the 50th Division remained in G.H.Q. reserve. The only armoured force that was yet available was one brigade of heavy infantry tanks. The code word "Birch" was to be used to put the Division under six hours' notice for action under Plan "D."

On the 11th of April the code word was received. Brigadier Massy, C.R.A., 50th Division, had been selected to control the traffic on the forward routes, and he went off to carry out his duty with the 4th Royal Northumberland Fusiliers and also with the 9th Durham Light Infantry, whose special task was control of refugees. This turned out, however, to be a false alarm; no action was taken and the move into Belgium was cancelled. Air-raid sirens sounded in Lille for the first time on the 27th of April, but no bombing occurred.

On the 9th of May the 50th Division held a boxing championship which included both a team and an individual championship. The Signals won the team trophy. When presenting the prizes at the end of the tournament at about 11 p.m. on the 9th of May, the G.O.C. stressed the value of boxing as training for war. He explained that in boxing you have to learn to keep your wits when all sorts of dreadful things are happening to you, and this is not unlike the first experience of a soldier in battle. If a soldier has learned to keep his head under those conditions in the ring it is easier for him to keep control of his wits when he first comes under heavy fire on the battlefield. The G.O.C. expressed his pleasure at the fine fighting spirit that had been shown, and said that he was sure that we would soon be tested on the battlefield against the enemy. He had no idea, of course, that the operations would be launched in the next few hours, but when this happened the men were convinced that the G.O.C. had known that the hour for the battle was at hand.

On the 10th of May at 6.30 a.m. the code word "Birch" was again received, and this time it was obviously no false alarm, for news was received of the German invasion of Holland and Belgium. Brigadier Massy went forward with the 4th Royal Northumberland Fusiliers to control the forward movement, and they did splendid work. The I and II Corps occupied a defensive position on the Dyle, with the First French Army on their right and the Belgian Army on their left. The 50th Division remained in G.H.Q. reserve.

During the next few days the Germans made alarming progress and crossed the Albert Canal in strength. Our small air forces carried out successful attacks against the enemy at bridges and defiles, but their numbers were becoming very depleted.

The B.E.F. could have held their positions with ease, but the situation on the front of the First French Army was becoming very serious, and the Germans were breaking through farther south.

On the 16th of May Lord Gort received orders for a withdrawal. On that same day the 50th Division was sent to take up a defensive position on the River Dendre behind Brussels. The position extended from Ath on the right to Ninove on the left. All three brigades were in the line, the 150th on the right, the 151st in the centre and the 25th on the left. 50th Division Headquarters took over from the 5th Division at Everbecq. The tail of the Division came into position on the morning of the 17th, and a little later news was received at Divisional Headquarters about the withdrawal of the B.E.F. The 50th Division was to come under the II Corps and to go back to the line of the River Escaut with the right at Pecq and a front extending for five miles farther north. The 25th Brigade was to remain at Ninove, and ceased to be under the orders of the 50th Division.

The withdrawal began at dawn, and the infantry had to march, as the troop-carrying companies were in use to bring back troops from the forward divisions. The move was completed during the night of the 18th. Divisional Headquarters was at Herceaux. On both the

Dendre and Escaut lines the divisional engineers had prepared all bridges for demolition, and handed them over in that state to the rearguards of the I and II Corps.

On the morning of the 19th information was received that the southern flank of the B.E.F. was endangered by the penetration of the German forces through the French lines. The 50th Division was to move down and hold the line of the canal from Raches to Bethune, and come under G.H.Q. control. The 25th Brigade was to revert to the 50th Division. Owing to the length of front to be held, all three brigades would have to be in line. The necessary orders were issued, but a new instruction was then received as to the portion of the line to be held from right to left by the 150th, 25th and 151st Brigades. Advance Divisional Headquarters opened at Loos at 1600 hrs. That night information was received at Divisional Headquarters that the position on the south flank had changed and that only one brigade would remain on the canal line and that the Division was to move to Arras for special operations. At first the 151st Brigade was detailed to remain on the canal, but owing to the position of the available troop-carrying companies this was changed and the 25th Brigade, under command of the Division again, was left there.

By this time the enemy had penetrated as far as Amiens with his armoured and mechanized forces. Our communications were still working through Abbeville, but it was almost certain that the enemy would penetrate through to the coast in the next few days. Our only armoured division had landed in a half-mobilized condition at Havre and was south of the Seine. The chance of this division reaching the B.E.F. as a reinforcement was very small. There was a great danger of the British, French and Belgian forces which were round or north of Arras being entirely cut off.

The Commander-in-Chief considered three possible plans for these forces, which included the whole of the B.E.F. except the 51st Division on the Saar front. First, a counter-attack southwards from Arras, combined with a northward attack from the Somme, might have closed this corridor and rendered the enemy's position very difficult. It might have been possible to stabilize the position along the frontier defences. Unfortunately, all the information that was available pointed to the unlikelihood of the French Ninth Army south of the Somme being able to concentrate sufficient force to carry out this counter-attack. Nor had the French and British forces in the north any substantial resources for such operations.

An alternative was to fall back along the whole front to the line of the Somme. This would have enabled us to re-establish our communications behind a firm front. It seemed unlikely, however, that such an operation could have been carried out successfully at this stage.

A third possibility was for the B.E.F. to concentrate round the Channel ports, holding a perimeter defence along the canals and rivers while the troops were withdrawn by sea. This last alternative would reduce the forces available for the defence of France, and a great quantity of equipment would have to be abandoned.

The most serious threat to the B.E.F. lay on the southern flank. A number of troops had been collected together round Arras under Major-General Petre, and the force was known as "Petre Force." Arras was a vital road junction and was becoming a bastion for the defence of the southern flank. Petre Force was, however, very weak, and it was for this reason that plans had been made to send the 50th Division to that area.

On the evening of the 19th of May the Commander-in-Chief, Lord Gort, sent for General Martel and informed him that a portion of his Division at any rate was to go south to Arras to deliver a counter-attack against this corridor, and that the 1st Army Tank Brigade would also be sent there and come under his orders. A little later it was decided that the 5th Division also would be sent there, and the G.O.C. 5th Division, Major-General Franklyn, who was the senior, took charge of the operations as a whole. The force became known as "Frankforce." Most of the account of the Battle of Arras which follows is taken from reports made at the time.

General Martel went to Arras at dawn on the 20th of May to ascertain the situation, and the leading infantry brigade group of the 50th Division (150th Brigade) followed and reached Vimy, just north of Arras, at midday. Much valuable information was obtained from the 12th Lancers, who had established posts along this front and did splendid work during all this difficult time.

Arras was being held by a battalion of Welsh Guards and a few odd units. They were, however, very thin on the ground and becoming exhausted; they were also very short of anti-tank guns. There was every indication that the enemy would soon deliver a heavy attack.

General Martel therefore at once sent one battalion from the 150th Infantry Brigade, one anti-tank battery and one field company, R.E., to help in the defence of Arras.

The French were holding positions on a line running east of Arras and then northwards to join up with the B.E.F. On the immediate east of Arras the French 1st Light Mechanized Division were in position along the River Scarpe. They had some seventy Somoa tanks (20-tonners), but their infantry were very weak and exhausted.

Major-General Franklyn arrived at Vimy on the afternoon of the

20th of May. He decided that the remainder of the 150th Infantry Brigade group and his own leading brigade (13th Infantry Brigade) should relieve the French 1st Division Leger Mechanisé that night, and this was duly carried out.

The position was now fairly secure. Arras had been reinforced and the two infantry brigade groups which were relieving the 1st Division Leger Mechanisé would hold the River Scarpe, east of Arras, without much difficulty. Moreover, this relief would allow the 1st Division Leger Mechanisé to co-operate with the offensive operations. They were tired troops, but they still had those seventy tanks with thick armour. At any rate, there was now a reasonably secure base or pivot from which the attack could be launched. A conference was held late that night, but no detailed plan for the offensive operations could be made, for no further troops had yet arrived. Moreover, the tactical situation might well change before this happened.

The 151st Brigade group, commanded by Brigadier Churchill, and some divisional troops of the 50th Division, and also the 1st Army Tank Brigade, arrived during the early hours of the morning of the 21st of May after a very tiring journey. These troops had had very little rest for several days. General Martel issued strict orders that all were to rest at once on arrival and obtain as much sleep as possible. No plans were to be discussed about impending operations, as that might easily result in commanders and staff not taking the necessary rest. Brigade commanders were to be at 50th Division Headquarters at 0730 hrs. on the 21st of May and troops were to be ready to move at 0800 hrs.

At 0600 hrs. General Franklyn held a conference. The general plan was that the 50th Division, which consisted mainly of the 151st Infantry Brigade and divisional troops, was to attack with the 1st Army Tank Brigade under its command. The attack was to be launched round the south of Arras, and to clear the area of the enemy as far round as the River Sensee. It was to be carried out in two phases—the first as far as the River Cojeul and the second to the Sensee.

During the second phase the 13th Infantry Brigade of the 5th Division was to co-operate by advancing over the River Scarpe. The whole attack was to be under the G.O.C. 50th Division. The 1st Division Leger Mechanisé were to move out on the right flank of the attack. It was hoped that further reinforcements would arrive, and that it would become possible to extend the operations on the next day in the direction of Cambrai and Bapaume and join up with the French.

The operation resolved itself into clearing an area about ten miles deep and four miles wide, and General Martel stated that he proposed to carry this out by advancing through the area with two mobile columns. The area was, of course, much too large to be dealt with by an advance with troops extended over this front when only such a comparatively small force was available. It was a case for attacking in two columns, each on a narrow front.

On the advice of the French the Arras—St. Pol road had been taken as the start line, and both columns were to pass this line at 1400 hrs. As it was now nearly 0700 hrs. and the troops would have an approach march of eight miles, General Martel asked that the time should be postponed to 1500 hrs., but General Franklyn pressed for the attack to be launched at 1400 hrs. In fact, it was eventually launched at 1430 hrs.

There were, of course, many difficulties. The troops had never had any previous training in working in a mobile column with tanks, and this was their first serious encounter with the Germans. The test was therefore a high one for a Territorial division. Then there was very little detailed information about the location of the enemy. The French had been in the line for some time, but had not kept very close contact with the Germans. They certainly held no defensive line, and the general opinion was that the enemy had troops in the villages and a considerable number of tanks ready for counter-attack if necessary. It was these tanks that the French feared.

With so little time and information available, it was not easy to decide the best tactics. If the main threat was the enemy tanks, then our tanks should lead, supported closely by infantry and guns. If, on the other hand, a defensive position or strong defensive localities were met, then a combined plan of attack, employing all arms, would be necessary. The plan which General Martel adopted was that the tanks should lead. If enemy tanks were met, our tanks, with their thick armour, should be able to deal with them without undue difficulty. If, however, defensive positions were met, then the tanks should pause until a combined plan could be made using all arms.

Unfortunately, very few tanks were available. The tank brigade consisted of only two battalions, the 4th and 7th Royal Tank Regiment, and they had marched long distances in the advance and subsequent withdrawal from Brussels. Tank tracks were very worn and were constantly breaking, and no spares could be obtained. There were only sixteen Matilda tanks available in the brigade, ten with the 4th Battalion and six with the 7th Battalion. There were also a larger number of Mark I tanks, which had heavy armour but were equipped only with a machine gun. The 4th Battalion had twenty-three of these and the 7th had thirty-five.

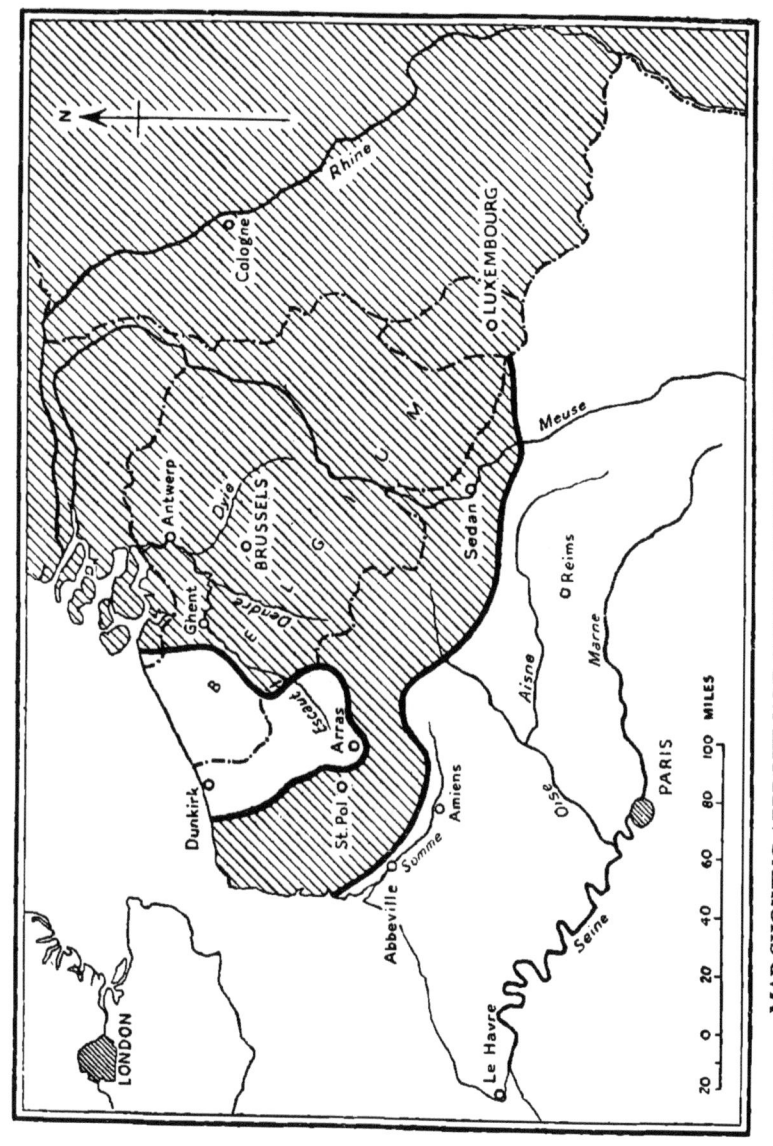

MAP SHOWING APPROXIMATE GERMAN ADVANCE BY THE 21st OF MAY, 1940

Brigadier Pratt commanded the brigade, and Lieutenant-Colonels FitzMaurice and Heyland commanded the 4th and 7th Battalions respectively.

General Martel had received his orders at 0700 hrs., and at 0730 hrs. gave his own orders to commanders at Divisional Headquarters at Vimy.

Each mobile column was made up as follows:

> One infantry battalion.
> One tank battalion.
> One battery 18-pounder, R.F.A.
> One anti-tank battery.
> One company of the motor-cycle battalion.

The 8th Durham Light Infantry, under Lieutenant-Colonel Beart, and the 7th Royal Tank Regiment were allotted to the right column, and the 6th Durham Light Infantry, under Lieutenant-Colonel Miller, and the 4th Royal Tank Regiment were in the left column. The infantry battalion commander was to command each column. The remainder of the troops were to be kept in hand in reserve.

Both columns were to move at once to assembly areas behind the start line on their respective routes, and there the commanders of the infantry battalions were to make detailed plans with the tank battalion commanders. Both tanks and infantry arrived a little late at the assembly area, and the advance was further delayed by the fact that the enemy were found to be holding posts on our side of the start line. These posts had remained silent during the preliminary reconnaissance, but had to be mopped up.

The 4th Royal Tank Regiment, advancing in front of the 6th Durham Light Infantry, met the enemy almost at once to the west of Dainville. They shot-up his transport and killed many men. The 6th Durham Light Infantry opened out into artillery formation. There was a good deal of sniping and artillery fire, but the infantry battalion continued the advance in a steady manner and mopped up the area round Dainville. Many prisoners were taken. The men had started rather tired from their march, but the sight of the damage caused by the 4th Royal Tank Regiment and the fact that they were capturing and killing many Germans gave them new energy.

The 4th Royal Tank Regiment continued their advance on Achicourt and knocked out many anti-tank guns. Several enemy tanks fled as ours approached. The battalion commander, Lieutenant-Colonel FitzMaurice, was killed at this time. He was commanding from a light tank which received a direct hit from a field gun. The tanks continued to find good targets and destroyed much enemy transport.

The infantry continued their advance through Achicourt on Beaurains; they encountered slight artillery fire, which increased as they approached that village.

In the meantime, the right column had not been progressing quite so well. The 7th Royal Tank Regiment were leading, and they arrived on the start line rather late. They proceeded at once through Duisans, where they shot-up enemy infantry and transport. They were followed by the 8th Durham Light Infantry, who entered Duisans at about 1500 hrs. Some sniping and machine-gun fire was encountered from the west and a certain amount of shell fire, but casualties were light. The whole area was mopped up and about a hundred prisoners were taken. Though the men were inevitably tired from their previous exertions, they were elated by these successes.

At this stage, however, the advance was held up by the enemy at or round Warlus. They were reported to be in some strength and supported by some medium tanks. The tank battalion commander, Lieutenant-Colonel Heyland, was killed by a direct hit on the light tank in which he was travelling.

At about 1530 hrs. General Martel motored up to the left column, where he met Brigadier Churchill and saw that they were pushing ahead much faster than the right column. They were moving out of supporting distance of each other, and the G.O.C. therefore ordered the left column to secure Beaurains and make it into a tank-proof locality.

General Martel reached the right column at about 1600 hrs., where he found the situation somewhat confused. The tanks appeared to have passed on the flank of Warlus, where the infantry was held up. Enemy tanks were soon in and round Warlus, and the G.O.C. impressed on the column commander the necessity to press hard and obtain further information so that the necessary forces or artillery support could be brought to bear to clear a way through.

A little later the French tanks, which were advancing rather slowly on our right flank, saw our anti-tank guns which were in position protecting the right of the 8th Durham Light Infantry. They turned towards them; the anti-tank battery presumed that they were French tanks, though they had no special marking. Suddenly the French tanks opened fire and knocked out an anti-tank gun, killing two men. Fire was then opened with one gun, and five shots were fired, which killed or wounded the crews of four tanks. The tanks were now coming to close quarters, and the French saw their mistake and emerged from their tanks. Their commander apologized.

The 4th Royal Tank Regiment, with the left column, was continuing the action with undiminished zest, though it had suffered many casualties.

Although the advance had been very successful as a whole, it now became clear that the original proposal to reach the Sensee River could not be achieved.

It was now necessary to decide on plans for that night and the following day, and General Martel returned to see General Franklyn. So far, heavy casualties had been inflicted on the enemy with only small losses on our side. It was, however, certain that the enemy would hit back, and that he could easily do so with much superior forces. It was therefore decided to hold a tank-proof locality at Beaurains and another at Duisans after the situation at Warlus had been cleared up.

The enemy had been shaken by the 50th Division's thrust. They had complete superiority in the air, and air observers had watched the whole progress of the battle. As soon as they saw our columns collecting in their tank-proof localities they made plans for a counter-attack, for which they had already concentrated the necessary forces. Their general plan was simple and sound. They had no intention of attacking if the British held a strong defensive position, especially in an anti-tank locality. The plan was therefore to use intensive air attack to drive the 50th Division out of such a position and then launch a tank attack in the open, using very large numbers of tanks. This plan met with a good deal of success.

At 1850 hrs. the enemy launched very heavy dive-bombing attacks on Beaurains, where the 6th Durham Light Infantry were forming a tank-proof locality, and also on the main body of the right column near Warlus. These attacks were delivered by over a hundred planes and lasted for twenty minutes. This was easily the most intensive air bombardment which our troops had yet encountered, and the troops were already exhausted. The 6th Durham Light Infantry were forced to extricate themselves from Beaurains and were then attacked by great numbers of tanks in the open. Major Jeffreys did particularly good work at this stage.

The 4th Royal Tank Regiment, though greatly outnumbered, helped to stem the tide, and the anti-tank guns did their best, but the column was forced to withdraw to Achicourt.

On the right flank the air bombardment was followed by heavy tank attacks on the troops from the south-west of Duisans and on Warlus. Anti-tank guns of Major Forrester's battery were quickly in action, and upwards of twenty tanks were knocked out and left burning on the ground.

After these attacks it became clear that the enemy was in much superior strength, and both columns were ordered to withdraw to our lines during the night.

To sum up, the result of the attack was that heavy casualties were inflicted on the enemy and over 400 prisoners were taken. More than twenty tanks were definitely destroyed. The advance of ten miles through enemy territory carried out by the 6th Durham Light Infantry and the left column showed remarkable powers of endurance, especially when it is remembered that the troops had been in action for several days with little rest and had an approach march of eight miles to the start line.

The 8th Durham Light Infantry, under Lieutenant-Colonel Beart, and the right column met stronger opposition and penetrated less deeply, but resisted the counter-attack in the evening. The 1st Army Tank Brigade showed great courage and fighting qualities.

The medium tanks used by the Germans in this battle were Marks III and IV, and were much the same as the models used later in the Middle East, except that the Germans had not then added any plates to increase the protection on the front of the tank. The Germans drove off the attack in the end because they were able to concentrate very superior numbers in both tanks and other arms and had complete air superiority; but it cost them dear in tanks. German tanks were knocked out by our 2-pounder anti-tank gun, whereas our infantry tanks resisted the shell fire of the corresponding enemy 37-mm. gun without difficulty. Some tanks were hit fifteen times without effect on tank or crew.

The attack probably delayed the main enemy encircling movement via Calais by two days, which may have had a considerable effect on the success of our operations to cover the eventual evacuation from Dunkirk.

Although this action of these forces round Arras was only a comparatively small affair, it has been discussed in some detail, as it was their first clash with the German tanks; also the enemy were 100 per cent. German, and they used the pick of their Army for this thrust through the Allied front. The forces that attacked the 50th Division were under the command of Rommel. It was the first of a succession of such encounters in widely separated parts of the world.

Frankforce now received orders to hold the position round Arras, and General Franklyn issued the necessary instructions for the two divisions and for what was left of the 1st Army Tank Brigade.

Frankforce was now practically isolated in this area, and the enemy were in great strength and closing in round the north of Arras. It looked like a fight to the finish. General Martel made this plain to the troops.

"There is no doubt," says General Martel, "that those North Countrymen would have fought to the last man, and this might have set a standard which we badly needed on one or two occasions later on in the war."

A little later, however, orders were received that the Division was to withdraw northwards on the night of the 23rd through the narrow corridor and rejoin the main body of the B.E.F. To do this they had to move radiator to tailboard and three abreast up the one remaining road, and in this way they extricated themselves in one night from a very precarious position. During this difficult time the 1st Army Tank Brigade continued to give valuable help.

ARRAS OPERATIONS

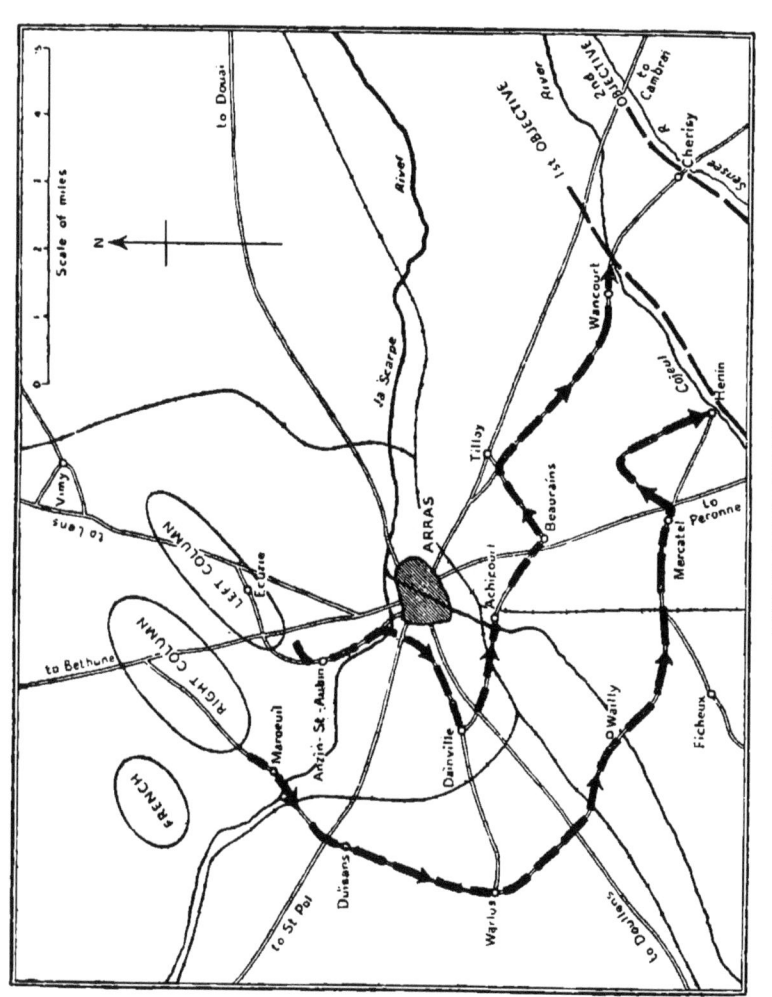

CHAPTER II

THE WITHDRAWAL TO THE COAST—PERIMETER DEFENCE—
THE LAST DIVISION TO LEAVE DUNKIRK

MAY TO JUNE, 1940

ON the 24th of May Divisional Headquarters was established at Loos for the third time. The 25th Infantry Brigade were still behind the canal line and the 150th and 151st Brigades came in to rest behind this line. Proposals for a new offensive southwards were still under discussion. General Martel had to go to G.H.Q. and attend conferences with Lieutenant-General Sir Ronald Adam, commanding the III Corps, but unfortunately nothing came of the proposals. It was far too late, and the resources were quite insufficient at this stage for a new offensive.

The 26th of May was a day of countless orders and inevitable changing of plans. At 0730 hrs. orders were received for the Division to move to high ground near Bailleul in case the enemy broke through the Belgians in the north. The necessary divisional orders were issued. Information came in that the 151st Brigade had been holding positions in the Provin—Carvin area behind the French. The 151st Brigade had been engaged on the 25th. While the orders for the move of the Division were being issued, information came in that the 151st Brigade was being shelled and bombed. The 6th Durham Light Infantry were moving back to Herrin and the 8th Durham Light Infantry would pull out as soon as possible, but the 9th Durham Light Infantry had been badly shot-up and there would be difficulty in disengaging this unit. The 8th Durham Light Infantry were counter-attacking a small number of Germans who had crossed the canal at Carvin. General Martel decided at 1100 hrs. that the Division could move as ordered, except for the 9th Durham Light Infantry, who would follow later.

Half an hour after this Brigadier Churchill, commanding the 151st Brigade, phoned to say that the Germans were penetrating through the French and engaging the 8th Durham Light Infantry at Camphin. General Martel gave orders that the enemy must be held and that this was the primary task of the brigade; he confirmed this after speaking on the phone to G.H.Q.

MAY TO JUNE, 1940 23

At 1145 hrs. new orders arrived from G.H.Q. The move of the Division to Bailleul was cancelled, but one brigade group was to move at once to Ypres. The G.O.C. was to go personally to Ypres, take command of any troops there, and organize the defence. He was then to hand over the defence to Major-General Franklyn, who was moving up just south of Ypres with the 5th Division.

General Martel at once phoned to Brigadier Haydon, commanding the 150th Brigade, giving him instructions to move forthwith to Ypres with the 72nd Field Regiment, 150th Field Ambulance, 232nd Field Company and the 6th Durham Light Infantry. The G.O.C. then left for Ypres, where he reconnoitred the position with Brigadier Haydon.

Meanwhile, the 151st Brigade were putting up a great fight. The 8th Durham Light Infantry recaptured Carvin that afternoon and the 9th Durham Light Infantry remained firmly established at Provin. General Langlois asked that the 8th and 9th Durham Light Infantry should remain in position until the 2nd North African Division arrived to support him. Brigadier Churchill agreed to this and G.H.Q. were informed. At 1730 hrs. the Division received the personal congratulations of the Commander-in-Chief on the action of the 151st Brigade and particularly on the counter-attack of the 8th Durham Light Infantry.

G.H.Q. plans were now that the whole Division should move to Ypres and come under the II Corps. At 2030 hrs. the G.O.C. returned from his reconnaissance around Ypres and went on almost at once to Headquarters, II Corps. He returned at midnight. The 150th Brigade had been held up by traffic blocks, and the whole Division was to move at dawn on the 27th to the area round Ypres. The necessary orders were issued at 0100 hrs. and Advanced Divisional Headquarters left at 0600 hrs. and moved to a report centre at the entrance to Ypres, where plans were made to allot areas to the incoming units.

The Commander of the II Corps, Lieutenant-General Sir Alan Brooke, came to the report centre and discussed matters. Ypres was under fairly continuous shell fire and so a more suitable Divisional Headquarters was sought and established in a small village a few miles north-west of Ypres. The 150th Brigade were holding Ypres on this day (the 27th of May). The 151st Brigade were still fighting during the night of the 26th/27th, but were able to disengage at dawn, and arrived at Poperinghe on the evening of the 27th. They moved on the left of the 150th Brigade. The Division was attacked on the 27th and 28th. The 4th Green Howards, on the right, were heavily engaged, but their commanding officer, Lieutenant-Colonel C. N. Littleboy (whose name was such a misnomer), was a powerfully built man, and whenever he moved up his great body seemed to fill any gap in the line. The men had a great respect for him and his second-in-command, Major E. C. Cooke-Collis.

The Division lost a little ground on the right, and a few Germans penetrated across the canal north of Ypres; reserve units had to be moved to stabilize the situation. The 150th Brigade fought particularly well, and their commander, Brigadier Haydon, handled a difficult situation in a very able manner.

It was now clear that there was no longer any hope of the French forces in the south taking any action which would result in reuniting these forces with those that were isolated in the north. On the 26th of May the Government authorized the Commander-in-Chief, B.E.F., to operate towards the coast in conjunction with French and Belgian forces. Plans were accordingly made to withdraw in stages to a perimeter defence round Dunkirk. Lieutenant-General Sir Ronald Adam was instructed to prepare the plans for the defence of and evacuation from Dunkirk. Troops began to withdraw behind the perimeter on the front of all three corps on the 27th of May. On the 28th of May information was received that the Belgian troops were capitulating at midnight.

On the 28th also the Division heard that it would shortly be embarking for England. That afternoon orders were received for a withdrawal to a line between Poperinghe and Elverdinghe. This was carried out without difficulty, the 150th Brigade holding the right and the 151st Brigade the left of the line. The enemy did not follow up the withdrawal that night, but was probing into our positions by the afternoon of the 29th.

The I Corps was on our right and the 5th Division on our left. That evening the 5th Division withdrew, and was followed during the night by the 50th Division, who retired into the bridgehead position along the Bergues—Fournes Canal. The II Corps were holding the eastern portion of the bridgehead with the 3rd Division on the left, the 50th Division on the right, and the 5th Division in reserve. The I Corps was still on the right. A certain proportion of motor transport was destroyed before the 50th Division entered the bridgehead, and guns were destroyed when supplies of ammunition ran out. Divisional Headquarters opened at Adinkerke shortly after midnight. The 150th Brigade was on the right, with its right flank near the frontier, and the 151st Brigade on the left near Bulscamp. The enemy closed up during the afternoon of the 30th and made a few light attacks. The 3rd Grenadier Guards, with 200 men, were placed under the orders of the Division and were sent up to deal with one of these attacks and did very good work. The 2nd Royal Northumberland Fusiliers and

[*British Official Photograph*] [*Crown Copyright Reserved*]

The scene as the last troops embarked at Dunkirk.

the 4th Gordon Highlanders (M.G.) were also put under the Division and fought splendidly, but they were much depleted in strength.

The results of the flooding which the Belgians had carried out began to affect the divisional area. Many fields were under water, and this caused considerable difficulty in the defences, though it probably hampered the enemy to a greater extent.

Orders were received that the 50th Division would embark from the beach at La Panne during the night of the 31st. At 0830 hrs. on the 31st, Brigadier Ritchie, B.G.S. Corps, arrived and said that there was a change of plan. The 50th Division would not now embark as planned, but was to pivot on the right and draw back and occupy the Franco-Belgian frontier with the 5th Division on the left. The 50th Division was to come under the I Corps at 1800 hrs. that day.

Heavy attacks were now launched on the 50th Division position and particularly on the left flank. The right flank of the 3rd Division on the left was driven back, and the 151st Brigade lost some ground on that flank. The enemy also made penetrations at other points, but the grim fighting qualities of these North Country troops restored the situation. The casualties in the 151st Brigade were very heavy.

The Division had now been fighting almost continuously since the 21st of May, and the way in which they resisted enemy attacks during the final few days in France restored the situation on many occasions.

That night and in the early hours of the 1st of June the Division withdrew to a position south of Bray Dunes and just behind the frontier, which was still held by a thin screen of French troops. The 150th Brigade held the position, and the 151st Brigade—which was now very weak—dug in on the sea shore behind them. The enemy did not close up to this position until the afternoon of the 1st of June.

The 50th Division was ordered to embark that night. Already a large proportion of R.A.S.C. personnel had been embarked and sent back to England. Gunners were also sent back in considerable numbers as ammunition gave out and the guns were destroyed. On this last day the final plans for evacuation were made. All vehicles and munitions which could be of use to the enemy had, of course, to be destroyed. The instructions which the Division had received were that the troops should embark with rifles or hand weapons alone, owing to the difficulty of salvaging any other weapons under existing conditions. In many places the troops had to wade through deep water to the boats.

The 50th Division made it a point of honour to take all machine guns back in spite of the difficulties. The artillery units also took back a considerable number of optical instruments which they knew were in short supply at home. When the time came, no unit in the Division failed to salve the machine guns and instruments.

By this time General Lord Gort had been ordered to return home, as the greater part of his command had already been evacuated. Lieutenant-General Alexander took over command and gave out his orders verbally at midday. The 50th Division now had only the 150th and 151st Brigades and some attached troops which had already been thinned out. The 25th Brigade, which had been parted from the Division during most of the fighting, had already been evacuated. The 150th Brigade was to embark from the east end of the beaches at Malo Les Bains, and the remainder were to leave from the mole at Dunkirk.

At 1700 hrs. the embarkation was due to start. The troops moved down to the beaches, where there was a little shelling and bombing. The embarkation went on smoothly, but it was very difficult to keep in touch with the 150th Brigade, which was on the extreme east of the beaches. By 0200 hrs. nearly all the troops of the 151st Brigade were known to have embarked and almost the whole Division was thought to have been taken off. It transpired afterwards that a large part of the 150th Brigade had failed to embark off the beaches, and they marched along the front and embarked at the mole with the few remaining divisional troops during the night of the 2nd of June. The 50th Division was the last division to leave Dunkirk.

Thus ended the Division's first campaign in France. The road back lay through many other theatres of war; but, as this story will show, the last division to leave Dunkirk shared the honour of being the first to land on the beaches of Normandy four years later.

CHAPTER III

LESSONS OF THE CAMPAIGN AND SOME REFLECTIONS ON MORALE—
50TH DIVISION MANS THE DORSET COAST—THE DESERT LOOMS AHEAD

JUNE TO DECEMBER, 1940

CONSIDERING the confusion and anxiety of the times, surprisingly complete arrangements had been made for the reception of the B.E.F. men returning from France. They went off to various camps, and the 50th Division was directed to a large camp near Knutsford, in Cheshire, there to get itself into working order.

Brigadier Massy volunteered to take charge of a report centre which the Division set up at the entrance to the park, and from which all personnel were directed to their respective units. It was an exhausting task, but it did much to get the Division going again. Units began to regain their old form. General Martel went round to explain what had happened and to discuss with officers and non-commissioned officers all the main lessons that had been learned. These lessons were set out and sent to G.H.Q., Home Forces, who issued them officially to all divisions.

One of the main lessons raised an interesting point. In the First World War young soldiers were put into the line in small parties among experienced troops so as to become used to shell fire before they went in as a formation. At the start of the Second World War this was clearly impossible. Formations had to go into the line composed almost entirely of young and inexperienced soldiers, and they had to face the full onslaught of the enemy at once. The Germans realized this, and made every effort to concentrate the most intense fire on certain parts of the front to break the spirit of the men.

All experienced soldiers know that troops may lose all power of self-control for a short time when they are heavily bombarded for the first time in their lives.

Every effort was made in the 50th Division to safeguard against this danger. The point was stressed that whenever the enemy concentrated a very heavy bombardment on any part of the front, a senior commander or staff officer should be ready behind that portion of the front and waiting for the inevitable reaction. Sometimes brigade commanders went there, sometimes the G.O.C. himself was there. After about an hour a few men would start to trickle back in a completely dazed condition. The senior officer dealing with the situation would go and talk to them. He would ask: "Do you mean that you—men of the 50th Division—are leaving your posts because of shell fire?"

Dazed as such men usually were, when they realized what they had done they were heartily ashamed of themselves. They were then taken back to the line. Neighbouring posts had often seen such men trickling back. They wondered whether a withdrawal had been ordered. Sometimes they had joined the trickle, but when they saw the men brought back with senior officers present confidence was at once restored.

The 50th Division took endless trouble to carry out this process of implanting confidence in the men for the first three or four days under heavy fire. The result was splendid. After that period there was never any necessity to take these precautions, for the men had gained their confidence in themselves and their comrades.

The effect on the Division was striking. Many divisions which had certainly had no more serious fighting than the 50th were down to half strength or less as they were withdrawing into the bridgehead. A considerable proportion of the missing had trickled back into the rear areas and did not join up again until their units entered the bridgehead. The 50th Division kept up their strength with practically no men missing right up to the last day, though the 151st Brigade had rather heavy casualties and lost a small batch of men who went astray after the Arras battle.

There was now time to look round and see how the various parts of the Division had carried out their tasks in France. The work of the 150th and 151st Infantry Brigades has been fully dealt with, but little has appeared about the 25th Brigade, as they were parted so soon from the Division, but they fought with great success under Brigadier W. H. C. Ramsden (who was later to command the Division) at various stages in the withdrawal to the perimeter defences.

Throughout this period, the divisional artillery had been a great source of strength and had supported the infantry at every stage. Some of the work of the C.R.A., Brigadier Massy, has already been mentioned, and his Brigade Major and Staff Captain, Captain Gibson and Major Priestman, were well-known figures throughout the Division. Lieutenant-Colonel R. M. Graham, who commanded the 72nd Field Regiment, had a splendid team, and they were in the thick of the fighting during all this time. Lieutenant-Colonel Graham remained for a long time with the Division, and served as C.R.A. for a period in North Africa.

As one might expect from a North Country division, the Engineers were a robust body of officers and men, and well skilled in their role.

Lieutenant-Colonel Spiers worked with untiring energy to make them into a first-class team and never spared himself.

An outstanding figure at Divisional Headquarters was Lieutenant-Colonel Sheffield as O.C. Signals, and his units carried out splendid work.

The R.A.S.C. units of the Division had been raised, trained and taken out to France by Lieutenant-Colonel Thompson, but he fell ill before operations started and Lieutenant-Colonel Divers became C.R.A.S.C. It was a large command with the additional troop-carrying companies, but they sailed through all the difficulties under the guidance of Lieutenant-Colonel Divers. The problem of supply became very difficult after the communications had been cut and the B.E.F. had become isolated, but they succeeded in collecting and bringing gun ammunition to the batteries right up to the last stages of the fighting.

The two field ambulances, the 149th and 150th, had much to learn after they had mobilized, but they were well up to their work by the time that the operations started in France. When the B.E.F. moved into Belgium the field ambulances established dressing stations along the forward routes. After the withdrawal from Belgium the bearer companies of the 149th Field Ambulance accompanied the 154th Brigade in their attack at Arras, and dressing stations were opened in rear. The field ambulance continued their good work during the withdrawal to Dunkirk and on the beaches under the leadership of the A.D.M.S., Colonel Errington, with the strong support of the D.A.D.M.S., Major McCracken. When the Division returned to England, the 186th Field Ambulance joined it as the third unit, and training was resumed in preparation for future operations.

After a short spell in camps in Cheshire, the Division moved to Dorsetshire to take over the role of defending that county in the event of invasion. Before the end of June the 69th Infantry Brigade joined the Division to make the third brigade. This was a brigade from the (duplicate) 23rd Division, with the 5th East Yorkshire Regiment and the 6th and 7th Green Howards as the infantry component. Many of the officers and non-commissioned officers had been at some time in the 50th Division.

Divisional Headquarters was at Blandford, where the accommodation was ideal. For physical fitness there were cross-country runs of four or five miles in length. Everyone had to take part. They could "run, walk or creep," but they had to finish the course. There was an outdoor boxing ring on the lawn by the headquarter mess. The nearest units had to send two men each evening to box with the G.O.C. There was also hunting at times with the Portman. Everyone became very fit. Colonel Everett had fallen sick, but Major Mitchell, who had supported him so well in France, was still with us, and Major R. H. Turton, M.P., had returned to help us on the administrative side and continued to give his valuable help to the Division for a long time, under Lieutenant-Colonel Benoy, who had been such a tower of strength to us in France.

The Division now had to prepare defences. Along the coast the 50th Division was responsible for the sector from Lyme Regis to Christchurch. Shell-proof machine-gun posts were made in concrete at many important localities and were carefully concealed or camouflaged as huts or buildings. The divisional engineers under Lieutenant-Colonel Kennedy, did splendid work and there were many "show places" visited by parties from other formations.

By this time Colonel Sir Donald Banks had taken charge of work in connection with flame-throwers, petrol bombs, etc., and he came to his old division for help in trying out submarine petrol pipes to produce fire on the sea. Some very interesting trials took place.

In September the Division heard that it had been earmarked as the first Territorial division to go to North Africa when the time came.

On the 8th of December it became known that General Martel was to become the commander of the Royal Armoured Corps, and he left the Division a few days later. He had commanded it for nearly two years. He issued the following message to all units:

"SPECIAL ORDER OF THE DAY

BY

MAJOR-GENERAL G. LE Q. MARTEL, C.B., D.S.O., M.C.,
Commander, 50th (Northumbrian) Division.

"HOME FORCES,
"10th December, 1940.

"Now that I am leaving the 50th (Northumbrian) Division, I want to remind all ranks about a few points. When war was upon us we likened it to a crusade. The badge for our hostel was a Crusader's shield, which represented the fight for right and freedom. This Division has always had a strong team spirit, but it became more than ever united in this righteous cause. There was no one who did not give of his best. The Church and the medical side as well as the combatant branches and the administrative side combined in a wonderful team spirit, and it is that spirit that wins wars.

"It is not necessary for me to thank units or branches of the Division for what they have done. They have all done well. They have done this in fulfilment of their faith and creed, and that brings its own reward.

"Never before have I been so sorry to leave an appointment, but never before have I felt so sure of the future well-being of a command. Nothing can stand against the deep-spirited determination of this Division.

"I wish the Division every good fortune and with the fullest confidence in ultimate success.

"G. LE Q. MARTEL, *Major-General.*"

APPENDIX TO PART ONE

ORDER OF BATTLE, 50TH DIVISION
10th May, 1940

G.O.C.	Major-General G. le Q. Martel, D.S.O., M.C.
A.D.C.	Second-Lieutenant J. G. F. Milbank.
G.S.O.1	Colonel M. Everett, D.S.O.
G.S.O.2	Major F. J. Mitchell, M.C.
G.S.O.3 (O.)	Major D. Grey.
G.S.O.3 (C.W.)	Captain W. S. Olleson.
D.I.C.	Captain M. J. Buckmaster.
Cipher	Lieutenant E. J. S. North.
A.A. and Q.M.G.	Lieutenant-Colonel J. M. Benoy, O.B.E.
D.A.Q.M.G.	Major T. E. H. Helby, M.C.
D.A.A.G.	Major H. V. Ewbank.
Camp Commandant	Lieutenant D. Wilkie.
Divisional Catering Officer	Captain R. I. Beattie.
Staff Captain	Captain H. T. Shean.
Assistant D.A.A.G.	Captain Welch.
S.C.F.	Reverend R. T. Newcombe, M.C., T.D.
Entertainments Officer	Captain Platts.
A.D.M.S.	Colonel R. Errington, C.B.E., M.C., T.D.
D.A.M.S.	Major J. D. W. McCracken.
D.A.D.O.S.	Major R. H. White.
S.O.M.E.	Lieutenant-Colonel W. G. Carrock.
C.R.A.S.C.	Lieutenant-Colonel S. T. Divers.
Adjutant	Captain R. W. S. Norfolk.
Salvage	Lieutenant J. Harris.
F.S.P.	Lieutenant A. P. Bryce.
D.A.P.M.	Captain R. A. Guild.
Provost Company	Captain W. G. Kelsey.
A.P.O.	Second-Lieutenant A. S. Gammon.

150TH INFANTRY BRIGADE

Commander	Brigadier C. W. Haydon, M.C.
Brigade Major	Captain K. G. F. Chevasse.
Staff Captain	Captain B. H. W. Jackson.
Intelligence Officer	Captain W. H. L. Urton.

4TH BN. THE EAST YORKSHIRE REGIMENT

Commanding Officer	Lieutenant-Colonel R. H. Martin.
Second-in-Command	Lieutenant-Colonel F. Willis, D.C.M.
Adjutant	Captain C. Middleton.

4TH BN. THE GREEN HOWARDS

Commanding Officer ..	Lieutenant-Colonel C. N. Littleboy, M.C., T.D.
Second-in-Command ..	Major E. C. Cooke-Collis.
Adjutant	Captain R. H. Turton, M.P.

5TH BN. THE GREEN HOWARDS

Commanding Officer ..	Lieutenant-Colonel W. E. Bush, M.C.
Second-in-Command ..	Major R. V. V. Guy.
Adjutant	Captain Wait.

151ST INFANTRY BRIGADE

Commander	Brigadier J. A. Churchill, M.C., A.D.C.
Brigade Major	Major A. F. L. Clive.
Staff Captain	Captain W. M. Fletcher Vane.
Intelligence Officer ..	Captain C. C. Ridley.

6TH BN. THE DURHAM LIGHT INFANTRY

Commanding Officer ..	Lieutenant-Colonel T. H. Miller, T.D.
Second-in-Command ..	Major P. J. Jeffreys.
Adjutant	Captain H. V. Ferens.

8TH BN. THE DURHAM LIGHT INFANTRY

Commanding Officer	Lieutenant-Colonel C. W. Beart, M.C.
Second-in-Command	Major P. S. McLaren.
Adjutant	Captain A. B. S. Clark.

9TH BN. THE DURHAM LIGHT INFANTRY

Commanding Officer ..	Major J. E. S. Percy, M.C.
Second-in-Command ..	
Adjutant	Captain W. Robinson.

4TH BN. THE ROYAL NORTHUMBERLAND FUSILIERS

Commanding Officer	Lieutenant-Colonel R. Wood, T.D.
Second-in-Command	Major J. Clark.
Adjutant	Major B. J. Leech.

25TH INFANTRY BRIGADE

Commander	Brigadier W. H. C. Ramsden, D.S.O., M.C.
Brigade Major	Captain K. T. Roper.
Staff Captain	Captain M. C. D. King.
Intelligence Officer ..	Second-Lieutenant D. H. Dismore.

7TH BN. THE QUEEN'S ROYAL REGIMENT

Commanding Officer ..	Lieutenant-Colonel G. A. Pilleau.
Second-in-Command ..	Major P. Adams.
Adjutant	Major D. C. G. Dickinson.

2ND BN. THE ESSEX REGIMENT

Commanding Officer	Lieutenant-Colonel A. H. Blest.
Second-in-Command	Major C. L. Wilson, M.C.
Adjutant	Captain P. C. Hinde.

1ST BN. THE ROYAL IRISH FUSILIERS

Commanding Officer	Lieutenant-Colonel G. H. Gough, M.C.
Second-in-Command	Major H. A. Davies, M.B.E., M.C.
Adjutant	Captain M. J. F. Palmer.

ROYAL ARTILLERY

C.R.A.	Brigadier C. W. Massy, M.C.
Brigade Major	Captain L. Y. Gibson.
Staff Captain	Major J. L. Priestman, M.C.
Intelligence Officer	Second-Lieutenant Harbottle.

72ND FIELD REGIMENT

Commanding Officer	Lieutenant-Colonel R. M. Graham, M.C., T.D.
Second-in-Command	Major H. H. Peile.
Adjutant	Captain R. J. H. Harding-Newman.
285 Battery	Major H. Clapham.
Battery	Major J. Lyall.

74TH FIELD REGIMENT

Commanding Officer	Lieutenant-Colonel R. T. Edwards, A.F.C., T.D.
Second-in-Command	
Adjutant	Captain J. B. Irvine.
293 Battery	Major H. W. Abey.
296 Battery	Major A. V. Brooke-Webb.

65TH ANTI-TANK REGIMENT

Commanding Officer	Lieutenant-Colonel K. W. Hervey.
Second-in-Command	Major R. P. Hogson-Makenzie.
Adjutant	Captain H. F. A. Moore.
257 Battery	Major A. R. Colman.
258 Battery	Major J. H. Boag.
259 Battery	Major H. E. Collet-White.
260 Battery	Major H. W. Forester.

ROYAL ENGINEERS

C.R.E.	Lieutenant-Colonel W. M. Spires (succeeded by Major Swan, 18th May).
Adjutant	Captain J. B. Dodds.
235 Field Park	Captain N. Pearson.
232 Field Company	Major R. W. S. Casebourne.
Field Park Company	Major C. W. Pegler.

ROYAL CORPS OF SIGNALS

Commanding Officer	Lieutenant-Colonel T. T. J. Sheffield, T.D.
Second-in-Command	Major R. M. Percival.
Adjutant	Captain J. G. Hopkins.
No. 1 Company	Captain Miner.
No. 2 Company	Major C. C. Fairweather.
No. 3 Company	Captain N. I. Bower.

ROYAL ARMY SERVICE CORPS

Ammunition Company ..	Captain E. E. Bonner.
Petrol Company..	Captain V. R. Bonner.
Supply Column	Major E. Steele.
3 Petrol Sub-Park	Captain C. E. Westmorland.
11 Troop Carrying Company	Major W. A. Woollam.
12 Troop Carrying Company	Major W. R. Bingham.

ROYAL ARMY MEDICAL CORPS

149th Field Ambulance ..	Lieutenant-Colonel G. G. Drummond.
150th Field Ambulance ..	Lieutenant-Colonel J. Morrison, M.C.
Hygiene Section..	Captain N. Baster.
Bath Unit	Second-Lieutenant G. M. Cooper.
Divisional Transport Officer	Second-Lieutenant F. G. Dawson.
Motor Contact Officer.. ..	Second-Lieutenant Ashburner.
French Liaison Officer ..	Captain De la Debutris.
Liaison Officers	Lieutenant Lour.
	Lieutenant Ritz.
	Lieutenant James.
	M. Beurgner.
Motor Contact Officers ..	Second-Lieutenant Wrightson.
	Second-Lieutenant Collett.

PART TWO

CHAPTER IV

Orders for Overseas—To Egypt via the Cape—The Division split up, then reunited in Cyprus—Another Separation—Into Iraq—50th Division enters the Desert

DECEMBER, 1940, TO JANUARY, 1942

MAJOR-GENERAL W. H. C. RAMSDEN succeeded to the command of the Division on the 12th of December, 1940, shortly after the Division moved to the north coast of Somerset, still in an anti-invasion role.

Detailed plans were made and full orders written to repel nearly twenty possible enemy landings. The filing and mastering of these orders were a formidable task, but a most necessary one, if only because the Divisional Commander was liable to order a rehearsal of any particular plan at very short notice.

The morale of the Division at this time was very high. It believed itself to be the only formed and effective division in the country—the only one that had proved itself ready for war—and this as a true Territorial division owing allegiance to nobody and drawing help from few Regulars. Allowing for a certain amount of prejudice, there is no doubt that this belief was well founded. It was an inspiring formation to join.

When orders to mobilize for overseas were received they were accepted as a due right, and the quartermaster's stores began to fill with tropical kit instead of with battledress and greatcoats.

Troops began to go on embarkation leave about Christmas, but departure was postponed and, in the New Year, there was very intensive training on the bleak moors of Somerset and Devon. Lieutenant-General Franklyn, Commander of the VIII Corps, set an exercise over Exmoor which ended in a fierce snow blizzard. For many of those taking part this exercise involved more physical hardship than most of the real battles to which it was the prelude. Some fifteen members of the Division, gassed in a troop carrier, lost their lives.

The Division had reached concert pitch in training. To have trained further would have brought only staleness and unsound theory. Now only active service could mould it once more into a fighting force. It was ready to tread that long road which was to lead it to the Normandy D Day as a spearhead of the British Army.

In March more embarkation leave was granted and the King went to the West Country to visit all units. He found them equipped, in great heart and ready for the adventure that lay ahead.

By the 21st of April the first units were moving towards their port of embarkation—Liverpool. They were the components of the 150th Brigade Group, together with an Advanced Divisional Headquarters, which included General Ramsden. They marched from the railway station to the docks in unseasonable heat. As the 4th Green Howards, burdened with their kit, marched steadily through mean streets, people gathered at their front doors and on the pavements to wish them "God-speed." Many infantrymen will remember how some of these poor folk pressed into their hands precious boxes of matches, odd, crumpled cigarettes, and even an occasional orange.

The ships that were to carry the greater part of the Brigade were the *Empress of Asia* and the *Empress of Russia*, sister vessels of the Canadian Pacific Railway built before the 1914 war for the Pacific passenger service. In the *Empress of Russia* went the party from Divisional Headquarters, Headquarters of the 150th Brigade, 4th East Yorkshire Regiment, 4th Green Howards and 232nd Field Company, R.E. In the other vessel were the 72nd Field Regiment, R.A., 5th Green Howards and 150th Field Ambulance.

Both ships joined a convoy which was assembling in the Clyde, and on the evening of the 26th of April warships led the ten or twelve large vessels towards the Atlantic. The naval escort was most imposing—H.M.S. *Repulse*, fourteen destroyers and an armed merchantman. Those were perilous days in the Atlantic.

The convoy had to be routed far out into the ocean, so that the journey to the Near East took six weeks. In the troops' overcrowded quarters, and in hot weather, everybody began to feel a bit "screwed up." Desert navigation was ardently studied. Most of the theory and many of the recommended sun compasses and gadgets proved to be unnecessary.

The remainder of the Division sailed around the end of April and early May. Part of these later convoys shared vicariously in the excitement of the *Bismarck* incident. Their escort was called away to join the hunt for the German warship, and the convoy was not very far away from the *Bismarck* when she was sunk. But let the story of the leading ship's journey serve for all. The voyages were similar in many respects.

The 150th Brigade, leading the way to the Middle East, touched at Freetown on the 16th of May, where the ships coaled, surrounded by native bumboats whose clamorous occupants dived for pennies and tried to persuade the troops lining the decks to exchange their boots, shirts or trousers for bananas and oranges.

Very few people got ashore, for the ships sailed again quickly, and rounding the Cape about a week later ran into what was described by seafaring folk at the time as the worst storm in that area for sixty years. Certainly to the three thousand and more landlubbers, cooped up in their rolling vessels, it looked impressive. During this storm the *Empress of Asia* proved to be a lame duck, and had to put in at Capetown. The rest of the convoy continued to Durban. They sailed into the bay on the evening of the 27th of May and saw spread before their eyes a beautiful waterfront of white buildings where lights were already beginning to twinkle. As the ships tied up, the men in them, who had been confined in stuffy and uncomfortable quarters during much of the journey through tropical waters, saw the first evidence of the generous South African hospitality that awaited them, as cars drew up to the dockside ready to take them to see the sights of the city as soon as they left the ship.

Four glorious days were spent in Durban, largely as guests of the Victoria League, and on the 1st of June the convoy, still without the *Empress of Asia,* sailed away for the Red Sea and Port Tewfik, near Suez, where the troops began to disembark on the 13th of June.

The *Empress of Asia* did not reach Suez until the 23rd of June. Before she left Capetown, many of her stokers had deserted, and the position in the stokehold was such that the troops had to go below and stoke the ship through the fiery heat of the Red Sea. This they did manfully under the direction of Lieutenant Black, of the 5th Green Howards.

The remainder of the Division arrived in the months of June and July.

A rude shock awaited the first troops of the Division to arrive in the Middle East. The 150th Brigade was snatched away for duty in the Western Desert—almost before they had had time, in the desert phrase, to get their knees brown—and Divisional Headquarters went to Mena to plan the now-historic Alamein position. The Divisional Headquarters later moved to Cyprus, being followed by the 151st Brigade. Later the 150th and 69th Brigades rejoined the Division in the island.

These moves were a double-edged disappointment. They meant that the Division was not to operate in the desert at once, and that it was not together for its Middle East initiation. Not until February of the following year did the 50th Division take the field as a division against Rommel's armies, and then it was in the remarkable position of being the only English infantry division in contact with the enemy in any part of the world.

The first move to Cyprus took place in July. During the summer the

British Expeditionary Force in Greece had been obliged to evacuate that country, and subsequently Crete, a bastion of the Eastern Mediterranean, had been captured by the Germans. The importance of Cyprus as a stepping-stone to Palestine and Syria became suddenly enhanced and thither units of the Division were sent with all speed to put the island in a state of defence.

The directive to Major-General Ramsden from General Auchinleck, G.O.C.-in-C., Middle East, was terse and to the point: "Hold the island for H.M. Government."

It was a big task, and time pressed. Airfields and roads had to be constructed and railways and docks reorganized. Supplies of food, water, petrol and ammunition for ninety-one days for thirty-one thousand troops (including Royal Air Force) had to be brought in and stored. Defensive positions for three brigades had to be built.

When the defensive plan was made, the troops had to be disposed in their battle stations and rehearsed to meet and defeat the German should he "try another Crete."

Inevitably, in planning for the defence of an island as large as Cyprus by one division, certain isolated defended areas had to be chosen. These were to be denied to the enemy, no matter what other ground he occupied. They could be held sometimes by a battalion with supporting arms, sometimes by a brigade. From these areas there could be no retreat—they were fortresses to be held to the last man.

A mobile reserve, consisting of part of the 3rd Hussars, refitting after Crete, the 74th Field Regiment, the pre-war garrison, the 1st Sherwood Foresters, and the Cyprus Regiment, was bivouacked around the capital, Nicosia, in the centre of the island. This was the Divisional Commander's only reserve.

Thus was born within the Division the idea of the "box" and of the brigade group in which the Brigadier commanded the artillery, engineers and machine guns.

Unsound as they were tactically, and against all rules for economic and effective use of supporting arms, these theories were forced on the Division by the desperate shortage of men and the large frontages to be held.

The North Countrymen of the 50th Division always had a reputation for hard work. Their efforts with pick and shovel in France with the B.E.F. had called forth admiration; and though by this time the men in the formation were changing, the original North Country spirit persisted. All ranks did a fine job against the clock.

Lieutenant-Colonel Kennedy, acting as Chief Engineer and assisted by Lieutenant-Colonel Peter Bickford, was a tower of strength, planning and guiding the work and using mass-production methods when he could. A labour directorate was set up, and at its peak controlled a civilian labour force of twenty-three thousand.

The Prime Minister was intensely interested in progress, and gave notice that he required to know when the first pillbox was completed. On the 31st of August General Auchinleck toured the island's defences and visited units, and when he went away he expressed himself as well satisfied.

By the end of the Division's stay in Cyprus it was estimated that it had achieved more in three months than had been expected of it in six.

All this hard work served as a useful introduction to the stern tasks that lay ahead. And in other ways, too, Cyprus was a pleasant prelude to the Middle East campaigns. The troops of the 69th and 151st Brigades were able to become acclimatized in surroundings less hostile to man than the desert.

They found, like the Crusaders before them, that Cyprus is a charming island of magnificent mountains and lovely colour, with a dusty central plain that gave some idea of what the real desert was like. It is washed by warm seas, in which many of the troops were able to bathe regularly. There are groves of pomegranate and an abundance of wines. Primitive villages house Cypriots who were in the main friendly and amusing, and the quaint and ancient capital, Nicosia, with its walls and its native quarter, boasted historic charms side by side with a couple of night clubs.

To the 150th Brigade, coming by warship from Egypt after over a month in the Western Desert, it seemed like an earthly paradise. Their sojourn in Egypt had brought them abruptly face to face with desert conditions, and had given them a short lead over the other brigades in desert experience. Later they were to return to the desert, again alone, and finally one of the heaviest battles ever fought in the barren lands was to destroy them.

But when they came to Cyprus they had not been involved in any desert fighting. Their main job had been defence of rear areas and airfields, which had necessitated dispersion by companies over big distances, and which precluded ambitious training. None the less, various members of the brigade were able to visit the forward areas, where the Western Desert Force—forerunner of the Eighth Army— was operating in the sandstorms and mirages, and begin to learn what desert veterans called "the form."

The reunited 50th Division remained in Cyprus until the 3rd of November. Then at three days' notice the task of defending the island, and with it all the divisional transport and many of its weapons, was handed over to the 5th Indian Division. The 50th Division stole away by night, crowded on the decks of warships, heading for Palestine with the ultimate object of concentrating in Iraq and moving on to fight side by side with the Russians in the Caucasus.

The Division concentrated in the area of Haifa with the object of re-equipping there preparatory to moving off on their long journey eastwards. They took over the weapons and transport left behind by the 5th Indian Division. In the exchange the 50th Division were heavy losers, for whereas the transport they had left the Indians on the island had been new and British, in first-rate condition, the Indians' transport, drawn originally from every dump in the East, had been through tough campaigns. Some nine hundred vehicles were found to be completely unserviceable.

There was a great urgency. A speaker from Headquarters, Middle East, addressed the officers of the Division. He forecast a German thrust by up to ten armoured divisions south-east into Persia via the corridor of level country to the east of the Caspian. This the 50th Division was to help to hold. It was vital that the Division should get to the forecast theatre of operations as soon as possible. With this somewhat alarming speech in mind, the Division laboured to re-equip itself.

At this time many stores were "controlled"—that is to say, in such short supply that they could be issued only with G.H.Q. sanction. It was soon found that it would be impossible to re-equip, within the set time limit, by normal methods.

It was decided, therefore, to strip the 150th Brigade of most of its transport and stores in order to make the other two brigades mobile. After a period of feverish work the 69th and 151st Brigades moved off over the desert via Baghdad to Kirkuk, in Iraq. So finely had the time been cut that soldiers could be seen running down the road alongside the trucks tossing in the last stores.

The 150th Brigade was to follow later, but plans were changed and it was to find itself separated from the Division once more.

The march across the Transjordan desert, which was done without maps, since no maps were available, was the Division's first real experience of desert driving.

The weather was good, the surface mostly hard gravel sand, and the Division, in authentic desert formation for the first time, bowled along merrily. An exception was the motor-cyclists—it was still thought that motor-cycles were a possible means of transport in the desert. The only man who thought so by the time Baghdad was reached was the concert party's eccentric dancer, who had somehow acquired a huge four-cylinder bike and sidecar.

Soon after the troops' arrival at Kirkuk the Caucasian project was cancelled. The 50th Division, however, stayed in Iraq for a time. The country was still a little "jumpy" after the German coup which had resulted in the capture of the oil wells and a rising in the Army. It was common, when calling on senior Iraqi officers, to be told that they were "on leave"—a polite euphemism for "in prison, and likely to stay there, having backed the wrong horse."

The 151st Brigade did another fine piece of digging, preparing a defensive position at Two Rivers, north and west of Kirkuk.

The weather was very bad, cold and with torrents of rain, and nearly all the troops were living in tents and bivouacs. The clay soil became as slippery as ice, and one exercise was carried out in 28 degrees of frost. It was not a luxurious life.

The Division, however, experimented doggedly in cooking and heating by crude oil in home-made stoves, drawing the oil from the large puddles to be found everywhere. Thus it kept up its spirits and toughened up daily.

On Christmas Day the concert party, under Lieutenant Stringer Davis, put on a pantomime at Kirkuk. The theatre was a wet marquee and the lighting was by oil lamp. Before its break-up in 1946 this concert party, virtually unchanged, was to give shows in seventeen different countries.

In January, 1942, the Division, still without the 150th Brigade, was ordered to Syria to relieve the 6th Australian Division in the Baalbek area. This division was needed in Australia to prepare against a possible Japanese invasion.

Against the background of the tragic fall of Singapore, the 69th Brigade laboured to dig defences which should hold the expected German thrust southwards through Syria. As in Cyprus, there was a tremendous building of pillboxes, arduous digging and much argument as to the best siting of infantry on an obstacle to check German tanks. The brigades were still working as brigade groups, and would have fought as groups, widely dispersed, had the Germans attacked. No other plan was possible.

At the end of the month, however, the atmosphere lightened. The Division was ordered to the Western Desert. It set off once more on the long march south and west, relieved at the prospect of action after so much preparation and at a time when British fortunes seemed to be so low. The 151st Brigade, which had not reached Syria, moved direct. The 150th Brigade was in the desert waiting for the remainder of the Division.

CHAPTER V

The Desert—Adventures of the 150th Brigade—In the Line—Operation "Full-size"—Last Preparations before the Storm, and some Misgivings

JANUARY TO MAY, 1942

The background to the story now changes to the North African desert, in the fastnesses of which the Division was to fight until 1943. It is unlikely that anyone who did not personally experience the desert in war will understand clearly the impressions of those who did. In the tales that will be told in the future will be many contradictions. Some people will dwell on the desert's hostility to all forms of life, and the discomforts it occasioned to those who had the temerity to try to support life in its sterile bosom. They will tell how myriads of flies, the most faithful camp followers in the history of warfare, plagued them throughout the day and sometimes clustered so thickly on their vehicles as to turn them from brown to black.

They will describe the abominable khamseen, the hot wind from the burning deserts of the south, which spread a smothering blanket of fine sand over everything, choked the nostrils, infiltrated into ears and eyes, and, when mouths were opened to swear, got into them too.

On the other hand, there will be others who will speak wistfully of sunsets, when coolness came upon the desert like a benediction after the heat of the day, and the sky was beautiful in pastel shades of heliotrope and pink; who will speak of long journeys through trackless wastes, accomplished by means of magnetic and sun compasses; who will affirm that there is a special joy in the desert in a beer or whisky and the light of a hurricane lamp at eventide.

The contradictions will be understandable to those who realize that the desert has many moods and is very large. The northern desert of Africa is, in fact, bigger than India.

The coastal strip, which is the part which concerned the Division, consists in Egypt of a coastal plain which is backed by an escarpment which runs parallel to it. From the top of the escarpment a plateau extends to the south.

Just east of the Libya-Egypt frontier this escarpment turns north and puts a barrier across the coastal plain, forming a natural frontier additional to that which the Italians wired with a broad entanglement before the war.

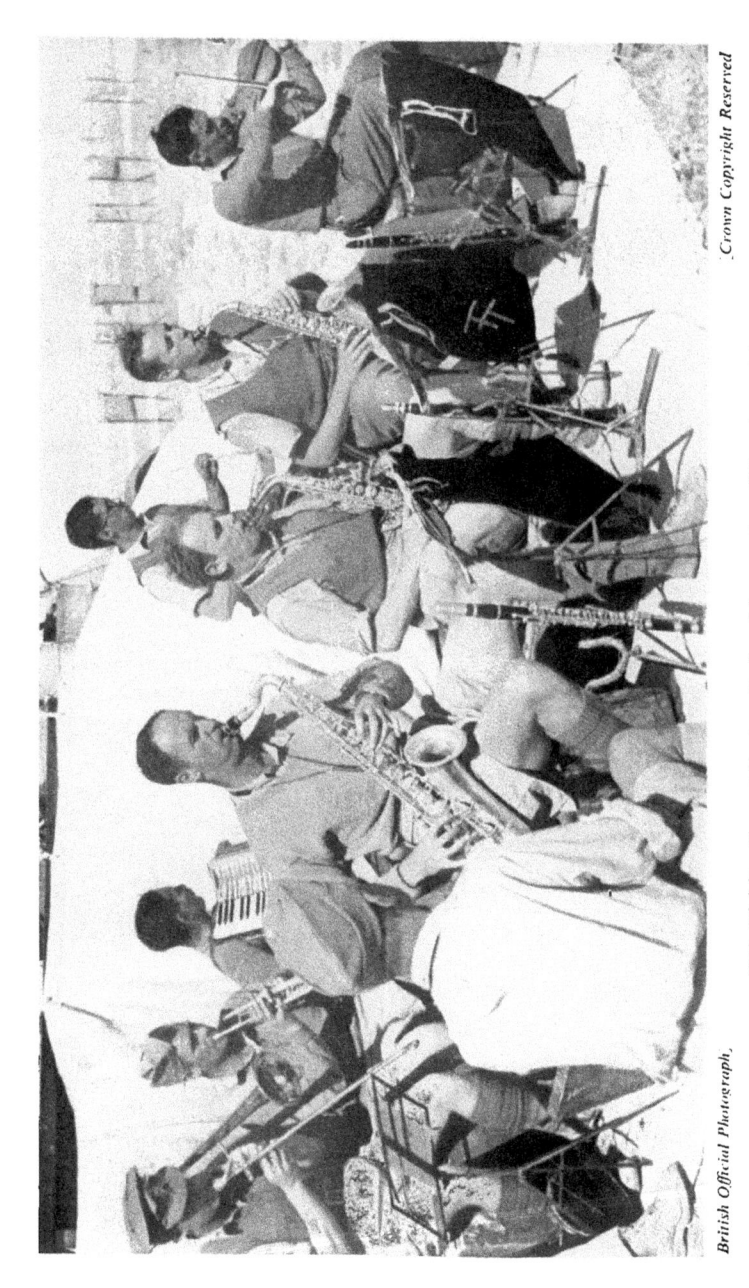

British Official Photograph. *Crown Copyright Reserved*

50th Division Concert Party. It played in seventeen different countries.

Face p. 46.

Up this barrier, at Sollum, the coastal road winds painfully; and a little to the south-east a secondary route—no more than a track—clambers to the top of Halfaya Pass.

Westward through Cyrenaica the escarpment is for the most part close to the coast, and in the semi-circular bulge between Gazala and Benghazi it develops into the Akhdar Hills, green and pleasant, and colonized before the war by Italian smallholders.

The Gebel, as this country was called in the Eighth Army, is one of the few green areas in Libya. Along the coastal strip there is, generally speaking, just sufficient rainfall to support a thin, sporadic vegetation. In places the desert suddenly blossoms, and in spring small depressions may be carpeted with flowers. Such oases in the barren lands seem doubly beautiful by contrast with their surroundings. Here and there the Bedouin succeed in growing a thin crop of cereals.

But in stark contrast to such glimpses of gentler country great tracts of sterile sand stretch away to far horizons under the staring sun, and fantastic mirages are the nearest thing to beauty which the traveller will find.

One piece of desert is very much like another, for the wilderness is full of repetitions. The newcomer, looking at a map produced in those early days, would sometimes say: "But why is all this space blank?" He would not yet have learned that the desert itself is sometimes blank for scores of miles.

Landmarks were few. Rock cisterns, dug and cemented by the Romans, and usually flanked by twin mounds of excavated material, were invaluable guides to one's position. "Bir" (pronounced "Beer") was their Arabic name. Occasionally the map would show the tomb of some desert personage. Sometimes it was just four low walls, like a miniature village penfold, with white rags fluttering from it. Occasionally the humble grave of a desert commoner, just a few stones apparently pitched on to the face of the desert, would help an anxious navigator.

Tracks there were, and when these were marked by route posts they were invaluable. But often the criss-cross comings and goings of the vehicles of two armies had resulted in a maze of tracks to which it was safest to pay no attention.

Natural features, with a few notable exceptions, did not exist in any marked form, though experience taught the soldier to recognize slight rises and falls in the desert for what they were. "Return to this depression tonight," said an officer to the leader of a small patrol. "What depression?" was the reply. "The one we're in now," said the officer.

This vast tract of open country made possible movement in a manner and on a scale that would have been out of the question in Europe. Mobile forces advanced in the desert not in single file but spread out like a fleet at sea, each vehicle in its station, and the whole company driving on a given compass bearing, led by a navigator.

The Army was highly mobile and detached forces were accustomed to operate over very wide areas indeed. The desert flank was usually open, and this resulted in deep patrolling to the south.

Everything which the Army needed to sustain it had to be brought from somewhere else. The desert produced nothing. Supplies came along the coast road, along the railway which, when the Division entered the desert, had been extended from Matruh to Bir Thalata, on top of the escarpment not far from the frontier, and by sea to Tobruk. These were the three pipelines to the Army. The farther the Army advanced the longer they became. The bigger the Army grew the greater the pressure on them.

So the Army lived hard . . . and the sum of all these circumstances produced the original "desertworthy" soldier. Accustomed to hardship and deprived of many of the amenities present in more conventional theatres of war, he became tough and resistant as a Bedouin, with a Bedouin-like knowledge of how to care for himself. He could find his way over the desert, theoretically by star and compass, but actually by some strange skill, based apparently on contempt of or disbelief in the difficulties involved. He had fought against odds since the beginning of the desert war and had known both reverses and splendid triumphs. He knew that his weapons could not stop the German tanks, but he was prepared to hold on somehow until the new armies arrived.

Into this goodly company, now holding a line from Gazala on the coast to Bir Hacheim in the south, motored the 50th Division in their battle-worn transport in the New Year of 1942. During the next few months they learnt to be "desertworthy"—and learnt with true North Country thoroughness.

It has already been stated that when the Division entered the desert they found the 150th Brigade Group there waiting for them. This story must now explain the brigade's activities during the period of separation.

When the main part of the Division left Haifa, the 150th Brigade remained there, under orders to follow as and when the transport situation permitted. But on the 19th of November the Eighth Army launched a major offensive in the Western Desert, and later in that month the 150th Brigade were suddenly ordered west to join them.

They moved initially to Baggush, where they had been on their first tour of duty in the desert in July.

There they trained for nearly three weeks, receiving valuable help from the 7th Indian Infantry Brigade and the New Zealanders, who were resting after their heavy battles at Sidi Rezegh and Bel Hamed.

On the 22nd of December they moved on to Bir Thalata, in the area of which was desert railhead. Before they went the divisional reconnaissance unit, the 4th Royal Northumberland Fusiliers, was detached from the brigade; and, as events turned out, this proved to be a final parting. To everyone's regret the Royal Northumberland Fusiliers never rejoined the Division. In the spring of the following year that battalion was decimated at Knightsbridge.

The Bir Thalata area was bleak at this time of year. By day there were frequent sandstorms and at nights white frosts. There the brigade, with a troop-carrying company under command, trained intensively in daylight and in darkness for operations which everyone felt could not now be long delayed.

The 72nd Field Regiment was temporarily detached to join the forces investing the Halfaya garrison, where a small German force was still holding out.

During the stay at Thalata Lieutenant-Colonel Caldwell relinquished command of the 4th East Yorkshire Regiment owing to illness, and the command passed to his second-in-command, Major Norman.

The Divisional Commander flew from Iraq to visit the Brigade on the 3rd of January. The intention then was that the Brigade should rejoin the Division, and shortly after General Ramsden's visit they were placed at twelve hours' notice to do so. In the midst of preparations to move east, however, they were suddenly placed at four hours' notice to move in the opposite direction. The situation at El Agheila had deteriorated and the Eighth Army were giving ground in the face of a swift attack by Rommel.

On the 25th of January the 150th Brigade Group set off for Bir Harmat, in Libya, one hundred and twenty miles farther west. They moved across the desert in four columns in one of the worst sandstorms they ever experienced. Swirling sand reduced visibility to a yard or two, and vehicles had to close together in night formation to keep touch. Some unfortunate navigators had to march on foot, compass in hand, through this stinging sand "fog" with the vehicles they guided grinding slowly along at their heels.

A twelve-hour halt was made at Harmat, where the brigade received its first anti-tank guns—eight 50-mm. German weapons. Then the troops pushed on for a further sixty miles to the area of

Garet el Auda. This was the southern limit of the line which British and Allied forces were holding temporarily, and through which the main body of the Eighth Army was falling back.

It was a very distinctive tract of desert, marked by depressions and small, dumpling-like sandhills, with very little vegetation. Even by desert standards it was desolate, forbidding and confusing, and the troops named it "The Land of the Moon," and, perhaps even more aptly, "The Bloodiness."

The 4th Green Howards, with the 285th Battery, R.A., were sent fifteen miles west of Garet el Auda to the area of Bir Tengeder. The armoured cars of the Royals were operating still farther to the west and south, and day by day units of the Eighth Army passed through on their way east, some of them after making long detours in the southern desert to avoid the Germans, who had cut them off.

The 150th Brigade patrolled strongly west, south and north for information, and to the 4th Green Howards fell the honour of capturing the Division's first prisoner in the desert. A small column of infantry and artillery under the command of Captain Peter Kirkby, working in co-operation with the Royals, seized a volkswagen containing a German sergeant-major, a fair part of the Christmas mail for a German unit, and some Christmas "comforts" (including the liquid variety) intended for the officers' mess.

By the 2nd of February the rearguard task at Bir Tengeder was deemed to have been accomplished, and the brigade began to withdraw by night through the soft sand of "The Bloodiness" to Bir Hacheim. Hacheim was the southern bastion of the position which became known as the Gazala Line, and on which the Eighth Army was to stand. It is a small fort, rather like an illustration from "Beau Geste." French Legionnaires were, in fact, destined to fight a famous battle there in defences which the 150th Brigade now began to devise "against the clock."

Mines were laid and wire erected, and infantry and gunners dug in as fast as they could. To the south light armour patrolled the open flank. To the north the 201st Guards Brigade, fifteen miles away, were the nearest neighbours. To the west, Licol, a small force of infantry from the 4th Green Howards, gunners from the 72nd Field Regiment, and sappers, in rickety vehicles with few spare wheels and fewer spanners, operated eighty miles from their base against the advancing enemy.

On the 15th of February the 150th Brigade began to move north to take over from the Free French. The 5th Green Howards went into the line on the right of the new brigade front at Bir Naghia, the 4th East Yorkshire Regiment were in the centre, and on the left the

4th Green Howards moved into position at Alem Hamza, a battlefield made famous by the Buffs.

The situation on the Eighth Army front had by now become stable. As foretold by General Cunningham, both sides reached the practicable limit for the length of their lines of communication by holding, the British the Gazala position, the Germans the Tmimi position. The flat stretch of country between them, often twenty-five miles wide, had no feature on which to hang an infantry defence. It became a No Man's Desert separating the two armies.

The main body of the 50th Division, coming from the east, took over from the 4th Indian Division. The frontages were very wide; roughly twenty-five miles had to be held. To the north was the 1st South African Division, and to the south the flank was refused. Thence a big "mine sea" ran down to Bir Hacheim which was held by the Free French. Behind the "mine sea" was the 1st Armoured Division. To the south of Bir Hacheim the country was open.

This was the time when the 50th Division was the only British infantry division in contact with the enemy in any part of the world.

It was intensely active. Each brigade, following the doctrine of fortresses to be held irrespective of enemy break-through, enclosed itself and its supporting arms in an intricate minefield, carefully covered by fire and giving all-round defence. All positions were dug flush with the ground without parapet, and were very hard to see. Overhead cover was provided nearly everywhere. There was a desperate shortage of anti-tank guns—only the 69th and 151st Brigades had 2-pounders (roughly twelve each). Field guns were all sited in anti-tank positions, and Italian guns, mostly 47-mm., were salvaged from old battlefields, though it was known that they were useless against German Mark III or IV tanks. Stocks of food, water and ammunition to stand a three-week siege were gradually built up in each brigade "box." A splendid defensive position was built up, very strong and inconspicuous.

"The contention was," writes Lieutenant-Colonel R. H. L. Wheeler, who was G.S.O.1 at about this time,[1] "that this position would be a secure base, holding fast in spite of enemy break-through and giving to our armoured forces a point of manœuvre. It is evident that this policy gave the Germans the initiative from the outset. It is hard to see what else could have been done with the resources then available.

---

[1] Lieutenant-Colonel Wheeler became G.1 in April. His predecessor was Lieutenant-Colonel L. G. Holmes, on whose shoulders fell the heavy burden of staff work in Cyprus. He left to command the 1st Field Regiment, R.A.

"The patrolling activity which the Division carried out was perhaps not based on such sound logic.

"Against the Italians small columns of all arms, perhaps two companies or a battalion of infantry with supporting arms, all motorized, and pursuing harassing tactics, had been very successful.

"This doctrine was handed on to the Division, who accepted it enthusiastically. Brigades took it in turn to find the column, which ranged No Man's Land, shelled enemy positions and then slipped away and sent out fighting patrols at night. This was excellent training for commanders, and for all ranks in 'desert drill.'

"The Germans, however, experienced and strong-nerved, did not react. They gave little sign that they had noticed our columns, but occasionally they would come out in force with tanks. A column could not take on a force of tanks, and had to retreat precipitately. Two columns got mauled. This was bad training, but it happened so seldom that, probably, little harm was done.

"It is certain that these sorties were necesary if the troops were to avoid clinging to the protection of their minefields with all the attendant loss of initiative and nerve.

"Fine work was done by many units and individuals. For instance, Captain Ian Donking and his specially picked patrol of the 4th Green Howards had at least two desperate night encounters with the entrenched enemy near Sidi Bregsic before they succeeded, on their third raid, in bringing back a German lorried infantryman. Donking was killed shortly afterwards in the bombing of a hospital ship, and the Division lost a brave fighting soldier.

"There were many other examples of individual spirit and initiative—such as that of Lieutenant E. W. Clay and Second-Lieutenant P. J. Howell, who lay hidden in the German lines for three days observing and noting what the Germans were up to."

Donking's prisoner was a fitting parting gift to the battalion commander, Lieutenant-Colonel C. N. Littleboy, who fell a victim to the age limit and handed over command to Lieutenant-Colonel L. Cooper.

Another change in command which occurred at about this time was that Lieutenant-Colonel S. V. Keeling succeeded Lieutenant-Colonel Gentry Birch as commanding officer of the 2nd Cheshire Regiment.

From the small-scale operations the Division went on to something much bigger in March. An attempt was made to get an important convoy to Malta, and the Eighth Army co-operated by seeking to divert the Luftwaffe at the critical moment.

The Division's share in this operation, known by the code word

"Full-size," was to send two columns to harass the enemy landing grounds at Tmimi and nearby Martuba. A third column was to move to Bir Temrad to cover the assembly of the Tmimi column, which was to include tanks, and to cover the withdrawal of both columns. The whole operation was under the command of Brigadier J. S. Nichols, Commander of the 151st Brigade.

The attacking columns moved off on the night of the 20th/21st March, the 4th East Yorkshire Regiment (150th Brigade) providing the infantry for the Martuba attack. This column included mortars, carriers, 25-pounders, Bofors, anti-tank guns, sappers and a field ambulance, and was commanded by Lieutenant-Colonel Norman, officer commanding the 4th East Yorkshire Regiment.

A small force under Captain D. E. Field was sent to secure the right flank of this column by seizing an enemy observation post at Ras el Eleba. This flankguard did its job after sharp fighting, during which Brigadier Haydon, Commander of the 150th Brigade, who turned up and took part in it, got a bullet through his forage cap.

The East Yorkshire column got to within two miles of Martuba aerodrome in broad daylight and opened fire. Of course, this frontal blow stirred up a hornets' nest, and throughout the remaining hours of daylight the enemy ran a shuttle service of aircraft between the aerodrome and the column, which they dive-bombed and machine-gunned. A large amount of Bofors ammunition was blown up early in the attacks, which weakened the column's A.A. defence. Before our troops withdrew at midnight they had lost several casualties and forty vehicles—but some of the Luftwaffe had been diverted.

The other principal column, under the direct command of Brigadier Nichols, had first to capture dominating ground at Gabr el Aleima, which barred their way to Tmimi. This was brilliantly achieved by tanks and infantry of the Durham Light Infantry, and over one hundred and fifty prisoners were captured. The column then pushed on and harassed Tmimi.

Thus the Division was, in a phrase of those times, "blooded" in desert warfare. Though the columns had losses, "Full-size" had been a success from the larger point of view, for the Malta convoy had got through.

There had been talk of withdrawing the Division for retraining and re-equipping ready for an offensive. Transport and equipment were certainly in a deplorable state, but it was soon clear that the Germans were not going to grant the necessary time.

On the 6th of April they suddenly narrowed No Man's Land by advancing in force and seizing key points on the Division's front where previously our columns had manœuvred—Bir Temrad, Sidi Bregisc and Rotunda Segnali.

It became increasingly clear that the German offensive would be ready before ours. The High Command therefore had to make its final defensive preparations.

A South African brigade was sent to relieve the 150th Brigade in the northern part of the 50th Division's position and the 150th Brigade was sent south to relieve the 201st Guards Brigade in the Ualeb area, south of the Trigh Capuzzo. This was a very poor exchange for the Division. The new 150th Brigade position with a perimeter of twenty miles was isolated from the 69th Brigade by a gap of six miles, was too big for three battalions, uncompleted, and very hard to defend in the rear. Yet it was obvious that the Germans would cut off this position and attack it in the rear—indeed, a map was captured showing a German line of advance which would result in this. However, all the supporting arms that could be spared were given to the 150th Brigade, and they settled down to improving the position with their usual energy.

Ten miles to the south of the 150th Brigade were the Free French in Bir Hacheim.

The two gaps in the line were covered by minefields, but it was obvious that the Germans would breach these fields, which were unprotected by fire. Indeed, the Commander of the 150th Brigade discovered that at one place the minefield, laid long before by other troops, and unrecorded, was only a few hundred yards wide. This weak patch was on the Trigh Capuzzo—the main track through the Imperial position.

Behind the entrenched infantry were the 1st and 7th Armoured Divisions, with the 201st Guards Brigade in a defended locality called Knightsbridge. In Knightsbridge were the first 6-pounder anti-tank guns to be seen in the desert—they had arrived a few days before the battle began. The Division still had its 2-pounders and 47-mms. The 1st Army Tank Brigade and the 7th Medium Regiment, R.A., were put under the command of the 50th Division.

From north to south the Army's dispositions were:

    Gazala.—1st South African Division.
    Alem Hamza.—One brigade of the 2nd South African Division.
        Behind this line: 201st Guards Brigade (Knightsbridge) and 1st Armoured Division.
    Alem Hamza to Gabriel.—151st Brigade. Behind this line: 7th Armoured Division.
    Fachri.—69th Brigade.

A six-mile gap.
Trigh Capuzzo to Ualeb.—150th Brigade.
A ten-mile gap.
Bir Hacheim.—Free French Brigade.

Tobruk was garrisoned by the rest of the 2nd South African Division, which had no transport.

It was therefore clear from the start that the battle would have to be fought as foreseen—each brigade fortress holding on until the armour could strike its blow and restore the balance.

But now a disturbing factor was that the 150th Brigade could not be supported by the other brigades, while under the original lay-out all three brigades were mutually self-supporting.

The equipment and transport of the Division were in a sorry state. The shortage of anti-tank guns has already been described. Moreover, it was common for field regiments to have at most one or two observation-post trucks with serviceable engines. With these they would tow the remaining trucks into position, coming back to fetch them when the tour of duty was over. Tyres, particularly for 8-cwt. trucks, were so scarce that many vehicles were permanently jacked up in the "boxes," their wheels being used on vehicles wanted for the desert columns. Divisional Headquarters had only five wireless sets. Scavenging parties went out daily to pick over stores long since abandoned after forgotten skirmishes. One lieutenant-colonel was particularly adept at refitting abandoned Italian anti-tank guns, which he would give, on persuasion, to what he called "good homes." One day, however, in mid-May, a Spitfire made a forced landing between the 69th and 151st Brigade "boxes." It was the first sign of equipment equal to that of the Germans.

As always in war, the margin of time was small but all-important.

The Americans had built Grant tanks—prototype of the Sherman and found to be unsatisfactory owing to the very limited traverse of the 75-mm. gun. These Grants now began to appear in the desert, and, badly designed as they were, they were the first tanks on our side to mount a gun comparable to that of the German Mark IV. The 6-pounder anti-tank gun was in production, but there was as yet no reinforcement of heavy or medium artillery. These new weapons began to trickle into the desert a short time—in some cases a few days—before the Germans struck; for late in May it became obvious that Rommel was ready to attack.

On the 26th of May the Axis forces began to move.

CHAPTER VI

THE AFRIKA KORPS STRIKES—THE CAULDRON—TRAGEDY OF
THE 150TH BRIGADE

MAY TO JUNE, 1942

ON the night of the 26th/27th May the greater part of the German Afrika Korps—90th Light Division, 15th Panzer Division and 21st Panzer Division—together with the Italian Ariete Armoured Division, made a rapid forced march round the open flank of the Eighth Army's position at Bir Hacheim, and turned north, directed on Tobruk. They ran into our armoured forces on the way and were jolted to a standstill around Harmat and Knightsbridge.

To the north and west the 1st South African Division and the 69th and 151st Brigades, only lightly attacked by Italian troops, remained in their fortresses as ordered.

To the south of the 69th Brigade the Germans quickly began to lift the stretch of undefended minefield, thus cutting off the 150th Brigade from the rest of the Division. This the 50th Division was not allowed to dispute.

Still farther south, in Bir Hacheim, the Free French fought stoutly.

Standing firm in their positions, these "garrison troops" waited for the armour to contact and destroy the enemy.

It was Rommel's purpose to shorten his lines of communication by lifting the minefield between the 69th and 150th Brigades, thus establishing a direct route along the Trigh Capuzzo east and west through this unoccupied stretch of desert.

The intention of our Higher Command was to enclose this piece of ground—which was nicknamed the Cauldron—and there destroy the enemy's armour. To this end all the "garrison troops" were to stand fast in their positions. The 50th Division was ordered to put out first one and, later, a second battalion in defended positions to the east of the 151st Brigade in order further to enclose the Cauldron. They were supported by the Army Tank Brigade.

Divisional Headquarters had already moved into the eastern end of the 151st Brigade position.

From these positions the rest of the Division was forced to watch the struggle of the 150th Brigade, who, with the Free French, were the only "garrison troops" to be heavily attacked. It was a bitter business, but there was no alternative. A direct attack by infantry on the armoured forces surrounding the 150th Brigade was unthinkable.

A plan to break out westward and get astride Rommel's rearward lines was made with representatives of the 1st Armoured Division. This attack was never launched, presumably because the armour could not be spared.

Lieutenant-General Gott, Commander of the XIII Corps, who motored frequently through the German lines to visit the Division, was not permitted to order any sorties.

There was nothing to do but to sit tight. That was the general position in the first days of the battle. Let us see now what happened in detail.

The British armoured divisions, positioned to meet such an offensive, came to grips with the enemy in the general areas of Harmat and Knightsbridge, and stopped the onrush.

The Divisional Mobile Reserve played a part in this battle. It consisted of:

> Headquarters, 1st Army Tank Brigade (Brigadier O'Carroll).
> 44th Royal Tank Regiment.
> One squadron, 42nd Royal Tank Regiment.
> One squadron, South African Armoured Cars.
> 287th Battery, 124th Field Regiment (Major Ian Bransom).
> 6th Green Howards (Lieutenant-Colonel E. C. Cooke-Collis).
> One company, 2nd Cheshire Regiment.

By 1015 hrs. on the 27th of May the reserve was on the way to occupy Bir Aslagh, about half-way between Harmat and Knightsbridge and a little to the west of the main track between the two points. It thus positioned itself between the enemy who had swept round the southern flank and the rear of the 150th Brigade. The intention was to establish a firm point protecting the 150th Brigade's rear, and also to establish an "anvil" against which our armour could hammer the enemy.

The mobile reserve was quickly in contact with an enemy force moving north, and in the resulting actions throughout the day it caused them losses, though several of its tanks were "brewed up." It is clear now that it was, in fact, skirmishing on the left flank of Rommel's main advance.

The 150th Brigade heard the noise of battle at their backs, but to their front no heavy fighting developed; nor was the experience markedly different on the remainder of the divisional front.

In general the enemy nosed forward against our western defences but did not develop a serious attack when checked. On the 150th

Brigade front he pushed along the lines of the Trigh Capuzzo and the Trigh el Abd. The 4th East Yorkshire Regiment, in their defences covering the latter track, destroyed thirteen Italian tanks, which discouraged the enemy for the rest of the day. To the north the 4th Green Howards established a fighting patrol under Captain A. P. Mitchell on rising ground about three-quarters of a mile in front of their foremost post on the Capuzzo Gap. The defence of this ground, known as the Disputed Ridge, both on this day and subsequently, was a fine and determined action.

The 150th Brigade also sent out a mobile column to assist the divisional mobile reserve, and the medium battery (Battle Axe) in the brigade "box" gave artillery support to the reserve.

The armoured battle was joined again on the 28th of May, and before 0700 hrs. the divisional mobile reserve was on the way to Knightsbridge, which they occupied without opposition. The 150th Brigade column took over at Aslagh, where the mobile reserve had left some of their tanks to support them. Later, a heavy attack forced our troops back from Aslagh.

On the remainder of the divisional front the enemy maintained pressure from the west, again devoting most of his attention to the 150th Brigade, who saw that he was trying to make gaps through the minefield north of the Trigh Capuzzo and south of the Trigh el Abd; ammunition restrictions—twenty-five rounds per gun on this day—made it difficult to put a stop to his ominous activity.

During the day trucks were sent to Tobruk for ammunition. They were not seen again by the 150th Brigade.

By evening it had become necessary to make radical alterations in the 150th Brigade's dispositions. "D" Company, 4th East Yorkshire Regiment, had replaced two platoons of the 5th Green Howards as the infantry component of the brigade mobile column, and their absence from the static defences of the "box" was felt. The remainder of the 4th East Yorkshire Regiment was now too extended.

With the increasing freedom of action of enemy armour the threat of attacks from the Cauldron had increased, and on that side of the "box" was a gap between the 4th Green Howards and the 232nd Field Company, R.E., who had provided infantry posts. The 4th East Yorkshire Regiment were therefore ordered to place their two remaining companies one on either side of the field company, the move to be made during the night. During the night, also, the brigade mobile column and the 44th Royal Tank Regiment withdrew into the "box."

The pattern of the battle on the 29th of May was roughly the same —the enemy continued to edge forward, and shelling of the divisional area increased. The enemy occupied the ground vacated by the 4th East Yorkshire Regiment—heavy artillery fire would have given them pause—and finally gained control of the Disputed Ridge with a full-scale attack which was halted in front of the Capuzzo Gap.

Lieutenant-Colonel Cooke-Collis, officer commanding 6th Green Howards, came into the "box" to ask for armoured protection to get his troops back to the 69th Brigade area. This was provided, and he was able to take with him General Cruewell, G.O.C. Afrika Korps, who had been shot down over the area of the 4th Green Howards while making a reconnaissance in a Feisler Storch.

Perhaps the most significant occurrence on the 29th of May was that the enemy managed to send supplies to his armour in the Cauldron—which had been severely embarrassed by lack of petrol and water—by way of the gap he had made north of Trigh Capuzzo. This, coupled with the serious shortage of ammunition, caused a grave deterioration in the situation of the 150th Brigade.

Elsewhere on the divisional front the situation was virtually unchanged.

On the night of the 29th/30th "D" Company, 4th East Yorkshire Regiment, moved from brigade reserve into position on the perimeter on the right of the 4th Green Howards. Night patrolling was carried out by weary men on all fronts, and Lieutenant Hopkins, with a patrol from the 5th Green Howards, inflicted heavy casualties on an enemy working party.

In the 150th Brigade position the next day was spent in the dispiriting process of "plugging up holes" as they were punched by an enemy who now encircled the entire position in superior strength.

The enemy attacked the 232nd Field Company on the eastern face of the defences, and overran them, gaining a vantage point from which a great part of the Brigade position could be overlooked. Gallant attacks by armour and infantry throughout the day failed to dislodge them.

In heavy fighting on the front of the 4th Green Howards the enemy was held, though the battalion lost one of its outstanding figures in Major Brian Jackson, who was mortally wounded.

The enemy, heavily concentrated on the front of the 5th Green Howards, put in an attack that was repulsed largely as a result of a carrier counter-attack led by Major Peter Fox, who was given command of what remained of the brigade reserve for the purpose. Both he and his gallant driver were severely wounded and made prisoner.

While the 150th Brigade struggled on during this bitter day attempts were being made from outside to relieve a situation that was growing desperate. On two successive nights Headquarters, 50th

Division, had tried to send ammunition through, but the enemy cordon round the Brigade was too strong. Continuous attempts were made to send forces to the rescue.

All other attempts failed, and on the 31st of May the enemy, heavily reinforced, broke into the north-east corner of the "box." There "B" Company, 4th East Yorkshire Regiment, under Captain Good (who was killed at his post), and "F" Troop, 286th Battery, R.A., fought from 1000 hrs. until 1600 hrs. before they were crushed. Second-Lieutenant Farmiloe, "A" Troop, 81st Battery, 25th Light A.A. Regiment, helped to pump Bofors shells into a Mark IV tank until a direct hit wounded him and the rest of his brave gun crew. The few remaining tanks were mustered to seal off this new penetration.

The enemy also attacked the south-east corner of the "box" at the junction of the 4th East Yorkshire Regiment and 5th Green Howards and gained ground and prisoners. The timely arrival of Major Jack Brewer and men of the East Yorkshire Regiment Battalion Headquarters helped to restore the situation.

The 4th Green Howards also withstood a heavy attack, during which the enemy breached the minefield and marked the way through by white tapes. When they were forced back Captain P. B. Watson bravely relaid the mines under heavy fire. Years later, when he returned from captivity, he was awarded the Distinguished Service Order for this.

As night fell the patchwork defence still held, but there were now no reserves with which to plug any further holes. Only thirteen tanks remained; there were six medium guns with twenty rounds each, and twelve 25-pounders with less than a hundred rounds among them. Most of the 2-pounder anti-tank guns had been destroyed, and the infantry battalions had hardly any ammunition left. If help did not arrive by early the next day the brigade was obviously finished as a fighting force.

The Army Commander sent a personal message over the air to Brigadier Haydon, urging him to hold on, for help was coming. At Divisional Headquarters there were very heavy hearts. It was expressly forbidden to go to the rescue, and all realized that to do so would indeed break up the pattern on which the Army Commander wished to fight this battle. The 69th and 151st Brigades were fighting fit. Could the battle be mounted by other forces in time to save the 150th Brigade?

Help did not arrive. At first light on the 1st of June the enemy attacked from all sides, and platoon by platoon the brigade was overrun and captured. The last sub-unit to go down was believed to be the platoon of the 5th Green Howards commanded by Captain "Bert" Dennis. Brigadier Haydon, who had commanded the brigade with conspicuous skill and gallantry both in France and the desert, was killed.

The Germans had not only eliminated the 150th Brigade: they had succeeded in lodging themselves in the very centre of the British positions in the Gazala Line.

This was the end of a chapter in the battle; it is a suitable moment to turn away from the main story to describe some of the experiences which befell the divisional field ambulances. Like many other units of the Eighth Army which would not normally expect to find themselves in the front line, the field ambulances, stationed in rear of the Gazala defences, were in the thick of the fray as a result of the enemy armoured sweep round the southern flank.

The 186th Field Ambulance was overrun on the 27th of May. A little later the enemy overran the main dressing station of the 150th Field Ambulance, under Lieutenant-Colonel Scriven, but it continued to operate for both British and German wounded. German medical arrangements were seen to be primitive in some respects. German doctors, though skilful, would often attempt to operate without anæsthetic. During the day Rommel visited the hospital area. It is reported that he used it as an advanced headquarters. Each night the hospital area was used by the Germans to leaguer their tanks.

After some days spent in this peculiar situation, the British medical unit was able to get away, complete with its wounded, and join the Guards Brigade at Knightsbridge.

The 149th Field Ambulance main dressing station shared in the general excitement. On the 29th of May German armoured forces entered its area no fewer than seven times. They looted the canteen and took away some of the unit transport. But the official report of the ambulance for this period says: "In fairness it must be stated that in general the terms of the Geneva Convention were adhered to. The enemy, especially officers, were punctilious in their compliments, and personal kit was not interfered with to any extent."

Rear Divisional Headquarters also found itself in or near the battle. The entire headquarters, including the services but excluding the medical units, formed a large and vulnerable prize of "soft-skinned" vehicles, and destruction or capture at the hands of the enemy would have spelled almost certain disaster for the 50th Division's fighting units.

Rear Headquarters' job was to position itself out of harm's way yet so as to continue to serve the fighting troops. This entailed several rapid moves. Night after night R.A.S.C. drivers took supplies from

Tobruk to the Gazala positions, often under heavy fire. Between spells of duty they bathed near Tobruk, where "Teecol" (code name for Rear Divisional Headquarters) was established for a time.

For a long time the unprotected Teecol lived dangerously; that it lived at all was due to the vigilance and devotion of all concerned, and in particular to the direction of Lieutenant-Colonel Divers (C.R.A.S.C.) and Major R. H. Turton, M.P. (D.A.A.G.), who was also the senior operational staff officer at the headquarters. Lieutenant-Colonel Divers was awarded the Distinguished Service Order and Major Turton the Military Cross.

CHAPTER VII

THE BATTLE LOST—50TH DIVISION BREAKS OUT—WITHDRAWAL TO THE FRONTIER—REARGUARD ACTION TO MATRUH, AND ANOTHER BREAK-OUT—THE STRUGGLE ON RUWEISAT RIDGE—THE GERMANS STOPPED

JUNE TO JULY, 1942

WITH the loss of the 150th Brigade the battle now entered a period of deadlock which lasted for several days. The remaining brigades of the 50th Division remained in occupation of their positions north and east of the Cauldron while the enemy established himself in the 150th Brigade positions and prepared energetically to renew full-scale operations.

The record of the Division's activities in this period is far from complete, but there are glimpses of small and fierce actions around the 69th and 151st Brigade positions against both Italians and Germans. By vigorous patrolling and aggressive action outside their own positions, the infantry gradually wrested the initiative from the enemy. The 151st Brigade in particular turned to the offensive and on one occasion brought back from a raid nearly a battalion as prisoners. The 7th Green Howards, who had won great distinction as part of the divisional mobile reserve, made a noteworthy attack with tanks against the enemy established in the Cauldron.

Of the smaller actions, one of the most remarkable was that of Captain Francis L. Cole and two sections of carriers of the 9th Durham Light Infantry. They attacked an enemy convoy on the 30th of May, captured a lorry complete with crew, destroyed two other lorries and shot-up two lorry loads of infantry.

The next day, with one section of carriers, four anti-tank guns and a section of machine guns from the 2nd Cheshire Regiment, Captain Cole attempted to disperse seventeen armoured fighting vehicles which were protecting the same convoy. A fierce action ensued in which Cole was severely wounded and his driver killed; he was obliged to disengage his small force in the face of very heavy fire. The withdrawal of his own vehicle presented him with a grim problem. In his weakened state Captain Cole was unable to move the body of his driver from the driving seat; he held the dead man's leg on the accelerator and steered the carrier out of action.

By such determined action the enemy facing the Division was robbed of morale—particularly the Italian infantry divisions who were dug in on the western perimeter.

As an illustration, it may be recalled that an enemy tank was chased by three British Bren carriers. Bullets from the carriers' Bren guns bounced harmlessly off its sides, but the tank stopped and the Italian crew surrendered. This incident caused a good deal of merriment in Durham Light Infantry circles, and shortly afterwards another patrol of three carriers was delighted to encounter a second Italian tank in similar circumstances. The carriers opened fire and the tank duly stopped. An Italian popped out his head and suggested that since he was "only on patrol" and had absolutely no aggressive intentions, he should be left alone.

In the air the enemy was much more aggressive. Stukas circled over various parts of the divisional area and carried out dive-bombing. This led to the celebrated incident in which the Divisional Commander, wearing only a towel, shot out of his dug-out and cheered on a Bofors gun crew so effectively that they blew the tail off a German fighter.

Though the Division was invested virtually on three sides—west, south and east—the enemy was really active only on the south. The eastern side of the defences was not attacked, though the main German armoured forces were manœuvring and fighting in that area. But though the 50th Division was holding its ground, taking prisoners and making the enemy's life as uncomfortable as possible, the overall picture was changing.

The Free French were withdrawn from Bir Hacheim by night after a resistance which has become an epic. The retreat from Hacheim left the desert to the south of the 69th Brigade in undisputed possession of the Germans.

On the 13th of June a decisive action was fought south-west of Tobruk. In this great armoured battle the Imperial forces lost a large number of tanks, which meant a breakdown of the battle plan. The 50th and 1st South African Divisions were now isolated. No longer were they a firm base round which the British armour could manœuvre, for the British armour was decimated. To continue to hold the positions would have been pointless; withdrawal became inevitable.

Yet, to the 69th and 151st Brigades, undefeated and indeed unchallenged, a withdrawal meant bitter disappointment. And when the orders came the Divisional Commander, who answered General Gott, spoke for the Division when he said: "This is a bitter blow, a very great disappointment." But, despite this setting of general misfortune, the 50th Division was destined to perform a feat of arms which made its name famous throughout the Empire.

Conventional withdrawal was impossible. The coast road and the desert immediately to the south of it were adequate only for the withdrawal of the 1st South African Division. For the 50th Division to have withdrawn due east would have brought them face to face with the main German armoured force. To go south would have resulted in collision with further German armoured forces.

It was therefore decided that the Division should withdraw by advancing westward through the Italian division. They were to break clean through the enemy positions; then turn south, driving across the enemy's lines of communication, turn eastward in a wide sweep round Bir Hacheim and then head for the frontier at Fort Maddalena, some one hundred and twenty miles from Bir Hacheim.

The 50th Division were ordered not to move until the 1st South African Division was clear of its position. This meant giving them twelve hours' start, thus reducing any chance of surprise.

It was a great gamble. The Eighth Army was leaving its only English infantry division holding the fort in isolation while other components were withdrawn. It was by no means certain that the Division would emerge from its battle with the entrenched enemy in a condition to continue the fight; it was by no means certain that those troops who broke out would make the long journey to the frontier without further desperate encounters; but, in fact, the 50th Division emerged triumphant from this desperate situation and lived to fight for many another day.

It was decided to break out through two bridgeheads in a large number of small columns of all arms. These columns, once clear of the enemy positions, were to travel independently. Thus the desert would be dotted with small mobile columns widely scattered. Though one column here might be checked by the enemy, two more elsewhere would slip past.

The immediate problem was that of transport. To lift the Division with all its stores and equipment would require one hundred and eighty three-ton lorries. Half that number were available, and no more could be obtained from outside sources. Therefore everything not required to fight the Division into the open desert and maintain it on its long journey was jettisoned. In addition to weapons and wireless, the Division carried with it petrol for three hundred miles and rations and water for three days. All that had to be abandoned was disposed of carefully. There could be no large-scale demolition or fires in case they should give notice to the enemy of the impending withdrawal.

A dust-storm blew up during the afternoon of the 14th of June and helped to mask much of the additional activity in the divisional area. Stores and equipment of all kinds were destroyed, booby-trapped or buried. Many of them probably lie under the sands to this day.[1]

There are several good stories of individual actions which took place either just before or just after the withdrawal began. Major Paul Parbury, commanding a battery of field artillery operating with the 5th East Yorkshire Regiment, was approached by an infantry subaltern about dusk and told to "damned well go" and silence a machine gun which was holding up the advance of the subaltern's platoon. The major's verbal reaction to this brusque order from so unexpected a source is not on record, but without hesitation he charged the position in his carrier and silenced the gun. He then returned and said: "I have done that." The subaltern was a hard man to please. He told him to "damned well" silence another post—and once again Major Parbury obliged.

The columns broke out in two principal groups, one based on the 69th Brigade, the other on the 151st Brigade. The 5th East Yorkshire Regiment made the bridgehead for the first, and the 8th Durham Light Infantry for the second. Both did a magnificent job. They were supported by one squadron of tanks under Major Lindsay which rendered yeoman service. They went into action with tins of Diesel oil strapped on to their sides because it was known that they would not be able to refuel by any other means until they reached the frontier. The squadron turned up, complete with all vehicles, at Maddalena.

The 5th East Yorkshire Regiment attacked the enemy in two waves. Two companies were held up temporarily, but when they were joined by a third they broke the enemy's resistance. One platoon advanced in step singing "Rule Britannia"; when they were within ten yards of the petrified Italians they suddenly brought their bayonets to the "on guard" position—and that was that.

Private Albert Robinson's company of East Yorks launched an attack on a strongly held position and were met with very heavy fire from artillery, Breda guns and heavy machine guns. Robinson crawled two hundred yards out in advance of his platoon and positioned himself between two enemy machine-gun positions, neither of

---

[1] During the subsequent advance of the Eighth Army many officers and men of the Division revisited the old battlefield; Lieutenant-Colonel M. L. P. Jackson, 8th Durham Light Infantry, found his old battalion mess practically as he had left it on the night of the 14th of June, with a book open on the table at the point where an officer had put it down to go out to battle. Shells which had been buried were dug up by the divisional gunners and used for practice.

which could fire at him without running the risk of hitting the other. From this advantageous position he proceeded to pick off the crews of both positions. He was awarded the Military Medal.

C.S.M. Thomas Mattock, accompanied by a private soldier, wiped out the entire crew of a machine-gun post. He was awarded the Distinguished Conduct Medal.

The 8th Durham Light Infantry, making the other bridgehead, operated in three columns. One advanced a mile and then came under fire from heavy machine guns and mortars. The vehicle of the column commander was blown from beneath him, but after a bitter struggle the troops reached their objective. The remainder of the battalion reached its objective in the face of opposition which cost it fifty casualties.

Thus the bridgeheads were established according to plan on the ridges two to three miles west of the Gazala position. There the bridgehead troops stayed until about 0400 hrs. on the 15th of June, after which they themselves moved off.

Not all the Division passed through the bridgeheads. The 9th Durham Light Infantry, owing to special circumstances, had been given the option of following the main bodies or of withdrawing via the coast road and Tobruk. This battalion and its attached troops attempted to move through the bridgeheads after the rest of the Division, but the commander decided that because the enemy was now thoroughly awake to what was going on it was advisable to exercise his option, turn about and retire along the coast road.

Lieutenant-Colonel Percy split the 9th Durham Light Infantry into two groups for the move, taking command of one half himself and giving command of the other half to Major J. C. Slight, his second-in-command. The columns moved on parallel routes, and Major Slight's column, shortly after daybreak on the 15th of June, reached the top of the escarpment near the Ageila Pass. This the South African rearguards had already blown, and the column turned east, feeling its way along the edge of the minefields parallel to the escarpment, and looking for an open pass down to the coastal plain. One was found within a mile or so, and the column (having almost been fired on by the South African engineers, who were preparing it for demolition), trickled down one vehicle at a time to the plain below. It transpired that the enemy had already reached the coast road with a handful of tanks some five miles to the east, and he had a battery of field guns on the escarpment in the same locality, covering the coastal plain.

In the meantime, Colonel Percy's column had reached an open pass about a mile east of the one used by the rest of the group, and were

F

sharply attacked by Stukas while descending it, with some casualties to men and vehicles. Colonel Percy also realized that the road was closed by the enemy and decided, as did Major Slight, to cross the road into the rough dune country near the coast, in the hope of slipping along a little-used track close to the beach, and so reaching Tobruk. There seemed little chance of getting through unopposed, but the dune country would suit the infantry better if it came to action.

The two columns were forced by the ground to converge as they neared the beach and serious congestion occurred on and near the track. Rearguards of the South African Division with their vehicles were also using the same route, and by the time the head of the now combined column approached M'Rassus water point a total of three of four hundred vehicles were on the scene. There the head of the column was heavily engaged by enemy ground troops in positions astride the track, supported by tanks near the coast road and by the artillery on the escarpment.

Colonel Percy realized that quick action gave the only chance of success, and ordered an immediate attack by such forces as could be quickly collected on the spot; in the meantime he put the composite column in a state of local defence. In particular he sited a number of anti-tank guns to protect the flank of the stationary column while the attack was carried out. As a result of the action which followed, Major Slight was awarded the Distinguished Service Order. The citation states:

> "It was vital to clear the enemy out to allow the move to continue. In circumstances of great difficulty Major Slight collected several platoons of infantry, formed them up and led them with great determination on the enemy position, which in spite of heavy enemy fire was captured, together with thirty German prisoners. Later Major Slight consolidated the area which had been held by the enemy and made arrangements to support the further move of the rest of the force. The action of this officer helped to retrieve a dangerous situation and to enable the group to reach the Tobruk perimeter."

The infantry which was so hurriedly collected from the nearest troop-carrying lorries was helped forward by the very bold use of a number of Bren-gun carriers, led by Major M. Ferens, of the 6th Durham Light Infantry, by close support, over open sights, from one South African 25-pounder, and by the very gallant manœuvres of one or two South African armoured cars which joined in.

The enemy who were captured claimed to have been landed some days before with the express purpose of cutting off the withdrawal of small formations along the coast. They had not yet made actual contact with the tanks on the road, although they had signalled their position to them. A message was sent back to Colonel Percy that the track was now clear and that the column could continue its withdrawal to Tobruk. At this moment seven enemy tanks, which had been lying near the main road, attacked the congested transport from the south-east, coming between the transport and the infantry which had carried out the attack. The tanks were engaged by the anti-tank guns and Bofors to such good effect that five were put out of action and the remainder withdrew at once.

By this time the enemy artillery on the escarpment had ranged on the track, and were able to prevent the column from making any progress along it. By the greatest good fortune Major Slight (who had been cut off with his infantry from the column by the tank attack, and who had sent the troops towards Tobruk on foot) made contact with a South African 25-pounder battery some three thousand yards east of the scene of the action, and was able to arrange for effective support in the form of smoke and high explosive to enable the advance to continue.

The column passed through Tobruk without further incident and reached the frontier wire on the 16th of June.

The rest of the Division picked its way through Italian and German positions. Part of Divisional Headquarters blundered straight into some German guns, which were fired off by the gun sentries. The result was frightening, but, of course, perfectly harmless, since the shells went off in the wrong direction. Later the same column was embarrassed by the offer of thirty Italians to become prisoners. Nothing could be done with them, so their boots were confiscated and they were left.

In general it was not difficult to avoid the enemy leaguers, which signalled their presence by flares, fired with great regularity. But small enemy posts were not so easy to avoid in the darkness. Lieutenant-Colonel Kennedy, the C.R.E., one of the outstanding engineers in the Middle East, was killed in these circumstances while leading a column.

During that night and the next day many vehicles lost their parent column. The stragglers, often private soldiers, formed impromptu columns of their own, navigating by the stars or sun.

The Divisional Signals had a rough passage, but from that unit comes a story typical of the resource and initiative displayed by all ranks during the break-out. A Signals vehicle was moving so near to an Italian leaguer during the darkness that the enemy's voices could be heard. Then the truck broke down. Nothing daunted, the crew decided to carry out repairs on the spot. They found that the fault was a burnt-out brush in the dynamo. They had no spares, but they remembered that there were similar brushes in the generator of their wireless set. They took one of them out and spent an hour adjusting it so that it would fit the dynamo. After a total of two hours' delay the vehicle moved again. The Italians' suspicions were belatedly aroused, and they gave the signallers a send-off with machine-gun fire which did no damage.

The Germans had obligingly lit up Bir Hacheim, which helped the columns in judging the correct spot to turn east. Ninety-six per cent. of those who started out eventually arrived on the frontier wire. This was an extraordinary performance when the sorry state of the divisional transport is remembered. It was common to see a troop carrier towing another, both grossly overladen with the crew of a third.

Many sweeps were made by the R.A.F. on the 15th, 16th and 17th of June to locate stranded vehicles. Two rescue parties went out, one led by the G.O.C. Nevertheless, of the missing, many must have been lost in the desert.

Many individual stories are told of this unconventional operation. An account by the Divisional Intelligence Officer, Lieutenant E. H. St. G. Moss, describes an experience which was probably typical of many:

"I did not see much of the making of the bridgeheads myself, but I have heard about it from others. The enemy here were Italians, apparently with a stiffening of a few German gunners, and they were very much taken by surprise; I think it was pretty late in the night before they realized what was happening and that a whole division was passing straight through their lines.

"Some vehicles went up on mines, others were shot-up; but on the whole we had very few casualties and both attacking battalions did their jobs successfully; the infantry went in with the bayonet and the Italians departed, in some cases leaving all their arms and equipment lying about the trenches.

"It was dark by now and there was a good deal of confusion; but, though not every position in the vicinity had been mopped up, there was a way through and the columns began to move.

"It was a black night, with brilliant stars, but not a wisp of moon. We started grinding and jolting off through the darkness at four or five miles an hour, nose to tail, with every now and then strange, unexplained halts, while we looked and listened and wondered what was happening. My own truck was spluttering and I had continually to ask for a push from the three-tonner behind me to get it started again.

"After a couple of miles, we came over a small rise and suddenly saw a glow of flames in front of us; a few tracer bullets came singing past; then the column came to a standstill and we sat and waited, a long line of black vehicles, with a few men talking in low voices here and there; not a cigarette end showing. In front of us on a low ridge three or four vehicles were burning and there seemed to be something moving against the glow of flames and lit-up smoke. Intermittently tracer bullets, red, green and purple, and occasional anti-tank shells, cracked past; they were nearly all over our heads, however, and as far as I know our column suffered no casualties here. Now and again there came the bigger crash of a shell somewhere beside us, but the enemy had not recovered from his surprise and it did not amount to very much.

"On the left we could see other fires in the distance and at one time we fancied we could hear the tanks with the 69th Brigade over in that direction. Nothing moved for some time. It was a curiously beautiful scene, with the little fireworks singing past us and over our heads, the dots of blazes of smoking light ahead of us and the long, dark column of vehicles, all drowned in an enormous glittering night. After half an hour or so . . . the firing was still going on and it looked as if it would be risking disaster for the whole column to go straight forward in crocodile, each vehicle coming over the ridge in turn and being silhouetted against the glow; but it was no good standing still. Soon we saw some trucks moving on in front of us past the fires, apparently without hurt (we probably did not realize what a smoke screen had been created round there) and presently we began to move ourselves. We safely ran the gauntlet past the first ridge; after that, we passed one or two more burning trucks or carriers and our column lost one or two vehicles on mines or from anti-tank shells, but as we went on our way the firing gradually died down and we had no desperate adventures. The night wore on and we kept grinding southwards, huddled in our greatcoats as it grew colder and colder.

"The extreme darkness was a great strain on the drivers, as there were many patches of rough going and obstacles reared up suddenly in the night. Some trucks got stuck and had to be man-handled out; others broke down; others ran into the trucks ahead of them and smashed their radiators; on one occasion our navigator swung off right to make a detour and we lost the tail of our column, which did not notice the manœuvre and completed the journey on its own. On the whole, however, all was well; and other columns had very similar experiences, though few had so smooth a passage as we did. One or two ran straight through the enemy camps, losing trucks in the slit trenches and picking up a few alarmed prisoners as they went; others were shot-up to some extent or ran into minefields and had to halt while engineers went forward and cleared a way through; but when a vehicle was lost the men climbed on to other vehicles and in the end very few were missing.

"In the south, as that morning broke it found us split up into small, scattered parties, each making its own way to the wire. Some were making for Fort Maddalena, others for a gap at Sheferzen farther north. It had been an exceptionally cold night and I remember the sun coming up, yellow and egg-shaped, through layers of mist, which hung in all the hollows and stretched out like a streaky sea to the horizon.

"We were now a small group of twenty or thirty vehicles crossing a smooth, undulating desert, good going except for occasional patches of camel hump. We dispersed out to two hundred yards between vehicles and moved on steadily all the morning at a good speed, with a few short pauses to collect ourselves and spy out the land. There were one or two alarms of enemy tanks or armoured cars as we went round Bir Hacheim; we stopped and sent on the two armoured cars that were with our own party to see what was happening, but nothing ever eventuated; nor did we see any aeroplanes.

"My own truck still seemed to be firing on only about five cylinders out of the eight, and we could hardly ever get out of third gear; she was eating up petrol, but she kept going all right and now she kept on steadily all day, though it was an effort at times not to fall behind. On one of our halts later on I was able to exchange some water for eight gallons of petrol from a three-tonner. Nearly every truck was crowded now with men picked up from others which had broken down or been shot-up during the night, and, naturally enough, most of the new arrivals had not been able to bring any water with them except what they had in their water-bottles.

"By the middle of the morning we were well beyond Bir Hacheim and we swung round south-east. The desert was now completely brown, bare and trackless; the ground became gradually more broken and the going varied from sandy patches to patches of stony ground or of small, black, sharp-edged pebbles; but never a bird or beast or tyre mark, only the continual, shimmering mirage, which closed in on us as the sun climbed higher and the heat grew. That was the hottest day I ever knew. There was no stir of wind and when we made a long halt in the middle of the day the heat came down in a flattening blaze which made one want to wriggle and twist for a moment of relief. One of the men on my truck had sunstroke.

"That day I think we made the acquaintance of the desert for the first time, and it was an acquaintance worth making. The scrubby

[British Official Photograph] [Crown Copyright Reserved]

"As that morning broke, it found us split up into small, scattered parties, each making its way to the wire."
Troops of 151st Brigade, who captured an enemy car during the break out, reach the frontier—and safety.

land near the coast, full of soldiers and trucks and roads and pipelines, was a very different thing. On that journey the desert was, in some ways, a more awful enemy than any insignificant human beings could be with their miserable guns and tanks. There were some of us, I suppose, those who were missing after it all and will never be accounted for, who did find themselves stranded and did come to their deaths out there; I can only hope for those whom I knew that they are prisoners now or else were killed in the action earlier on. There were others who were stranded for as much as eight hours and then miraculously were picked up: they must know something.

"One does not hate the desert; after all, it swallowed up very few of us in the end; and, in fact, it is almost fascinating in its huge indifference; but when one is really brought up against it the desert, like the sea, is very strong and terrible.

"By six o'clock the heat was abating and we were within thirty or forty miles of the frontier. Here we came across the first sign that day of other human beings (apart from the bones of a Wellington bomber, which we passed during the afternoon). A solitary smudge in the distance gradually resolved itself into a carrier with four men in it. My truck was going better by then, and I was deputed to go and pick them up. I found that they were four men from the 69th Brigade whose carrier had given trouble, fallen back and eventually petered out. They were quite alone and had no water except what was in the radiator. What was worse, they had no compass and they were completely lost. They had worked continuously on the engine and, while I was there, they at last managed to make it start, but there was still no hope of keeping up with the convoy and I told them to abandon the carrier and pile on my truck. There was no room, however, for the machine gun and its tripod. When the corporal in charge saw this he said that rather than abandon their gun they would stay with the carrier and take their chance alone. It was a very brave thing to say in the circumstances, and I have a great admiration for those men.

"By now the convoy had moved off again; I had a compass and the rough bearing (I well remember it was 110 degrees), so I decided to stay with them and accompany them back at their own speed. We went on for another fifteen or twenty miles, when we saw another convoy coming over the horizon, which we were able to join.

"The various parties scattered over the desert were now gradually converging on Maddalena. From now on it was only a question of following tyre tracks. I gave the carrier crew some water and rations and left them with a gunner officer who had had a breakdown and was completing the course at a slow speed. They arrived safely at Maddalena.

"The next morning, after another cold and very dewy night, we set off again; by eight o'clock we had met the wire a couple of miles south of Maddalena and then, at last, coming out of a fold in the ground, we saw the fort itself, a small, white-stone ruin on the top of a low rise in the desert; not much to look at, but it had a well with plenty of fresh, cold water, and I have seldom been more glad to see a place.

"Several parties had arrived the night before and stragglers were coming in all day. The Division was to gather itself together at Bir Thalata, south of Sidi Barrani. It took several days to sort everything out and people kept coming in from most unexpected places; one batch, for instance, had found its way right through to Mersa Matruh. Armoured-car squadrons and R.A.F. also went out to locate and pick up lost sheep west of the wire.

"One of the grimmest stories I know of the campaign is that of the crew of a carrier who were picked up well east of the frontier four days or so after we arrived. They had somehow become separated from their group, but had made good time and found their way through the wire earlier than most of us, without realizing where they were; then they ran out of petrol and were stranded actually well inside our country and probably only a few miles from one of the main convoy routes. But the desert is a big place and no one is particularly likely to investigate a single vehicle in the distance. No one found them and two of the men went mad with thirst and marched off by themselves into the desert before the rest were finally picked up."

But though the Division had so successfully broken out of Gazala, it had suffered a very severe blow. The work of collecting the columns and vehicles scattered over a hundred miles was tremendous. The divisional transport, on its last legs before the break-out, was now in an appalling state. No more was forthcoming. Kits, equipment, reserve ammunition and weapons, stores, all had been jettisoned to make room for the extra men who had to be carried on each vehicle—and for the crews of stranded vehicles. More serious still, vital signal stores and wireless trucks had been destroyed or lost during the operation.

Little could be done to make up these deficiencies. There was no possibility of refitting. But in the break-out from Mersa Matruh which was to follow the Division was to suffer heavily for these things.

The Division gathered itself together and rested for a few days in the area known as "The Kennels" near Bir Thalata. News of the battle was scarce, although it was known that the Eighth Army rearguards were falling back towards the frontier. Nothing was known about the fate of Tobruk, although there was a general impression that the port would be held as it had been before. News of the fall of this famous little Libyan town came like a thunderbolt, and was followed by a decision not to hold the line of the frontier.

To the ordinary soldier these two events illustrated more than anything else the magnitude of the defeat which the Eighth Army had suffered. In the minds of most the frontier had become the classic dividing line between two armies when neither was in the ascendant; and the earlier epic defence of Tobruk had somehow made it difficult to realize that this port could ever be held by the enemy.

Gradually it dawned upon us all that the retreat was only beginning; that the road eastward was a long one; and there was food for thought that at the end of it lay Alexandria, Cairo and the Suez Canal, the very heart of the Imperial positions in the Middle East.

The greater part of the 50th Division was ordered back to the area of Mersa Matruh to reorganize, but a strong group from the 69th Brigade, with a small Divisional Headquarters, was dispatched northwards with orders to take up a defensive position in the area of Buq Buq on the coast, preparatory to fighting a rearguard action along the coastal road. The rearguard on the desert flank was formed by the 7th Armoured Division.

The 69th Brigade force was commanded by Lieutenant-Colonel E. C. Cooke-Collis, who had commanded the brigade for much of the fighting in Libya owing to the ill-health of Brigadier Hassett. Lieutenant-Colonel Cooke-Collis was later awarded the Distinguished Service Order for his part in this campaign. He had been wounded at an early stage, but had refused to be evacuated. With his arm in a sling he could be seen in most places where there was action during the course of the arduous retreat.

On the night of the 22nd/23rd of June the 10th Indian Division withdrew through the position held by the 50th Division rearguard. The next day the German advance guards came into contact with the 50th Division and the rearguard action began. The troops fell back steadily in contact with the enemy, delaying him where they could and shelling his forward troops.

Not the least important of the duties falling to the 50th Division was the demolition of stores which could not be got away in time, and of communications and water supplies. Parties of engineers worked doggedly, until they were nearly dropping from exhaustion, to destroy water points. Time was short, and it was no easy task to put out of action the elaborate system of water supply which the Eighth Army had built up to maintain itself in this hostile wilderness.

As the column retreated down the road individual officers and men could be seen hurrying off to push down a telegraph pole here, set fire to an abandoned lorry there and set fire to stores at another place. At a point just before Sidi Barrani two staff officers of 50th Division Headquarters could be seen trying to disable a Matilda tank by the use of pickaxes. At Sidi Barrani itself great dumps of food were soaked in petrol and set on fire—but not until the troops had helped themselves freely to tinned pineapples, pears and other delicacies which they had not seen for a very long time.

On the afternoon of the 23rd of June a pall of black smoke drifted over the little village of Sidi Barrani as the British stores were reduced to ashes and "Finis" was being written to a melancholy chapter in the Eighth Army's history.

As the rearguard force approached Mersa Matruh, which was its destination, reports reached the commander that enemy forces had slipped round them on the desert flank and were astride the road ahead of them, thus blocking their line of withdrawal.

The rearguard switched off the road on to a precipitous track nearer the coast, along which their vehicles crawled painfully in single file for most of one night. They reached Matruh safely.

The whole Division was now brought together and disposed in a defensive position south-east of Matruh. The 10th Indian Division was garrisoning the port. The enemy came on with unabated speed despite the fact that his lines of communication had now become very long, that air support was becoming difficult for him as the bases in Cyrenaica were left farther behind, and that his tanks were nearing the end of their endurance.

The German forces bumped up against the defences of Matruh and were brought to a halt, but the main armoured force swept on past the town, bypassing the 10th Indian Division and the 50th Division and continuing to press the main body of the Eighth Army, now withdrawing towards the Alamein position.

By the 27th of June the Germans had cut the road east of Matruh and the two divisions in and around the port were isolated, in the same way that the Tobruk garrison was isolated in 1941.

Once more troops of the 50th Division, already weary from weeks of fighting, were called upon to wage heavy defensive battles against an enemy still superior in numbers and resources.

Much of the heaviest fighting fell to the lot of the 151st Brigade. Let one outstanding incident on the 27th of June speak for the many individual acts of devotion, so many of them unrecorded or even unnoticed, which kept the divisional positions intact in those desperate days. It is the story of Private Adam Wakenshaw, of the 9th Durham Light Infantry, whose feat of arms won for him the Victoria Cross, the first V.C. won by a member of the Division in this war.

Wakenshaw was a member of the crew of a 2-pounder anti-tank gun on a forward slope in front of a position held by the 9th Durham Light Infantry. Shortly after dawn the enemy attacked, and a tracked vehicle mounting a light gun was brought to within short range of the position. The British gun crew opened fire and succeeded in putting a round through the engine, immobilizing the enemy vehicle.

Another mobile gun then came into action. All members of the crew of the 2-pounder, including Wakenshaw, became casualties, and the 2-pounder was temporarily silenced. During this respite the enemy moved forward towards their damaged vehicle to get the light gun into action against the Durham Light Infantry.

Realizing the danger to his comrades, Wakenshaw crawled back to his gun under intense mortar and artillery fire. Although his left arm had been blown off at the shoulder, he loaded the gun with one arm and fired five more rounds, setting the damaged vehicle on fire and damaging the light gun.

A near miss then killed the gun aimer, who had been helping Wakenshaw, and blew the latter away from the gun, inflicting further severe wounds. He slowly dragged himself back to the gun, placed a round in the breech, and was preparing to fire when a direct hit on the ammunition destroyed the gun and this brave man.

In the evening after the action the body of Wakenshaw was found stretched out alongside the ammunition box.

On the night of the 27th/28th of June the Division was ordered to attack southwards across the enemy's lines of communication to destroy transport and disorganize supply services. This attack was carried out in moonlight in several columns. It was virtually a fighting advance into the unknown, and the cost of the operation was high in British lives and equipment.

One column, with which the Divisional Commander moved, and which included the 5th East Yorkshire Regiment, under the command of Lieutenant-Colonel Guy Stansfield, came into conflict with an enemy position on a small plateau. Fire was exchanged in the darkness and casualties were caused on both sides. Eventually the enemy brought field artillery to bear on the column and set fire to several trucks. But the column gave as good as it got.

It was during this bitter and confused encounter that a senior officer approached General Ramsden in a state of great excitement and said that he had laid hands on an enemy vehicle of new design. From it he had taken a pigskin case which he proposed to present to the Divisional Commander. Not until the next morning was it known that a divisional liaison officer had complained bitterly that somebody had been trying to take away from him one of the first jeeps to reach the desert, and with it the small amount of kit which remained to him.

To left and right of this column could be seen the lights of conflict —tracer shells moving across the night sky, flashes of high explosives and occasionally the red glow of burning vehicles and guns.

As the Divisional Commander's column disengaged itself from this muddled battle, a message was received ordering the attacking columns to return to the area of Matruh. This difficult night march was accomplished by dawn.

On the 29th of June the situation of the Division was becoming desperate; the German armour was making raids into its area—even Divisional Headquarters was attacked by tanks—and the whole of the divisional position was under constant shell fire. It was obvious that the time had come for the Division either to make a last stand or attempt to break out once more.

That day orders were received from the X Corps to break out and rally farther east in the area of Fuka. A plan very similar to that of Gazala was made, but this time conditions were even less favourable. The troops were exhausted. They were short of weapons and of serviceable transport. The enemy was in close contact and was not Italian but German, not infantry but armour, strongly supported by 88-mm. guns. Instead of a dark night there was now a full moon. The ground was very unfavourable, since it was necessary to debouch from a few steep ravines on to a plain held by the enemy. And, worst of all—there was now no surprise.

As the grim day wore on, the enemy's shell fire increased. Across the divisional area spouts of sand rose in regular ranks as the German batteries poured their shells into the basin in which the Division was disposed. Continually, enemy infantry and anti-tank guns strove to penetrate our thinly held positions. It is a remarkable reflection that in many instances they were driven off by the sustained rifle fire of batmen, cooks and orderlies pressed into service in the thinly held firing line.

After dusk had fallen the 50th Division formed itself into several small columns of all arms. Orders were given that these columns were to make their way through ravines, on to the plain, through the enemy positions, and then were to swing eastwards to rejoin the main part of the Eighth Army.

The scene was tense as the columns, each of about thirty vehicles, formed up at about 2100 hrs. and waited for the word to move off. Many of those waiting with their small groups of trucks under the large, bright moon felt rather "naked." And before long, indeed, the enemy did discover that the defences held so resolutely during the day had now been abandoned, and that he had a nice little target in front of him. A heavy anti-tank shell crashed into the rear of one group with a clang, followed by one or two more. A few trucks were hit, with some casualties, and Major W. H. L. Urton, D.A.Q.M.G. at 50th Division Headquarters, remained behind to bring along the survivors while the rest of the group moved off.

It had been impossible to reconnoitre the ravines (or wadis) before the break-out began, and therefore it was not surprising that there were some delay and turns-about before the columns found suitable routes out of the basin.

The Divisional Commander's column found itself winding up a long, narrow wadi in single file; the sides were steep and rocky, but the bed of the wadi was soft sand. Vehicle after vehicle stuck fast and had to be pushed on to firmer ground. The sticking of any vehicle invariably halted the whole column.

At one bend in the wadi the sand was so soft as to constitute an almost impassable obstacle. To overcome it tarpaulin sheets were whipped off the tops of three-ton lorries and spread on the ground, and over this improvised bridge a surprising number of heavy vehicles passed without trouble.

Such delays and misadventures cost time—and time was precious. It was realized that if daylight came with the column still trapped in the wadi the enemy could destroy it at leisure. However, with much of the soft sand passed and various other obstacles overcome, it seemed that the Divisional Commander's column was, in fact, to be lucky—until suddenly the leading vehicle ran up against a very steep hillside. This was the end of the wadi and there seemed to be no way out of it.

At about this time a few shells and bullets flew over the column from the surrounding high ground—a grim foretaste of what was to come if the vehicles quickly did not find a way of escape from the cul-de-sac in which they were trapped. It was a nightmare scene. Attempts were made to drive vehicles up the steep and rocky hillside facing them, but all failed.

The Divisional Commander threw off his overcoat. He made a running reconnaissance of the end of the wadi, and returned after ten minutes, out of breath and perspiring but with a plan. He had found a possible way out. Everyone got out of their trucks and formed man-handling parties. One of the few jeeps in the Division was driven to the front of the column and vehicles were pushed out of the wadi one by one by the united efforts of a fatigue party of perhaps forty men aided by the pushing power of the indomitable little jeep, which must have made thirty or forty journeys to the top.

Once out of the wadi the column formed up again and moved off, passing groups of enemy vehicles which did not, however, display any hostile intentions. By the morning most of the columns were turning east—and by that time also the Germans knew that the 50th Division was once again in a fair way to escape the net which had been drawn about it.

Groups of tanks appeared on the desert and gave chase to the various columns, firing as they moved, but the columns moved faster. Some of them, unfortunately, failed to receive later orders, and went to Fuka. They found the Germans waiting for them there. Among those captured were the G.1 (Lieutenant-Colonel R. H. L. Wheeler) and the A.Q. (Lieutenant-Colonel Steele). The senior Padre, the Reverend Harlow, whose car was riddled with bullets, knocked out two Germans with his hands and feet before he was made prisoner. The rest of the Division collected itself behind the El Alamein position. Casualties as a whole had been heavier than in the Gazala break-out.

But the 50th Division had not yet finished its job in this phase of the campaign. By the 1st of July it was back again in the line, with a small tactical headquarters operating a number of battle groups, some from the 50th Division, some from other formations, on the celebrated Ruweisat Ridge. (Battle groups were strong mobile columns consisting of a few infantry and a lot of guns—the word soon went out of fashion.)

Along Ruweisat Ridge the battle edged back and forth, but the 50th Division and its stout-hearted associates hung on grimly—and the crisis passed. The El Alamein position was the limit of the German advance. It is interesting to recall that the planning of this position was the first job given to Divisional Headquarters on its arrival in the Middle East from England.

The Germans were much disappointed in those early July days. They thought they had the Eighth Army on the run, and it appears that they certainly did not expect to come up against such strongly organized defences as they found at El Alamein. Some Italian prisoners captured at this time were stuffed with stories that Alexandria and Malta had already fallen, and some Italian commanders were already issuing rather ridiculous orders about the manner in which their troops were to parade through Alexandria.

On the 4th of July the 50th Division was relieved in the line and withdrew to Mareopolis (south-west of Alexandria) to reorganize. It was battered and weary, and had lost eight thousand eight hundred and seventy-five casualties since the opening of the Battle of Gazala.

On the 7th of July General Ramsden left the Division to command the XXX Corps.

EL GAZALA

APPENDIX TO PART TWO

ORDER OF BATTLE OF THE 50TH DIVISION ON ARRIVAL IN THE MIDDLE EAST, JUNE, 1941

Commander	Major-General W. H. C. Ramsden, C.B.E., D.S.O., M.C.
G.S.O.1	Lieutenant-Colonel L. G. Holmes (R.A.).
A.A.Q.M.G.	Lieutenant-Colonel Firth (Gloucestershire Regiment).
C.R.A.	Brigadier G. N. C. Martin, D.S.O., M.C.
C.R.E.	Lieutenant-Colonel Kennedy, D.S.O.
A.D.M.S.	Colonel Pirrie, M.C.
C.R.A.S.C.	Lieutenant-Colonel Divers, O.B.E.
A.D.O.S.	Lieutenant-Colonel Russell, O.B.E.
2nd Cheshire Regiment	Lieutenant-Colonel Gentry Birch.
65th A.T. Regiment (Norfolk Yeomanry)	Lieutenant-Colonel Harvey.

69TH INFANTRY BRIGADE

Commander	Brigadier R. E. Erskine, M.C.
5th East Yorkshire Regiment	Lieutenant-Colonel T. Thornhill.
6th Green Howards	Lieutenant-Colonel E. C. Cooke-Collis.
7th Green Howards	Lieutenant-Colonel MacDonnell.

150TH INFANTRY BRIGADE

Commander	Brigadier Haydon, D.S.O., M.C.
4th East Yorkshire Regiment	Colonel Caldwell.
4th Green Howards	Colonel C. N. Littleboy, D.S.O., M.C.
5th Green Howards	Colonel G. Bush, M.C.

151ST INFANTRY BRIGADE

Commander	Brigadier Redman.
6th Durham Light Infantry	Lieutenant-Colonel Battiscombe.
8th Durham Light Infantry	Lieutenant-Colonel Beart.
9th Durham Light Infantry	Lieutenant-Colonel Percy.

50TH DIVISION RECONNAISSANCE REGIMENT

4th Royal Northumberland Fusiliers	Lieutenant-Colonel De Graz.

PART THREE

CHAPTER VIII

REORGANIZING IN THE DELTA—BACK TO THE RUWEISAT AREA—ADVENTURES OF THE 69TH BRIGADE—50TH DIVISION ON GUARD IN THE DELTA

JULY TO SEPTEMBER, 1942

BACK in the Delta the Division took stock. It was not in very good shape. The field artillery had lost many of their guns and from thirty to forty per cent. of their strength in addition to the loss of the 72nd Field Regiment, which had been with the 150th Brigade in the last desperate stand at Gazala. Engineers, machine gunners, signals, supply, ordnance and medical services—all had had heavy losses.

The infantry, however, had suffered worst of all. In the two remaining brigades—the 69th and 151st—the average strength of battalions was now only three hundred, and of their transport very little remained. In these circumstances it might have been expected that morale would not be very high, but the reverse was in fact the case. The Division had done a remarkably fine job in the gruelling withdrawal to Alamein, and all ranks were conscious of the fact. In good spirits, and with high hopes, they set about the task of reorganization.

On the 11th of July Major-General J. S. Nichols, D.S.O., M.C., assumed command of the Division. Lieutenant-Colonel C. Olivier, R.A., had already arrived to replace Lieutenant-Colonel Wheeler as G.S.O.1. A welcome batch of reinforcements reached the Division at this time to bring infantry battalion strengths up to four hundred to four hundred and fifty, and training in both brigades, which had been in the Amiriya area, was begun in earnest. The divisional artillery had been collected at the School of Artillery at Almaza, while Divisional Headquarters and the other arms and services were all in the area Mareopolis—Amiriya.

It had been hoped that the Division would be able to spend at least a fortnight in the Delta, thus gaining a well-earned rest and the time to reorganize and train new arrivals without too much haste. This was not to be, however, for on the 15th of July orders were received to start without delay the construction of reserve localities in the area immediately east of the Ruweisat Ridge. The scope of this work made it necessary to employ the whole of the 69th Brigade and part of the Divisional Engineers; and since the 21st Indian Infantry Brigade and a motorized infantry brigade had been placed under General Nichols's command for similar work in the same area a small Divisional Tactical Headquarters also moved forward on the 16th of July to a position west of Burgh el Arab.

This was a most trying few days for the Division. The task, though of considerable importance, was dull and extremely arduous, and involved long hours of toil under a merciless sun in an atmosphere thick with flies. The work went forward with remarkable speed, however, and by the evening of the 18th of July the major part of the new defences was complete.

There was unfortunately to be no rest for the 69th Brigade, for that same evening orders were received for one brigade group to move forward and come under the command of the 5th Indian Division on Ruweisat Ridge by first light the following day. After hasty reorganization in order to bring two battalions (5th East Yorkshire Regiment and 6th Green Howards) up to full strength by drawing on the third (7th Green Howards), the 69th Brigade moved off with "B" Company, 2nd Cheshire Regiment (machine guns), and the 233rd Field Company, R.E. In spite of the short notice, they were not late at the rendezvous. The task allotted was the occupation of a defensive position on the ridge to act as a "backstop" in case of an enemy break-through, and the prospects of a short respite and a chance to continue the training of the new reinforcements seemed good.

On the 20th of July fresh orders were received, and the brigade found itself heading south to come under the command of the 7th Armoured Division.

The Brigade Commander was given orders for an attack on strong enemy positions in the south sector of the armoured division's line. A composite battalion from the 201st Guards Brigade was placed under his command for the operation. It was to be carried out in three phases on the night of the 21st/22nd of July. Phases 1 and 2 were to be undertaken by the 69th Brigade and included, in Phase 1, the capture of Taqa Plateau and, in Phase 2, the capture of Jebel Kalakh. Phase 3 was to be carried out resultant upon the success of Phases 1 and 2. In this event the 4th Light Armoured Brigade, of the 7th Armoured Division, would pass through the gap made, and work behind the enemy's lines with the object of forcing them to withdraw. All phases were to be supported by the divisional artillery.

Brigadier Cooke-Collis, now confirmed in his command of the 69th Brigade, found that little was known about the enemy in the area in which he was expected to attack, nor was there much information available about the state of the going about Taqa Plateau and Jebel Kalakh. Detailed reconnaissance was impossible by day, as the whole area was under direct enemy observation, and any movement forward brought an immediate reply from hostile artillery.

Moreover, it was clear that the attacking troops were in no state to carry out a major operation of this nature. The 69th Brigade was merely a composite force scratched together for limited operations. The Guards battalion was very much under strength and was very tired after continuous fighting, and the 4th Armoured Brigade consisted of only small Stuart tanks and armoured cars. It was clear to the Brigade Commander from the start that the whole operation was extremely ambitious and difficult.

He decided that the Guards battalion should attack and capture the east end of the Taqa Plateau and Naqb el Khadin, as it was hoped that this would not be strongly held and would be within the powers of this rather weak battalion. On completion of this operation the 5th East Yorkshire Regiment and the 6th Green Howards were to attack the Taqa Plateau from the south. Little was known of the actual localities occupied by the enemy, and, ammunition being short, it was decided that the attack would be carried out without a preliminary bombardment.

Before dark on the evening of the 21st of July the 5th East Yorkshire Regiment and the 6th Green Howards moved to the area of Garet el Himeimat, which was as far as they could go without coming under enemy observation. As soon as the sun set they began the long move forward to the chosen debussing areas, about six miles south of Taqa. Considerable difficulties were encountered on this move, as the sand proved to be very soft in places, involving much pushing, towing and digging, but both battalions completed their forming up by 0100 hrs. While this advance was going on the Guards battalion carried out its attack and had reached its objectives without any difficulty and with little opposition by 2300 hrs.

At 0130 hrs. the 6th Green Howards on the right and the 5th East Yorkshire Regiment on the left began their advance and by first light both battalions had reached the southern edge of the plateau. So far, no enemy had been encountered, but as soon as it became light they came under heavy machine-gun fire. By 0830 hrs. the 6th Green Howards had managed to get two companies firmly established on the plateau, but they were under heavy mortar and machine-gun fire and could make no further progress. On the left the leading companies of the 5th East Yorkshire Regiment managed to reach the southern flank of the plateau only and could make no more headway. Both battalions had suffered casualties. During the morning the leading companies of the 6th Green Howards were withdrawn to the southern edge of the plateau to conform to the position held by the 5th East Yorkshire Regiment. This limited withdrawal made the position more secure and the Brigade Commander felt that he was better able to withstand the enemy counter-attack which was clearly brewing up.

Both battalions spent a very unhappy day on this plateau. They were subjected to continuous artillery and mortar fire, which caused a considerable number of casualties, and the commanding officer of the 6th Green Howards was wounded. Besides casualties from enemy fire a number of men suffered from heat exhaustion.

At 1600 hrs. the expected counter-attack fell on both battalions. It was supported by armoured cars. The attack was, however, beaten off by artillery and mortar fire. During the following night both battalions patrolled, and from the information which they obtained it was clear that the enemy was reinforcing his position and meditating further action. Accordingly, the Brigade Commander told General Renton, commanding the armoured division, that he could see no hope of further progress. He asked for permission to withdraw his brigade during the night of the 23rd/24th of July, which was granted.

During the 23rd of July both battalions were subjected to heavy artillery and mortar fire and the enemy counter-attacked twice, mainly against the 5th East Yorkshire Regiment. Both attacks were beaten off, though not without loss to the East Yorkshire Regiment. At 2100 hrs. on the 23rd of July the withdrawal started and it was successfully carried out during the night without further interference from the enemy. On relief the 69th Brigade rejoined the 50th Division.

At the end of July the 50th Division was given the role of securing the defence of the Northern Delta area, for which task the Division, although remaining in the Eighth Army order of battle, was to come under the command of Headquarters, British Troops in Egypt. The prospect was formidable in its complications. In the first place, in order adequately to defend this vast area, stretching from the sea to Halfway House (fifty miles south of Alexandria on the road to Cairo), and including all the Delta area behind this line, the following additional formations were placed under General Nichols's command: 26th Indian Infantry Brigade, 1st Greek Brigade, 2nd Free French Brigade, Guides Cavalry (armoured cars) and the Alexandria Garrison. Later the 7th Indian Infantry Brigade and 1st Armoured Brigade were also placed under command.

To control this not inconsiderable force, General Nichols had to assist him only a much-depleted Divisional Headquarters staff, since at this period both the G.S.O.1 and G.S.O.2 were in hospital and much of the work of taking over the existing defence plans from the X Corps, which had until then been responsible for the Northern Delta, devolved upon the G.S.O.3, Captain Parker (Essex Regiment). This officer, to whom General Nichols referred as his "Chief of Staff," carried out his arduous duties with great skill until the return of his absent seniors.

The complications of command were further added to by the heterogeneous nature of the artillery available to support the Northern Delta Defence Force. The divisional artillery was not available, as it was moved straight from Almaza to reinforce the artillery of the XIII Corps, where it was destined to play a distinguished part in the halting of Rommel's drive in August. It did not rejoin the Division until shortly before the Battle of Alamein. Instead, General Nichols had at his disposal the 75's of the 1st Free French Brigade, the 25-pounder battery of the 1st Greek Brigade, some heavy anti-aircraft batteries around Alexandria, and the Alexandria coast defence batteries, which could fire inland as well as out to sea. The coordination of these mixed resources was no mean task, and General Nichols was lucky to have the services of Brigadier Fowler, C.R.A., 1st Armoured Division.

General Nichols decided to form a number of defended localities to withstand any enemy advance which might result from a break through the Eighth Army main positions. In addition, the possibility of airborne attack and seaborne raids, and the chance that the enemy might attack across the Qattara Depression round the southern flank of the Eighth Army positions, to cut the Cairo—Alexandria road and penetrate the Delta, all had to be considered. The possibility of internal trouble in Egypt and fifth-column activities was also a constant worry.

To meet these various contingencies the defence was based primarily on a series of mutually supporting defended localities on the commanding hill features around Amiriya, west of Alexandria. In addition, a curtain of defended posts was organized along the most western canals to delay and give warning of any enemy penetration between the main positions and the southern end of the area. A system of patrols watched the desert between the Northern Delta defences and the Eighth Army to the west, and as far south as Halfway House.

It was well known at this time that Rommel was preparing his final bid to reach Cairo, and though there was the utmost confidence throughout the Eighth Army that he would fail, nothing could be left to chance. By the middle of August the Northern Delta defences were ready and had been inspected by General Alexander and Mr.

Casey, the Resident Minister in the Middle East. A period of expectant waiting followed, during which the only event of note was the capture by the Free French of an over-bold Italian raiding party which had used the sea approach.

In the middle of August major changes took place in the Middle East Command. General Alexander relieved General Auchinleck in Cairo and General Montgomery took over command of the Eighth Army. The Division lost an old friend with the departure of "The Auk," who had been its Army Commander in Southern Command and had always taken great interest in it. The changes in command were accompanied by the arrival of large quantities of modern equipment which enabled the Desert Army to meet the Afrika Korps for the first time on equal terms.

By the end of the month Rommel had attacked and been thrown back. The Afrika Korps had taken a knock and its offensive power had been diminished.

The need for strong Delta defences was therefore removed, and the question of the future employment of the 50th Division again arose. At this time the Division was still well below establishment, particularly in infantry, but reinforcements were on the way and General Montgomery informed General Nichols that the Division would be employed in a coming attack by the Eighth Army.

At the beginning of September the 151st Brigade was moved forward to come under the command of the New Zealand Division. The brigade was made up to strength from the 69th Brigade, and, with one company of the 2nd Cheshire Regiment and the 505th Field Company, R.E., under command, it took over part of the line in the New Zealand "box."

For the remainder of the Division intensive training now began. The 69th Brigade set up an organization to train infantry reinforcements for the whole Division, and though these reinforcements did not arrive until the 12th of September, such were the enthusiasm and keenness of all ranks that by the end of the month they were ready to take their place in battalions.

The Northumberland Hussars (102nd Anti-Tank Regiment) were allotted to the Division, as was the 25th Light A.A. Regiment, though this latter unit did not join until October. Equipment, transport and supplies arrived to bring units up to establishment, and by the 30th of September the portions of the Division in the Delta were ready to move forward and join up with other divisional units already operating in the X, XIII and XXX Corps. Divisional Headquarters, which had been without a G.S.O.1 for some time owing to the illness of

Lieutenant-Colonel Olivier, was completed by the arrival of Lieutenant-Colonel R. G. B. Innes (Seaforth Highlanders), who in 1940 and 1941 had been Brigade Major of the 151st Brigade and knew the Division well.

CHAPTER IX

151st Brigade in the New Zealand "Box"—50th Division in the Line Again—Preparations for the Battle of El Alamein—The Battle—151st Brigade in "Supercharge"—Break-through and Pursuit

SEPTEMBER TO NOVEMBER, 1942

MEANWHILE, the 151st Brigade, in the New Zealand "box," passed to the command of the 44th Division at the end of the month and remained in the line.

Their part of our front was just south of Ruweisat Ridge, where the line swung sharply eastwards along the northern edge of the Munassib Depression. In the middle of the "box" stood a somewhat prominent feature, Alam Nayil. It was from this feature that the New Zealanders had made a gallant but unsuccessful attempt to pinch out the salient which had been left in August, after Rommel's final attempt to break through to Alexandria. Considerable portions of the line were overlooked by the enemy, therefore much movement during the day was impossible.

As can be imagined, the 151st Brigade gained a great deal of experience in this area and their standard of patrolling reached a very high level. They completely dominated No Man's Land from the start, and made many and varied excursions into the enemy's positions. Germans and Italians in general never had the reputation of being fond of work at night, but this was not true of the Italian Folgore Division of parachutists, with whom patrols had many small clashes. An early feature of this night work was the recovery of derelict carriers and other vehicles which the New Zealanders had been forced to abandon in their efforts to regain the Depression. Covering patrols would go out at night in front of our minefields while breakdown parties got to work to bring in the broken vehicles.

The following examples are taken from the war diary of one of the Durham battalions and show the sort of work that was carried out each night:

> "*Night, 13/14 Oct.*—A Reconnaissance Patrol under Captain Lindrea went out to reconnoitre area ———. The patrol came under heavy fire when it approached the area and had to dodge a strong enemy patrol on the way out. On the way back

one patrol engaged an enemy patrol believed to be German, 30 yards south of west end of 'Jarrow' Gap, and had to make a detour through the 'Don' minefield to get back to our lines. On Captain Lindrea's return a strong fighting patrol under Lieut. Lawrence was sent out to try and destroy the enemy ambushing party. The enemy had withdrawn.

"*Night, 14/15 Oct.*—Reconnaissance Patrol under Lieut. Galloway encountered a strong enemy force at ——. His patrol was fired on by several machine guns and mortars from this area."

It was found that the area opposite to the brigade was extremely strongly held, that it was covered by a belt of minefields containing some anti-personnel mines and with barbed-wire obstacles, and that every feature was accurately registered both by artillery and mortars.

Starting on the 1st of October, the remainder of the Division began to move up to the area of the XIII Corps in the south, where it continued in reserve. During the whole of this week the 151st Brigade remained under the command of the 44th Division and did not revert to the 50th Division until the 10th of October.

On the night of the 9th/10th of October the 69th Brigade, with the 124th Regiment, R.A., batteries from the 102nd Anti-Tank Regiment (Northumberland Hussars) and 25th Light A.A. Regiment, and the 233rd Field Company, R.E., relieved the 132nd Brigade of the 44th Division in the Munassib Depression area.

The 1st Greek Brigade, which had for a few days been under the command of the 44th Division and was in the sector on the immediate right of the 151st Brigade, also joined the 50th Division. Excellent relations were soon established with this brigade, commanded by Colonel Katsotos, with a well-trained staff. They were enthusiastic and ever ready to carry out orders, both in the spirit and to the letter, and their information was always reliable and up to date. They revelled in patrolling at night.

And so by the 10th of October the 50th Division had once more taken its position on the front of the Eighth Army and was holding a sector reaching from just south of the Ruweisat Ridge in the north up to and including the Munassib Depression in the south. This latter feature, which later proved to be formidably held, was not unlike a deep, wide river bed of very irregular shape. Worn away by the wind and sand of many ages, it had high and precipitous sides which dropped abruptly below the level of the surrounding desert. Within the Depression the enemy was well concealed, for it was quite impossible to look down on to the sandy floor. All movement there could be carried out unobserved, except perhaps for a tell-tale cloud of dust rising high into the air as some convoy passed up or down. A vast network of defences protected by broad minefields had been dug along the lip of the Depression, whose occupants were safe from artillery and mortar fire, for unless such fire was particularly accurate the shells were likely to fall harmlessly behind and many feet below the defenders.

The three brigades were in the line as follows:

    Right: 1st Greek Brigade with its own supporting arms.
    Centre: 151st Brigade.
    Left: 69th Brigade.

There was a considerable gap between the two latter brigades which was covered by minefields only. Subsequently it was filled by the 132nd Brigade from the 44th Division, which came under the command of the 50th Division for a short time.

Between the 10th and 23rd of October as much training as possible was carried out behind the lines. Immediately after "stand down" in the morning battalions would send back a company to carry out some form of training until the late afternoon, when the usual sandstorm or the shimmer due to heat concealed their return.

Added to this there was much planning to be done for the forthcoming attack, as well as the hundred and one tasks required in defence. In order to make sure of our positions, which would be thinly held when once the attack began, a great deal of work had to be carried out by way of minelaying and construction of wire obstacles. Staffs had to be trained, and the many new reinforcements of both officers and men had to be welded together into one team, with *esprit de corps*, which would enable the Division to play its part in one of the most important battles in history.

The Army plan for the defeat of the Afrika Korps at Alamein differed from most of the previous desert offensives in that the initial attack involved a break into the line rather than an outflanking movement round the enemy's southern flank. The outflanking mentality was deeply ingrained in the Eighth Army, and there were many senior officers who believed that it was the only way in which successes could be achieved. The enemy, too, who had studied the British desert mentality, had formed a firm opinion that the coming offensive would take much the same form as its predecessors, though the possibility of attack in the centre was not overlooked.

General Montgomery, however, had come to the desert with no preconceived idea and had set about the task of planning the defeat of his enemy with a free mind. He was faced with the situation of two armies firmly entrenched facing one another in the 1914-18 style. The northern flanks rested on the sea; in the south the Qattara Depression was impassable to a mechanized force. Both sides were stronger in the north because there the desert was firm and the road and railway gave communications required for any advance either way, but the Germans held the south of the line with a series of formidable fortresses connected by deep and elaborate minefields. Behind their main positions they had stationed reserves consisting chiefly of the veteran 15th and 21st Panzer Divisions and the 90th Light Division. This armoured reserve lay behind a deep minefield separating the northern and southern sectors of the enemy front. It was therefore able to move north or south at will to back up either flank, but once committed to one flank it could be extricated only with some difficulty to move to the other. It was essential to the enemy, therefore, that he should diagnose our main threat correctly at the earliest moment in our offensive.

The British line was held with the XXX Corps in the north and the XIII Corps in the south, the dividing line being roughly the Ruweisat Ridge. In reserve and carrying out training was the X Armoured Corps astride the Alexandria—Cairo road.

General Montgomery's plan, therefore, was to attack in the south with the XIII Corps to draw the German armoured reserve away from the north. This had to be a major threat. Meanwhile, in the north, the XXX Corps was slowly and methodically to drive a hole into the German positions and through this hole the X Corps would eventually penetrate.

The preliminary arrangements for the attack involved an elaborate deception plan. The X Corps was kept well back on the fringe of the Delta up to the last moment. When it was moved forward it came up behind the XIII Corps in the first instance and was moved north only at the last moment.

The full-scale attack was planned to start on the 23rd of October with a full moon. On the northern front the assault was to be carried out by the 9th Australian, 51st Highland, 2nd New Zealand and 1st South African Divisions, supported by a great weight of artillery. Their task was to destroy the various German positions systematically until the break-through was effected.

The XIII Corps, in the south, consisted of the 50th, 44th (Home Counties), 4th Indian and 7th Armoured Divisions, with Free French and Greek troops in addition. The first attack was planned to drive a hole through the enemy's line at its weakest point between Munassib Depression and Himeimat, with the object of drawing the enemy armoured reserve south. A formidable weight of artillery supported this attack also.

The enemy positions in the south were protected by a belt of minefields. The 44th Division was given the task of breaking through them, and as soon as a bridgehead had been secured the 7th Armoured Division was to pass through, turn north and roll up the enemy defence in the rear of the Munassib area.

Whilst the latter phase of the operation was taking place, the 50th Division was to attack the Munassib area frontally east and north of the Depression to a depth of some one thousand two hundred yards, starting from its original position in the line. Additional artillery was to be available, including two medium regiments.

The Corps Commander decided that the attack of the 50th Division would take place on a night subsequent to the attack of the 44th Division, and not until the 7th Armoured Division had succeeded in reaching its objectives behind the enemy facing the Division.

The main attack was to be made by the 69th Brigade, supported by the divisional artillery from the 50th, 44th and 7th Armoured Divisions.

The first objective for this attack was a strongly defended "island" in the Depression given the code name of "The Moor," and an isolated strong-point on the plateau on the south side of the Depression given the code name of "The Cape." The second objective was a line of defences about three hundred yards in rear of these strong-points. The final and last objective could not be laid down definitely. It was anticipated that it would be the ground farther west lying between the second objective and the positions secured by the 7th Armoured Division.

The attack was to be carried out by the 6th Green Howards on the right and by the 5th East Yorkshire Regiment on the left.

To the north the task of the 151st Brigade was more complicated, although the opposition on the actual objective was thought to be less. The brigade was to push forward one battalion group silently during the night to take up positions on the plateau north of the Munassib Depression and east of the enemy main defensive minefield so as to be in a position to dominate the Depression when dawn broke.

A second battalion was to be ready at dawn to mop up the enemy position on the north side of the Depression in co-operation with the 69th Brigade. Two field regiments, R.A., were allotted to support the 151st Brigade at call.

Still farther north were the 1st Greek Brigade. They had no actual integral part in the attack, but were to make a raid with a view to dissipating the enemy's resources, and preventing movement of reserves.

The Division was then to hold these positions as a firm base for further operations by the XIII Corps. It was thought that it would not be required for any follow-up operations.

Although the plan was not ambitious it involved considerable administrative arrangements. The main difficulty arose from the fact that all the ground in rear of the divisional positions was overlooked by the enemy; therefore the problem of supply to the attacking battalions, once the attack had begun, was not easy.

Such, then, was the role of the 50th Division. When it was explained to all ranks, there was considerable disappointment that it was not to be more important.

The Division was, however, only partially trained and, though the keenness of all was of the greatest value, the 50th Division was in no fit state to take part in the extremely complicated operations which were about to start in the north.

Those who fought in the desert will always remember the relief that was experienced when the sun finally disappeared behind the horizon. The scorched ground began to cool, the flies gave up their torment, a nightly breeze arose and once more it was possible to move about without being visible to the eyes of the enemy.

The night of the 23rd of October was no exception: a full moon shone, and the desert was still. But in the Eighth Army there was an air of suspense.

Promptly at 2140 hrs. the massed guns of the army opened fire.

The 50th Division had no part to play on this opening night except in a very small way. A company of the 9th Durham Light Infantry carried out a raid, the object of which was to test the strength of the enemy positions to the north of the Munassib Depression, but it was not a success, and it was obvious that the positions were stronger than was previously thought. Likewise, the 1st Greek Brigade carried out a raid on posts immediately opposite them, to distract the attention of the enemy.

The next day it was learnt that the attack in the north had met with success, but in the south the 44th Division had failed to secure a bridgehead through the minefields. New and uncharted fields had been encountered which had caused both delay and confusion. Further attacks were made by this division, closely supported by the 4th Armoured Brigade of the 7th Armoured Division, but although some ground was gained no gap was secured to permit the exploitation by the armoured division. Casualties had been heavy.

In an attempt to relieve the pressure in front of the 44th Division orders were received from the XIII Corps on the morning of the 25th that the attack of the 69th Brigade on "The Cape" and "The Moor" was to take place that night. The 4th Armoured Brigade, which had moved up on the south of the 69th Brigade, was ordered to support this attack by fire and to keep the enemy defences to the south neutralized.

On the night of the 25th the attack started. At first everything went according to plan. On the right the 6th Green Howards breached the obstacle and minefield satisfactorily and secured the east end of "The Moor." Here, however, they "lost" their artillery support, but, led by their commanding officer, Lieutenant-Colonel Lance, they fought their way forward to within three hundred yards of their final objective.

On the other flank the 5th East Yorkshire Regiment were less fortunate. They got forward to their assaulting positions without much difficulty, but two of the three Bren carriers which were leading the attack with grappling irons to tear away the minefield wire were destroyed by mines. The attacking infantry were now in an extremely difficult position and quite unable to penetrate the defences. Twice the acting commanding officer, Major Edgar, called for a repeat of the artillery programme, but failed to get his companies into the enemy defences, which were surrounded by booby-trapped barbed wire and a belt of anti-personnel mines. After a third attempt had failed, the Divisional Commander ordered Brigadier Cooke-Collis to withdraw the battalion to a reverse slope some three or four hundred yards short of the enemy position and there to dig in.

The next morning, the 26th of October, the situation was as follows:

On the right the 6th Green Howards had secured about two-thirds of "The Moor" and had made quite an adequate gap through the minefields and obstacles together with a useful mechanical-transport track to the objective. Casualties had been about a hundred of all ranks.

The 5th East Yorkshire Regiment were dug in some seven hundred yards in advance of their starting line and about four hundred yards from "The Cape." Their casualties were about one hundred and fifty of all ranks.

Later in the afternoon the 6th Green Howards renewed their attack, but it was beaten off by very accurate enemy mortar and artillery defensive fire just as they were reaching their objective. Casualties amounted to about a further sixty.

As there was little chance of success against this extremely difficult position, General Nichols decided to discontinue the operation.

Throughout this period the 151st Brigade had been busy preparing for their attack. Extra gaps had been made in their own minefields, intensive patrolling had been carried out, and stores of all descriptions had been concealed in No Man's Land.

During the next few days the 69th Brigade carried out an intensive programme of mortar harassing fire each day. This was particularly well maintained by the 7th Green Howards, commanded by Lieutenant-Colonel Seagrim, on the north side of the position. It was subsequently learnt that the enemy had suffered heavy casualties from this mortar fire and amongst them was an Italian corps commander who was killed while visiting the forward positions.

During the operations in the south the XXX Corps in the north had continued to hammer away in its efforts to break the line and let the X Corps out. Though the line had been considerably dented, no gap had appeared. Most of the units in the XXX Corps had already been committed at some time or other during the course of the battle; it was not therefore surprising that a warning order was received at 50th Divisional Headquarters that the Division would be required to extend its front to the north and that a brigade might be moved north for operations under the XXX Corps.

On the night of the 28th of October the 151st Brigade was taken out of the line to join the XXX Corps, together with the 505th Field Company, R.E., 149th Field Ambulance and a battery of the Northumberland Hussars. All were to take part in Operation "Supercharge," the culminating phase of the Battle of Alamein. This meant a night move from a position in the south of the line to a concentration area in the north behind Tel el Eisa.

The 2nd Free French Brigade, which had rejoined the Division on the 23rd of October, moved up between the 1st Greek Brigade and the 69th Brigade. As the Free French Brigade were unable to move up immediately, the line in parts was held by small battalion rear parties of the 151st Brigade, consisting of one officer and a handful of men with even smaller advance parties from the Free French.

The object of Operation "Supercharge," originally intended for the night of 31st of October/1st of November, but later postponed for twenty-four hours, was to make a bridgehead as far west as the notorious Rahman Track. This desert route started from the lone mosque of Sidi el Rahman on the coast and ran into the wastes in a south-westerly direction, to the distant oasis of Bahariya. Throughout its length it was clearly marked by a line of telegraph poles.

The attack was to be carried out under cover of darkness by the 151st Brigade on the right and the 152nd Brigade, from the 51st (Highland) Division, on the left; whilst the 28th (Maori) Battalion from the New Zealand Division was to put in a local attack to secure the right flank of the Durham Light Infantry.

To assist in keeping direction, Bofors guns were to fire red tracer along the brigade boundaries.

There were to be two phases, first an advance to an intermediate objective followed by a pause for half an hour, and then an attack to the final objective. These objectives were strongly held by the German 90th Light and 164th Infantry Divisions and the Italian Trento and Littoria Armoured Divisions.

Artillery support was to be given by thirteen field and two medium regiments in the form of a creeping barrage, and armoured support consisted of the 8th Royal Tank Regiment with a battle group of Shermans to exploit and break through before first light.

The countryside was flat and open, almost imperceptibly rising on a stony, barren waste to the track itself. It was known, too, that in this area the Germans had been laying mines with all speed, but the fields as yet were incomplete and unidentified. In consequence, the infantry were ordered to advance straight through, risking casualties, after which the Royal Engineers were to make the normal vehicle gaps. On this occasion two gaps were to be made on the front of each brigade.

Detailed information about the enemy was hard to obtain, and as is so often the case there was little time for commanders to make a thorough reconnaissance of the ground. Such information as was forthcoming was taken from a study of the overprints of the enemy defences made from air photographs, which later proved extremely accurate. It appeared that, in addition to the usual infantry positions, there was a row of dug-in tanks or self-propelled guns and in one place a strong "box" position which contained 88-mm. guns.

On the 1st of November the brigade moved to an assembly area immediately east of Tel el Eisa Station, and just as the sun set—at 1900 hrs.—it started its move forward to the forming-up positions where it was due to arrive at 2200 hrs., by which hour all marching troops were to be clear of the track.

The march was particularly long and dusty and the night seemed warm and sticky. There were the usual unpleasant smells of battle: of burnt explosive and rotting corpses. Then came the New Zealand gun positions with the crews stripped to the waist, with sweating bodies shining in the flashes of their guns. Their battle had already started, for they were making a diversion between the coast road and the sea.

The 8th Durham Light Infantry was to attack on the right, the 9th Durham Light Infantry on the left, while the 6th Durham Light Infantry was to move in rear to mop up any isolated enemy posts left by the other battalions. Thereafter the 6th Durham Light Infantry was to advance some two thousand five hundred yards to take up positions facing north while the others faced west; thus making two sides of the bridgehead.

This latter operation naturally meant a complete right wheel for the 6th Durham Light Infantry, to be effected during the lull in the barrage, when they should have reached the line of dug-in tanks or self-propelled guns.

So in this array the Durhams lay down on their forming-up positions to snatch whatever sleep was possible before they made their great effort. The wait, however, was long. Although it afforded ample time to make the usual last-minute checks, it meant that after the hot march everyone soon began to feel the cold night air of the desert intensifying the usual suspense of waiting.

Promptly at 0055 hrs. the spell was broken. The supporting barrage opened up with all its fury, and ten minutes later the leading battalions crossed the start line dead on time.

The partial moon was completely veiled in dust and smoke; visibility was little more than fifty yards, but the infantry moved steadily forward. After advancing five hundred yards, scattered minelaying parties of Germans were encountered. Completely stunned and deafened by the noise, they offered little resistance.

The first sign of enemy reaction to the attack, apart from the usual flares, was machine-gun fire from the immediate front of the 8th Durham Light Infantry. There were also some desultory shelling and mortar fire, which caused but few casualties.

Then the leading battalions came up against the enemy's main position, broke into it after a fight, and then moved into the heart of his lines, past his advanced ambulance posts, his headquarters and finally through his gun lines. There they paused on their intermediate objective.

As far as the reserve battalion was concerned, it was its right-hand company that first met the enemy. This company, after an advance of nearly a thousand yards, came under fixed-line machine-gun fire from an enemy position in the north, and one or two posts that had been bypassed by the other battalions. It was here, too, that Regimental Sergeant-Major Page accounted for at least one enemy position with his rifle and bayonet; he was killed later that night.

Commanding officers found control of their companies and the keeping of direction increasingly difficult. Major Worral, of the Somerset Light Infantry, serving with the 9th Durham Light Infantry, kept excellent control of his company with a hunting horn. Leading companies invariably increased their pace as each small post was rushed. There was no holding them back. The blood of these North Countrymen was up in truth, and Sergeant Dunn, of one of the battalions, was a typical example. He rushed a post at point-blank range, making certain of the five occupants with his bayonet.

The first objective coincided with the areas where the enemy was known to have dug in his tanks and self-propelled guns. The leading battalions kept close to the barrage, and when it halted on the first objective they found themselves in amongst these tanks and guns. Some of them had been put out of action by shell fire, but several showed plenty of life and were dealt with by the infantry in hand-to-hand combat with the crews.

It was then that the reserve battalion, the 6th Durham Light Infantry, started to take up its position facing north. A wheel in the dark is no easy task, but this was accomplished satisfactorily.

At 0200 hrs. the leading battalions struck out on the last phase of their grim journey towards the Rahman Track, and by 0400 hrs. they had reached their positions and had started to dig in. By 0500 hrs. the battalions' "A" echelon transport had navigated the gaps so speedily made by the Royal Engineers and had joined their individual units.

First light was at 0630 hrs. and at that time tanks of the 9th Armoured Brigade began to move through the infantry and out towards the enemy beyond. Almost immediately they came under heavy fire from what in the end proved to be the enemy's last screen of 88-mm. guns, and suffered considerable casualties.

As the sun rose and the early morning mist cleared it became possible for the battalion commanders to take stock of their positions. All round a number of enemy posts were visible and any movement brought prompt and heavy fire from their forward troops and supporting machine gunners. Digging had been difficult owing to the nature of the ground, and cover extremely hard to find.

Throughout the morning there was intermittent small-arms fire accompanied by a certain amount of shelling, particularly of the "soft-skinned" vehicles following the armour on its way through the minefield gaps. This shelling increased as the day wore on. There was also considerable anti-tank gun fire directed at our tanks operating in the area.

To the west on the Rahman Track it was obvious that a desperate tank battle was in progress. At about midday the enemy tried to counter-attack with some twenty tanks, but was beaten back by our armour, although at least one tank was knocked out by a 2-pounder gun of one of the battalions. And so the morning passed to afternoon and the battle continued.

During the later afternoon a considerable number of our tanks attempted to pass through the positions of the 6th Durham Light

British Official Photograph] [*Crown Copyright Reserved*

"Leading companies invariably increased their pace as each small post was rushed. There was no holding them back. . . . The blood of these North Countrymen was up."

A picture taken during "Supercharge."

Face p. 102]

Infantry into the desert beyond, but were again met by heavy anti-tank fire and compelled to withdraw. These tanks, however, must have had a very demoralizing effect on the German infantry so close to their own posts, for dejected groups got up out of their positions with their hands up and a total of ninety men walked over and surrendered. With them came the commanding officer of a regiment of panzer grenadiers, still most immaculately dressed.

At 1900 hrs. there was some intense enemy shelling, but it stopped before dusk.

With darkness came the news that the brigade was to be relieved, and at last the battle quieted down. The firing ceased and all round the battle area the glow from burning tanks faded out.

At 2230 hrs. from the north-west came sounds of distant transport moving. Later a German 88-mm. gun, driven straight into one of the forward companies, was stopped by a burst of tracer through its petrol tank. Few of the crew escaped, but those who did confirmed the hope that the Germans were pulling out. This crew had lost their way.

In the very early hours of the next day the battalions marched back, somewhat wearily, the seven miles to their own concentration areas. But their job had been well done in the highest traditions of the Division.

While the X Corps later successfully moved through the breach and won the great tank battle of El Aqqaqir, the brigade was put under the command of the 9th Australian Division.

Two days later, on the 5th of November, the brigade moved forward to mop up as far west as Daba, but on the 12th of November it once more came under the orders of the 50th Division. Casualties had not been light; almost four hundred of all ranks had been killed or wounded.

In an account of this kind it is impossible to tell of all the other arms, but a special mention must be made of the Royal Engineers. Their work was of the highest order. There was never delay. The gaps through the uncharted minefields were clearly marked and in the early hours of the 2nd of November the transport came forward smoothly and punctually to the forward battalions.

Meanwhile, the great events in the north were having their effect in the south. During the first few days of November the 7th Armoured Division had moved north, which in consequence left the XIII Corps with only two Divisions—the 44th and 50th. The 50th Division still possessed a decidedly international complexion, consisting of the 69th British Brigade, the 1st Greek Brigade and the 2nd Free French Brigade.

In turn the 2nd Free French Brigade relieved the 69th Brigade, and the 69th Brigade took over the Ruweisat Ridge from the 4th Indian Division. Opposite the 69th Brigade lay a very strong locality on the western edge of the ridge, with Deir el Shein immediately to the north of it.

Facing the 1st Greek Brigade was a series of less formidable positions. In front of the 2nd Free French Brigade stood the formidable Fortress "A" (Bab el Qattara), one of the main defences in the original Alamein Line which unfortunately fell to the enemy in his last desperate effort to break through to Alexandria early in July.

Far to the west, behind all these defences, ran the Rahman Track.

This, then, was the situation as the final blow was being struck in the north.

On the night of the 3rd/4th of November the nightly patrols from all brigades found the forward positions only partially occupied. Junior commanders, with the later experience of the Axis withdrawal through Africa and Italy, were wont to say that it was possible to sense an enemy pulling out. On more than one occasion an early morning "tap" would find that the birds had flown. Much forced activity in the early hours of the night might be the prelude to a quiet withdrawal before daybreak. And so it happened on this occasion. It was obvious, too, that opposition was cracking all down the front.

In preparation for this eventuality Corps Headquarters had given orders that the 50th Division in two or more foot columns was to advance to the Rahman Track and no farther, clearing up all enemy pockets in the area.

The Division was relieved of all its second-line transport, which was lent to the 44th Division. This was a bitter blow, for it implied that the advance of the 50th Division was to be very limited.

On the morning of the 4th of November the pursuit began. Vast minefields lay ahead. Progress could not be fast. By nightfall the 69th Brigade had secured the western edge of Ruweisat Ridge, and the 1st Greek Brigade had reached positions on a ridge a little more than a mile in front of their original line, but the 2nd Free French Brigade had made only small progress, as Fortress "A" was strongly held by rearguards supported by field and medium artillery.

In the late afternoon General Nichols visited all brigades and subsequently made the following plan:

The 69th Brigade was to force a way through the minefield confronting it, to strike direct for the Rahman Track and seize a commanding feature some twelve miles west of Ruweisat Ridge. The 1st Greek Brigade in two columns was to move at once by night and work round the northern flank of Fortress "A" with the object of cutting off the retreat of the enemy rearguards still holding out. The 2nd Free French Brigade was to hold a firm base on the high ground in front of Fortress "A" to keep the enemy heavily engaged and to be ready to advance and mop up the fortress as opportunity occurred.

Throughout the night the 69th Brigade continued clearing passages through the minefields in front of them. These proved to have a depth of some two thousand yards. The next day, the 6th of November, their advance at first was slow, but the objective was reached, without opposition, before dark.

A very fine display of dogged perseverance was given by the Greeks. All through the night they pushed on round the north flank of Fortress "A." Many prisoners were taken and by 1100 hrs. the next day they too had reached the Rahman Track. This meant a march of thirteen miles through the difficulties of enemy defences and broken ground.

On the other hand, the Free French encountered considerable opposition and it was not until noon that resistance weakened and the brigade was at last able to penetrate Fortress "A." By night it was completely secured.

Progress so far had not been fast. There were still opposition and vast minefields to be faced. Although the enemy was disintegrating quickly, the final collapse had yet to come.

The next day the long-hoped-for opportunity had arrived. At 2000 hrs. additional orders were received from Corps Headquarters to the effect that the 50th Division would form one mobile brigade column. This column would strike hard due west with the utmost speed and cross the Rahman Track at 0800 hrs. on the 7th of November. In preparation the G.O.C. ordered every available vehicle within the Division to be sent to the 69th Brigade during the course of the night and sent his orders to the Brigade by a liaison officer, who reached the Brigade Commander at 0200 hrs. Thanks to the past experience of the Division in a mobile role, the hurried reorganization that these orders meant was completed in the remaining hours of darkness.

Formed into battalion groups, the 69th Brigade started off in the early hours of the morning with the greatest enthusiasm. The track was crossed on time and a four-day dash to the west began.

General Nichols's orders to Brigadier Cooke-Collis were: "Advance as fast as possible; accept big risks and attack the enemy with the utmost dash." And it was not long before an opportunity arose to carry them out to the very letter.

After the Brigade had gone some six miles a small enemy defensive locality was encountered. With the anti-tank guns firing at point-blank range, the infantry charged in their motor transport, shooting from their vehicles. These somewhat unorthodox tactics were completely successful. The locality was captured without loss, and it was found to contain the headquarters of the Italian Brescia Division, including the divisional commander and his staff.

During the rest of the day several thousands of prisoners were taken. All had to return on foot, as there was no transport available. Long trains of weary and disillusioned Italians streamed back through the divisional area. Their feeding proved to be a big problem, and later a dump of six hundred prisoners' rations was maintained at Divisional Tactical Headquarters.

So the pursuit continued for a further three days. Eventually the brigade crossed the Matruh—Siwa track, level with the leading troops of the X Corps, the main pursuing force of the Eighth Army.

As no enemy had been encountered or prisoners collected for over twenty-four hours, and as supply was becoming increasingly difficult, the brigade was ordered on the 9th of November to withdraw. Three days later it had returned.

Throughout this time Divisional Main Headquarters had stayed in its original position and the remainder of the Division had been working hard in clearing the battle area and collecting the spoils of war. Vast numbers of prisoners had been captured.

So ended the Battle of El Alamein.

In considering the achievement of the Division throughout this phase it must be remembered that neither the 69th nor the 151st Brigade regained its individual identity until after the first week in October—three weeks before the battle started; that reinforcements came from far afield and that time was all too short to weld them into one formation. Training of the individual was difficult, and training collectively had been well-nigh impossible.

Despite these many handicaps, a very good credit balance was ultimately disclosed. It was obvious that patrolling had been brought to a very high standard. This, combined with other small operations carried out at night, was good training for the junior officers and non-commissioned officers. Leadership was not lacking. As a result of these experiences many useful lessons were learned, particularly in the method of crossing and breaching minefields, which were ultimately embodied in a very useful divisional training instruction. There was no doubt, too, that the Division ably fulfilled its defensive role on a much-extended front; at improvisation it was not amiss, and when the time came to attack it gained considerable success. Finally, and above all, it had reaffirmed its excellent reputation.

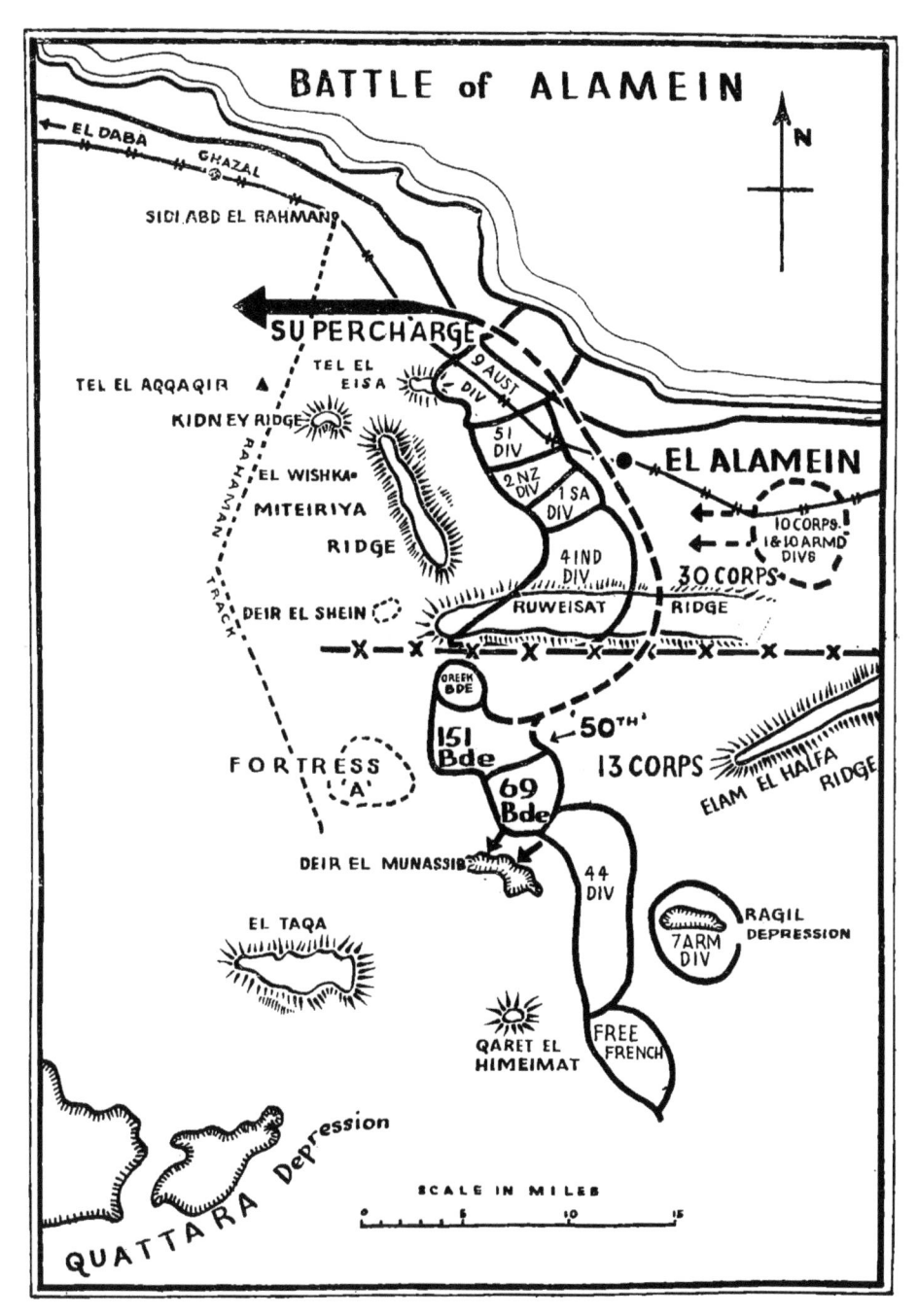

BATTLE of ALAMEIN

After the Battle of Alamein Brigadier Beake, V.C., took over the command of the 151st Brigade from Brigadier J. E. S. Percy, D.S.O., M.C. Brigadier Percy had served with the Division as a brigade major, a commanding officer and a brigade commander since 1938.

CHAPTER X

50TH DIVISION'S FATE IN THE BALANCE—A PERIOD OF TRAINING—
FORWARD TO MARETH

NOVEMBER, 1942, TO MARCH, 1943

THE Division was now withdrawn behind the old Alamein positions and given the task of clearing the battlefield. The 151st Brigade rejoined the Division, and gradually all the Allied contingents which had fought with it at Alamein departed. The clearing of the battlefield took a fortnight.

At this time the fate of the Division hung in the balance. The man-power situation in the Middle East became so acute as to make it necessary to disband one division. For a time it seemed as if the 50th Division was to be selected, but to the relief of all who knew the situation another division was chosen instead.

As a result of the decision, the Division was joined by the 50th Field Regiment from the 44th Division, and the divisional order of battle for the future became firm by the permanent inclusion of the 102nd Anti-Tank Regiment (Northumberland Hussars) and the 25th Light Anti-Aircraft Regiment, R.A. For a short time also the 44th Reconnaissance Regiment served with the Division.

Meanwhile, the advance of the Eighth Army was continuing. Mersa Matruh was retaken, and in a short time the remnants of the Afrika Korps were out of Egypt; most of the Italian army stayed as prisoners. Though much weakened, the Afrika Korps still maintained the ability to delay the advance, as was shown during the next two months.

Training became the order of the day within the 50th Division. By the first week in December the Division was concentrated in the area of El Adem, sixteen miles south of Tobruk.

The XXX Corps now took over the advance from the X Corps, and the X Corps was withdrawn into reserve, of which the Division formed part. This Corps was taken over by General Horrocks, who had commanded the XIII Corps, under which the Division had served at Alamein. Christmas was passed in comparative comfort at El Adem.

During December the enemy withdrew from the Agheila position to Buerat, at the western end of the Gulf of Sirte. The Division was ordered forward to take part in the forcing of the Buerat position, the first halt on the long journey to be made at Agedabia.

During the desert journey a violent storm caused a major alteration of plans. The mole of Benghazi was severely damaged, several ships being wrecked or rendered unserviceable. As a result it was impossible to maintain further troops forward at Buerat. Consequently, the Division was ordered to Benghazi, where it could be maintained from the port on its own transport.

The storm also affected the journey across the desert. What had once been firm, fine sand suddenly became a morass. Hundreds of vehicles became bogged in the area of Msus, and were pulled out only with the greatest difficulty. It was a muddy and weary force which eventually joined the coast road south of Benghazi.

The Division moved into a bivouac area on the hills above Regina, some fifteen miles east of Benghazi. There was an acute shortage of tents, but with remarkable improvisation all somehow got under rudimentary cover. January and February were wet and cold months, but by the end of the latter month the desert in this area blossomed like a rose, and few will forget the wonderful show of wild flowers that abounded everywhere, and the mushrooms.

Meanwhile, the maintenance situation in the forward areas was becoming increasingly difficult, and all units of the X Corps were called upon to make up improvised transport platoons to carry ammunition, petrol and rations from Tobruk to the Army railhead in the Marble Arch area. The X Corps arranged a competition between the various units, marks being awarded for quantity of stores carried, freedom from accidents, maintenance of vehicles and fitness of crews. The Division came out of the competition with flying colours, having five platoons amongst the first six.

At the beginning of the period out of the line there was little guidance as to the trend that training should take, due to uncertainty as to the form of the next operation in which the Division would be engaged. As the enemy was chased in turn from the Agheila and Buerat positions, and then out of Tripoli, it soon became clear that his next stand would be on the Mareth Line, in Tunisia. Accordingly, the X Corps started discussions to study the conditions of an attack on such a position. A very detailed divisional drill had been produced for an attack through enemy minefields and across obstacles. A rehearsal of this, combined with training attacks against the rocky escarpment on which the Division was bivouacked, did much to prepare the troops for the forthcoming battle. A street-fighting school was also opened in Benghazi. The less reputable part of the town was reduced to an even finer state of rubble than had been produced by two years of bombing.

The Division had not been long in the Benghazi area before some units were called forward. The first to go were the two field companies, R.E., who went to open up ports and improve roads behind the leading divisions. The port of Sirte, the bulk petrol installation at Tripoli, and the causeways across the salt marshes on the Tunisian border bear their mark. As a result of this, when the Division entered the battle again at Mareth, the divisional engineers were much less rested and trained than the remainder of the Division. The 25th Light Anti-Aircraft Regiment was moved forward to protect landing grounds.

Another handicap to effective training was the absence of carrier platoons of the infantry battalions. They had been moved forward from El Alamein on transporters and had not been halted when the Division was ordered to stop at Benghazi. As a result they spent two lonely months at Sirte.

In spite of these handicaps, a considerable amount of very valuable training was carried out, and by the end of February it could be said that the Division was in fine fighting trim. Numbers had mostly been made up.

No record of this period would be complete without mention of the divisional concert party. Under the direction of Lieutenant Stringer-Davis, a very good pantomime was produced, with several original songs, and the cast included a most personable female impersonator. The party became most popular, not only with the divisional troops but with other units of the X Corps in the area.

During this period several changes occurred in the divisional staff. Lieutenant-Colonel R. H. Batten replaced Lieutenant-Colonel P. K. Chance as A.A. and Q.M.G., Brigadier R. Hall, D.S.O., replaced Brigadier C. Eastman, O.B.E., as C.R.A., Lieutenant-Colonel C. Brownrigg, M.C., came as C.R.E., Major James, D.S.O., Brigade Major of the 151st Brigade, took command of the 5th East Yorkshire Regiment, and Colonel Melvin replaced Colonel Morrison as A.D.M.S.

During the last week of February the Division was once more on the road, this time to a concentration area south of Tripoli, a move forward of over seven hundred miles. It was once more a powerful fighting force, and as keen as mustard to avenge the withdrawal from Gazala and the losses incurred during that long retreat. It still had only two infantry brigades.

The Eighth Army entered Tripoli on the 23rd of January, 1943, three months to the day after the opening of the Battle of El Alamein, and the German forces withdrew slowly towards the Tunisian frontier. The leading formations of the Eighth Army crossed the frontier between Tripolitania and Tunisia, seized the important road centre of Medenine and approached the main defences of the Mareth Line.

Marshal Rommel's reaction was twofold: he manned the Mareth position and assembled his remaining armour for a desperate throw.

To the 50th Division at Benghazi went a dual summons. The machine-gun and anti-tank regiments (2nd Cheshire Regiment and the Northumberland Hussars) were ordered to move at once to the Medenine area to assist in repelling Rommel's expected attack. The main body of the 50th Division was ordered to follow with a view to a subsequent attack on the Mareth position. The Cheshire Regiment and the Northumberland Hussars averaged two hundred and fifty miles a day in convoy along the narrow coast road, and on the 6th of March, when Rommel ordered his armour forward against the Eighth Army's positions at Medenine, they were dug in and ready to take their part in a highly successful defensive battle. Meanwhile the 50th Division was arriving in its concentration area behind the Eighth Army. It was no light task which faced them, and in the long history of their campaign in the Second World War the Mareth battle stands out as a particularly grim encounter.

The Mareth Line, which took its name from the town in front of which this great barrier stood, was a miniature African counterpart of the Maginot Line. It had been built by the French in pre-war days, when Mussolini dreamed of a great African empire.

The coastal plain, bounded on one side by the Matmata Hills and on the other by the Mediterranean, was barred here by a natural obstacle in the form of a valley known as the Wadi Zigzaou. The Mareth defences were based on this wadi. They were sited with great skill and stiffened with wire, mines and anti-tank ditches. Before the retreating Axis forces reached them they formed a strong defensive system; after Rommel's engineers had been at work on them for a few weeks they were formidable indeed.

To the 50th Division was given the task of making a frontal assault on this position to secure a bridgehead through which the main body of the Eighth Army could be passed, while a mobile force based on the New Zealand Division was ordered to make an outflanking move on the other side of the Matmata Hills.

The setting for the 50th Division's operation was a type of country with which the Eighth Army had become familiar since leaving the true desert. The sandy coastal plain has scattered clumps of palms, small ridges, wadis which intersect it laterally, and very few roads. The wadis are deep near the Matmata Hills, but become shallow valleys nearer the coast, and most were dry at the season when the Battle of Mareth was fought. The Zigzaou is one of the more difficult wadis. Near the coast it is tidal, and there is water in it for some part of its length even during the dry season.

The tarmac road between Medenine and Mareth crossed the Zigzaou and passed through strong fixed defences at Arram—not unnaturally one of the strongest redoubts in the Mareth position.

In the sector chosen for attack by the 50th Division there was no similar road and crossing, though there were crossing places which had been used in fine weather. The whole of the Division's area was overlooked by the defences, and observation of enemy positions was well-nigh impossible. Knowledge of the defences was based on very good air photographs and on what Fighting French officers could remember of them.

Few people in the 50th Division who were concerned in the intensive planning for this attack will forget the invaluable help of Captain Paul Mezan, formerly an officer of a Tunisian rifle battalion who had helped to plan and build that part of the position which the 50th Division was to attack. This engaging and picturesque young man had requisitioned a black taxi in the name of De Gaulle from the inhabitants of the Isle of Djerba, off the coast of Tunisia, whom the tide of war seemed to have passed over. It was a very ancient taxi, but Paul Mezan used it as caravan, office and fighting vehicle. In the front he stacked his weapons of war, and in the back, on coat-hangers, was his dress uniform.

Captain Mezan's exact military memory was often tested against air photographs, and he was never wrong. He knew the vital parts of the Mareth Line inside out; he knew a great deal about crossing places over the wadi; from study of air photographs he could appreciate and describe with an amazing minuteness of detail how the enemy engineers had developed the position he once helped to build.[1]

The defences which the 50th Division now faced were a series of forts along the north-west bank of the wadi, each containing some six pillboxes. There was a second line of forts in the rear, on top of a ridge covering the other positions and protecting their rear. Most pillboxes were surrounded by a maze of tunnels and trenches, many of them concreted. From this miniature Maginot Line fire of all calibres could be directed into the wadi and on to the gentle slopes leading down to it.

The enemy's main improvements to the position in the sector

---

[1] Captain Mezan was later awarded the Military Cross for his part in the Tunisian campaign.

chosen for attack were threefold—the obstacle was increased by the construction of anti-tank ditches and the laying of minefields; a position of great strength was built forward of the wadi on high ground (the Bastion)²; and the line of outposts was constructed to impose delay and prevent close reconnaissance of the main defences.

As the Division faced the Mareth Line the forward enemy redoubts were, from right to left, Ksiba Est, Ksiba Ouest, Ouerzi, Zarat Sudest and the Bastion. Behind them were an enemy locality marked "X" on the map, Ouerzi Est and Ouerzi Ouest. Still farther back were the palm trees and wadis of the village of Zarat, and nearer the sea was a solitary and fantastic mansion called Maison Triolet, from the roof of which the enemy was able to command a wide view of the country towards Medenine.

The defences facing the 50th Division were manned by the Italian Young Fascists Division and the 164th German Infantry Division. The greater part of the armour of the Afrika Korps was in reserve south of Gabes.

The sector selected for attack was between Ksiba Ouest and Ouerzi. There were two main advantages to be foreseen from attacking on this frontage, and one big disadvantage. The advantages were that this part of the enemy line was not covered by an advanced main position, which meant that the crossing and the breaching of the defences could be carried out in one operation; and that at two points there were old crossing places. The disadvantage was that the entire sector was overlooked from the left flank by the powerful Bastion.

It was therefore decided to attack the Bastion on the same night as the main attack was to be delivered, and a little before it.

The main assault was to be made by the 151st Brigade, supported by the 50th Royal Tank Regiment, and the assault on the Bastion by the 69th Brigade. Meanwhile, the front was to be held by the 69th Brigade, which was also given the job of eliminating the outposts and closing up to the main position.

This it did on the nights of the 16th/17th and the 17th/18th of March, with clockwork precision, the last phase of the attacks giving the infantry possession of a low ridge facing the Bastion and dominating the Chet Meskine, a more or less covered approach to the wadi. All three battalions—the 6th and 7th Green Howards and the 5th East Yorkshire Regiment—were used in these attacks, and a special technique was employed. Each battalion was preceded by a picked fighting patrol known as "The Thugs," led by an experienced officer and accompanied by engineers to deal with minefields. The Thugs'

---

²See sketch map facing page 122.

technique was to advance to the edge of the minefield before the British artillery fire was opened. As soon as this fire came down the engineers made personnel gaps under its cover, and when the fire lifted the infantry raced through and attacked the nearest enemy post.

On the first night this procedure was completely successful on the right. A patrol of the 5th East Yorkshire Regiment, led by Lieutenant Watney, did exceptionally well and captured a strong enemy post without loss to themselves; the remainder of the 5th East Yorkshire Regiment followed through the gap in the minefield and soon dealt with the shaken defenders. In the centre the 6th Green Howards' patrol lost their commander in capturing the position and the battalion fought hard hand-to-hand before capturing their objectives.

The most difficult operation was on the left. A brigade of the 51st Division was to attack on the left of the 50th Division, but because their artillery was required for a time for another task their attack had to begin later. The 7th Green Howards on the left of the 50th Division front therefore had an exposed left flank and suffered a good deal from small-arms fire. The battalion's initial attack was helped by heavy fire. Lieutenant-Colonel "Bunny" Seagrim decided to use his reserve company to work round the left flank of the enemy positions and the battalion captured the whole of their objectives after heavy fighting.

The final phase of this preliminary operation was carried out the next night by two companies of the 5th East Yorkshire Regiment, whose attack succeeded with very few casualties. By the morning of the 18th of March the 69th Brigade were in possession of the ridge overlooking the Zigzaou, which enabled reconnaissance of the wadi to be made for the first time.

From the 151st Brigade, busy training for their tremendous task in a divisional rear area, patrols came forward to examine the wadi. On the night of the 18th/19th of March these patrols examined the bed of the wadi, crossed it and reconnoitred the anti-tank ditch on the other side. They found that the slopes leading down to the wadi were mined, as was the wadi itself. They reported that there was some water in it, but that it had a firm bottom at the places where they examined it. The Corps Commander and the Army Commander sent special congratulations on these daring patrols.

The stage was now set. The 151st Brigade, with its supporting arms, had been training intensively near the sea and assembling special equipment. This included short wooden ladders to be used in crossing anti-tank ditches, and fascines to be rolled off the front of the tanks to form temporary crossings over the wadis and ditches. No other bridging equipment was available.

I

The plan was for an attack in three phases.

At H hour (2200 hrs.) the 7th Green Howards were to assault the Bastion. Half an hour later the 151st Brigade, forming up in the Chet Meskine, were to capture an initial bridgehead from Ksiba Ouest to Ouerzi, with two battalions. Shortly after midnight the third phase was due to begin, the third battalion of the 151st Brigade, with any other reserves available, attacking the localities on top of the ridge from locality "X" to Ouerzi Ouest. The whole of the Corps artillery was to support all phases, firing on a timed programme. One field regiment (the 74th) was to be superimposed and available on call to the 151st Brigade for close support.

The sappers faced a very heavy task. One field company was to be in close support of the infantry with a view to gapping minefields, helping to cross anti-tank ditches, and generally assisting as assault engineers. The remainder were to tackle the all-important job of making two vehicle crossings over the wadi.

A last-minute misfortune, which had far-reaching effects on the battle, was that Divisional Headquarters found itself unable to move into its selected battle position chiefly owing to congestion in the area. Consequently, communications were stretched to the limit.

By H hour on the night of the 20th/21st of March, however, the Division was in all other respects ready for battle; the full weight of the Corps artillery crashed down on the Bastion, and the 7th Green Howards braced themselves to strike the first blow in the historic battle. Their action was memorable for heavy hand-to-hand fighting with German infantry. The battalion advanced in two columns. When the right-hand one reached the anti-tank ditch and minefield they were temporarily stopped by fire from a strong-point which had escaped the worst of the bombardment.

The Thug patrol leading this column suffered heavy casualties. The battalion commander, Lieutenant-Colonel Seagrim, who was at the head of the leading company, saw what was happening. He placed himself at the head of the patrol and led them through the minefield and straight in to attack the post that was causing all the trouble. Seagrim is reported to have killed or wounded, single-handed, some ten or twelve Germans, and this spirited attack caused the surviving defenders of the locality to surrender.

This was but one example of Seagrim's brilliant leadership that night. Even after both columns had penetrated the defences, the Bastion remained a tough spot for the rest of that troubled night. Seagrim's powerful personal example was an inspiration to the troops. For this night's work he was awarded the Victoria Cross, but he never lived to know it. He was killed at the Battle of the Wadi Akarit shortly afterwards.

British Official Photograph] *[Crown. Copyright Reserved*

"Small-arms fire poured down the wadi as the troops struggled desperately for a foothold"

Men of the D.L.I. "reconstruct" their human-pyramid technique in the Mareth anti-tank ditch, a few days after the battle, for the benefit of cameramen making the film "Desert Victory."

Thus the Green Howards captured the Bastion, marshalled their two hundred prisoners and proceeded to patrol into and even across the Wadi Zigzaou.

Later, to avoid our own artillery supporting fire, the patrols of the 7th Green Howards which were across the wadi were recalled.

Meanwhile, the Durham Light Infantry had launched the main attack. Their forming-up position in the Chet Meskine was packed with troops, and movement was made difficult by disused enemy slit trenches and old gun positions.

The 9th Durham Light Infantry on the right, approaching the wadi in the moonlight, were met by a hail of fire from artillery, mortars and machine guns, but much of it was inaccurate. The rumbling Scorpions and the gapping parties led the way through the minefields, and the leading company crossed the anti-tank ditch by means of their ladders, waded across the wadi and reached the far side without having suffered serious casualties. There they encountered Italians, who were holding out in strong, dug-in positions, and there was hand-to-hand fighting before the position finally caved in.

While this fight was in progress, the second company, under Major Worrall, was advancing through the minefield on the British side of the wadi, nearly fifteen minutes behind schedule. The company commander, knowing that he was committed to a timed artillery programme, led his men through the last part of the minefield without waiting for a gap to be cleared, and this brave gamble succeeded, the company suffering only a few casualties.

They reached the far side of the wadi at a point where the bank was very steep, and as they were struggling to get up it they came under very heavy fire from Ksiba Ouest. Small-arms fire poured in enfilade down the wadi as the troops struggled desperately for a foothold. For a few moments it was touch and go; then some of the men formed a human ladder against the bank, and the remainder scrambled up and out on top.

Their orders were to attack Ksiba Ouest from the rear. After fierce fighting they established themselves in the enemy trenches about a hundred yards from the main position. Worrall's second-in-command had been killed, one of his platoon commanders was wounded, and Worrall himself had been hit in the chest. He elected to stay on and continue the fight. He collected his company and, cheering them on with his hunting horn, he led the way into the strong-point, which was captured by 0100 hrs.

The third company followed the others without much difficulty, and well before daylight the battalion was established on its objective.

The 8th Durham Light Infantry, on the left, had to tackle the

Ouerzi strong-point. Early in the operation their commanding officer, Lieutenant-Colonel "Jake" Jackson, had been killed in the wadi; it fell to the second-in-command, Major Lidwell, to direct the battalion into an attack on a strong-point that proved to be bigger and more strongly held than had been thought. Its capture by 0200 hrs. by a battalion already depleted by casualties was a fine performance.

At about midnight the leading tank of the centre column of the 50th Royal Tank Regiment tried to cross the wadi—and stuck irretrievably. Engineers with the tanks at once began to make a crossing with fascines, but by daylight only four tanks had got across.

General Nichols had decided that the latest time at which phase three could begin was 0300 hrs., which would leave three hours of darkness. But at that time all that was known at Divisional Headquarters was that both the leading battalions had got some sort of footing on the far side of the Zigzaou. (They were, in fact, established in Ksiba Ouest and Ouerzi, but the slender infantry communications of those days had proved inadequate, and the true situation was not apparent.) The Divisional Commander therefore ordered a postponement of the third phase.

At first light the overall situation was promising, but there remained for solution the central problem in the whole Mareth operation—the Wadi Zigzaou. True, the assault infantry were across this formidable obstacle. But now they had to be supplied and reinforced. Only four tanks were with them, and it remained to pass the rest of the 50th Royal Tank Regiment across with the least possible delay. A few anti-tank guns were on the other side. The 2nd Cheshire Regiment had gallantly man-handled their machine guns across, and two troops of light anti-aircraft guns were in position near the very rudimentary crossing which had been made during the night.

The engineer crossing reconnaissance party with the 9th Durham Light Infantry had been wiped out, and no reconnaissance had been made on this sector. The party with the 8th Durham Light Infantry had reported that the only practicable site for a crossing was where the tanks had crossed. A decision was taken to concentrate all efforts there.

The enemy was obviously shaken and in some confusion. He still held commanding ground, but seemed to have little idea of the extent of the Division's penetration. He was unable to mount any major counter-attack during the day, though his gunners and machine gunners made life very unpleasant for those at work on the wadi crossing. Two hundred and fifty Italians from three strong-points gave up the fight and crossed over into the British bridgehead, being shot-up as they came by stouter hearts who remained at their posts.

Meanwhile, the Division prepared to enlarge the bridgehead by carrying out phase three that night. Slight changes were made in the original plan. The 69th Brigade were ordered to relieve the Durham Light Infantry in Ksiba Ouest as soon as it was dark. Thereafter they were to attack Ksiba Est. The 151st Brigade were to attack locality "X," Ouerzi Est, Ouerzi Ouest and Zarat Sudest.

It was decided at a higher level that the 51st Division should take over the Bastion. This was a hurried relief, without proper reconnaissance, and the newcomers had little chance to get a real grip on the situation.

Throughout the day working parties at the crossing and those going into the bridgehead had been subjected to very heavy fire, and as night fell the fire on to the crossing rose to a crescendo as the enemy tried to block the only route into the bridgehead.

The infantry crossed the Zigzaou and met the same sort of bitter, hand-to-hand fighting as the Durham Light Infantry had met the night before.

The 5th East Yorkshire Regiment, on the right, advanced without difficulty up to the near end of Ksiba Est. There they found a network of deep, narrow trenches which they entered and cleared. By the time, however, that they had reached the concrete pillboxes the artillery had lifted and they were unable to make further progress. It appeared that Ksiba Est was a much larger fortress than had been anticipated, and it was subsequently discovered that it had a length of one thousand two hundred yards and a depth of nearly four hundred yards, and had also been prepared for occupation by a complete battalion.

In the centre two companies of the 9th Durham Light Infantry reached their respective objectives, where they had in both cases a hard hand-to-hand fight. Before they succeeded in clearing out the enemy they took a number of prisoners, but themselves suffered considerable casualties. As a result of this, both of these companies were really too weak to hold their objective satisfactorily.

On the left the 6th Durham Light Infantry secured both their objectives comparatively easily, the enemy clearing out just before their assault on the objective. Ouerzi Ouest was found to be a position of great importance, standing on top of the ridge and commanding the country in all directions. Zarat, like Ksiba Est, proved to be much larger than had been anticipated and contained a network of deep, narrow trenches in which platoons and sections easily became detached and out of control. Forty-two tanks crossed into the bridgehead.

Thus the actual attack had, in general, gone fairly well. But the decisive point was not the perimeter of the bridgehead, but the crossing that was the lifeline to it. There matters were by no means so satisfactory. The tanks had so damaged the crossing that the anti-tank guns could not get over, while the infantry had not received adequate supplies of ammunition.

The tanks of the 50th Royal Tank Regiment provided some anti-tank protection, but it was realized that they alone could not repel a determined armoured counter-attack.

The enemy had managed to leave behind several snipers, some of whom were on the east bank, and they succeeded in putting a stop to all work on the wadi crossing as soon as it became light. The enemy still had observation over the crossing and over the slopes leading up from it on the west side. As a result, the work of consolidating and improving the position was particularly difficult. Finally, daylight showed how really extensive the enemy positions were, and it was doubtful if they had been completely mopped up.

Although no work was possible on the crossings in daylight, a few more tanks of the 50th Royal Tank Regiment managed to cross. One squadron were pushing forward in support of each battalion in the bridgehead. They gave much assistance in mopping up, but their power of manœuvre was considerably restricted by mines, which were everywhere.

Shortly after first light the R.A.F. began to note changes in the enemy's dispositions. They reported that there were considerable numbers of guns, tanks and transport in the woods around Zarat. By night the enemy had obviously moved forward part of his reserve from the Gabes area, and it was clear that a major counter-attack was brewing. This concentration of the enemy should have provided a wonderful target for our Air Force.

Throughout the morning all enemy attempts to move forward were stopped by our artillery. Then a disaster occurred: it rained. It was only a short, sharp shower, but it caused the water in the wadi to rise. It also prevented our air striking force using their airfields, and gave the enemy the chance to move his tanks into the open and to mount his counter-attack.

By this time troops in the bridgehead and many in the remainder of the divisional area were extremely tired. Other difficulties also cropped up. Means of intercommunication were failing, cables were frequently cut, many wireless sets had been hit and others required new batteries which could not be taken forward to them across the wadi. Consequently the information reaching Brigade and Divisional Headquarters was extremely scanty.

At midday on the 22nd of March the Corps Commander visited

Divisional Headquarters and discussed plans for the night. It was assumed at that time that, with the aid of the R.A.F., the impending counter-attack could be beaten off, but it was not then known that no anti-tank guns had crossed the wadi, otherwise a less optimistic view might have been taken about the prospects for that night.

At about 1300 hrs. the enemy launched his counter-attack, supported by heavy artillery concentrations and some aircraft. The attack was made in three columns from forming-up places in the palm trees around Zarat, each column containing Mark IV tanks, anti-tank guns and large numbers of infantry. One column was directed on Ouerzi Est and tackled this post from the north. The second column struck between Ouerzi Est and Ouerzi Ouest, and the third column came in along a shallow valley between Ouerzi Ouest and Ouerzi.

The line of approach for these attacks had been very carefully selected, and in many instances the attacking enemy were defiladed from the fire of our troops in the bridgehead. The infantry were running out of ammunition, and the tanks were badly situated and in any case had not large enough guns to deal with the enemy Mark IV tanks.

The enemy first directed his main efforts against the Valentine tanks of the 50th Royal Tank Regiment, and by about 1700 hrs. some thirty of these had been knocked out, and their commanding officer, Lieutenant-Colonel Cairns, killed. The remaining fifteen tanks withdrew to cover near the wadi crossing, where they remained in action until night. The enemy then proceeded to attack each post in turn with his infantry, his tanks giving close supporting fire from hull-down positions. As the afternoon wore on, the ammunition of the defending companies ran very low, and towards evening the company commander in Ouerzi Est withdrew his company to the wadi bank under cover of smoke from the few tanks that remained. The company commander in locality "X" was forced to take similar action soon afterwards, and in this move a large proportion of his company was lost. Ouerzi Ouest held firm, but also suffered considerable casualties. It was not clear what happened to the garrison of Zarat, but the enemy was in possession of this post by 1800 hrs.

By 1700 hrs. the situation in the bridgehead was clearly so serious that all plans for any attack that night were abandoned, and attention concentrated on attempts to restore the situation. The whole of the 151st Brigade and one battalion (the 5th East Yorkshire Regiment) of the 69th Brigade were already committed in the bridgehead. There were varying reports of the condition of the troops on the west side of the wadi, and the making of any plan was much complicated by the constantly changing situation. Information became more and more conflicting, and the exact positions and condition of the troops more and more difficult to assess.

By the evening a bloody and desperate battle was being fought out west of the Wadi Zigzaou, and slowly but surely the infantry were driven back to the wadi edge, until by midnight, except for the East Yorkshire Regiment holding out in Ksiba Ouest, there was no depth whatever in the bridgehead. Though tremendous casualties had been inflicted by the supporting artillery, whose concentrations had been kept going ceaselessly in support of the infantry, they failed to stop the enemy attack. Later in the evening even this support flagged as wireless sets with the forward troops, the essential links between the observation posts and the guns, were gradually knocked out or failed owing to exhausted batteries.

The men of the 6th, 8th and 9th Durham Light Infantry were inextricably mixed up, many without commanders, all hungry, tired and desperately short of ammunition. The whole area was lit up by burning tanks of the 50th Royal Tank Regiment where they had been fought to a standstill by superior enemy armour. Such was the picture as seen by a liaison officer whom the Divisional Commander sent forward when he visited the forward areas shortly after midnight.

General Nichols therefore decided that the situation was such that he had no option but to withdraw the remnants of the 151st Brigade to the east of the wadi, leaving the 5th East Yorkshire Regiment in Ksiba Ouest as a pivot on which to resume his attack on the 23rd of March.

The withdrawal took place according to plan with little loss, and dawn found the 5th East Yorkshire Regiment alone on the west side of the Wadi Zigzaou. The east bank was held by the remaining two battalions of the 69th Brigade, while the 151st Brigade was withdrawn to rest and refit. Battalions proved to have suffered somewhat fewer casualties than was expected, but all the troops were extremely tired and the loss of equipment had been very considerable.

On this day the 5th East Yorkshire Regiment was repeatedly attacked, but on every occasion the enemy was driven off. The divisional artillery did excellent work in supporting their defence, being in action all day, and firing with devastating effect every time the enemy formed up to attack.

The counter-attack on the Wadi Zigzaou contributed to the undoing of the enemy. During the 50th Division's operations, the New Zealand Division had been gradually working round his exposed flank in the desert south of the Matmata Hills. The move forward of part of his armoured reserve to the Wadi Zigzaou on the night of the 21st/22nd of March had left the southern flank relatively lightly

MARETH

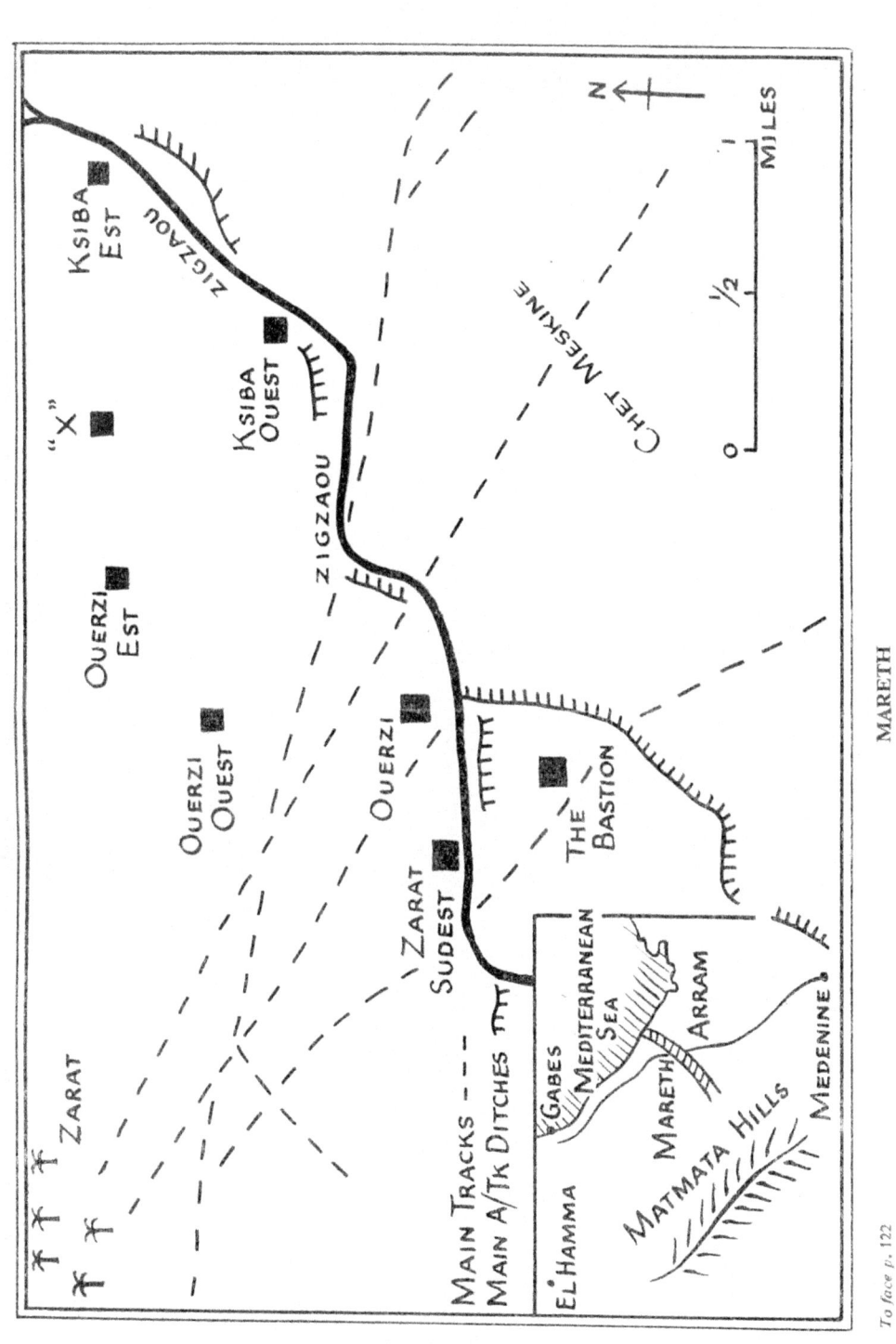

unprotected. His counter-attack at Mareth had cost him dearly, and he was so short of troops that he had no alternative but to leave armour forward at Mareth to hold the line.

General Montgomery seized the opportunity. The New Zealand Division was considerably reinforced, while the 4th Indian Division was moved into the Matmata Hills to provide a link between the main forces on the coastal plain and the mobile forces in the desert.

As a result, on the night of the 23rd/24th of March the 5th East Yorkshire Regiment was withdrawn to the east side of the Wadi Zigzaou, and the whole of the 50th Division was back on its original line. Later the Highland Division took over the positions held by the 69th Brigade, and eventually the whole Division was withdrawn into reserve to rest.

So ended the main part of the Battle of Mareth as far as the 50th Division was concerned.

The end of the battle found the 50th Division tired and battered, but it had played a notable and gallant part in the major victory that Mareth proved to be. North Countrymen had assaulted the enemy at his strongest point, they had driven a hole through it, and it is no discredit to them that they could not retain the positions which they had won.

CHAPTER XI

A Brief Rest, and a Sudden Call to Action—The Battle of the Wadi Akarit—Two Victoria Crosses

MARCH TO APRIL, 1943

The Division was withdrawn to reserve on the night of the 23rd/24th of March and on the 25th it was ordered to relieve the 7th Armoured Division in a quiet sector of the line in positions astride the Medenine—Mareth road. Meanwhile, the New Zealanders in the south were bringing increasing pressure to bear on the enemy south of Gabes, which was having its effect on the Mareth front. On the morning of the 27th of March patrols reported that some of the enemy positions were unoccupied and the advance began. Mareth was occupied by the 69th Brigade the next day.

The Division took no further part in the subsequent advance through Gabes and northwards to the Wadi Akarit. The next day it moved north and west of Mareth, and the following days were spent in clearing up the Mareth battlefield, burying the dead, and recovering much of the lost equipment. During this period Brigadier R. Senior, D.S.O., relieved Brigadier Beake, V.C., as Commander of the 151st Infantry Brigade, and Brigadier Hill became C.R.A. in place of Brigadier Hall.

No sooner had the Division settled down to this well-earned rest than its second-line transport, and much of its first-line as well, was removed to assist the maintenance of the remainder of the Eighth Army forward at Gabes and the build-up for a further attack at Akarit.

Northwards from Gabes the next natural defensive position on the line of advance of the Eighth Army was this wadi and the hills behind it. Together they formed a natural obstacle from the sea to the salt marshes inland, known as the Sebket el Hamma, which were impassable to all forms of transport.

On the 2nd of April the Divisional Commander attended a conference at Headquarters, XXX Corps, at which the Corps Commander outlined his plan for the attack on the Akarit position. The 50th Division was not to take any part. In the evening, however, on his return to Divisional Headquarters at Zaret, he was told on the telephone that the Division would after all be required. As the attack was to take place at dawn on the 6th of April, little time was available for planning and preliminary moves.

The first plan outlined by the Corps Commander on the 2nd of April involved an attack by two infantry divisions, the Highland Division on the right and the 4th Indian Division on the left, with the X Corps held in reserve to take advantage of a break-through. The Akarit position, however, was of some considerable natural strength and it was felt, after more consideration, that there might be insufficient troops on the ground to capture and completely clear such large and intricate positions. General Nichols was therefore ordered to use one brigade of the 50th Division to attack in the centre. The general plan for the battle was therefore as follows:

The coastal plain between the hill known as Jebel Romana and the sea was to be held by the 7th Armoured Division. No attack was contemplated in this area. The attack would be carried out by three divisions, as follows:

On the right the 51st Division would attack Jebel Romana and such enemy positions as there were between Jebel Romana and the coast road, employing two brigades for the purpose.

On the left the 4th Indian Division would seize the Fatnassa Hills and the Jebel Meida.

In the centre the 50th Division with one brigade was to capture the Hachana Ridge and a known enemy post between the Hachana Ridge and the Jebel Romana over which a track crossed into the plains of Southern Tunisia.

General Nichols returned to his headquarters at Zarat late on the night of the 2nd of April with this plan. The Division was in no state for any immediate action. It was scattered over a wide area; it had been deprived of a large proportion of its transport and none was to be returned. To enable a brigade from the Division to become operational, the Division's artillery was completely grounded. All support for the attack was to be given by the gunners of the New Zealand Division. As a result, the attacking battalions of the 50th Division were to face the further disadvantage of having strange artillery officers to work with them, though, as it turned out, thanks to the co-operative attitude and the high technical ability of the officers concerned, the arrangements worked most satisfactorily on the day.

On the afternoon of the 3rd of April the 69th Brigade moved forward.

A shallow, open valley separated the hills of the Akarit position from the forward positions taken over by the 69th Brigade. All movement in this valley, which was some three or four miles wide, could be seen by the enemy and the troops in position on the forward slopes were confined to their cover by day. It was possible during daylight, however, to get a good view of the enemy positions, though at a distance.

The attack on the Akarit position opened on the front of the 4th Indian Division. These experienced troops, accustomed to individual action by night, advanced as soon as it was dark into the Tebaga Fatnassa and the Mesreb el Alig without artillery support and set to work destroying Germans and Italians silently and effectively. On the right the Highland Division started their attack at 0430 hrs. and it was soon known that all was going well on both flanks.

Meanwhile, on the 50th Division's front the 7th Green Howards on the right and the 5th East Yorkshire Regiment on the left, with their supporting arms, started their advance up to time and according to plan. One company of the 7th Green Howards attacked and captured a small feature short of the anti-tank ditch on the right known as "The Pimple" without much difficulty, the infantry breaching the minefields and wire with their own resources.

The remainder of the 7th Green Howards approached the anti-tank ditch which turned out to be on the reverse slope of a low ridge. This had not previously been appreciated from the air photographs, and because the anti-tank ditch itself could be seen only in part before the battle. There the forward troops took up position while gapping parties went to work making passages through the minefields, which turned out to be less formidable than had been expected.

Unfortunately, the artillery barrage had been of insufficient density to subdue the enemy forward positions. As soon as the leading company started to cross the ridge, they came under devastating fire from the enemy's foremost defended localities, most of which contained 47-mm. guns firing at short range. Heavy casualties occurred and the advance was held up.

Lieutenant-Colonel Seagrim then once again organized a party himself and endeavoured to work forward, but in doing so he was wounded in the arm and shoulder. For the time being the 7th Green Howards were held up on this ridge some three hundred yards short of the ditch.

Meanwhile, on the left the advance of the East Yorkshire Regiment had suffered a similar fate. They too had come under devastating fire as soon as they crossed the first subsidiary ridge, and the leading company suffered about seventy per cent. casualties. Colonel James, the commanding officer, therefore decided to keep his battalion back behind the ridge until effective fire could be brought to bear on the enemy localities which were holding him up.

Meanwhile, little was known of the progress of the 4th Indian

Division on the left. Considerable fire met by the forward troops of the 69th Brigade had come from the high ground of the Tebaga Fatnassa, so it was certain that this Division had not secured its final objective. On the right it was known that the 152nd Brigade of the Highland Division had secured the top of the Jebel Romana, but were having a bad time there. The other attacking Highland brigade had suffered heavy casualties on the right flank, and no sooner had they crossed the crest of the hill on to their objective than the enemy had counter-attacked heavily, making their position very insecure.

By 0900 hrs. the picture was not too bright. General Nichols went forward to the Pimple on the 7th Green Howards' front to see the state of affairs for himself. At about this time events began to take a turn for the better. Forward troops of the 4th Indian Division began to arrive on the Jebel Meida, and, on the left, the Highlanders began to make their presence felt from the top of the Jebel Romana. Meanwhile, a squadron of tanks of the 3rd County of London Yeomanry under Major Cameron managed to infiltrate across the right corner of the anti-tank ditch where a crossing had been made by some troops of the Highland Division. As a result, first the 5th East Yorkshire Regiment and later the 7th Green Howards started to advance, supported by their own fire, and were soon over the anti-tank ditch.

The attack was considerably helped forward by the supporting fire of the machine guns of a company of the 2nd Cheshire Regiment who were now in position on the Pimple and who were able to bring really effective fire to bear on the enemy positions. Seeing this progress, General Nichols ordered Brigadier Cooke-Collis to start phase two of the operation. At 1015 hrs. the 6th Green Howards passed through the 7th Green Howards into the attack, and by 1100 hrs. it was clear that the enemy's resistance had been broken. This news was passed back immediately, and in the early afternoon the armour of the X Corps began to form up on the routes through the divisional area ready to start off in pursuit.

During the night the enemy made a faint attempt to counter-attack the 6th Green Howards. This was quickly beaten off and proved to be the end of the battle.

On the 7th of April the X Corps began to pass through the front of the 50th Division and the view of large numbers of tanks and other armoured vehicles spreading out across the Plain of Tunisia was a heartening sight for the battle-weary men of the 50th Division on the Ouidane el Hachana. On the 8th of April the Division concentrated in the area which had been No Man's Land before the battle for another rest and for a continuation of the refit which had been interrupted at Zarat.

Shortly afterwards orders were received for a further move forward. This time the route lay through a smiling olive country, a welcome contrast to the hundreds of miles of desert previously traversed by the Division, and the whole Division concentrated south of Sousse. There Major-General J. S. Nichols, D.S.O., M.C., who had led the Division with such gallantry all the way since the dark days in Alexandria, left, to be relieved by Major-General S. C. Kirkman, O.B.E., M.C.

* * *

This is a convenient moment to mention two Victoria Crosses gained during this stage of the North African campaign. It has been mentioned already that Lieutenant-Colonel Anthony Seagrim, 7th Green Howards, who was killed at the Wadi Akarit, was awarded the Victoria Cross for his outstanding leadership and valour at Mareth in the attack on the Bastion. The citation reads:

"The defence of this feature was very strong. It was protected by an anti-tank ditch twelve feet wide and eight feet deep, with minefields on both sides.

"From the time the attack was launched the battalion was subjected to the most intense fire from artillery, machine guns and mortars.

"Realizing the seriousness of the situation Lieutenant-Colonel Seagrim placed himself at the head of his battalion, which was at the time suffering heavy casualties, and led it through the hail of fire.

"He personally helped the team which was placing the scaling ladder over the anti-tank ditch, and was himself the first to cross it.

"He led the assault, firing his pistol, throwing grenades and personally assaulting two machine-gun posts which were holding up the advance of one of his companies. It is estimated that in this phase he killed or captured twenty Germans.

"This display of leadership and personal courage led directly to the capture of the objective. When dawn broke the battalion was firmly established on the position, which was of obvious importance to the enemy, who immediately made every effort to regain it, but Lieutenant-Colonel Seagrim was quite undeterred. He moved from post to post organizing and directing the fire until the attackers were wiped out to a man.

"By his valour, disregard for personal safety and outstanding example he so inspired his men that the battalion successfully took and held its objective, thereby allowing the attack to proceed."

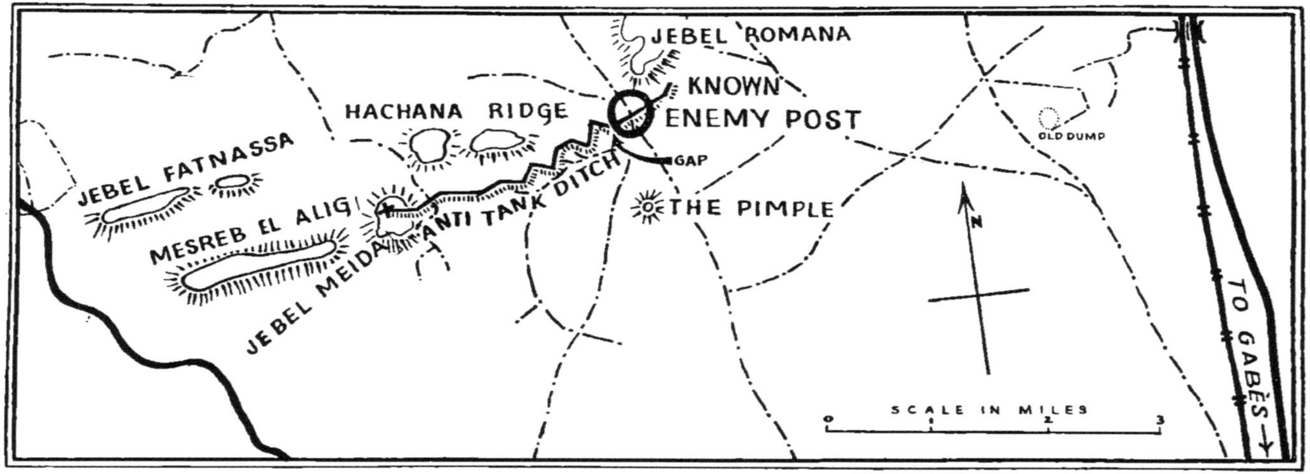

AKARIT.

Private Anderson, 5th East Yorkshire Regiment, was awarded the Victoria Cross for his actions during the Battle of Wadi Akarit. The citation reads:

"On the 6th of April, 1943, a battalion of the East Yorkshire Regiment was making a dawn attack on a strong enemy locality on the Wadi Akarit with 'A' Company leading. After some progress had been made, and 'A' Company was advancing over an exposed forward slope, it suddenly came under most intense and accurate machine-gun and mortar fire from well-concealed enemy strong-points not more than two hundred yards away. Further advance in that direction was impossible, and 'A' Company was able to withdraw behind the crest of a hill with the exception of a few men who were wounded and pinned to the ground.

"Private Anderson, a stretcher-bearer attached to 'A' Company, seeing these men lying wounded in No Man's Land, quite regardless of his personal safety, went forward alone through intense fire and single-handed carried back a wounded soldier to a place of safety where medical attention could be given.

"Knowing that more men were lying wounded in the open, he again went out to the bullet-swept slope, located a second wounded man and carried him to safety.

"Private Anderson went forward once again and safely evacuated a third casualty.

"Without any hesitation or consideration for himself he went out for a fourth time, but by now he was the only target the enemy had to shoot at, and when he reached the fourth wounded man and was administering such first aid as he could to prepare for the return journey he was himself hit and mortally wounded.

"Private Anderson by his valour, complete disregard for his personal safety and courage under fire probably saved the lives of three of his comrades, and his example was an inspiration to all who witnessed his gallant acts."

APPENDIX TO PART THREE

50TH (NORTHUMBRIAN) DIVISION

COMMANDS AND STAFF LIST, OCTOBER, 1942

G.O.C.	Major-General J. S. Nichols, D.S.O., M.C.
A.D.C.	Lieutenant D. Peck (2nd Cheshire Regiment).
G.S.O.1	Lieutenant-Colonel R. G. B. Innes (Seaforth Highlanders).
G.S.O.2	Major R. J. H. de Brett (East Yorkshire Regiment).
G.S.O.3 (O.)	Captain C. P. N. Parker (Essex Regiment).
G.S.O.3 (I.)	Captain E. W. Clay (Green Howards).
G.S.O.3 (C.W.)	Captain P. Markham (Foresters).
G.S.O.3 (Cam.)	Captain A. H. Hazell (Durham Light Infantry).
A.A. and Q.M.G.	Lieutenant-Colonel P. K. Chance (Warwick Yeomanry).
D.A.A.G.	Major W. H. L. Urton (East Yorkshire Regiment).
D.A.Q.M.G.	Major T. J. Black (Durham Light Infantry).
Intelligence Officer	Captain E. H. St. G. Moss (Intelligence Corps).
S.C.F.	Reverend J. C. Starkey.
A.D.M.S.	Colonel J. Melvin (R.A.M.C.).
A.D.O.S.	Lieutenant-Colonel R. C. Gibb.
C.R.E.M.E.	Lieutenant-Colonel W. J. Lyon (R.E.M.E.).
A.P.M.	Major D. McL. Douglas (Royal Northumberland Fusiliers).
Camp Commandant	Captain Smith.
O.C. D./E. Platoon	Lieutenant R. S. Kelly (2nd Cheshire Regiment).

69TH INFANTRY BRIGADE

Commander	Brigadier E. C. Cooke-Collis, D.S.O.
Brigade Major	Major J. F. C. Mellor (King's Royal Rifle Corps).
Staff Captain	Captain G. W. Thrift (Green Howards).
Intelligence Officer	Captain R. Turton (Green Howards).

5TH BN. THE EAST YORKSHIRE REGIMENT

Officer Commanding	Lieutenant-Colonel T. W. G. Stansfield.

6TH BN. THE GREEN HOWARDS

Officer Commanding	Lieutenant-Colonel G. C. P. Lance.

7TH BN. THE GREEN HOWARDS

Officer Commanding	Lieutenant-Colonel A. Seagrim.

151st INFANTRY BRIGADE

Commander	Brigadier J. E. S. Percy, D.S.O., M.C.
Brigade Major	Major R. B. James, D.S.O. (Essex Regiment).
Staff Captain	Captain W. A. Lowth (R.A.).
Intelligence Officer	Lieutenant T. H. Thackrah (Durham Light Infantry).

6TH BN. THE DURHAM LIGHT INFANTRY
Officer Commanding .. .. Lieutenant-Colonel W. I. Watson.

8TH BN. THE DURHAM LIGHT INFANTRY
Officer Commanding .. .. Lieutenant-Colonel M. L. P. Jackson, D.S.O.

9TH BN. THE DURHAM LIGHT INFANTRY
Officer Commanding .. .. Lieutenant-Colonel A. Clark, D.S.O.

1st GREEK BRIGADE
Commander .. Colonel Katsotos.

2ND FREE FRENCH BRIGADE
Commander .. Lieutenant-Colonel Alessandrie.

HEADQUARTERS, ROYAL ARTILLERY

C.R.A.	Brigadier H. R. Hall, D.S.O., M.C.
Brigade Major, R.A.	Major W. D. E. Brown, M.B.E.
Staff Captain, R.A.	Captain R. A. C. Sayer.
Intelligence Officer, R.A.	Captain J. G. Wood.

65TH FIELD REGIMENT
Officer Commanding .. .. Lieutenant-Colonel J. St. C. Holbrook.

25TH LIGHT ANTI-AIRCRAFT REGIMENT
Officer Commanding .. .. Lieutenant-Colonel Orme.

74TH FIELD REGIMENT
Officer Commanding .. .. Lieutenant-Colonel Collett White.

111TH FIELD REGIMENT
Officer Commanding .. .. Lieutenant-Colonel J. Hill.

124TH FIELD REGIMENT
Officer Commanding .. .. Colonel C. F. Todd.

HEADQUARTERS, ROYAL ENGINEERS

C.R.E. .. .. Lieutenant-Colonel Lindsay.

233RD FIELD COMPANY
Officer Commanding .. .. Major Osborne.

505TH FIELD COMPANY
Officer Commanding .. .. Major J. Wood.

FIELD PARK COMPANY
Officer Commanding .. .. Major Revers.

DIVISIONAL SIGNALS
Officer Commanding .. Lieutenant-Colonel J. B. de Lisle.

2ND BN. THE CHESHIRE REGIMENT
Officer Commanding .. .. Lieutenant-Colonel S. V. Keeling.

PART FOUR

CHAPTER XII

CLOSING STAGES IN TUNISIA—THE TWO THOUSAND MILE TREK BACK TO EGYPT

APRIL, 1943

By the middle of April the X Corps, under whose command was the 50th Division, was in close contact with the enemy position on the hills which run inland from Enfidaville. In the coastal sector the enemy's position was formidable. South of the village the ground is very open and flat, but to the north, except for a narrow coastal plain some two miles wide and much of it marshy, the hills rise abruptly and in places precipitously.

As in all the previous Eighth Army battles since El Alamein, the enemy held a position which he had been able to select and organize at leisure. He held Enfidaville and the high ground behind, and whilst his own troops found ample natural cover he was able to overlook the bare, grassy plain from which any attack would have to be launched and where the guns would have to be sited. The Corps plan was for the New Zealand Division, 4th Indian Division and 7th Armoured Division to attack on the night of the 19th/20th.

Enfidaville itself was not to be directly attacked, as it was considered likely that were the New Zealand Division to secure the high ground slightly farther inland the enemy's position would become untenable. If, on the other hand, he did not voluntarily withdraw, both the New Zealanders and the Indians were to wheel right through the hills and cut the main road north of Enfidaville.

On the 14th of April Major-General S. C. Kirkman, C.B.E., M.C., took over command of the Division from Major-General Nichols. General Kirkman was a gunner who came out to the Eighth Army as B.R.A. shortly after General Montgomery's arrival. He came to the Division from Tunisia, where for two months he had been with General Alexander as B.R.A., 18th Army Group. The Division was at the time in Corps reserve near Sousse, but on the next day orders were received for it to take over that part of the New Zealanders' position facing Enfidaville, so as to allow them to concentrate farther inland. In addition, artillery and machine-gun support was to be provided for the New Zealanders' attack, and plans were to be made for the Division to attack Enfidaville frontally should the attacks as planned fail or be held up.

In pursuance of these orders, the 201st Guards Brigade, then under command, took over positions some four thousand yards short of Enfidaville on the night of 16th/17th of April, whilst the rest of the Division concentrated in rear. It was found that the Guards Brigade had an open right flank resting on marshy ground, so the 151st Brigade, who were in reserve on the coast, pushed forward patrols along the narrow belt of low sand-dunes which runs along the coast, to give some protection to the Guards' right flank.

Reconnaissance by these patrols revealed that there was a narrow covered approach towards the enemy's position through the sand-dunes, and that the enemy's left flank was sharply thrown back between Enfidaville and the sea. Advantage was taken of this situation and at various times individual field guns and on one occasion a section of field guns were sent with an infantry escort to work along the coast until a position was reached from which the road north of Enfidaville could be seen. Laying direct, the guns then opened fire on enemy motor transport using the road. Several vehicles were hit and "brewed-up" before the enemy spotted where the fire was coming from, and started ranging on the positions. The guns then slipped away under cover, and the gunners had the satisfaction of seeing the enemy shell their vacated positions.

The task of supporting the New Zealanders' attack with the divisional artillery presented a difficult problem. On coming into action, positions under cover were occupied as far forward as possible, but it was found that from them the range of the bulk of the fire required by the New Zealanders was far too great. The attack was to be by night, so positions much farther forward and in the open could be occupied after dark; but however successful the New Zealanders' attack, these positions would not only be within full view of the enemy at dawn but would be within effective machine-gun range. Careful calculations showed that there was just time for the guns and ammunition to be brought up after dark, for the whole programme to be fired, and for the guns to be back again behind the crest by dawn, so this was arranged. There would be little time for digging, and there was some risk that the enemy at Enfidaville, seeing the flashes, would open fire during the night with his Spandaus. To lessen the chances of this, the Cheshire Regiment gave machine-gun covering fire on to the Enfidaville defences, an arrangement which fortunately also suited the New Zealanders, and in addition one troop of 25-pounders was held ready to smoke Enfidaville if there was any trouble. In the event, the supporting programme was fired with no interference from the enemy.

On the 18th General Montgomery held his final conference before the attack. On the 19th Major-General Kirkman carried out two reconnaissances, the first with Brigadier Senior, Commander of the 151st Brigade, the second with Brigadier Cooke-Collis, Commander of the 69th Brigade, both with the object of planning attacks which might have to be launched if the main Corps attack failed. They found the prospect of attacking over the open flat plains exceedingly distasteful, but alternative plans were made in sufficient detail to allow of reconnaissances being made that night for possible start lines.

Late that night, when the reconnaissances had started, the Divisional Commander was told that the Division was shortly to be withdrawn from the battle, and that no attacks were to be launched without the permission of the Army Commander. The next morning further details were given confidentially to the Divisional Commander. The Division was to be relieved by the 56th (London) Division in two days' time, and on relief was to proceed to Egypt, where it would come under the command of the XIII Corps. There it would plan and train for the invasion of Sicily. The 201st Guards Brigade, who in previous fighting had had heavy casualties, were to be left behind, and in their place the 168th Infantry Brigade, of the 56th Division, were to join the Division. With them were to come the 90th Field Regiment, R.A., 295th Field Company, R.E., and the 140th Field Ambulance, as the whole brigade group was at the time training for amphibious operations at the Combined Training Centre at Kabrit on the Suez Canal. It was with regret that the decision had to be accepted to leave behind the 65th Field Regiment, who had supported the infantry of the Division so well during the fighting of the previous two months. The regiment had joined the Division on the disbandment of the 44th Division after the Battle of El Alamein.

Whilst plans for the future were being considered the X Corps attack had been partially successful. The New Zealand Division was temporarily held up by the very formidable enemy position at Takruna, but sufficient progress had been made to cause the enemy to fall back from Enfidaville. The village was occupied by the 201st Guards Brigade on the morning of the 20th, and by the evening they had established themselves some three thousand yards beyond it, with the 69th Brigade in reserve in and to the east of the village.

Enfidaville will be remembered by those in the Division who saw it as an unpleasant place, full of disagreeable smells from olive-oil presses, which was constantly shelled and bombed by the enemy. But these conditions had not to be endured for long; the 151st Brigade was withdrawn on the 21st and the 69th Brigade was relieved on the 22nd and 23rd, on which date command of the sector passed to the 56th Division.

On the 24th the Divisional Commander and the G.S.O.1, Lieutenant-Colonel R. G. B. Innes, left Tunisia by air for Cairo, and the Division started its long march back by road to its new concentration area at Alexandria, a distance of nearly two thousand miles. Further members of the divisional staff followed by air on the 27th. The two infantry brigadiers arrived by car a few days later. Thus, for the Division, the fighting in North Africa was finished. There were some regrets that, after campaigning for so long in Africa, the Division was not to be present at the final destruction of the enemy's forces; on the other hand, there was considerable joy over the immediate prospect of enjoying a few days' leave in Egypt. There were few regrets at leaving the enemy's famous 90th Light Division occupying the forbidding mountains beyond Enfidaville.

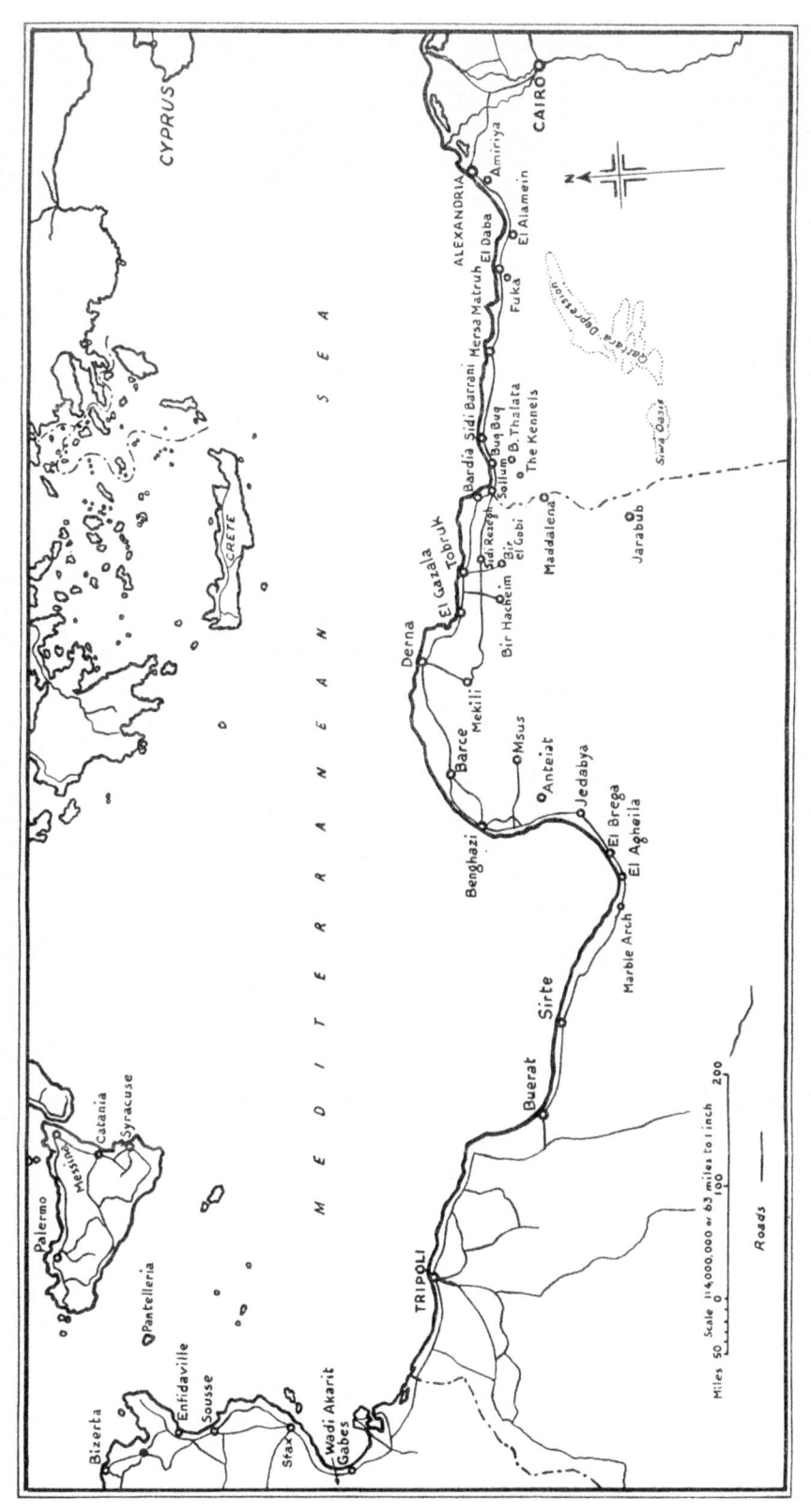

NORTH AFRICA

CHAPTER XIII

PLANNING FOR THE INVASION—151ST BRIGADE SELECTED TO ASSAULT—
TRAINING AT KABRIT—A REHEARSAL AT AKABA—EMBARKATION AT SUEZ

APRIL TO JULY, 1943

PLANNING for the invasion of Sicily had to start the moment the senior commanders and their staffs reached Cairo, for, although it was known that the expedition would not sail for some two months, there was much to be done in the time. From the point of view of a division, the work to be done in planning is in its broader outline simple, though it involves many detailed calculations. The commander is given his task; this will include a sector of the enemy's coast, where he will have to establish a beach-head position. He will be given the type and number of personnel ships (L.S.I.), mechanized transport ships (L.S.T.) and L.C.Ts. (Landing Craft Tank, which can discharge directly on to the beaches) which will be available for him in the D-Day convoys; the capacity of these ships will dictate the number of troops, the total weight of ammunition and the number of guns and vehicles which can sail with the D-Day convoys. Lastly, he will be given the number of Infantry Assault Craft (L.C.As.) and other small craft which can be carried on the big ships and be used to transfer troops and their equipment from ship to shore; the capacity of these craft will dictate the number of men who can land in the first flights, and, allowing for reasonable casualties, the rate of build-up on shore, as the same craft will return to the ships to run a ferry service.

The detailed calculations are not so simple. It will quickly be obvious whether one, two or three brigades can be used on the first day, but there will be many alternatives as to the number of other units who can be used, and the exact number of men and vehicles of the units forming the first flights that can be put on shore. The Royal Navy control the bringing in and unloading of craft on the beaches, and some of their personnel will require to land early.

A large organization is necessary to run the whole business of the disembarkation of troops, vehicles and stores on an open beach once the assaulting troops have passed inland. For this purpose an infantry battalion is considerably increased in size by the addition of other arms to form a "beach group," or, as it was called in Egypt, a "beach brick." The beach brick is responsible on shore for all development work such as putting down roads, making exits from the beach, and marking assembly areas for troops, vehicles and stores, and for the reception, stacking and issue of all commodities as directed by the "Q" staff of the division. They also therefore want their reconnaissance parties ashore early. The forward observation officers who are to observe the fire of naval guns against targets on land have equal claims for priority. All these experts will want to travel in the leading L.C.As. The result is that there will be many conflicting demands for accommodation, all at the expense of riflemen required to capture the beaches from which the specialists wish to work.

It is the same with vehicles—nearly everyone requires a vehicle as soon as possible in order to carry out his task efficiently, but vehicles rule out guns, tanks and carriers. It will be clear that after the commander has made his tentative plan there will be much juggling with figures and alterations to detail as conflicting interests make their weight felt. Finally, loading tables have to be made out showing what individuals are to travel in each craft and what units, or parts of units, and what mechanized transport is to be embarked on each ship.

All these calculations take time, and as they progress they may necessitate some modification to the commander's plan, which again entails fresh calculations. Losses of craft at sea before assembly may make it necessary for higher formations to change the first allotment of landing craft, which will again upset the details of the plan.

When the final plan is made and the loading tables are complete, the troops have to be rehearsed and trained with those individuals of other arms and services who will land with them, and arrangements have to be made for waterproofing vehicles which are to be landed on the beaches. These are the reasons why time was precious.

In fact, no time was wasted. On the 25th of April, the day after Major-General Kirkman and the senior members of his staff had arrived in Cairo, the Army Commander held a conference and gave his outline plan. The Allied landing was to be made in the south-eastern part of Sicily. The Eighth Army, consisting of the XIII and XXX Corps, was to land on the east coast and the south-eastern corner, whilst the American Army assaulted the southern coast. As in any landing on a hostile shore, the general area for the landing having been selected, it was necessary to select as immediate objectives a suitable port through which the army could be maintained and aerodromes from which fighter aircraft could operate. When these objectives had been selected the next step was to decide on the best beaches.

The port selected was Syracuse, and the task of capturing it was given to the XIII Corps, consisting of the 5th and 50th Divisions. The XXX Corps was to land at the south-east corner of the island and secure the aerodromes in the vicinity of Pachino.

Lieutenant-General Dempsey, commanding the XIII Corps, and his staff had been working in Cairo for some time, so their plan was ready. On the right the 5th Division were to land in the Cassibile area with the immediate task of turning north and capturing Syracuse. They were to be assisted by one parachute brigade, which would be dropped near the port. On the left the 50th Division was to land in the neighbourhood of Avola and protect the left flank and rear of the 5th Division. The relative positions of the beaches to be used by the two Corps would leave a gap of some ten miles between the left of the 50th Division and the right of the 51st Division, the right-hand division of the XXX Corps.

Once ashore and the immediate objectives captured, operations were to be developed by the XXX Corps turning north, first to gain touch with the 50th Division in the neighbourhood of Noto, and later to take over the ground it had gained, so that in its turn the 50th Division could move north to reinforce the 5th Division. Strong divisional thrusts were then to be made to the north and north-east towards the Plain of Catania, in order to gain ground whilst the enemy was still in a state of disorganization, and before he could concentrate and regroup his forces. The final objective was to be Messina, the port from which the enemy supplied, and would eventually attempt to evacuate, his forces.

The shipping allotted to the 50th Division allowed of two brigade groups sailing with the D-Day convoys, and the third brigade group arriving on D+3. The number of landing craft of various types which, at the time, it was thought would be available was known. Maps, air photographs and notes on the beaches and on the country were issued by the XIII Corps. There was only one good beach in the sector of coast allotted to the Division. This, apart from other factors, limited the Division's initial effort to an assault by one infantry brigade group.

All the information necessary for planning at Divisional Headquarters had therefore been given. Accommodation for a tactical headquarters in Cairo had been earmarked, and the dates by which the various stages of planning were to be complete had been laid down by the Army Planning Staff. Experts were available to be consulted, and the Division's S.N.O.L. (Senior Naval Officer Landing) Captain P. S. Smith, R.N., with his staff, joined Divisional Headquarters. Additional troops were allotted to the Division for the operation. These were the 98th (Army) Field Regiment (self-propelled guns), under the command of Lieutenant-Colonel The Hon. C. G. Cubitt, D.S.O.; the 44th Royal Tank Regiment, under the command of Lieutenant-Colonel E. D. Rash; "A" Squadron of the famous Royals' armoured-car regiment; and No. 34 Beach Brick, chiefly composed of the 1st Welch Regiment, under the command of Colonel J. T. Gibson.

At Divisional Headquarters the first few days were spent partly in consulting the experts on combined operations and partly in making considerable calculations to discover approximately who could be landed with the assault flight. The Divisional Commander made his plan, and the staff satisfied themselves that it was feasible with the craft available. Work was hampered because Lieutenant-Colonel Innes fell sick and went to hospital on the 5th, where he remained for a month, during which time the direction of the very considerable staff work fell to the G.S.O.2, Major M. A. C. Osborne, D.S.O., M.C.

On the 7th of May a conference for all brigadiers was held, at which the Divisional Commander gave his appreciation and plan. The bulk of the work then fell to the staff of the leading brigade. It was known that time for specialized training would be short, and it was therefore at first intended that the 168th Brigade, who had done the full course at the Combined Training Centre at Kabrit, should carry out the initial assault, but this brigade had never been in battle or experienced hostile fire, and when it was found that another brigade could do a shortened course at Kabrit the Divisional Commander decided that the 151st Brigade should take their place.

Planning had finished by the 16th of May, but constant minor changes had to be made up to the day of sailing, as information about the exact number of craft, and the type of L.C.T. which would be available, varied almost from day to day. As late as the 18th of June a certain number of "Dukws" (amphibious lorries), which had never been seen by anyone in the Division, were offered and a few accepted, though they displaced other vehicles which had already proceeded to the port of embarkation. These changes were further complicated by the fact that the personnel of the Division embarked at Suez, vehicles which were to go in M.T. ships were loaded at Alexandria, whilst those to go the whole way in L.C.Ts. were to be loaded at Benghazi.

The last crisis occurred on the 29th of June, when it became known that of the L.C.Ts. promised three would not be available. Those available had loaded at Benghazi and sailed for Tripoli. The vehicles left on the quay at Benghazi had therefore to be driven some seven hundred miles to Tripoli, where some reshuffling of vehicles took place in order that vehicles left behind should be the lowest on the priority lists.

During the first stages of planning, the Division was driving back from Tunisia to Egypt. Many of the vehicles had already traversed much of the well-known road several times, and were no longer renowned for their reliability, and as the journey progressed more and more vehicles had to be towed, but by the 11th of May the whole Division had arrived at Alexandria without leaving a single vehicle behind. On arrival the first necessity was to give as many men as possible four days' leave, many having had no leave for two years. At the same time, the overhaul of mechanized transport, the drawing of new vehicles, and the waterproofing of all vehicles which were likely to have to land on a beach had to be undertaken.

It was unpleasantly hot in Cairo, but quite bearable at Alexandria. It was a time of great activity, of hard work with as much sea bathing as possible, and of much coming and going of commanders and staff officers between Cairo and Alexandria and Gaza, where the 168th Brigade Group was stationed after it left Kabrit.

The next problem was the specialized training necessary for troops who had never before taken part in an invasion by sea. The training of No. 34 Beach Brick had begun before it joined the Division, and was continued under the 168th Brigade at Gaza. The training of the 151st Brigade took place at Kabrit from the 25th of May to the 6th of June. It included a landing exercise by night from L.C.As. and a few L.C.Ts. on the eastern shores of the Bitter Lake. As far as possible the defences were arranged to correspond with what was to be expected at Avola. This exercise, which was taken very seriously by all ranks of the 151st Brigade, was invaluable.

A second exercise for both divisions of the XIII Corps took place in the Gulf of Akaba. For this exercise Divisional Headquarters, the 151st Brigade and No. 34 Beach Brick sailed from Suez on the 10th of June, returning on the 15th. Those who took part will long remember the barrenness and heat of the country and the dust-storm which arose shortly after a successful landing had been made.

During this time the 69th Brigade managed to get a few days' training at Kabrit, and during the first week in June many officers and senior non-commissioned officers from the 69th and 168th Brigades attended a special course at the Mountain Training Centre near Tripoli in Syria. During the mobile fighting in Sicily this brief course was found to have been of definite value, particularly to the 5th East Yorkshire Regiment when, just short of Messina, they were issued with mules.

Immediately after the Akaba exercise the whole Division, less transport, concentrated at Ataka, just south of Suez. Commanders were worried at this time about the state of the men's feet. The warfare up to Enfidaville had been on the mechanized transport basis, and the inevitable relaxation at Alexandria had not helped. The result of a two-day march by the 69th Brigade from Kabrit to Suez was disquieting, and it was realized that the sea voyage would do further harm.

Suez is not a health resort at the end of June; not only was it very hot, but every evening brought the inevitable dust-storm. Everything possible, however, was done to harden the men's feet, and training with this object in view, as well as exercises in mountain warfare on the nearby hills, was carried out.

On the 23rd of June the Secretary of State for War, Sir James Grigg, spent a morning seeing units training. On the morning of the 24th Field-Marshal (then General) Montgomery addressed all senior officers of the XIII Corps, and in the evening he addressed all officers of the Division. The next day, the 25th, he carried out an informal inspection of all units of the Division. For three and a half hours he motored through the specially selected training area, seeing one company or battery after another. He had a great reception, all ranks crowding round his car to hear him speak. Nobody present doubted that the Division was at the top of its form, and that all ranks were fully prepared for the great adventure which lay ahead.

The same day the C.R.A., Brigadier Hill, who was unfortunately sick, left the Division and was replaced by Brigadier C. H. Norton, D.S.O., O.B.E. A final exercise was held on land on the 26th. Though the Division's real destination was still known only to the senior members of Divisional Headquarters, brigadiers and unit commanders of the assaulting brigade, an imaginary coastline and roads had been taped to represent the beaches and high ground which the Division was to assault in Sicily. Assembly and maintenance areas were marked with notice boards, and the exercise took the form of a final walk over the course.

The loading of vehicles at Alexandria and Benghazi had by now been completed, though, as has already been stated, there was still to be some reshuffling of vehicles at Tripoli. The period of training was over, and it was a great relief to everyone when they embarked at Suez. On board ship there was a welcome variety of food, and there was no sand. As someone said at the time, we left the flies and the dirt and the heat for the clean-smelling Anglo-Saxon world represented by life on board ship. The ships in which the bulk of the assaulting personnel sailed were the *Winchester Castle, Orontes,*

Devonshire, Ruys and *Christian Huygens,* whilst the D+3 convoy sailed in the *Kosciesko, Takliwa, Karao, Oronda* and *City of Canterbury.* Embarkation was complete by the 29th of June. On the 30th of June and the 1st of July the personnel ships passed through the Canal. The ships carrying Divisional Headquarters and the 69th and 151st Brigade Groups, together with the XIII Corps Headquarters ship, the *Bulolo,* and the ships carrying the assaulting units of the 5th Division, anchored at Port Said, whilst the D+3 convoy, which included the 168th Brigade Group, went on to wait at Alexandria. There had been a great mass of shipping at Suez, but there is there no lack of sea room, and the ships at anchor were well dispersed. At Port Said it is very different, and for the five days spent there some twenty big ships lay close together in the Canal immediately opposite the town, making a fine target for enemy bombers had they known what was afoot. All communication with the shore was prohibited, but it must have been obvious to anyone on land that no ordinary movement of troops was about to take place. As the great ships passed slowly through the Canal troops in camp in the desert seemed to assume, for the most part, that they carried new arrivals from England. "Get your knees brown!" they shouted to the veterans of the desert campaigns in the ships, who were, of course, speechless with fury.

During the wait at Port Said Major-General Kirkman visited each ship in turn and personally addressed all ranks on the task ahead of them. Everyone knew that they were about to assault the enemy's shores, but the exact destination was still a secret from most, and speculation was more or less equally divided between Rhodes, Crete, Sicily and Sardinia, though there were some who were prepared to put their money on the Balkans.

This secrecy was preserved until the expedition sailed, after which full details were made known to everyone; models of the Division's sector of the coast of Sicily appeared, aeroplane photographs were handed round, and everywhere junior officers and non-commissioned officers were to be seen studying the problems which faced them.

CHAPTER XIV

Target in Sicily and the Plan—Order of Battle of 50th Division—The Assault goes in—Landings in the Wrong Place—Into the Fortress of Europe

JULY, 1943

The sector where the Division was to land in Sicily was not ideal for the purpose. Much of the coastline consisted of cliffs about twenty to twenty-five feet high; they were scaleable in places, but it was difficult to tell from air photographs exactly which places could or could not be climbed. In the sea, particularly opposite the cliffs, there were a good many rocks which were a danger to navigation. In the centre of the sector and about a thousand yards inland lay Avola, a town of nearly twenty-two thousand inhabitants, and about one and a half miles to the north of it was the only beach over which vehicles could for certain be landed.

There the water off shore was deep, the beach consisted of fairly hard sand, and, though no exits for wheels existed, it was known that there would be no difficulty in making them by bulldozing a passage through the low sand-bank bordering the beach, and making gaps in the stone walls with which the whole cultivated area was covered. This beach, marked as No. 47 on the special charts which were prepared for the operation, was given the code name of "Jig Green." Its left-hand limits were clearly marked by two concrete pillars and a circular concrete platform just in the sea, the locality being known as the Lido d'Avola.

Opposite the town was a second landing place, possible for infantry only, which was given the code name of "Jig Amber." Immediately to the south was the Marina d'Avola, which consisted of a very small anchorage and pier used by local fishing boats, but it was well fortified, and considered unsuitable for the discharge of vehicles.

The enemy defences consisted of a succession of pillboxes and entrenched localities along the coast, fifty yards apart on an average. Likely exits from the shore had been wired. There were few mines, though before landing this fact was not known. Once the troops got ashore they would have to operate in a coastal plain intensely cultivated with vineyards, olive groves and citrus orchards. In addition to the stone walls which bordered every field and road, the ground was crossed by many dry water courses and some ditches, many of which were tank obstacles. From the coast the ground rose slowly for about one to two thousand yards and thereafter more sharply. At three thousand yards from the coast, hills rose steeply. The summits, which were about a thousand feet above sea-level, lay some seven thousand yards from the coast. The hills were rocky, or covered with grass or low scrub. One good lateral road ran through Avola roughly parallel to the coast, leading to the north to the village of Cassibile just outside the Divisional sector, and to the south to the town of Noto, on the edge of the area which the Division was initially to occupy. Another good road ran inland from Avola to Palazzolo Acreide, ascending the hills in a succession of hairpin bends, and roads connected the town with the Lido and Marina. In the Divisional sector there were no coast-defence or field guns in action, but just outside field guns manned by Italians were in action in a coast-defence role.

The beaches were to be assaulted by the 151st Brigade in the dark, H hour being laid down by Army as 0245 hrs., two hours before first light. The operation was to take place in three phases. The first task was to secure the two landing places and mop up all the enemy on the coast who could bring small-arms fire to bear on the beaches. This task was to be carried out by the 9th Durham Light Infantry, who would land on "Jig Green," and the 6th Durham Light Infantry, who would land on "Jig Amber." In the second phase the two battalions were to secure a beach-head so that any enemy inland would be prevented from bringing effective small-arms fire to bear on the beaches. The limits of the beach-head were defined by the interdivisional boundary, which ran inland about three thousand yards north of Avola, the railway, which ran parallel to the coast from one to two thousand yards inland, and the River Mammeledi, which flowed into the sea about a mile south of Avola.

To accomplish these two tasks the two leading battalions were to turn south and mop up all beach defences within the beach-head position, later establishing themselves on the main road and seaward exits from the town of Avola; at first light they were to advance to the railway. The third phase was to consist of seizing a covering position on the high ground to deny to the enemy observation on to the beaches or the Divisional maintenance area. The conformation of the ground dictated the depth inland to which the covering position must go. In order to go far enough to secure some depth for battalion and company localities in the hills, it was calculated that it would eventually be necessary to hold a position the perimeter of which would be some nineteen thousand yards in length. This was a somewhat excessive frontage for two brigades, and more so for one brigade, but anything less ambitious would have resulted in leaving in the enemy's hands high ground from which he could get excellent observation on to the beaches. Defence would be facilitated, however, by the fact that the hills themselves were fairly open, and it would be necessary initially to hold only certain key summits, and to dominate the intervening country with machine-gun fire.

The place of landing of the 8th Durham Light Infantry, who were in brigade reserve, was to depend on conditions at the time, but it was hoped to land them at "Jig Green." The intention was that they should be ready to pass through the beach-head just after first light to seize the most important positions in the hills. Later the covering position would, if necessary, be reinforced by the 69th Brigade.

It was not known to what extent the enemy would attempt to hold the town of Avola, but it was appreciated that it might be necessary to secure the beach-head and covering positions before the town had fallen. The 151st Brigade was to have under command the following additional troops:

    98th (Army) Field Regiment (self-propelled).
    107th Anti-Tank Battery (less the 17-pounder troop, but made up to three 6-pounder troops).
    Reconnaissance party of the 3rd Survey Regiment.
    505th Field Company, R.E.
    No. 3 Platoon, 233rd Field Company, R.E.
    "A" and "C" Companies, 2nd Cheshire Regiment.
    Detachment of the 149th Field Ambulance.
    34th Beach Brick.

The role of the follow-up brigade group, the 69th, was not laid down in the operation order. It was to land on orders from Divisional Headquarters, and brigadiers were informed in the operation instruction that it was the Divisional Commander's intention that it should take over the left sector of the covering position.

Any units of the 151st Brigade were, however, to remain in that sector so that the 69th Brigade could, if desirable, be withdrawn to move farther north to relieve units of the 5th Division. The 69th Brigade was also to organize a mobile column to be ready to deal with any enemy batteries in action south of and outside the covering position. Additional troops placed under command of the 69th Brigade were:

    124th Field Regiment.
    99th Anti-Tank Battery (less one 17-pounder troop).
    233rd Field Company (less one platoon).

One troop of 44th Royal Tank Regiment.
"B" and "D" Companies, 2nd Cheshire Regiment.
186th Field Ambulance.

Other units to be landed on the first day were:

Divisional Headquarters.
One squadron of the Royals.
25th Light A.A. Regiment (less one battery).
44th Royal Tank Regiment (less one troop).
235th Field Park Company, R.E.
A proportion of the services and the remainder of any units under command of the two leading brigades.

The 168th Infantry Brigade was to land on D+3 with the following units under command:

74th Field Regiment.
90th Field Regiment.
289th Anti-Tank Battery.
501st Field Company.
140th Field Ambulance.
Proportion of services.

The loading of L.C.Ts. was planned so that essential vehicles and guns would arrive at approximately the same time as the personnel of units. It was hoped that the principal units of the assaulting brigade group with assault scales of transport would be complete on shore by the following times:

H+30: Two assaulting battalions, less transport.
H+50: 505th Field Company complete.
H+60: Carriers and portees of two leading battalions.
H+90: 107th Anti-Tank Battery.
H+100: Reserve battalion; one machine-gun company.
H+2 hours: One light A.A. battery (beach brick).
H+3 hours: 98th Field Regiment.
H+4 hours: 44th Royal Tank Regiment (in divisional reserve).

Elements of the 34th Beach Brick were interspersed with the above units, and it was hoped that about nine hundred personnel and one hundred and ten vehicles of this formation would be ashore by H+5 hours. Stores, including ammunition, were to be landed throughout the day. Instructions were given to infantry brigadiers that guns were to be deployed centrally and revert to the control of the C.R.A. as soon as he had established his headquarters ashore.

Such was the plan which had been worked out in Cairo. It was the plan on which units had trained at Kabrit and at Suez. It was altered only in minor details owing primarily to the fluctuations in the number of landing craft which at various times it was thought would be available. One of the planned places of landing was slightly altered at the last minute when new and better air photographs became available. The necessary written orders had been prepared in great detail, and were made known as soon as the convoy left Port Said to those who had previously been kept in the dark.

The ships started to leave the harbour early on the 5th of July and, escorted by destroyers, sailed in a westerly direction roughly parallel to the North African coast. The slower-moving M.T. convoy had already sailed from Alexandria. The L.C.Ts. loaded with the most important D-Day M.T. and guns were assembling at Tripoli. All ranks expected that sooner or later the convoy would be bombed. On the 6th of July a report was received of an enemy reconnaissance plane flying over the convoy at forty thousand feet, and there were a few air-raid warnings, but throughout the voyage no hostile aircraft were seen and no bombs were dropped. An M.T. ship of the slow M.T. convoy carrying the transport for the 5th Division was torpedoed on the 6th of July, and later sank.

Throughout the voyage training was carried out on assembling and assaulting troops on their correct deck, and embarking them in their L.C.As. This training was started in daylight and continued by darkness, so that when the time came each man could find his way from his troop deck to his landing craft without confusion.

During the 7th and 8th the wind had dropped and conditions were ideal for a landing. On the 9th, however, the last day at sea, when the convoy was sailing north towards Sicily, the wind freshened and by midday a rough sea was running. During the afternoon the personnel convoy caught up with and passed the M.T. convoy and at this time some seventy ships were in sight of each other. A little later some of the L.C.Ts. and L.C.Is. were in sight. The rough sea had little effect on the big ships, though two of them, built as troopers before the war, were unable to keep up, and gradually fell behind. It was also clear that the L.C.Ts. and L.C.Is. were dropping behind and would be late at the "release position." During the afternoon the possibilities of having to postpone the landing were discussed between the Divisional Commander and S.N.O.L. (Senior Naval Officer Landing). It was not known with whom would lie the decision whether to land or not; and there was speculation as to whether, in any event, local sea conditions would be known by that authority. Anxiety was somewhat allayed at sunset, for the wind dropped considerably, although at intervals afterwards it increased temporarily. At 2000 hrs., just before dark, the summit of Mount Etna could clearly be seen, appearing above the clouds with a curious appearance of detachment from the earth.

The ships stopped at their supposed release positions a short time before midnight. A strong off-shore wind was blowing, but though there was some swell the surface of the sea at this time was fairly smooth.

At about midnight the assaulting troops paraded on their mess decks. Then after about a quarter of an hour the calling forward of each L.C.A.'s complement on the ship's loud-speaker began. Silently a regular flow of men in single file came up from below, passed out from the dimly lit lounge to the darkness of the decks, and embarked in their craft. After much practice this had become a drill; there was no shouting and no confusion.

At 0100 hrs. the first wave was lowered, followed a quarter of an hour later by the second wave. Some difficulties were experienced in casting off the craft owing to the swell, and as soon as the L.C.As. left the ship's side there was some confusion and lack of control. Many craft were temporarily lost and circled their parent ship more than once, trying to form up in their correct flotillas. One flotilla failed to form up at all before leaving for the shore.

It was exceedingly dark and the sea was sufficiently choppy for water to be shipped. There was a good deal of sea-sickness. Conditions became better, however, when the L.C.As. eventually moved nearer the shore, and continued to improve as the land was approached. Shortly after 0200 hrs. Brigadier Senior, commanding the assault brigade, and the reserve battalion left their respective ships. It had been decided that the Brigadier's L.C.A. should move with the reserve battalion, as it was hoped that he would then be in the best position to decide where they should land. He had with him wireless sets to provide radio-telephonic communication to all his three battalions and to Main Divisional Headquarters on board the *Winchester Castle*.

To those still on board the ships, the continuous bombing of Syracuse was clearly visible, and anti-aircraft searchlights and much flak were seen. Some flak was also seen much farther south. There were, however, no signs from the shore that the defenders suspected the presence of the large invasion fleet, though once a seaward searchlight to the south exposed for a few moments. Those sitting at the bottom of the L.C.As. saw nothing and heard only the drone of the engines and the noise of the water against the blunt bows of the craft. From time to time there were changes of direction and occasional shouts between the naval officers in charge of check bearings.

At 0245 hrs., when the leading L.C.As. should have reached the shore, they were still at sea, and it became apparent to the assaulting troops that they would be late. As time slipped by it was clear to the naval officers in charge that the craft had become scattered; flotillas were no longer together and some craft were quite out of touch with their neighbours. Most naval officers were uncertain as to their whereabouts.

It will be remembered that the left-hand battalion, the 6th Durham Light Infantry, was to land at "Jig Amber." "B" and "A" Companies were to land at 0245 hrs., "C" Company at 0300 hrs. and "D" Company at 0315 hrs. The task given to the battalion was to clear the coast south of "Jig Amber," to establish themselves on the left of the beach-head position from Avola exclusive along the line of the railway and the River Mammaledi, and finally to clear the coast to the River Noto, which marked the limit of the covering position in their sector. The first company ashore was "B," who landed, less one platoon, one and a half hours late, at about 0415 hrs., just north of Punta Giorgi outside the beach-head position, and some three thousand yards south of "Jig Amber." After mopping up the beach defences they identified their position and proceeded towards their objective, Avola railway station, being joined on the way by a company of the King's Own Yorkshire Light Infantry of the 5th Division, who should have been landed some six miles north of Avola. Later they were joined by some American parachute troops who had been dropped near Avola, many miles from their own area, and who had been fighting there earlier in the morning. In the end, some two hundred Americans were collected and released from operations in the Avola area to join up with their own army.

The remaining companies landed at 0430 hrs. "A" Company, together with the missing platoon from "B" Company, landed some four thousand five hundred yards south of "Jig Amber" just north of the little village of Calabernardo, which was pointed out to them by their naval officers as the Marina d'Avola. As they approached the shore they encountered a considerable amount of enemy shell and mortar fire and machine-gun fire, but it was very inaccurate and no casualties were suffered. A searchlight in the village was successfully extinguished by light machine-gun fire. The Italians were completely surprised, and all opposition was quickly overcome.

The company commander, Major Galloway, still thinking that he was at the Marina d'Avola, turned south to carry out his task of mopping up the defences along the coast, and it was not until he had proceeded for about four miles, accepting the surrender of each Italian post in turn, that he realized that he was many miles south of where he should be. Out of wireless touch with his battalion headquarters, he withdrew a short distance and took up a defensive position, where the company remained until about 1100 hrs., when the battalion intelligence officer found them and brought them back into reserve.

"C" Company landed even farther south, just south of Calabernardo and some five thousand yards from "Jig Amber." They encountered the same heavy but inaccurate fire as "A" Company had experienced, but were less fortunate in that they lost their acting commander, Captain H. E. Walton, who was killed as he stepped ashore. Being a follow-up company, they blew a gap in the barbed wire and proceeded inland, and thus missed "A" Company, who, moving south, must have passed just behind them, except that one "A" Company platoon became detached and joined "C" Company.

On reaching the railway Lieutenant D. A. ffrench-Kihoe, who had assumed command, realized that the company had been landed in the wrong place, and proceeded across country towards Avola, encountering no opposition.

"D" Company was put ashore farther north, in approximately the same place as "B" Company had already landed. In spite of "B" Company's having been there before them, they encountered shell and machine-gun fire, but they found the gap made in the wire and reorganized clear of the beach without casualties.

It was soon light and the distillery chimney which marked their objective was picked up far to the north, and it was realized that they were in the wrong place. This was confirmed by the second-in-command, Major E. W. H. Worrall, D.S.O., M.C., who, landing a little later, had now joined company headquarters. The company moved northwards along the Calabernardo—Avola road until the River Mammeledi was reached, when it turned left up the river bed towards its objective astride the Avola—Noto road.

While in the river bed, the company came under fire, with the result that the situation became somewhat confused. Whilst a platoon was sent to Avola to contact battalion headquarters, the remainder of the company took up a position on the north bank of the river. Here it was later joined by a single 105-mm. self-propelled gun of the 98th Field Regiment. With this reinforcement Major G. L. Wood, M.C., the company commander, decided to attack the enemy position which had by now been located on the Noto road. As the company moved forward to attack it came upon some carriers of the 9th Durham Light Infantry, who, it was found, were also attacking the position, but from the north. The appearance of all this force was too much for the Italians, who surrendered, and it was then found that they had already suffered very heavy casualties from the American parachutists.

Whilst the battalion was thus accomplishing its task from an unexpected direction, the commanding officer, Lieutenant-Colonel W. I. Watson, whose L.C.A. had become detached during the night, attempted with his small party to land at his correct beach, "Jig Amber," but he was met by considerable shell and machine-gun fire, and it was clear that no previous landing had been made there. He therefore landed at "Jig Green," where the 9th Durham Light Infantry were already established, and after the enemy at the Lido had been mopped up he proceeded to Avola, where, at approximately 1000 hrs., he eventually found his battalion headquarters, which had been established by his second-in-command some two hours previously.

The activities of the 6th Durham Light Infantry have been given in some detail, as the battalion was more scattered than the other two. But the experience of the other leading battalion, the 9th Durham Light Infantry, was not very different. They also were about one and a half hours late, but they were luckier in that two companies were landed just south of the Lido only some five hundred yards from "Jig Green," their correct beach. The main beach was therefore cleared of the enemy fairly easily, though hostile shelling prevented its being fully used for some little time. The remainder of the battalion was landed with its platoons much scattered up to three thousand yards south of "Jig Green," except the second-in-command's party, which was put ashore too far to the north. The reserve battalion of the 8th Durham Light Infantry spent some time at sea out of wireless touch with their brigadier, and consequently without orders, but at about dawn they were ordered by Divisional Headquarters, with whom they were still in touch, to land wherever they could, but on "Jig Green" if possible.

The battalion commander, Lieutenant-Colonel R. B. Lidwell, D.S.O., asked the naval officer in charge of the flotilla to land the battalion at "Jig Green." The landing was made in broad daylight, but once ashore the battalion found itself at "How Amber," the left-hand beach of the 5th Division, some three thousand yards north of "Jig Green." The battalion therefore started on its three-mile march to Avola, as a preliminary to proceeding with its task of securing the more important features on the perimeter of the covering position.

At about dawn carriers, tanks, self-propelled guns and some wheeled vehicles began to come ashore in small numbers, and gunners and other personnel not carried in the 151st Brigade's assault craft began to land from L.C.Is. Though these landings were made in daylight, many of the early arrivals were, like the assaulting infantry, landed in the wrong place. Many craft had little idea of their whereabouts. Army officers had to take a hand in navigation, and had they not done so many craft would have beached still farther from their correct places. It was natural, once daylight had come, that experienced Army officers who had studied maps, aeroplane photographs and models should be better able to recognize landmarks on shore than young and often inexperienced naval officers. Once off shore there were delays through the difficulty of controlling landing craft. Signals were not always acknowledged, and many L.C.Ts. failed to obey the orders of the beachmaster. Some, in consequence, beached at unsuitable places. A typical example of what occurred were the voyage and landing of the tactical headquarters of the 102nd (N.H.) Anti-Tank Regiment, R.A. This tactical headquarters came from the *Devonshire* and, with about two hundred personnel from various units, was due to land on "Jig Green" from an L.C.I. at about 0425 hrs. The L.C.I. was late coming alongside, and because of the swell the time allowed for loading was not adequate. The L.C.I. finally left the ship at 0435 hrs., making for "Jig Green." There was considerable doubt about the direction and the craft circled many times. Eventually it arrived at what was hoped was the flotilla rendezvous, but no other craft were met there. After waiting, the craft proceeded on its course, but as it became light and the pillars of the Lido d'Avola became visible, it was clear to the senior Army officer that the craft was going too far to the north. There was then some discussion between the senior Army officer and the naval officer in charge, but the former was reluctant to be too dogmatic about the correct landing place while the craft was still some distance out to sea. Course was, however, altered to the direction of "Jig Green," but shells were later seen falling on that beach and craft were seen leaving under cover of smoke floats, so the L.C.I. again altered course to well north of any signs of shell or smoke.

At 0655 hrs., two and a half hours late, the L.C.I. beached in a well-sheltered cove some five thousand yards north of "Jig Green." The beach was then found to be very small; it was wired and mined, and came under shell fire before a gap could be cleared. There were some casualties and the craft was hit. The troops then had to start their three-mile march to their correct place.

In the meantime, while so much was happening on shore, Divisional Headquarters was very much out of touch with the situation. It was seen that all was quiet at H hour. The first eagerly awaited signal message came at 0325 hrs. and read: "Owing to heavy weather only half the leading L.C.As. arrived. D./S.N.O.L. looking for remainder. Will be directed to beaches when found."

Shortly after 0400 hrs. the first signs of life from the shore could be seen—a string of tracer ammunition from a heavy machine gun from what was thought to be the direction of Avola. Thereafter, gun flashes and a few Very lights were observed. By dawn, knowledge of events ashore was still strictly limited, and what was known was not reassuring. The 6th Durham Light Infantry on the left were reported to be ashore, there was no news of the 9th Durham Light Infantry, and the 8th Durham Light Infantry, who were still at sea and out of touch with their brigadier, had, as has already been described, been ordered to land on "Jig Green" if possible. At 0500 hrs. the main beach signal station, which had been established on the right-hand edge of "Jig Green," began to function, and the first message from it reported that its personnel had got ashore without casualties. At about the same time, the D./S.N.O.L. reported that enemy batteries were shelling both beaches. He reported that the northern beach was under heavy fire, that one L.C.I. had been hit and sunk, and that the beach could not be used as long as this fire continued. As it became light, this shelling could be seen from the *Winchester Castle*, and it appeared not to be heavy, and to come from a single battery in the 5th Division area. A message was sent to that formation asking for naval support. This was forthcoming, and by about 0700 hrs. had been entirely effective. In view of the uncertainty of the situation Major-General Kirkman decided shortly after dawn to go ashore and find out for himself what was happening, and his L.C.A. was ordered to be made ready.

As it became light, however, two things became apparent: first, it was obvious that the transports were very much farther off shore than they should have been. One estimate was that they were twelve miles off shore instead of seven. This to some extent accounted for the lack of news, as many wireless sets would be at the extreme limit of their range. Secondly, there was no enemy coast-defence artillery fire. It was therefore agreed that the flotilla should steam in towards the shore, and this was done at half-speed. The Divisional Commander therefore deferred his departure until the ships should reach a suitable position nearer the shore.

To any of the enemy who were on the hills overlooking Avola the sight must have been alarming. Ships of all sizes and types, from a monitor to an L.C.A., were slowly steaming towards the coast without interference. At 0700 hrs., whilst the ships were approaching the shore, the 6th Durham Light Infantry reported the capture of "Jig Green," and at 0752 hrs. the A.M.L.O. asked for bulldozers to be sent in urgently to make tracks from the exits of the beaches to the main road. Shortly afterwards, the *Winchester Castle* stopped, and

British Official Photograph [*Crown Copyright Reserved*]

"The coast looked most attractive in the sunlight, and all shelling of the beaches had ceased."
Landing craft off shore near Avola.

the Divisional Commander, having ordered the 69th Brigade to land at once on "Jig Green," left the ship to take over control of events on shore. It was now quite light, the water was calmer and there was no question of sea-sickness. The coast looked most attractive in the sunlight and all shelling of the beaches had ceased. On his way to the shore the Divisional Commander met Brigadier Cooke-Collis, commanding the 69th Brigade. They both landed at 0820 hrs. on "Jig Green," where they found that some vehicles were already ashore, that an exit from the beach had been made, and that the work of making gaps in the many stone walls was in hand. They proceeded on foot to the headquarters of the 151st Brigade, which was on the side of the main Cassibile—Avola road about one thousand yards inland from the beach.

The situation as known to Brigadier Senior, commanding the 151st Brigade, was that the 9th Durham Light Infantry had been landed somewhere near the right place, with the 6th Durham Light Infantry much too far to the south. The 8th Durham Light Infantry, who, it will be remembered, had landed on the 5th Division beaches, had already arrived and was starting to move to the high ground overlooking the coastal plain. The inhabitants were reported to be friendly as soon as they realized that our troops were not Germans—the first direct evidence we had of the hatred felt by the Sicilians for their Axis partners.

A little later, Avola was reported to be in our hands, and the situation seemed so favourable to Major-General Kirkman that shortly after 0900 hrs. he spoke to the Corps Commander on the wireless and said that he proposed to keep the 69th Brigade Group concentrated instead of sending it to take over the left sector of the covering position; also that he was prepared if necessary to send the brigade to take over from the 5th Division north of the Cassibile River so as to release the latter to advance towards Syracuse. The Corps Commander agreed to the 69th Brigade's being kept concentrated, and said that he would give orders as to its further actions when he visited the headquarters during the morning. As soon as this decision was made the Divisional Commander agreed with Brigadier Senior's plan to locate one battalion in the foothills north of Noto, one battalion on the high ground overlooking Avola, and one battalion holding the town itself and the line of the River Mammaledi. The defence company of No. 34 Beach Brick was at this time taking over the close defence of the Divisional maintenance area. Shortly after 0900 hrs. the advance party from Divisional Headquarters landed and started to function from a position on the main road near to Headquarters, 151st Brigade.

The landing of the 69th Brigade took some time. The ferry service did not run efficiently, and L.C.As. frequently returned singly instead of in flotillas, so that there were often no officers landed with parties of men. Many coxswains had to be firmly dissuaded from returning to the beaches from which they had come, far away from the proper place; even so, "B" Company and battalion headquarters of the 5th East Yorkshire Regiment were landed a mile to the north of "Jig Green." In order to collect battalions some companies were held in the assembly area, and men had the unexpected experience of spending the first hours inside the European Fortress lying under almond trees cracking almonds.

At 1330 hrs. General Dempsey arrived at Divisional Headquarters and the Divisional Commander was able to tell him that the Division's first task was practically complete, and that everywhere forward troops were out of touch with the enemy except in the vicinity of Noto. The Corps Commander gave orders that the 69th Brigade should take over a defensive position from the 17th Brigade (5th Division) south of Floridia, and that the 15th Brigade (5th Division), which was holding a defensive position north-west of Cassibile, should come under the command of the 50th (Northumbrian) Division. The 69th Brigade then began the first of a series of long marches which characterized the work of both brigades during the ensuing week. Transport was lacking and units moved with the aid of donkeys and mules; the brigade headquarters wireless sets were carried in a donkey cart requisitioned at Avola. It was very hot, the roads were dusty, and the only water available was that brought in water-bottles from the ships. Orders had been issued that water from local wells was not to be drunk until tested by the medical authorities, but junior commanders found it quite impracticable to enforce the order, as water carts were not available. For the next few days men had to march long distances, and the lack of water, the prevention of sore feet, and the heat were for a time the main problems to be dealt with.

Throughout the day the work of disembarking such vehicles and weapons as arrived at "Jig Green" went on smoothly and quickly, and during peak periods the rate of discharge was quicker than was expected. Exits from the beach had been quickly made and there was no confusion in assembly areas. Elsewhere, unloading did not go so smoothly, and there were some delays before any responsible person took charge. The unloading of vehicles took place at a beach discovered south of the Marina d'Avola and at the Marina itself, where a floating pier was used. It was at one time broken owing to an attempt to pull the landing end in to the shore at a time when the far end was still attached to an L.C.T. at anchor; it was only then that "Dukws" (amphibious lorries) were successfully driven from the L.C.Ts. straight into the sea and swam ashore. These vehicles would have been invaluable earlier, and should have been put straight into the sea on arrival. When available they carried out a ferry service from ship to shore.

The general scene was well described by Lieutenant R. J. Gilmour, a New Zealand reporter who was present. He wrote, in the Middle East weekly, *Parade,* as follows:

"0900 hours. Ashore in an L.C.A., passing three different types of amphibious vehicles 'driving' ashore under own steam. Beach as busy as a country fair. From dozens of landing craft with their fronts let down trucks, carriers, quads and jeeps, previously waterproofed, bounce into four and five feet of water. With sea water gushing from driving cabs and tool-boxes they roar up on to the beach in first gear. Wiremesh track leads across the soft sand and up a wadi to the 'de-waterproofing park,' where R.E.M.E. specialists strip adhesive tape and grease and waterproof cloth from ignition and induction systems.

"Down on the beach clanking bulldozers splash into the sea to extract the one vehicle in twenty that stalls in the big splash. Without the bulldozers and their drivers—and R.E.M.E.—there would be chaos.

"Through a loud-speaker the Navy's beachmaster harangues the tardy, abuses the odd fool and stage manages the whole incredibly efficient show. 'L.C.T. 313, come in now. Come on! Hurry! There's ample depth. What are you waiting for? Come on, that Dodge truck in L.C.T. 198. Give her everything you've got. L.C.A. 190, get the hell out of here. Get to your proper place along the beach. Party loafing near the wire track, get in the water and push that jeep. Party landing from L.C.I. 786, double off the beach and get inland. Enemy aircraft approaching from the west. Come on, double! At any moment you are likely to be dive-bombed and machine-gunned.'"

By last light the 69th Brigade was in position and the two brigades of the Division with a third from the 5th Division under command held a defensive position from Floridia exclusive to Noto exclusive, still in enemy hands, a frontage of about twelve miles. Casualties during the day had, on the whole, been light. Except at Noto, there was no contact with formed bodies of the enemy. Divisional Headquarters had been established near Cassibile. Farther north the 5th Division had occupied Syracuse. To the south the XXX Corps had landed successfully and captured their objectives. Prisoners captured by the Division during the day numbered three hundred, all Italians with the exception of three Germans. The remainder of the defenders, after but a slight resistance, simply walked out of their positions and made for their homes. Prisoners confirmed the conclusion reached during the planning days in Egypt, that the coastal defences on the Divisional front were manned by the 374th and 437th Battalions, both of the 146th Infantry Regiment of the 206th Coastal Division, with the 102nd and 84th Batteries in support.

Hostile air attacks started in the middle of the afternoon just as the 69th Brigade moved off. The first machines to appear were mainly fighters (Me.109's): they left the brigade alone as they moved close to the stone walls lining the roads, and in the shadow of olive trees, and instead indiscriminately machine-gunned the beaches and ships. These attacks increased in intensity during the evening and continued during the early part of the night. The enemy aircraft were engaged by the guns of the 25th Light A.A. Regiment and the A.A. Regiment under the command of No. 34 Beach Brick. No ships allotted to the Division were lost from bombing on the first day, but the luck was not to hold, and three of the Division's M.T. ships were lost on subsequent days. Largely during these attacks some one hundred and twenty-five men of the Division lost their lives at sea.

The first day had therefore been singularly successful. In spite of the storm which delayed the arrival of many craft, in spite of the ships halting too far out to sea, thus causing the L.C.As. to approach the shore late and in the wrong place, and in spite of the wireless failures due to the same cause, the Navy put the Army ashore, whilst the assaulting troops had seized the beaches on which they found themselves, overcome the enemy, and secured their objectives with the minimum of confusion and delays. The Divisional Commander had throughout the training period stressed the need for speed, and his instructions were everywhere followed. Junior commanders who landed with the intention of carrying out a detailed plan evolved from a careful study of models and air photographs, had, when they found themselves in unexpected surroundings, acted with initiative, speed and determination. The enemy's resistance had admittedly been slight, but the whole landing operation showed what determined, well-trained and properly briefed troops could achieve against an enemy who had been surprised, even when the troops had not been launched into battle precisely according to plan.

This, then, was the manner in which the 50th Division returned to Europe after its long sojourn in the barren and semi-barren lands of the Middle East. The desert predominated in the memory of most

"These things delighted the eye and refreshed the mind."
Troops with a suspect civilian in a beautiful Sicilian grove.

members of the Division. The majority had lived in it for at least a year, and some even longer, up to the time they returned to Egypt to prepare for the invasion.

The burning wilderness, almost devoid of life save for that of the contending armies, had been the unvarying background to existence, save for a brief glimpse of Tunisia.

On this memorable day in July, however, they entered an island which was of the same parent continent as their own. And they were quick to note the change: green fields where formerly there was sand, fruit and vegetables where there had been an arid waste, towns instead of camel-skin tents and tumbledown villages, women and children, and homes that bore at least some resemblance to their own.

These things delighted the eye and refreshed the mind. It was as though another step had been taken on the road that led to home.

In the intervals and periods of rest in the relatively short campaign that lay ahead the troops swam gratefully in the mild blue waters of the Ionian Sea, and ate the grapes that often grew alongside their battle stations, with the feeling that this campaign was not so completely divorced from the amenities of life as had been its predecessors.

CHAPTER XV

The Thrust North—69th Brigade's Struggle to reach Lentini—
First Stage of the Battle of Primosole Bridge—Over the River
Simeto, and 168th Brigade's first Battle

JULY, 1943

DURING the first night ashore all was quiet on the Divisional front and patrols advanced some four thousand yards without making contact. At dawn carrier patrols were sent out to seek the enemy, and Canicattini Bagni, twelve miles west of Syracuse, was found to be clear of the enemy. In the south Noto was occupied, and shortly afterwards contact was made with the XXX Corps. Later in the day a patrol from the 8th Durham Light Infantry was ambushed five miles east of Palazzolo and two carriers were destroyed.

At 0700 hrs. General Dempsey arrived at Divisional Headquarters and gave the Divisional Commander the plan for the day. The 51st Division, part of the XXX Corps, who were advancing from the south, were to take over the area held by the 151st Brigade round Avola. The 151st Brigade was then to take over from the 15th Brigade in the central sector, thus relieving that brigade to revert to the 5th Division. At the suggestion of the Divisional Commander, it was agreed that the 69th Brigade should extend their right to the River Ierna. Additional orders were received from Corps at 1100 hrs. which placed No. 3 Commando, then concentrated in the Divisional area, under command for the purpose of immediately relieving two battalions of the 15th Brigade. During the afternoon, therefore, these moves began, and everywhere parties of infantry were to be seen moving northwards. At the same time, the 69th Brigade, south of Floridia, advanced some three miles westward into more open country in the foothills. The only further information arriving during the day was of enemy movement on the road running south from Canicattini. This was part of the Napoli Division, which had a counter-attack role. They were later to be destroyed or captured before they could achieve anything.

At 1930 hrs. the Corps Commander again visited Divisional Headquarters and gave orders for the following day. The 51st Division was again to relieve our Division; the first brigade group was to relieve the 69th Brigade, and the second the 151st Brigade. On relief the Division was to relieve the 13th Brigade of the 5th Division in the Floridia—Solarino area and the Division was to be prepared to push north through the foothills to Lentini, at the southern edge of the Plain of Catania.

To fix up the details of the relief of the 13th Brigade, Major-General Kirkman visited the headquarters of the 5th Division at 0830 hrs. the next morning. He found the division in touch with the enemy in the area of Priolo. On return at 0945 hrs. he gave the brigadiers verbal orders for the forthcoming moves. The 151st Brigade, as soon as it was relieved, was to take over the existing positions of the 13th Brigade in the Floridia—Solarino area (Solarino is between Floridia and Palazzolo). This brigade was in touch with an enemy force of unknown strength who were active with guns, mortars and machine guns. The 69th Brigade on relief was to concentrate southeast of Floridia ready for the advance on Lentini. In the meantime, the Brigadier was ordered to send out a mobile column of one squadron of tanks, carriers and self-propelled guns to advance through Canicattini Bagni, first to cut and block the Solarino—Palazzolo road, then to attack the enemy facing our troops at Solarino in rear, and finally to join up with the 13th Brigade, or the 151st Brigade if the relief was completed.

At 1145 hrs., after the Divisional Commander's conference was over, the Corps Commander spoke to him on the wireless and told him to start the proposed moves without waiting for relief. Orders were therefore issued for all moves to proceed, and the 69th Brigade was ordered to send one battalion with one battery to capture Sortino during the night.

A problem which was causing anxiety and which was dealt with by the Divisional Commander at his conference with the brigadiers was the general administrative situation and in particular the acute shortage of R.A.S.C. vehicles. In the original plan sufficient R.A.S.C. load-carrying vehicles to maintain that part of the Division landed were to be ashore by, at the latest, the evening of $D+1$. In fact, at this time there were only six lorries ashore. This was largely due to the fact that on this day an M.T. ship was lost by bomb splinters puncturing the hull and igniting the petrol. A similar loss occurred on the third day, and a third M.T. ship was sunk on the fourth day by a direct hit. The total losses included two hundred and thirty-four M.T., eight 25-pounder guns and tractors, and nine tanks. By the end of the third day there were only fifteen R.A.S.C. load-carrying vehicles ashore, and it was not until $D+3$—by which time the Division had assumed a mobile role—that any number of vehicles were available. Amongst other troubles these losses caused a shortage of much-needed Bofors ammunition, and the priority of unloading had at one time to be changed from food to ammunition.

Many other administrative troubles occurred. R.E.M.E. tractors, essential for beach recovery, timed ashore at H+4 hours on the first day, finally arrived on D+2. Fortunately the beach was satisfactory, bulldozers and other tractors were available, all vehicles had been waterproofed, and only two in the Division were "drowned" on landing; but several had to be towed out of the water. The vehicles of the second field ambulance, which it was not planned to open initially, arrived before those of the first. The first field ambulance had opened on land, but could not function to the best advantage owing to the fact that the equipment carried in their own vehicles had not arrived.

Reverting to the situation as it existed on the morning of the 12th of July, when only six R.A.S.C. load-carrying vehicles were ashore, it was pointed out by the "Q" staff that the Division could be maintained with advanced elements only as far north as Solarino. In order to overcome this unsatisfactory situation, the Divisional Commander ordered brigadiers to arrange for the dumping of all possible ammunition and stores from unit lorries. These lorries were then to go back to Avola to bring forward food and ammunition and dump them near Floridia, after which they were to return to lift the stores which had been off-loaded. Had these steps not been taken there would undoubtedly have been an administrative breakdown during the succeeding days.

The mobile column found by the 69th Brigade was late in assembling and was hindered in its operations by difficult country. After some fighting and after taking some prisoners, it established contact with the enemy west of Solarino; but it never seriously engaged them, and instead of breaking through it returned by the way it had come. Possibly owing to the action of this column and in an endeavour to escape, the Italian troops west of Solarino attacked twice unsuccessfully, once with infantry and tanks and once with infantry alone. The tanks consisted of five light French tanks, R35's, manned by Italians. They came down the road from Palazzolo towards Solarino in line ahead at full speed. Four were quickly disposed of, but the leading tank got through the forward defences, passed through Solarino and down the long, straight road to Floridia, firing its machine gun at everything it could see. The 6th Durham Light Infantry and the 5th East Yorkshire Regiment were moving up, the former to take over from the 2nd Wiltshire Regiment (5th Division) in front of Solarino, and the latter to pass through Solarino on their way to Sortino. A

15-cwt. ammunition truck was hit and set on fire and everyone scattered off the road extremely hastily.

Lieutenant-Colonel James, commanding the 5th East Yorkshire Regiment, was on his way forward, riding a motor-cycle, half-way between Floridia and Solarino, accompanied by his intelligence officer in a carrier. Both turned round with expedition and went back the way they had come. A light shell knocked a track off the carrier and it swung on to the verge, and for half a mile the tank chased the commanding officer down the road, firing machine-gun bursts at him. He reached sanctuary in Floridia, where a 105-mm. self-propelled gun swung broadside across the road between the houses, and the enemy tank ended its career by running into a lamp-post.

The purely infantry attack which was launched after the 6th Durham Light Infantry had relieved the 2nd Wiltshire Regiment was stopped by artillery fire. Though held by the 151st Brigade, this force, if not eliminated, would become a potential threat to the Division's communications, and arrangements had to be made to deal with it on the next day. The Divisional orders issued late in the evening, which directed the 69th Brigade to continue the advance through Sortino to Lentini, also therefore instructed the 151st Brigade to overcome the enemy facing the 6th Durham Light Infantry and to make contact with the XXX Corps in the direction of Palazzolo. The brigade was also warned to be ready to take over Sortino after it had been captured by the 69th Brigade, and the whole brigade was eventually to be concentrated there when the task of establishing touch with the XXX Corps had been completed. The 151st Brigade was also to patrol the plateau which overlooks the Sortino road from the east, as there were indications of scattered parties of Italians occupying the area.

To follow the operations which started with the advance of the 69th Brigade and continued for the next two days, it is necessary to appreciate the nature of the country. A coastal plain some seven miles in width runs between Cassibile and Syracuse. To the north of the road Syracuse—Floridia—Solarino lies a mass of broken, hilly country which extends to the Plain of Catania. There were two roads running northwards, the good coastal road along which the 5th Division was already advancing, and the inland road which runs through the hills from Floridia through Sortino. These two roads meet at Lentini on the edge of the Plain of Catania, and from there one main road crosses the Leonardo River and then runs along the top of a low but commanding ridge until it drops again to the Primosole bridge over the Simeto River. Beyond this the road runs over quite flat country, overlooked by Mount Etna, to Catania.

The inland road along which the Division was about to advance runs for much of the way along valleys dominated on both sides by precipitous hills rising some two to three hundred feet above it. As it nears Sortino the hills are nearer the road and become steeper, until they form a gorge whose sides are covered with trees and shrubs. Only about a mile and a half from Sortino does the road begin to climb in a series of sharp bends to the town on the top of a ridge which forms a watershed.

Beyond Sortino the country is more open, and the road passes over a second watershed before dropping to Carlentini and Lentini. Throughout its length it is narrow, dusty and winding, and really fit only for one-way traffic. It is bordered by stone walls and, in the valleys, by olive groves, and over the two passes the road ascends in a succession of turns, often with hairpin bends. Sortino lies about half-way between Floridia and Lentini.

The 5th East Yorkshire Regiment had been ordered by the 69th Brigade to capture Sortino, and by about 1700 hrs. they had passed through the forward troops of the 8th Durham Light Infantry holding the ground north of Solarino. The 8th Durham Light Infantry were not in touch with the enemy.

The operations in which the 5th East Yorkshire Regiment were about to engage are of interest, as they illustrate the risks which were taken at this stage of the Sicilian campaign. As already recounted, the Division on landing had encountered not very determined Italian opposition, which had been quickly brushed aside. Further fighting of a more determined nature had actually taken place during the afternoon and evening with the enemy west of Solarino, but except for the mobile column which had not yet returned from engaging the rear of the enemy formation, and the incident of the tank which broke through to Floridia, the 69th Brigade had so far not encountered any enemy. The brigade did not therefore expect much serious opposition; it was clearly desirable to get through the difficult country ahead before the enemy's resistance stiffened, and any methodical combing of the olive groves, vineyards and scrub-covered ground which bordered the road would have been a very slow and laborious process. The leading troops therefore pushed on with speed, more or less confining themselves to the road, and taking what seemed reasonable risks.

"C" Company of the 5th East Yorkshire Regiment, commanded by Captain Owen, who was killed two nights later near Lentini, formed the advance guard, "D" Company, under Captain Penwell, followed, and the remainder of the Battalion came on behind.

Unknown to the Battalion, an enemy force of Germans and Italians had taken up well-concealed positions on both sides of the gorge just south-east of Sortino. The Germans were all to the north of the road, where their line of retreat was secure. The Italians had been given the position to the south of the road, whence there was no easy retreat. Both the commanding officer and the brigadier were with the leading company, Brigadier Cooke-Collis urging them on with his fly-whisk.

By about 1820 hrs. they were in sight of Sortino. Some apprehension was felt, as there had been a rifle shot fired as the company approached the gorge, but it was apparently assumed that it was a stray sniper rather than any form of signal.

The enemy opened fire with only "C" Company within effective range. An anti-tank portee had come too far up the column and reached the head of "D" Company just as it was turning a slight bend in the road. The sight of this large vehicle with its crew was apparently too much for the No. 1 of a Spandau, and he let go a long burst. The burst was not repeated, but the Italians on the left of the road had now opened fire on the head of "C" Company. It was a half-hearted effort, and they were quickly routed out of some stone houses and taken prisoner. "D" Company had halted on being fired on, but almost at once the intelligence officer brought orders from Lieutenant-Colonel James that the company was to come forward at once. Thus "D" Company also entered the stretch of road dominated by the enemy, and for that reason probably the Germans allowed it to move forward unmolested.

In the meantime "C" Company deployed on the right of the road and started to move up the steep slopes. On arrival "D" Company was ordered to follow "C" Company. At this stage heavy firing broke out on both sides of the gorge and a platoon of "D" Company gave covering fire whilst the remainder of the two forward companies continued to work forward; casualties were fairly heavy, but the immediate high ground was eventually cleared, and some German prisoners were taken. The heavy firing prevented the remainder of the Battalion from closing up, and they also left the road for the high ground on their right; thus the battalion was split into two parts and remained divided until 0200 hrs. the next morning, when the enemy withdrew and the battalion was reunited.

The Italians on the left of the road had for the most part surrendered. Some were found trying to change into civilian clothes—possibly an excellent thing from the point of view of the invasion as a whole, but very reprehensible from the point of view of our troops who had recently been fired on.

The reader will have noticed that the companies principally engaged were "C" and "D." Yet the others were not inactive, and the following account from the pen of Major K. C. Harrison, who was at that time a platoon commander in the 5th East Yorkshire Regiment, gives an impression of the ambush as experienced from the rear of the column:

"Sudden and exciting, I heard from my position in 'B' Company the unmistakable burr of Spandaus. Bren guns replied from our leading companies, then the heavy thump of German mortar bombs echoed down the valley. We halted for a while, hoping that 'D' and 'C' Companies might soon overrun the enemy. But the noises of battle continued spasmodically, and without being told much about the situation 'B' Company was ordered to advance farther down the narrowing valley. Farther ahead, at a road junction, we were ordered to establish ourselves on a hill to our right.

"The enemy could not see to fire his Spandaus at us, but a regular procession of mortar bombs hit the valley below, near the road junction we had just left.

"Dusk was rapidly approaching, and in my platoon area I found the C.O. with my company commander. The C.O.'s plan was that 'B' Company should occupy one of the enemy hills during the darkness, while 'D' and 'C' Companies were given similar assignments.

"Although the men were tired, hungry and thirsty after the long march in the almost tropical sun, they welcomed the move and set off with a good heart. The C.O. led us in the darkness, the company commander with him. I was immediately behind with my platoon, but the exceedingly rough ground and the many stone walls made it hard going for my men with their rifles, Brens and other platoon weapons.

"After a long and tortuous march we finally arrived at the foot of a hill terraced with many stone walls. It was about 0230 hrs. and the moon had put in a welcome appearance. I was told to occupy this hill with my platoon. It was one of the hills that the enemy had been firing from in the afternoon. Everything was quiet now; the Spandaus had not been heard for a long time, and although the mortar bombs had still been dropping in the valley at irregular intervals, even they had ceased at about 0100 hrs. So we thought there was a fair chance that the enemy had gone.

"It was a terrific toil climbing the many walls of the terraced hill. To be silent was impossible, and if the enemy was still on top as we clambered up he must have thought a division rather than a platoon was approaching. We eventually reached the summit and after a detailed search aided by the moonlight and the approaching dawn we found several abandoned German positions. When it was quite evident that the entire area had been completely abandoned by the enemy, I arranged for sentries and most of us got a couple of hours' sleep before the hot morning sun woke us at about 0700 hrs.

"On our way to rejoin the battalion in the valley we heard bursts of Bren-gun fire in front. An Italian had been seen on the hillside, but he now had his hands up and was coming to surrender.

"Lieut. Lowe and myself hastened to him: he was an Italian officer and was shaking with nerves, understandable in view of the many near misses he must have had from the Bren bullets. I questioned him in Italian, but as his English was rather better than my Italian we carried on the conversation in English. He was quite ready to talk, and said that he was an artillery officer of the Napoli Division. He said that his division was smashed and that all was lost. He then said, 'I suppose you are going to shoot me?' I replied that the English didn't shoot prisoners and added, as an afterthought, "unless you try to escape." It was strange that I should have said this, for afterwards he did try to escape and was promptly shot in the leg by the C.O.'s batman."

At 0600 hrs. the next morning the 6th Green Howards were able to pass through and occupy Sortino itself. Some more prisoners were taken, from whom it was known that the enemy's main body had withdrawn at 0200 hrs. They were part of a German battle group which had been in the area of Catania and had been rushed forward to assist a battalion of the Napoli Division, supported by some R35 French tanks, to delay our advance.

By shortly after dawn on the 13th of July the 69th Brigade was firmly established on the high ground beyond Sortino and not in contact with the enemy. Troops who had marched during the previous day and during much of the night were being fed, but were naturally tired. It was, however, most important to attempt to seize the high ground overlooking the Plain of Catania before the enemy could co-ordinate any serious opposition in this difficult country. The 151st Brigade had had a night's rest, but though one battalion was now moving forward from the Floridia—Solarino area the remainder were still engaged in dealing with the enemy west of Solarino, who were some eight miles in rear of the 69th Brigade, and a direct threat to their communications. The Divisional Commander, who was present with Brigadier Cooke-Collis north of Sortino, therefore ordered him to resume the advance northwards on Lentini, leaving one battalion at Sortino until relieved by the 151st Brigade, as it was still essential that this place, with roads coming into it from both flanks, and with the country all round not cleared of the enemy, should be firmly held. The 124th Field Regiment was already supporting the 69th Brigade, and the 151st Brigade was ordered to send forward the 98th Army Field Regiment (self-propelled guns as soon as they had finished with it in the Solarino area.

Major-General Kirkman was still forward in the Sortino area when at about midday he received a message by wireless to return to his headquarters near Floridia to see the Army Commander. He was back by 1415 hrs. General Montgomery and General Dempsey, who was also present, said that the 5th Division had been ordered to advance on Augusta, and after capturing the place were to concentrate in the open country north-west of the town. The 50th Division was to capture Carlentini and Lentini during the night. At the time this seemed quite possible, since as far as was known the 69th Brigade were already advancing on these places out of contact with the enemy. During the night one airborne brigade was to be dropped to capture the Primosole bridge over the Simeto River. No. 3 Commando was to land from the sea during the night with the object of capturing intact the bridge over the Leonardo River some three thousand yards north of Lentini. The final task for the Division on the next day was to take over the Primosole bridge from the airborne brigade. The approximate distances involved in these operations were Solarino to Sortino, ten miles; Sortino to Lentini, ten miles; Lentini to the Primosole bridge, ten miles.

The Divisional Commander found other visitors at his headquarters. General Porgini, commander of the Napoli Division, and his Chief of Staff, who as will be related below were captured during the morning, were standing disconsolately by the entrance, waiting to be taken away.

Brigadier Davidson, commanding the 168th Brigade, had come to report that the personnel of his brigade group had that morning landed at Syracuse with little transport, and had moved to a concentration area east of Floridia. He was ordered to march his brigade the next day to an area north of Melilli, permission to use the 5th Division's good tarmac road instead of the Division's dusty and congested road having been obtained from the XIII Corps.

While the 69th Brigade had been occupying Sortino and preparing to continue the advance, the 6th Durham Light Infantry, supported by the 98th Field Regiment and tanks of the 44th Royal Tank Regiment, were dealing with the enemy west of Solarino. It had been decided that the 6th Durham Light Infantry should attack the enemy opposing them at dawn. The enemy was known to consist of a force of all arms, including tanks, for, as already related, the enemy had attacked with infantry and tanks on the previous afternoon, and later with infantry alone, supported by mortar and artillery fire. The enemy's position was well concealed amongst boulders and olive trees, but his three main localities had been identified, and were subjected to heavy artillery concentrations, when the attack was launched at 0445 hrs. By 0500 hrs. the leading companies met heavy but inaccurate machine-gun fire, but the enemy had suffered heavy casualties from our artillery fire, he was completely demoralized, and by 0530 hrs. the position had been overrun and many prisoners, including the commanding officer of the unit, had been taken.

At 0800 hrs. a mobile force consisting of two sections of carriers and a troop of tanks was sent forward through the now completely disorganized resistance along the road to Palazzolo, whilst the reserve company started a sweep to round up snipers and any enemy who attempted to get away to the hills. The mobile force was more or less confined to the road, but was in every way successful. Two enemy tanks and an ammunition lorry were quickly disposed of with a shell apiece.

Two miles farther on a staff car containing General Porgini and his Chief of Staff was taken. Then a battery of field guns were engaged and after a sharp exchange of fire were all knocked out or captured. Next a group of sixteen R35 tanks were found in a field and engaged. The crews quickly surrendered, but not before the leading Sherman tank had received a direct hit on its gun which put it out of action. At 1130 hrs. an ammunition dump was set alight and one 75-mm. gun with five more trucks destroyed. During the afternoon Palazzolo was reached and contact made with the 51st Division, and by 1700 hrs. the column, weary but happy, had returned safely and rejoined its battalion.

That was the end of the ill-fated Napoli Division.

Casualties to the 6th Durham Light Infantry had been light, but they included two company commanders. Three hundred and twenty prisoners had been captured, and equipment taken included sixteen R35 tanks, thirteen field and anti-tank guns of various calibres, six mortars, thirteen Bredas, twelve Lancia ten-tonners, three Fiat 15-cwts. and thirteen motor-cycles. The fifteen lorries were a valuable addition to the Division's limited resources of mechanical transport. Another fifteen lorries had unfortunately been burnt out.

In the meantime the 6th Green Howards, the leading battalion of the 69th Brigade, were meeting gradually increasing opposition. Just before dark they were some three miles south of Carlentini and in contact with enemy rearguards; any further advance was temporarily held up by fairly heavy machine-gun fire from two features, the first a low hill astride the main road and the second Mount Pancali, a high, stony and somewhat precipitous hill slightly farther on and to the left of the road. Both features overlooked the road for some distance. The 6th Green Howards were very tired and artillery support would not be very effective, as batteries were only just coming into action in forward positions, and exact details of the enemy dispositions were unknown, but it was felt that if the enemy were Italians—and there was some evidence to suggest that the rearguard was partly composed of them—artillery fire, even if not very accurate, might frighten them away.

The 7th Green Howards were still moving forward some three to four miles farther back, and the 5th East Yorkshire Regiment were resting just north of Sortino, having been relieved at that place by the 8th Durham Light Infantry.

It was clear to the Divisional Commander and Brigadier Cooke-Collis, who at last light were together just in rear of the 6th Green Howards, that the first of the Army Commander's requirements, the capture of Lentini during the night, was unlikely to be achieved. Though wireless communication existed from the Divisional Commander's jeep to Divisional Headquarters and thence to Main Corps Headquarters still at sea on the headquarters ship, it was clearly too late to suggest a postponement of the projected operations, nor indeed was this desirable, as there was every reason to suppose that the Division would capture Lentini early the next day, and a twenty-four-hour postponement might well end in the two bridges being destroyed by the enemy—and no Bailey bridging was yet available. General Kirkman therefore ordered the 69th Brigade to work forward during the night and at any rate eject the enemy from his first position.

It will be remembered that the coastal road along which the 5th Division had been advancing and our Division's road through Sortino meet just south of Carlentini. Though unknown at the time, the enemy situation was that they had two German battalions of the 115th Panzer Grenadier Regiment on the main road south-east of Carlentini, one battalion from the same regiment in Carlentini and Lentini, and one company of Germans supported by one troop of self-propelled guns and some tanks on and near Mount Pancali. In addition, an Italian battalion, the 904th Fortress Battalion, was just north-west of Lentini, and an Italian force, Mobile Column "D," consisting of five hundred men, twelve tanks and two guns, was between Lentini and the sea. On the coast were Italian coast-defence troops.

During the evening of the 13th of July the 7th Green Howards moved into an assembly area astride the road Sortino—Lentini behind the 6th Green Howards, who were preparing to clear the road to Lentini by the capture of Mount Pancali and the neighbouring feature. Orders were given that if the attack was successful the 7th Green Howards were to pass through to Lentini and the Leonardo bridge beyond.

By midnight the 6th Green Howards had captured the first feature held by the enemy, but any further advance was held up by fire from Mount Pancali. At 0500 hrs. on the 14th of July the 7th Green Howards were ordered to capture Mount Pancali as soon as possible. The attack was to be supported by the Divisional artillery (98th and 124th Field Regiments) and all the available machine guns of the 2nd Cheshire Regiment. The attack was timed to start at 0700 hrs., but was postponed at the request of the battalion to 0800 hrs. and then to 0830 hrs., as the communications of the 124th Field Regiment were not working properly.

Just before the attack started some enemy tanks approached our positions and one machine gun was knocked out by their fire. These tanks did not unfortunately come within the arcs of fire of our anti-tank guns, and they eventually withdrew when the artillery fire to support the attack started.

The story of the attack from the point of view of the infantryman who took part in it is well described in the following extract from an officer's diary:

> "0530. O Group. We are to attack Mt. Pancali, a high hill on our left, alive with M.Gs. 'A' company goes left and we make a frontal assault. I can see the objective rising suddenly about 2000 yards away with a flat plain between us. H Hour is 0800.
>
> "0745. Hell! Start time altered to 0830—Gunners not ready yet. This waiting before an attack is bloody, especially when shelling is on. The men don't like it—neither do I. Pedestrian Smith seems quite cheery and is telling his platoon it will be dead easy. He and I found out some time ago that the best way to spend this last hour is to joke with the men—it's good for them and good for you. I pick out the Company 'funny man' and he gets cracking about his 'Missus,' who, according to him, gets all his money and weighs 15 stone.

"0830. The guns open up, and we move forward into the open —6th Battalion on our right are going to have a grandstand view of this attack.

"0900. At the foot of the hill at last. Looks bloody steep from here. I stop the artillery over the wireless, we're not going to get our own barrage. . . . There are big boulders as we climb. The men are splendid, climbing up grimly not knowing what to expect at the top. I move over right to search for Nigel's platoon, but cannot see them. We reach a ledge just before the summit and pause for breath and then I hear 'Pedestrian' shout, 'Follow me, 11 platoon,' and I find myself on the top.

"We have been covered during the climb by the steep sides and boulders, but now M.Gs. open up all round. The ground now is flat but covered with rocks. A miserable Boche crawls from behind a boulder about 10 yards in front shouting the inevitable 'Kamerad.' He could have killed me 20 times over as I stood there, but he's too shaken to press the trigger. I run past him—Gosh, this is great fun now. Bullets are whining everywhere, but our blood is up—we are shouting, swearing, cheering, it's easy, they're giving themselves up. . . . They've had it! Except that over on the right there's no sign of Nigel and a lot of fire is coming from behind that wall. I see Boche moving, but not away—they are advancing in the copse where I think Nigel's crowd is—three Spandaus open up on us and I drop to cover just in time.

"I look round, Gosh I've only one section with me. The rest of the Company have swept forward. I can hear the C.S.M. yelling encouragement to them—Geoff is quiet and looks bad, he was hit in the thigh but staggered on to the top to collapse in a hail of bullets.

"I am as excited as hell and get a Bren to open up towards the copse and Jerry quietens down. I must be excited now as I do a damn silly thing—I zig-zag forward under cover of the Bren . . . only half a dozen Boche there at the most I should think . . . two blokes say 'Good luck, Sir,' and a voice says 'I'm coming with you, Sir.' Grand troops; it's Cpl. Kendrick. We dash forward amongst the Spandau lead; our Bren silences one M.G.

"Another twenty yards then more Spandau and a dash for cover behind a great boulder—I turn round to see Kendrick shot clean through the throat.

"I grab his tommy and loose off the magazine. Poor Kendrick; courage evaporates. I hug the ground and pray, then

Jerry starts shelling us. I shout back for a smoke screen on the copse. The first smoke bomb lands nearer to me than the copse and I shout a correction only to find that the mortar crew have been knocked out. I lie there nearly half an hour sweating. Presently the Boche get browned off and come out with their hands up—about 30 of them, armed to the teeth. What a morning."

An observer who was at battalion headquarters that morning wrote:

"Watching the attack from a good vantage point near the 6th Battalion was an experience not to be missed, and the 'show' would put in the shade any demonstration which an Infantry School could produce. The planning of the attack was a masterpiece and the carrying out of the plan (under intense fire) was brilliant. When it is considered that 30 German M.Gs. under excellent cover, and cunningly concealed, swept the entire area continually, and that the climbing of the hill would have been unpleasant under peace conditions, some idea of the stupendous task which was undertaken can be imagined. Every little cog in the machine worked smoothly. The Gunners (90th Fd, bless them) the 3-in. mortars, the M.M.Gs., the wireless men all played their part—also under heavy fire from all types of enemy weapons, including air-bursts. What finer tribute could be paid to the officers and men of the battalion than the words of a German desert veteran, captured on Pancali, 'Since Britain started this war against my Fatherland' (or words to that effect), 'I have been against many British attacks, but that was the finest I have ever seen. I congratulate you.' "

"A" and "B" Companies had led the attack, followed by "C" and "D" respectively, with the carrier platoon covering the open left flank. On closing with their objective the leading companies had come under heavy machine-gun fire. The enemy also made full use of their mortars and self-propelled guns, though the fire of the latter was to some extent ineffective owing to the steepness of the mountain. "A" and "B" Companies, pressing home the assault with skill and determination, and in spite of the difficult going, had captured their objective by 1000 hrs., without it being necessary to employ the reserve companies. The Germans left many dead on the ground and twenty-nine enemy machine guns were found on top of the mountain. Some of the enemy machine-gun detachments continued to fire until the end.

As soon as the objective had been captured "D" Company were

ordered to clear the eastern slope of the mountain, from which the road drops steeply to Carlentini. Here they came under heavy fire from self-propelled guns, and considerable casualties were suffered. Before continuing the advance it was necessary to collect and reorganize the battalion, who were by now very tired. Inevitably this took time, and the advance was not resumed until 1300 hrs.

The 151st Brigade were not yet available in the forward area, but they had been ordered forward so as to be ready to pass through the 69th Brigade as soon as Lentini had been captured. When eventually the 7th Green Howards got on the move again they encountered sporadic opposition from enemy machine guns, self-propelled guns and tanks. Other enemy forces were also being driven into Carlentini by the 4th Armoured Brigade, who were advancing in front of the 5th Division along the coastal road. During the morning they reported ten tanks and 88-mm. guns on their front, and later that these troops had been driven back by our own shelling with the loss to the enemy of one tank and two 88-mm. guns. The brigade, which had previously been operating under the 5th Division, came under the command of the Division at 1300 hrs.

The fatigue of the troops and opposition from enemy rearguards were not the only factors making for delay. The countryside south of Lentini and Carlentini bore witness to the hard fighting that had taken place. The road from Sortino was obstructed at several points by burnt-out and burning enemy vehicles. During the morning the enemy air force had been active, and bombing and ground strafing continued for the greater part of the afternoon. Several carriers were destroyed and quite a number of casualties were incurred.

These conditions combined to cause considerable congestion, and on the other road the 4th Armoured Brigade fared little better, for they encountered the first major demolition of the campaign, a blown bridge a couple of miles from Carlentini. By early in the afternoon, however, Carlentini and Lentini had been secured by the 69th Brigade.

By 1700 hrs. the 5th East Yorkshire Regiment, who had passed through the other two battalions, were some three miles north of Lentini and had joined up with No. 3 Commando, who had landed during the previous night without difficulty. The bridge over the Leonardo River was intact.

At the same time, the leading tanks of the 4th Armoured Brigade, who had succeeded in bypassing the demolition, were passing through the town with the object of pressing on to the Primosole bridge to relieve the Airborne Brigade. Half an hour later the leading battalion of the 151st Brigade, the 9th Durham Light Infantry, reached Carlentini. Strange to relate, the inhabitants of Lentini and Carlentini seemed delighted to see the British troops, and gave them a great welcome.

By dusk on the 14th of July the 4th Armoured Brigade and the 6th Durham Light Infantry were only a mile south of Primosole bridge. They had joined up with elements of the Airborne Brigade and were in contact with the enemy. The airborne men had landed according to plan, seized the bridge and withdrawn all the demolition charges. As the day wore on they had to face a series of strong counter-attacks. These they repulsed, but, at about 1930 hrs.—only two hours before the 9th Durham Light Infantry arrived—lack of ammunition forced them to withdraw from the bridge in face of yet another counter-attack. Thanks to their foresight in removing the charges, the bridge, though in enemy hands, was still intact and under small-arms fire from our own forward troops.

When at about 2130 hrs. the 9th Durham Light Infantry joined up with the paratroops, the 8th Durham Light Infantry were some way behind and still south of Lentini. A little later the guns of the two field regiments came into action north of the village. By the time the situation was clear to the brigade commander darkness had fallen and it was clearly impossible to do anything that night to recapture the bridge. It had been very hot, and the 9th Durham Light Infantry were very tired: with one small break both brigades had been marching all the time since landing in Sicily on the morning of the 10th of July; little or no reconnaissance of possible crossing places over the river had been carried out; the 8th Durham Light Infantry were even more tired and hungry after a forced march, and in no state to carry out an attack; while the 6th Durham Light Infantry would not be up until about midnight.

Accordingly, Brigadier Senior decided that an attack supported by the two field regiments would be made by the 9th Durham Light Infantry at 0730 hrs. the next morning, to secure a bridgehead. This would give time for the necessary reconnaissance by daylight.

While during the last hours of daylight the 151st Brigade were closing up south of the Simeto River, the 69th Brigade, who had been ordered to hold all the approaches to Lentini, were taking up defensive positions, with the 7th Green Howards holding the area of the Leonardo bridge some three thousand five hundred yards north of Lentini, the 6th Green Howards covering the western approaches to the town and the 5th East Yorkshire Regiment in brigade reserve just north of Lentini, with one company covering the town from the east. There was thus a gap of some six miles between the two brigades.

The situation was unusual in that the enemy still remained between the road Lentini—Primosole bridge, along which ran the 151st Brigade's communications, and the sea, and between Lentini and the forward troops of the 5th Division, now stationary, north-west of Augusta. Some of these enemy were later to break through the gap by night and escape.

To the west the whereabouts of the enemy, or at this stage even of our own troops, were unknown. From the road south of the bridge, where it ran along a ridge, the Plain of Catania to the westward was overlooked for many miles, and no movement whatever could be seen. If any enemy threat was to come from the west it would be likely at this stage to follow the roads which lead either to the Primosole bridge or to Lentini. Lentini, a centre of communications, had clearly to be held, and the Divisional Commander decided to keep the 69th Brigade fairly concentrated in that area rather than to attempt to spread them out in a thin line to join up with the 151st Brigade, when they would not have been strong anywhere, and so scattered that they would not have been readily available as a reserve if required. The gap, at times lightly held by machine guns of the 2nd Cheshire Regiment and patrolled by tanks, was to remain for two days until the 168th Brigade arrived to fill it. On this night the 168th Brigade leaguered south of Melilli.

It was intended that all Divisional troops in the forward areas should harbour either in the 151st Brigade area or in the 69th Brigade area. The 24th Army Field Regiment (self-propelled), who had come forward under the command of the 4th Armoured Brigade, and the 98th Field Regiment deployed immediately in rear of the 151st Brigade area. The 124th Field Regiment reconnoitred suitable positions east of Carlentini, but the 69th Brigade was already too dispersed to provide any local protection.

There were some incidents before the guns of the 124th Field Regiment arrived. Two officers and some other ranks approached a lorry to accept the surrender of a number of Italians, when a German bolted from the lorry, after which there was a heavy explosion which killed both officers, two other ranks and several Italian prisoners. Another lorry full of Italians was halted only after it had been fired on, and many small parties of Germans and Italians were rounded up. The 489th Battery came into action just before dark, and the 441st Battery just after dark, and owing to subsequent developments and the late hour of its arival, the 288th Battery bivouacked in the streets of Carlentini, through which town a steady stream of troops and transport was still proceeding. Owing to the number of small parties of enemy about, steps were taken to picquet all routes leading into the gun area.

As it was getting dark the sound of tracked vehicles could be heard coming up the hill towards the 489th Battery from the north-east, and the alarm was given. The first vehicle to arrive was a large lorry towing a field kitchen; it was allowed to pass, as there was some doubt as to its identity. It was later stopped at a road block in rear of the battery. It was followed by several motor-cyclists; no one fired until the leading cyclist disclosed his identity by firing the machine gun mounted on his cycle. They were surrounded and captured. Three minutes later tanks could be heard approaching the last bend in the road. As the leading tank rounded the corner two 25-pounders opened fire, but the guns could not be sufficiently depressed to hit the tanks, which were low down in a sunken road; however, the effect of the fire was sufficient to make the leading tank swerve, hit a wall and block the road. More tanks halted in rear. Fire was now opened on the tanks with rifles and Bren guns, many firing at point-blank range. Since the enemy could not use their guns, as they were below the level of the walls, they returned the fire with automatics and threw a few grenades. For a few minutes there was a general uproar of shooting and shouting, which was momentarily increased by men of the 441st Battery near by also opening fire, but they were soon stopped. Order was quickly restored and the Italians were summoned to surrender, which they were quite ready to do as soon as the gunners could be restrained from shooting at them.

Shortly afterwards a patrol was sent down the road and captured two more tanks which were halted, and a third which came forward firing its machine guns. The bag so far was eight tanks. Preparations were now made to ambush any further enemy who might appear, and in due course M.T. was heard coming down the opposite hill and over the bridge at the bottom, but before it reached the bend on which fire was to be opened it stopped. A patrol went forward and opened fire, under cover of which another party charged the enemy, who immediately surrendered. More enemy were later found hiding in a cave near the bridge, and though bulging with grenades they also surrendered.

The action was over by 0100 hrs. The battery had captured intact the 4th Battalion Contracarro Semoventi of the 33rd Regiment (Parma) of the Livorno Division. Including those taken during the evening, one hundred and ninety-nine prisoners, among whom were five Germans, had been taken by the 124th Field Regiment; the booty consisted of twelve tanks—S47/32 Samevento, open at the top and armed with one 47-mm. gun and one machine gun—fifty motor-cycles, each armed with a machine gun, six lorries, three motor-tri-cycles, many automatic weapons, and two German 75-mm. pack howitzers. Undoubtedly the Italians had been much surprised, and their fire was very wild. Also—a typical Italian touch, this—an orange was found stored in the breech of one of the tank guns. Our success must be attributed to the determination of the gunners rather than to the accuracy of their fire. The total casualties were one officer killed and one officer and one gunner wounded; the enemy lost their colonel and two men killed, and about a dozen wounded.

Reconnaissance at dawn on the 15th of July disclosed that from the northern end of the ridge about one thousand yards south of the River Simeto a good view of both the Primosole bridge and the flat country beyond was obtainable. The bridge is about four hundred feet long and has a superstructure of iron girders. It is about eight feet above the river, which in most places is sluggish and deep and bordered by reeds. Neither bank commands the other: the southern bank gives some good cover, but except for a few scattered trees the country to the south is open. Immediately north of the bridge were two small farms, one on either side of the road. These consisted of two or three buildings with a barn which, being easy to pick up, formed useful points on which the guns could be registered. Northwards from the river bank thick vineyards dotted with olive trees extended to a depth of some four to five hundred yards. The vineyards were very close, the vines being about three to five feet high and some three feet apart. The olive trees which were scattered about among the vines were thicker near the two farms. Visibility in the vineyards when lying down was practically nil, except between and along the rows of vines, when it was not much more than ten yards.

On the left of the road on the far side of the vineyards and running parallel to the river was a sunken track, later to be known as "Stink Alley," but the fact that it was sunken was not at this time known, nor could it be seen from south of the river.

Beyond the vineyards the country is quite open for some four miles except for a belt of woods a thousand yards to the right of the road and running parallel to the sea. This open country is traversed by a few ditches and dotted with farms. Rather more than two miles beyond the river is the dry Bottaceto Ditch, with banks on both sides, the southern one being some ten feet high. This ditch, which runs at right angles to the main road, was a good tank obstacle. It formed the southern edge of the permanent defences of the Catania aerodrome, which included wired-in concrete pillboxes. From the bridge to Catania the main road runs absolutely straight between two lines of poplars.

The 9th Durham Light Infantry's attack went in as planned at 0730 hrs. on the 15th of July, supported by the 24th and 98th Field

Regiments. Odd platoons managed to get across the river, but once on the other side they came up against fierce resistance from the enemy, who were discovered to be German paratroops, concealed in considerable strength in the vineyards. After hand-to-hand fighting those of our men who had managed to get across the river were driven back.

For the remainder of the day our forward troops lined the southern bank, facing the Germans in a similar situation across the river. There was heavy mortaring by the enemy and any movement on the flat ground south of the river at once drew fire. Casualties at this stage were luckily light. Any approach by our own tanks was met by the fire of 88-mm. guns firing over open sights from the north bank. The enemy made several unsuccessful attempts to blow up the bridge, but was prevented from doing so by small-arms fire.

At about 1000 hrs. the Divisional Commander arrived at Headquarters, 151st Brigade, and after consulting with the brigadier ordered that plans should be made for attacking the position again, with stronger artillery support. The time for the attack was tentatively fixed for 1600 hrs.

Just before midday the Corps Commander arrived at Divisional Headquarters at Lentini, to which Major-General Kirkman had returned to meet him. General Dempsey gave the Divisional Commander his plan for the night of the 16th/17th of July—that is to say, the night after next. Seaborne troops were to land north of Catania and seize the port and hold the high ground immediately south-west of Catania. At the same time the 50th Division was to capture a bridgehead over the river, exploiting up to but exclusive of Catania. The 5th Division was then to pass through.

It was clear from these orders that there was no immediate urgency for the capture of the bridgehead, provided that the Division had a proper footing on the far side of the river on the 16th of July. The Divisional Commander therefore decided to postpone the 151st Brigade's attack until moonlight.

To support the attack there would be, in addition to the 24th and 98th Field Regiments, the 124th Field Regiment, who had moved forward from the site of their previous night's battle, the 92nd Field Regiment of the 5th Division, and one medium battery. To control the artillery Brigadier Norton, the C.R.A., had moved his headquarters forward alongside Headquarters, 151st Brigade. The guns and tractors of the 74th and 90th Field Regiments were still being unloaded at Syracuse, but it was hoped that these two regiments would be in action on the 16th of July. The 168th Brigade had left the Melilli area at 0700 hrs. and was on the way to its next halting place east of Carlentini, and it was expected that about half its transport would be unloaded by the evening. Brigadier Davidson was told that the next day, the 16th, he would move into the gap between the 151st and 69th Brigades, taking over from the reserve battalion of the 151st Brigade a locality around the junction of the Scordia road with the road Lentini—Primosole, later known as "Dead Horse Corner." Subsequently he was told that on their way forward his battalions were to carry out a sweep over the coastal belt between the Leonardo River and the 151st Brigade to mop up any enemy still at large in the area.

The Divisional Commander returned to the 151st Brigade during the afternoon and approved the plan, and the decision to attack with one battalion by moonlight at 0100 hrs. While the plan was being discussed between the Divisional and Brigade Commanders and the C.R.A., a message was received saying that enemy columns were advancing on Lentini from both the east and the west. This information did not affect the plan, as it was to meet precisely such a contingency that the 69th Brigade had been disposed around Lentini. In point of fact, the column from the west was later identified as friendly. It had become clear, however, that there were still considerable numbers of enemy east of Lentini. The 5th Division had reported that they were operating in the area of Agnone, and were driving the enemy, believed to be one thousand five hundred strong, towards Lentini. The Divisional Commander on returning to his headquarters at Lentini replied that he would much rather they were driven into the sea.

There had in fact been a series of reports during the day of enemy in the area south of the River Leonardo, between Lentini and the sea. At dusk on the previous day, the 14th, the 5th East Yorkshire Regiment had concentrated on the right of the main road in some orange groves just north of Lentini. Unknown to the battalion, the other end of the same orange groves was occupied by some three hundred German parachute troops. With them were three self-propelled 75-mm. guns from the Hermann Goering Division. Another body of Germans, whose presence also was unknown, was occupying some hilly ground about three miles east of Lentini. There was also in the area the Italian mobile column which, as has already been related, was rounded up early in the night by the 124th Field Regiment. As a result of the action the 124th Field Regiment asked again for infantry protection, and "C" Company of the 5th East Yorkshire Regiment was sent out at about 0200 hrs. to a position roughly two miles east of Lentini, and about a mile south-west of the German battalion referred to above. The first clash occurred at about midday, when a platoon patrol from "C" Company established contact with the Germans in the hills. The company commander, who accompanied the patrol, and the patrol commander were killed, and the bulk of the platoon captured. During the next night they were found locked in a house after the Germans had gone, but the action resulted in the commanding officer receiving a somewhat exaggerated report which caused him to move his reserve company to the scene of the action. The departure of the commanding officer and the reserve company was seen by the three hundred parachute troops in the north of the orange groves, and their commander organized a raid on battalion headquarters. At about 1500 hrs. the headquarters was fired on from the east at a range of about one hundred and fifty yards. The troops still remaining at the headquarters charged the enemy, who later withdrew, leaving several wounded, who were taken prisoner.

Soon afterwards a soldier from the Commandos arrived at the headquarters and reported the location of the German headquarters in some barns in the northern part of the orange groves. A platoon from "D" Company was therefore dispatched to attack it. The platoon commander was killed and the attack was stopped by heavy fire. The strength of the enemy had still not been realized. Five minutes' rapid fire by four 3-inch mortars was later directed against the enemy's position. This shoot was most successful; when the position was occupied the next day the barns were found to have been destroyed and several Germans killed.

Late in the evening the 69th Brigade was ordered to clear up the area between Lentini and the sea and to block all roads and tracks leading to the town from the east. A squadron of tanks was placed under command. The 69th Brigade ordered the bulk of the 5th East Yorkshire Regiment to move to the east of Lentini. This prevented further investigations being made in the area occupied by the three hundred parachutists, and during the night they made their escape. They first attacked "B" Echelon of the 7th Green Howards, and passed through their area, moving north-west. They caused a stoppage of traffic on the main road for a considerable period by setting fire to vehicles and firing at all comers. Later they passed out of the Division's area into that of the 51st Division, where they caused a considerable amount of trouble. They left behind the three self-propelled guns and a great quantity of airborne equipment.

The actions of one platoon of the 5th East Yorkshire Regiment that day—the 15th of July—are set down here in some detail to illustrate what the 69th Brigade as a whole was doing:

"We spent a quiet night amongst the orange trees, and the next morning we were still static. We began weapon cleaning and washing of clothes, but before long my platoon was given its first job of what later proved to be one of our busiest days. The order was to go out as a fighting patrol over ground where there were supposed to be pockets of enemy resistance, but although we combed the suspect area for 2 or 3 hours we saw no sign of the enemy, and returned to our leaguer about midday.

"The orange groves we were in were rather thick with trees and undergrowth and, generally speaking, it wasn't possible to see more than 20 yards. After lunch, however, the C.Q.M.S. drew my attention to movements about 200 yards away: a lane of trees in the grove afforded us this long view. Some troops were moving alongside a small wall, and we felt certain that they weren't Eighth Army, as they were wearing khaki drill slacks and not shorts. Whilst we were debating who they might be, the question was solved by the rapid burr of a Spandau not very far away. The bullets did not come in our direction, but we immediately stood-to, and the company 2 i/c led my own platoon and 10 platoon to overrun the enemy.

"Amongst the thickening groves we came to a house surrounded by a high wall, and from the wall a British paratrooper hissed to me to look out. He pointed in the direction of the enemy. We advanced a little further, and I suddenly saw that one of my section commanders had grabbed a German officer and was propelling him in front. The German officer was yelling something, but my men were right on top of their form now, and the air was ringing with shouts of 'Come out, you bastards,' and similar remarks. I felt sure that the officer was calling upon his men to surrender, so I shouted to my men to stop the noise. Soon the Boches appeared, several from a deep ditch and others from various hiding places in the undergrowth. We combed the area and our final bag was the officer and 18 men, with one Spandau.

"We had no sooner reorganized than up came the company commander in a hurry and told us to get ready for another job. This time we had to go out as a company mobile column to put in an attack on a farmhouse where a respectable number of Germans were holding out. We went off on portees, but when we reached the area the C.O. had decided that the battalion was already strung out too far, and in any case the attack was more than a company could tackle, so it was called off.

"Once again we returned to our orange grove, and once again we found a job already 'lined up' for us. This time we had to attack a farmhouse where a small number of enemy paratroops had been holding out. Fortunately for us, the C.O. decided to try his mortars first, and our mortar platoon laid down such an effective 'stonk' that the Boches came out and surrendered, obviating the necessity for our attack. Some British paratroops who had been captured came out with them and testified to the deadly accuracy of our mortars.

"Our last assignment on this busy day was to go a little further north and provide local protection for the artillery supporting the D.L.I. This was necessary owing to the numbers of enemy paratroops that had been dropped. Another task here was to ambush any enemy who might be driven into our area by the advancing troops of 5 Div. on the coastal sector. We spent a chilly and sleepless night, disturbed by the guns, which were firing all the time. We were not involved with the enemy, but 'A' Company and the anti-tank platoon fought a confused action in the darkness, capturing some enemy paratroops and releasing some British paratroops."

To return to the 151st Brigade's plans. Reconnaissance during the day made it clear that the task before the 8th Durham Light Infantry was no easy one. The eventual plan was based on information given by the commander of the parachute battalion which had taken part in the capture of the bridge on the previous day. He is Lieutenant-Colonel Pearson, D.S.O., M.C., a veteran of airborne soldiering, whose help was greatly appreciated by the Durhams. He was able to provide much useful information about the nature of the ground and in particular as to where the river could be forded.

The final plan was as follows. The assault was to take place at 0210 hrs. Artillery concentrations lasting for eighty minutes were to be put down in the area of the bridge and in the vineyards immediately north of the river, extending approximately five hundred yards to the west of the bridge. For the last ten minutes the entire artillery support was to concentrate on the area of the bridge itself. One squadron of tanks from the low ground south of the river and one machine-gun platoon of the 2nd Cheshire Regiment from the high ground overlooking the bridge were to thicken up the barrage. Two companies of the 8th Durham Light Infantry were to ford the river at a point approximately four hundred yards west of the bridge and then work their way downstream through the vineyards in an easterly direction towards their objective—the bridge.

The decision to risk the ford was made, as, although assault boats might have been forthcoming, there had been no chance of reconnoitring the river bank for suitable launching sites. Actually the river where crossed was found to be some thirty yards wide and about four feet deep, with a muddy bottom.

The remainder of the battalion and supporting arms were to cross the river by the bridge and enlarge the bridgehead. The position to be consolidated was approximately one thousand five hundred yards in depth and some two thousand yards in breadth. Owing to the northward curve of the river on both sides of the bridge, both flanks would rest on it.

It was a clear, moonlight night when, at 2200 hrs., the assaulting companies began to move forward towards the forming-up position. It had originally been decided to form up behind the embankment which ran roughly parallel with the river and about one hundred and fifty yards from it. On arrival, however, a narrow ditch, running at right angles to the embankment, was chosen, as it appeared to give better protection in case of any shells of the barrage dropping short. Contact was made on the forming-up position with Lieutenant-Colonel Pearson, who had gone down at dusk to tape a route from there to the river. Meanwhile, the supporting arms—carriers, anti-tank guns and mortars—the remaining two companies and battalion headquarters moved to their respective assembly areas east and west of the main road some one thousand and eighty yards south of the bridge.

At 0100 hrs. the barrage began. Some guns were firing short, but as the assault companies were to all intents and purposes entrenched in the ditch there were no casualties. The effect of the artillery and machine-gun fire appeared devastating. At zero hour the leading companies crossed the river in single file at two points about fifty yards apart. Although the average depth was four feet, there were deep holes, possibly caused by shelling, and many men were submerged. The companies formed up rapidly under cover of the far bank and started to move forward in an easterly direction, "A" Company on the right and "B" Company on the left, the right of "A" Company moving along the river bank. The vines were thick and closely planted, and as they were much entwined movement was difficult. There was a certain amount of enemy automatic fire from the left. This was, however, ignored, as the main task was to capture the bridge intact and speed was essential. Moreover, these automatics were using tracer and the fire was easily avoided. In the area of the bridge not a great number of enemy were encountered; these were speedily disposed of with bayonets, grenades and tommy-guns. The artillery had accounted for quite a number, and many others had withdrawn northwards.

The first phase had been successfully carried out and the remainder of the battalion could now come forward. Since it was essential that there should be no delay in getting the necessary orders through, four alternative methods of communication had been arranged: four —to make sure. The first was to use 2-inch mortar signal flares; the mortar and bombs unfortunately became separated in the dark, and in the chaos of the assault only one flare went up. This was not acted upon. Secondly, by wireless; each company carried a set, but despite all precautions both these sets became "drowned." Thirdly, as a stand-by, it had been arranged that the Royal Engineer officer, whose task it was to reconnoitre the bridge, and the carrier platoon commander were to be posted with a wireless set in a carrier on the south side of the bridge. Lieutenant-Colonel Lidwell accompanied the assaulting companies, and he was naturally most anxious to get news of the success of the attack back at once to his headquarters. When the first two methods failed he went back himself over the bridge in search of this the third link, only to find that the carrier had received a direct hit. The two officers were dead, the crew severely wounded and the wireless set out of action.

There remained the fourth and last method of communication. The tanks which had been giving covering fire from the south side of the river had a wireless link to brigade headquarters, which was in line communication with the battalion headquarters. Lieutenant-Colonel Lidwell found a tank with its engine running. It was still dark and there was a lot of firing going on, so to attract attention he climbed on to the side of the tank and with his stick tapped the commander on the head; the only result was that the lid of the tank was closed down hurriedly. Possibly the commander thought he had been hit. So, for the time being at any rate, this method failed too.

Incredible though it may seem, at that moment a War Office "observer" officer, Major Wigram, turned up riding a bicycle. He could not have arrived at a more opportune moment, and at once went back to bring the remainder of the battalion forward.

This unfortunate chapter of events had, however, delayed things considerably and dawn was just breaking as "B" and "C" Companies crossed the bridge. They extended at once east and west of the main road and advanced towards their respective objectives. But as they went forward they came under withering small-arms fire from the until then unsuspected sunken track which ran west from the road. This fire checked them, casualties were heavy and no further advance appeared possible.

By 0600 hrs., by which time battalion headquarters was established about two hundred yards north of the bridge and on the west of the road, the situation as known at battalion headquarters was as follows: "A" Company, on the right of the road, had lost all its officers and the company was badly scattered. "B" Company, on the left, was in position behind a steep earth bank surrounding the farm building near the road; it had only one officer and about twenty men left. "C" Company, which had exploited some way to the east of the road towards the sea, had been heavily counter-attacked and one platoon had been driven back across the river. "D" Company, the only one which had not suffered heavily, was in position east of the road near the bridge.

By this time it was clear that the enemy resistance was very considerable and the original plan for the 8th Durham Light Infantry to extend the bridgehead had to be abandoned. Instead, companies were reorganized so as to hold a small bridgehead about three hundred yards in depth and extending one hundred and fifty yards on either side of the road. The battalion was in close contact with the enemy, and lively fire was exchanged on both sides at ranges decreasing to twenty yards.

The brigade commander, who had crossed the bridge and reached battalion headquarters by dawn, was unable to return, as the bridge was under constant and accurate small-arms fire. He was, however, in touch with his headquarters by wireless. At 0600 hrs. the Divisional Commander had arrived at the brigade headquarters, and shortly afterwards Brigadier Senior, talking over the wireless, was able to give him more or less the true situation.

As so often happens in war, the picture gained at Divisional Headquarters from first reports had been inaccurate, and the Divisional Commander had left his headquarters under the impression that the attack had been entirely successful. There was some discussion as to whether another battalion should attempt to cross the river to reinforce the 8th Durham Light Infantry, but the Divisional Commander decided against it, as it seemed to him that they would only incur casualties and become pinned to the ground by the opposition which was holding the 8th Durham Light Infantry. Efficient artillery support for the advance of another battalion would at this time have been virtually impossible, as the exact dispositions of the 8th Durham Light Infantry were not known. Instead, a company of the 6th Durham Light Infantry was ordered to move to the tower and buildings south of and in the loop of the Simeto River between the bridge and the sea, as it seemed that from this position it should be possible to dominate the bridgehead area with machine-gun fire.

It was clear that the enemy opposition was determined and considerable. The Divisional Commander therefore returned to Main Divisional Headquarters and at about 1000 hrs. got in touch with Corps and told them that the Division would not be able to cooperate efficiently in the plan for the capture of Catania; he suggested that this plan be modified or postponed.

At 1040 hrs. the Commander of the 151st Brigade returned across the bridge safely in a carrier. He confirmed what was known about the situation on the other side and said in addition that there was much machine-gun fire and sniping from both sides of the road in the vineyards, and that the tanks were unable to help on account of two 88-mm. guns. He said that these guns were then being dealt with, but that the tanks had withdrawn south of the river. A tentative plan was made that when the 88-mm. guns had been knocked out a smoke screen would be put down and the tanks would clear the vineyard beyond the river. Later in the day the tank commander reported that this was impossible, as the ditches and undergrowth were impassable to tanks. Though unknown at the time, this was faulty appreciation of the ground.

At 1330 hrs. the Army and Corps Commanders arrived at Divisional Headquarters. They told the Divisional Commander that the plan to capture Catania was postponed for twenty-four hours, and that the task of the Division was to enlarge the bridgehead during the night.

At 1400 hrs. the Divisional Commander returned to the 151st Brigade. He discussed with the brigade commander whether the troops to enlarge the bridgehead should cross by the bridge or ford the river by the same route as had been used by the 8th Durham Light Infantry. In either case the artillery fire plan presented considerable difficulties, as it was impossible to identify the position of our own forward troops in the undergrowth from any observation post other than one in the forward defences themselves, where the view was very limited. Moreover, if the ford on the left of the 8th Durham Light Infantry was used, any barrage would have to swing round and across the front of the existing bridgehead to cover the attacking infantry on to the right of their objective.

As the main bridge was still under fixed-line machine-gun fire, it was decided to put the remaining two battalions of the 151st Brigade across the ford to the left of the 8th Durham Light Infantry which had previously been used. To cover the approach march a standing barrage was to be put down on the enemy's bank of the river to the left of the bridgehead. It was then to lift about two hundred yards north of the river to cover the actual crossing and forming up. The infantry were to assemble behind this barrage, after which they were to clear the wood and advance behind a creeping barrage to the final objective, a line about one thousand five hundred yards beyond the bridge, and between the two bends in the river. At the same time, a barrage was to be put down across the front of the 8th Durham Light Infantry bridgehead, and when the main barrage came up level with it. it also was to creep forward to the right of the objective. Heavy concentrations were to be put down on enemy positions on the river east of the bridgehead in order to confuse the enemy as to the actual point of attack. The 9th Durham Light Infantry was to end up on the right of the road, the 6th Durham Light Infantry on the left. Zero was to be 0100 hrs.

Throughout the day conditions in the bridgehead had continued to be most unpleasant. Very early two Sherman tanks crossed the bridge, but coming under fire from 88-mm. guns they had, as reported by Brigadier Senior, withdrawn to the south side again. The artillery officers who had accompanied the assaulting companies had established an observation post in the small farm on the right of the road and were engaging targets whenever their knowledge of the position of our own troops permitted. At 0630 hrs. the carriers and 3-inch mortars had been ordered forward. Despite very heavy small-arms fire, they succeeded in crossing the bridge and were able to take cover behind the farm. Here for the moment they were safe owing to the absence of enemy mortar and artillery fire. Several of their crews were detailed to assist "B" Company in dismounted action, whilst the remainder maintained a precarious supply of ammunition and food across the bridge and assisted in the evacuation of the wounded.

Using the house as an observation post, the 3-inch mortars gave extremely effective covering fire, more particularly to the companies on the right, as observation of the enemy on this flank was good. On the left there was a great deal more cover, and results were difficult to ascertain. Attempts by the enemy to infiltrate were beaten off by "B" Company and the carriers. Two anti-tank guns were towed over by carriers and placed in position at the northern end of the bridge. Later three Sherman tanks again tried to deploy to the east of the road, but were unsuccessful, two of them being destroyed by fire from the 88-mm. gun down the road. Shortly afterwards, however, this gun was put out of action by artillery fire.

Throughout the day the enemy attempted to launch counter-attacks against our small bridgehead with tanks and infantry. The infantry attacks were successfully dealt with by machine-gun, mortar and light-automatic fire and all attempts were foiled. The mortar platoon, which incidentally fired over six hundred bombs, and one machine-gun platoon of the 2nd Cheshire Regiment engaged numerous targets and made any movement by the enemy very costly. Close support by artillery was impossible on account of the nearness of the enemy. The artillery, however, were seldom silent and, judging by the number of dead found later on, their fire was most effective.

The 69th Brigade, back at Lentini, still had contact with the enemy from time to time throughout the day. An officer who had been captured during the night, and who subsequently escaped, reported that the enemy were hiding in a railway tunnel north-west of Lentini; the 69th Brigade cleared the tunnel and captured twelve Italians, but some Germans were still at large in the general area of Lentini; a band of forty were reported to have looted a farm and then made off in the direction of Mount Pancali; the 6th Green Howards had been ordered to deal with this situation, and during the afternoon they attacked a farm, which was by then found to be empty.

The squadron of the Royals were used to patrol westwards and north-westwards into the Plain of Catania, and they made contact with the enemy on the general line of the River Gornalunga, which runs south of but roughly parallel to the Simeto, and joins it just west of the Primosole bridge. One patrol reconnoitring out to the west flank engaged an enemy leaguer, killing and wounding fifteen of the enemy and capturing four guns and three Italians. Four vehicles and four store tents were left burning.

In the evening the 168th Brigade reported that the 1st London Scottish was taking over the locality at the north end of the ridge overlooking Primosole bridge, and the 10th Royal Berkshire Regiment and the 1st London Irish Rifles were on the ridge to the southwest protecting the main road from the north-west. During the day the brigade had taken eighty prisoners, mostly Italian, between the main road and the sea. They were ordered to send infantry patrols to reconnoitre river crossings farther inland, in case the night attack should not be successful.

The attack by the 6th and 9th Durham Light Infantry went in as planned. The river was crossed without difficulty and the two battalions formed up for the assault without any trouble, but during the subsequent advance companies became split up, and owing to the difficulty of movement through the vineyards several small isolated encounters took place in the thick undergrowth. As our troops fought their way forward in the moonlight they cleared up any opposition in their path, but inevitably left pockets of resistance on their flanks. Even when they reached their final objective there were still small nests of enemy left in the vineyards behind them.

The experience of a company of the 6th Durham Light Infantry is typical of the type of fighting that occurred. Once the company advanced into the vineyards it was met by intense automatic fire from the enemy, who were dug in along the near bank of the sunken lane. Almost a whole platoon was lost, but the rest pressed on in the darkness and cleared the undergrowth. Next they got into the sunken lane and cleared the enemy out of that. The company commander was wounded, but, led by a subaltern, and using both bayonets and grenades, they struggled to their objective commanding the main road, and established themselves in a shallow ditch and a large shell hole. At dawn some Germans managed once more to work their way back into the sunken road behind the position, whilst others were attempting to make their way down the main road from the direction of Catania to reinforce their comrades. This sadly reduced company was thus hemmed in on two sides and the situation was for a time awkward. For three and a half hours the enemy was held at bay by Brens and rifles, and finally driven back.

"A" Company of the 9th Durham Light Infantry was less fortunate. The company, made up into two strong platoons, Nos. 16 and 17, moved forward behind the barrage, No. 16 Platoon leading. Almost at once they came under heavy enemy fire and their advance was hampered by loose telephone and barbed wire. There were a number of casualties. Still under fire, they pushed on towards the main road, where they captured a machine-gun post, taking three prisoners. They then crossed the road, and reaching open ground came under fire from a white farmhouse. Covered by fire from Bren guns and 2-inch mortars, this in turn was successfully attacked. Casualties were caused to the enemy and nine prisoners were taken.

Having cleared the farm, the company moved another two or three hundred yards towards their objective without further incident, except that several Germans were killed on the way. The company commander, Captain Hudson, found that by this time he had only fifteen men left, two of them wounded. They were all from No. 16 Platoon, No. 17 Platoon having been lost in the advance.

Heavy machine-gun fire was now opened on the small party from a wood to their right rear; their position was considered untenable, and they started withdrawing towards the main road. As it began to get light fire was opened on them from the road itself, but Captain Hudson recognized the commander of another company advancing on the far side of the road and, managing to attract his attention, signalled to him that he would attack the post on the road from his own side. They attacked, but were eventually halted by heavy fire.

Finding himself short of ammunition, Captain Hudson managed to get his men across the road to join up with the other company of his battalion beyond, but found that he had by then only seven unwounded men left, with one Bren gun and very little ammunition. At this moment machine-gun fire suddenly opened on them from bushes to their rear. As ammunition was by now almost exhausted, Captain Hudson ordered his men to try to get back to the battalion. He himself had been wounded, and at about this time he was captured by the enemy.

Other companies of these two battalions were more successful in keeping together, and by 0515 hrs. the 9th Durham Light Infantry had crossed the road on the way to their objective, and the 6th Durham Light Infantry were steadily working forward. At about 0600 hrs. the enemy counter-attacked with tanks down the road from the direction of Catania. This was broken by fire called for by the artillery observing officers with the battalions.

At about 0615 hrs. both battalions were reported to be about a thousand yards beyond the bridge. At dawn our tanks again crossed the bridge. They were met by Brigadier Senior, who had come forward, and he ordered them to deploy on both sides of the road, himself pointing o t to them the enemy positions. The effect of their presence was seen almost at once. Movement began in the enemy lines, a few white handkerchiefs appeared, and soon everywhere the enemy were surrendering.

Whereas on the previous day the country had been considered to be too difficult for tanks, on this day they proved to be the key to the destruction of the enemy in the undergrowth immediately north of the river. The process of mopping up continued for some time, the tired battalions of the Durham Light Infantry being assisted in this work by a company of the London Scottish brought forward to help them. By 1000 hrs. mopping up had been completed, and all resistance in the area immediately beyond the bridge had ceased.

The leading troops of the 6th and 9th Durham Light Infantry were on their objective. One hundred and fifty-five German parachutists had been captured, and the enemy dead on the ground were estimated to number about three hundred. The battle for the bridgehead was over.

The prisoners taken were all parachutists. Nazi zealots to a man, and highly experienced veterans of Crete and Russia, they had fought as savagely as any Germans whom the Division had previously encountered. Within the bridgehead area had been three battalions of the 3rd Parachute Regiment, reinforced by the German 904th Fortress Battalion. Two days before the fighting started the German troops had been resting in the South of France.

At 1000 hrs. the Corps Commander visited Divisional Headquarters and gave the plan for the next night. The plan to attack Catania from the sea was abandoned. The Corps Commander's orders were that the Division was to enlarge the bridgehead by some two thousand five hundred yards to the ditch on the southern edge of the aerodrome.

By 1100 hrs. the position on the front of the 151st Brigade had stabilized with the 9th Durham Light Infantry on the right of the

o

road, the 6th Durham Light Infantry on the left, and the 8th Durham Light Infantry just north of the bridge for its close defence. The enemy was believed to hold the line of the river on either side of the 151st Brigade bridgehead, and to be facing our forward troops. At 1100 hrs. the Divisional Commander met all infantry brigadiers and the C.R.A. at Headquarters, 151st Brigade, and gave orders for the attack that night—the 17th/18th of July. The plan was for the 168th Brigade to pass through the 151st Brigade bridgehead and advance covered by a barrage, with its centre line on the main road and with the Bottaceto Ditch as its objective. After completion of this phase the 69th Brigade would pass through the bridgehead, swing to the west and, under a barrage, capture the line of the railway and secure the left flank of the 168th Brigade. The attack was to be supported by eight field regiments and one medium regiment.

During the day the squadron of the Royals had again been operating on the left flank. They had shot up the enemy in the area of some tents, inflicting casualties, setting fire to the tents and causing several explosions. In the afternoon they were attacked by sixty infantry, whom they beat off with a loss to the enemy of about twenty casualties.

At 1615 hrs. Major-General Kirkman, then at Divisional Headquarters, was informed by Brigadier Curry, commanding the 4th Armoured Brigade, that he thought the enemy had probably retired. The General therefore went forward to the 151st Brigade and ordered a reconnaissance to be carried out by tanks and two platoons of carriers from the 168th Brigade, to discover the approximate location of the enemy, and his strength.

There was one place—the crossing of the main road over the Fosso Bottaceto—where there was thought to be an 88-mm. in an anti-tank role in action, and covering fire of high explosive and smoke was put down on this locality throughout the reconnaissance. Brigadier Davidson, commanding the 168th Brigade, was told that as a result of the reconnaissance the plan might have to be changed. The reconnaissance was slow in starting—the carriers of one of the battalions of the 168th Brigade took a long time to arrive, and the tanks were even slower. It was probably not until about 1915 hrs. that the reconnaissance began. Though it was still light when the tanks and carriers were seen, from an observation post in front of Headquarters, 151st Brigade, to be returning, the light was definitely beginning to fail.

At 1915 hrs. reports were received from the Headquarters of the 4th Armoured Brigade stating that there was no enemy south of the Bottaceto Ditch and that they were probably only in small numbers on the line of the ditch itself. There was hardly any Spandau fire. It was also reported that no enemy fire could be drawn from the locality thought to exist on the right of the road, and that there were few, if any, enemy in the woods on the extreme right. It was stated that the commanders of the carrier platoons agreed with this report.

This report was misleading, as some four hours later, when the attack went in, the enemy was quite definitely in considerable strength.

Exactly to what factors this was due it is difficult to say. Lieutenant Duff, of the London Scottish, who was wounded and captured during the attack but who later returned to his unit when the enemy finally evacuated the island, states that his captors consisted of parachutists who said that they had been dropped on the Catania aerodrome only that afternoon and had come straight into the line. This information was partially substantiated by a wounded American pilot, Charles Kennard, who was in an enemy hospital with Lieutenant Duff, who told him too that he had seen fifty to sixty Ju.52's flying low over the Catania aerodrome and "dropping things" which he could not identify. Whether the parachutists went into the line before or after dark is unknown.

Whatever was the true state of affairs, the information on which plans had to be based was the report that the enemy was very weak, with few, if any, Spandaus. There were three courses open:

1. To attack as planned with a barrage going the whole way. This course was likely to give away surprise, and would be uneconomical in ammunition, which was not over-plentiful.
2. To postpone the attack on the enemy's new position until the next night, and confine the immediate action to gaining touch with the enemy. In this case, his dispositions might be more precisely determined the next day, but it would give the enemy another twenty-four hours in which to organize his defences.
3. To carry out the attack as arranged but to give up the barrage and to confine the supporting fire to a concentration on the final objective—the southern boundary of the aerodrome and the woods to the right of the road.

The third course was adopted, and while it was still light, at about 2015 hrs., Brigadier Davidson and the C.R.A. were so informed. Timings were not altered; the leading battalions were to leave the start line near our own forward defensive localities at 2200 hrs., and the barrage on the objective was to go down from 2245 to 2300 hrs.

In the case of the right-hand battalion, the London Scottish, the change in plan was not known to company commanders until just after they had left the start line; this was because the brigadier was unable to find the commanding officer. A further mistake was that the arrangements made for Bofors to fire tracer shells every three minutes to mark the flanks were not cancelled in time owing to difficulties in finding the guns, which had gone to special positions. This fire therefore was put down during the start of the attack, and may have lessened surprise. Machine-gun fire was put down to neutralize the enemy who might be on the eastern edge of the wood between the main road and the sea.

As the hour for the attack approached, some concern was caused at Divisional Headquarters by reports of paratroops landing in the Divisional rear areas, and of two craft the size of L.C.Is. moving south. Between 2140 and 2340 hrs. there were two reports of several L.C.Is. off shore. All troops in the Divisional area were warned, and a mobile patrol was sent out into the area between Divisional Headquarters and the sea to watch for a landing. This was reported to Corps Headquarters, who later informed Divisional Headquarters that these craft were friendly. "Stand down" was ordered. Reports from several sources about midnight stated that parachutists had landed in the rear areas of the Division. These reports proved false, but were an added anxiety at Divisional Headquarters.

Early reports from the 168th Brigade indicated that the attack was going well. Both leading battalions, the 1st London Scottish on the right and the 1st London Irish on the left, had left the start line as ordered and halted in approximately their correct positions three to four hundred yards short of the objective to wait for the standing barrage to come down. Up to this time the enemy had taken no action and no enemy machine guns had opened fire. During the fifteen minutes' standing barrage the London Irish on the left closed up to within a hundred yards of the shells; on the right, however, the London Scottish unfortunately remained where they were, some four to five hundred yards from the artillery fire, instead of closing up. When they advanced it was found that the enemy had some defences in a farm in front of the line of the aerodrome defences, and in consequence this pocket of enemy failed to receive any neutralizing fire. The right-hand company of the London Scottish reached its objective; the centre company was delayed by hand-to-hand fighting round the farm; the left-hand company was held up short of the objective. In the case of the London Irish, elements of all three forward companies reached their objectives.

The commanding officer of the London Scottish was out of touch with his companies except those troops in his immediate vicinity, and did not know the whereabouts of his right-hand company. Not realizing that they were on their objective, he asked for a repetition of the artillery concentration on his front, so that his troops could get forward under cover of the artillery fire into a better position from which to assault the final objective. This led to some casualties in the right-hand company, who were shelled by their own artillery. After the concentration had been repeated the left-hand company got on to its objective, but the centre company was still short of it.

Considerable confusion was caused when the enemy in the wood on the right opened up with Spandaus from the rear on troops on and short of the objective. This confusion was increased owing to the fact that this was the first attack that the 168th Brigade had ever made. Previous to this they had had little contact with the enemy, other than mopping-up operations. Stragglers brought back exaggerated reports of heavy casualties, of whole companies being overrun by the enemy, and Brigadier Davidson had a false impression of the situation. At 0245 hrs. he telephoned the Divisional Commander and said that at hardly any place were his troops on the objective and that generally speaking they were pinned to the ground some two hundred yards short of the objective, and in consequence about that distance from the pillboxes which formed part of the permanent defences of the Catania aerodrome.

It was considered that it would be undesirable to ask the troops to remain in this very open country in such a position, and the General therefore ordered the brigade to take up a position on the general line of a ditch about a thousand yards short of the objective.

The 69th Brigade had started to move out towards the left flank, and at 0200 hrs. were informed of the failure of the 168th Brigade and told to conform by locating their forward defensive localities in prolongation of the position given to the 168th Brigade. The 7th Green Howards had already, however, after some fighting, got on to their objective, and were in touch with the London Irish on their right. They were, however, able to extricate themselves and withdraw as ordered.

> "It was," writes an officer of the 7th Green Howards, "what might be described as the queerest night attack of all time. The orders were to move in several bounds by means of a compass bearing for so many paces, but on arrival at the start line all was chaos, and nearly 40% had failed to arrive, having become mixed up with the Scottish. Things were very quiet away towards our objective—the pillboxes surrounding the airfield—so we felt easier as we started off with our 'skeleton' battalion,

especially as some artillery support was provided at the last moment.

"The barrage unfortunately went wrong and two companies had a number of casualties from it before it could be stopped over the wireless. This caused a further splitting up of companies, and odd men were wandering about all over the place, completely lost. 'B' Company reached their objective, but as the Company Commander (Capt. Ian Hay) crept forward unseen to deal with the first M.G. post a fool N.C.O. with a machine-gun opened up and gave away the show. Hay collapsed, riddled with Spandau bullets, and it was only with great difficulty that the company was able to extricate itself. Orders had now come through to everyone except Tac Bn H.Q. that the 168 Brigade were unable to progress and we were to withdraw to a continuation of the ditch line which they held.

"Thanks to the energy and courage of the C.O.—the wireless was working only spasmodically at this stage—the companies were informed of the new orders and withdrew (in some confusion admittedly, for it was very dark and everyone had by this time more than lost their bearings), leaving Tac H.Q. in a farm 150 yards from the Boche. Just before dawn the Brigadier arrived, and Tac H.Q. learned of their predicament for the first time as the wireless had been out of action some hours. Luckily, ditches were plentiful, and a successful withdrawal was made before the enemy realized that he had 'easy meat' so near him.

"The night's 'escapes' included the crew of a carrier which received a direct hit from an 88 mm solid shot which went right through the vehicle and left the men untouched. One of the most trying facts about the operation was the great use made by the Boche of the searchlights on the airfield, which continually swept the ground over which we passed. The objective remained untaken—through no fault of the 7th—but at least the Simeto bridgehead was firmly in Div hands, and there remained only the burial of some 500 Boche and many of the Division's heroes."

The situation at first light was that the 168th and 69th Brigades held the line which they had been ordered to occupy. One battery of the 102nd Anti-Tank Regiment had been placed under command of each of the brigades, the whole of the Divisional artillery was in support of the bridgehead with a call on the 5th Divisional artillery, and the whole of the 2nd Cheshire Regiment was being moved forward to support the bridgehead with a battalion machine-gun plan. The 4th Armoured Brigade had the bulk of two battalions of tanks in the bridgehead. The crossing over the Simeto River was therefore firmly in our hands.

Now came a change in the character of the operations undertaken by the 50th Division. As an infantry officer wrote at the time: "The static period loathed by all P.B.I. had begun, but it produced no incidents of note, just the usual blood, sweat and toil—quite a bit of blood too."

CHAPTER XVI

Static Warfare at Primosole Bridge—The Enemy withdraws—An exacting Pursuit and a Seaborne Landing—Capture of Messina and the End of the Campaign

JULY TO AUGUST, 1943

The Army Commander and the Corps Commander arrived at Divisional Headquarters at 0900 hrs. on the 18th of July. The general plan for the Corps was changed. Thus far the intention had been to continue the advance up the coast, but it was now apparent that the Division was faced by strong opposition based on the permanent defences of Catania aerodrome, which had been constructed long before the invasion. They contained concrete pillboxes and belts of wire. In consequence the Division was ordered temporarily to assume a defensive role, and hold its present position, while the 5th Division attempted to gain ground on the left into the Etna foothills.

Thus there began for the Division a period of static warfare which was to last for a fortnight. The first phase, the period of strong Divisional thrusts into the enemy's territory whilst he was still disorganized, was nearly over. The efforts of the 5th Division to get forward failed, and they eventually held ground on the left of the Division. Farther left the XXX Corps were held. The enemy, reinforced from the mainland, succeeded in establishing a defensive position which ran from the Catania aerodrome defences across the island in front of Mount Etna. The next step was for the XXX Corps, reinforced by the 78th Division, a fresh division, to break this line at Adrano, south of Etna, on the enemy's one remaining lateral road this side of the mountain.

As far as the Division was concerned, the first problem was the organization of the defensive position. It was unfortunate that the enemy still held the Bottaceto Ditch, which, quite apart from its permanent defences, was so deep that it was easy for him to dig shelters which gave the defenders some security from our shell fire. Moreover, the high banks, which gave him some observation of our forward area, entirely concealed the enemy's rear from our own infantry, though it was overlooked, at a range of seven thousand yards, from the end of the ridge south of the Primosole bridge. On the right the enemy still held the belt of woods running parallel to the sea coast some one thousand yards inland, and our own right flank rested on the Simeto River midway between the bridge and the sea. The possibility of clearing the wood so that the line of forward defensive localities facing the Bottaceto Ditch should continue eastwards to the sea was considered, but after the recent experience of the 151st Brigade at the Primosole bridge it was felt that to attack the enemy in this type of country would result in casualties to no good purpose, as our position would not be greatly strengthened.

It was necessary to give the battalions some rest, and the forward troops were therefore reduced in numbers. The front was held with two brigades: in the left sector with two battalions forward and one in reserve near the river, and in the right sector with one battalion forward, one in reserve, but with a company holding the right flank, and one in reserve near the sea south of the river. The brigade in reserve was moved back to the coast some miles south of the river to bathe and rest. Battle positions for this brigade were reconnoitred on the high ground south of the bridge. Anti-tank and motor machine-gun positions were co-ordinated on the Divisional front by their respective commanding officers. Brigade reliefs took place every four days, except that the right sector was initially held by the 168th Brigade for a longer period so that they could have experience of this type of warfare.

In order to wear down the enemy and detain as many of his troops as possible on the Divisional front, a very active defence policy was pursued. Any movement was at once engaged by artillery and medium machine guns. Pillboxes were shelled, whilst medium machine guns stood by to engage the enemy should he leave them. Many were destroyed and it is believed that the enemy gave up holding them by day. We used two captured 28-cm. Italian howitzers, from their positions south of the river, to shell the enemy. Active night patrolling was carried out. Many hostile batteries were driven out of their positions by our counter-battery fire.

The enemy on his part was not inactive. In the initial stages he was quick to shell or mortar our localities if any movement was seen. The Primosole bridge was constantly shelled at irregular intervals nearly every day by big guns firing at long range. The bridge itself, screened by trees and the two farms, could hardly have been visible, yet the enemy fire was extremely accurate, and though his guns were firing diagonally across the bridge it was hit at least four times. It is believed that he fired at a visible "witness point" to adjust his fire each day. The enemy also shelled transport using the lateral tracks north of the river whenever vehicles moved fast enough to raise dust.

So that the bridge and dusty tracks could be avoided, two bridges were constructed across the river and a third was finally added just before the enemy retired, to facilitate the rapid move forward of guns and transport. The Primosole bridge was by this time out of action, to avoid needless casualties to working parties repairing it.

The extent of the enemy's fire can be judged by the fact that a herd of some twenty to thirty head of cattle, which could not be driven away from their usual grazing ground, were all, without exception, killed by shell or mortar fire in about a week. During this period our casualty list increased slowly but steadily, but the enemy probably suffered more heavily, as we had a considerable preponderance of artillery, and the handling of his artillery was not good. He had not yet appreciated the moral and destructive effect of concentrated shell fire. His tendency was to range on a target, fire four or eight rounds and then stop. The enemy never shelled the bridge we had put up, nor the transport moving along the main road where, south of the river, it runs along the top of the ridge, which must have been visible. Possibly it was out of range. The enemy's efforts at counter-battery fire were usually ineffective.

A few days after the arrival of the Division in this area the Royal Air Force had virtually complete superiority, and except for the first few days the enemy air force was rarely seen. The area was highly malarious, and, like other divisions, the 50th Division from now onwards suffered fairly heavily from this disease.

During the latter half of the period it became obvious that the enemy contemplated a withdrawal. Great explosions on the Catania aerodrome occurred daily—probably bombs were being destroyed. During the last few days he certainly thinned out his defences by day, and instead of maintaining his activity as might have been expected he became singularly quiet, and fired at daylight patrols only when they approached near to his positions. This may to some extent have been due to the fact that by the end of the period our artillery and medium machine guns dominated the battlefield.

Some information is now available about the enemy opposing the Division. At this time the 1st and 3rd Battalions of the 4th Parachute Regiment provided the backbone of the German defence, one on either side of the road and on the right spreading into the wood. An Italian battalion was also in the wood. These forces were supported by 88-mm. guns from the Hermann Goering Flak Regiment and some nebelwerfers. In addition, the 3rd Battalion of the Hermann Goering Artillery Regiment was in support, with self-propelled guns on light tank chassis, and there were a number of guns of heavier calibre. It was never proved whether or not the enemy kept a duty squadron of tanks forward in support; there were frequent reports of Mark VI tanks in the area, but no positive identification.

On the 3rd of August the XXX Corps captured Centuripe, five miles south-west of Adrano. The enemy's forces south of Mount Etna were not yet split into two parts, but it was clear that they shortly would be, and in fact on the 6th of August the XXX Corps captured Adrano, on the enemy's last lateral road south-west of Mount Etna.

On the Divisional front on the 3rd of August it seemed clear that the enemy were about to withdraw: there was little mortaring, no shelling, but more explosions behind his lines than ever. None the less, during the day our patrols were still fired at. Preparations were made to start the advance again the next day on a two-brigade front, with the 151st Brigade on the right, the 69th Brigade on the left, and the 168th Brigade in reserve. Strong night patrols were sent out, and by dawn our own troops were on the Bottaceto Ditch. The enemy had gone. On the 4th of August the Division started its pursuit of the enemy rearguards, which was to end only with the capture of the island.

The country was exceedingly difficult. Immediately north of Catania the plain ceases, and from the lower slopes of Mount Etna proper the ground falls away fairly steeply to the sea. It is intersected at frequent intervals by deep river beds, nearly all dry at this time of year, but none the less complete obstacles to tracks and wheels owing to their steep and often precipitous sides. The Division, advancing along roads near the coast, was always overlooked from the higher ground inland. The whole countryside between Mount Etna and the sea is intensely cultivated with vineyards, olive groves and citrus trees, except where it is covered with lava. So that the soil should not be washed away in the winter, much of the ground is terraced and the lava walls which support the terraces are often ten or twelve feet high. Nearly all roads are bordered by similar walls varying from four to twelve feet in height. These walls give good cover, but many are unscaleable, and a man caught against or between them by machine-gun fire is trapped. Up to Taomina there was always one and sometimes two good main roads, running parallel to the coast within the Divisional boundary, but the remainder were very rough, steep and narrow; and many were so narrow as to be impassable by lorries.

The country is thickly dotted with villages and farms, all of which have good fields of fire.

Beyond Riposto there is again a narrow, fairly heavily cultivated coastal plain to the bare hills at Taormina: beyond this the road runs for thirty-five miles to Messina, and throughout its distance it is dominated by precipitous hills rising to some two to three thousand feet above the sea. So steep are these hills that the road is in places cut into the side of the rock. There is little cultivation except in the numerous valleys, but the hills are in parts covered with trees and undergrowth.

The enemy took full advantage of this difficult country. All bridges on the main roads and many on the side roads were prepared for demolition, and he succeeded in blowing practically all the big ones and about fifty per cent. of the small ones. In the later stages the road where it was cut into the cliff was in several places blown away. The Division was faced with demolitions on a scale which it had never before encountered. Mines were freely laid on the roads, in the cultivation adjacent to the roads, in farms, and in particular around demolitions where diversions had to be made. These demolitions and mines caused great delays, often to the infantry and always to supporting arms and transport.

The work of the sappers became of paramount importance. They had heavy casualties and little rest, and were always in demand. Blown bridges were usually bypassed by diversions, bridges being constructed only at a later date. Bulldozers were essential. Field companies of the Royal Engineers, less mine-lifting detachments with the infantry, were always retained under command of the C.R.E., who allotted his resources to the roads where they were most needed.

The enemy held a succession of rearguard positions usually a day's march apart. His positions were probably not very strongly held, but his troops were well supplied with automatic weapons, which were skilfully deployed, well concealed, and always with alternative positions to which they could be moved under cover. His forward troops were supported by mortars and artillery. Concealment for the enemy was so easy that it was difficult to make a quick fire plan. The enemy defences were strongest adjacent to the better roads, and as movement across country was so difficult operations developed generally into road warfare. It was difficult for our forward troops to avoid being surprised, casualties were fairly heavy, and the daily task arduous. Between Mount Etna and the area through which the Division operated first the 5th Division and later the 51st Division advanced, but their axis of advance, along a main road on the higher slopes, was so far away that except on one occasion their action had little effect on the enemy facing the Division. It was difficult to follow up the enemy otherwise than by direct pursuit.

It is known that at one stage the instructions to the enemy rearguards were to hold their positions until pressed and then withdraw ten kilometres. Generally they stayed in a position for only one day, and retired again during the night, but on two occasions they stayed for two nights, withdrawing only their most advanced troops on the first night. On both these occasions an outflanking movement over the high ground on the left flank was carried out, but it was a slow process, and on the second occasion the battalion carrying out this task was supplied with mules to carry supporting weapons and food. Outflanking movements by sea were also considered, but generally the rocky coast was unsuitable for a landing and it was done on only one occasion. In addition to holding definite positions, the enemy generally opposed our advance during the day with light forces holding localities overlooking the main roads. Gun positions were difficult to find. The artillery was throughout kept centralized under the C.R.A. On no occasion did the enemy stay in one position long enough for any brigade to launch a deliberate attack, though such attacks were planned. The Divisional frontage was on an average one of about seven thousand yards.

On the 4th of August, the first day of the advance, progress was much hindered by minefields, craters, mortar and machine-gun fire; both brigades advanced some six thousand yards, and were held up by determined resistance about a thousand yards south of Catania. Three hundred and sixteen prisoners, mostly Italian, were captured that day.

That was the general picture, but of course it was not the picture as seen by the individual soldier, pressing forward with his rifle and bayonet in the heat and dust of that summer's day, wondering when and where he would hear the furious rattle of a Spandau, indicating that once more he was in contact with the enemy. An infantry platoon commander of the 69th Brigade gives that side of the story in the following words:

"Wednesday 4 August was our ninth consecutive day in the front line. It was also one of the worst days I have ever experienced. Soon after breakfast the battalion began to advance. 'B' Company was chosen to lead, and my platoon led the company. The first quarter of a mile or so was all right as it had previously been recced by strong patrols.

"We soon found ourselves advancing along a dusty road past evacuated enemy pillboxes, and on our left were troops of 5 Div, also advancing. We came to a level crossing, and a blow in the road held up our carriers for a time. With my leading section were sappers with mine detectors, and progress was slow on account of this.

"It was while we were near the level crossing that we first became aware that the enemy had not retreated very far: for over on our right, where the D.L.I. were advancing towards Catania, we heard the sinister whine of Nebelwerfers. We pushed on, more cautiously, and passed first one, then another of the pre-arranged report lines with their fishy code-names. I have a vivid memory of my batman's persevering voice on the 38 set repeating 'Baker Two Baker reporting Sprat—Baker Two Baker reporting Sprat.' Soon after 'Sprat,' however, we ran into trouble. As we threaded our way up a narrow lane Spandaus rattled at us from our right front, and a fusillade of air-burst shells came uncomfortably close. We grounded, and the company commander came up and tried a series of plans which were bound to fail because the country was so close that we never really pinpointed the enemy.

"The first plan was for 12 platoon and my own to do a left flanking attack. We went a little further up the lane but as we turned right to cross the valley an enemy tank opened up on us at point-blank range from further up the valley. With my platoon H.Q. and two sections I scampered on into the valley, where we were temporarily safe in a defiladed position. My third section was nowhere to be seen. Meanwhile, 12 platoon had pushed on, but as they topped the rise they ran into heavy machine-gun fire and had some casualties. It was obvious that with our depleted strength we could not hope to make more progress. The enemy's clever mutually supporting positions made it impossible for us to attack one post without running into heavy fire from the others.

"Having learnt some valuable information about the enemy's whereabouts and strength we decided to return to the company commander so that we could regroup and a fresh plan could be made. I was reluctant to turn back without my lost section, but the problem was solved immediately, for the section commander and his section rejoined us. Having been caught on the open hillside in full view of the tank, he and his section had gone to ground and remained perfectly still for some minutes until they got a chance to move.

"On meeting the company commander again we found that 10 platoon had forced the enemy out of one position but had then been held up in the same way as us. They too had had some casualties. While the company commander was planning a fresh approach, we occupied a rough defensive box. The enemy was still mortaring, and the air-burst shells were still coming over.

"The next plan was for my platoon to try a right flanking movement, and to do this meant getting into the next valley. I led my platoon round the spur to our rear, but as we entered the next valley we found ourselves in the unenviable position of being in the middle of a fire fight. Spandaus from up the valley were firing on to a hilltop, and from the hilltop came the answering bursts of Brens. We scuttled to safety, and it was obvious that we could not continue our plan until I had identified the troops firing the Brens and told them of our intention.

"I then did a rather silly thing. If I had had the patience I ought to have taken a roundabout route towards the Brens, but I felt that enough time had already been wasted: so, leaving the platoon under the platoon sergeant, I ran directly up the hill in full view of the Spandaus. They soon saw me and began firing, the bullets spitting all round my heels. As I neared the top of the hill frantic voices shouted 'Hurry up, sir.' I tumbled into a ditch occupied by our own troops just as a fierce burst of Spandau fire skimmed the top. When I had got my breath I learnt that the troops were Green Howards who had been ordered to advance up the same valley as myself, but who had been held up. 'He's got this place taped, sir,' they said.

"There was nothing to do except report back to the company commander, so I braved myself for a chancy descent the way I had come. I started slowly, but by dint of using all available cover, and dashing from tree to tree I made my way back without being spotted. The company commander was with my platoon, and agreed on the impossibility of the plan, but he asked me to go again to try and see the Green Howards company commander and find out what he was going to do. This time, taking one man with me, I chose a safer, defiladed route, and eventually found their company H.Q. The Green Howards company commander told me that he thought a further advance was impossible, and that he was going to stay where he was, pending further orders.

"When I eventually got this information back to my own company H.Q., I found that yet another attempt to dislodge the enemy had been made, but it was still unsuccessful. More serious casualties had occurred within the company. By this time it was dusk, and it was decided to rest and lick our wounds."

The enemy withdrew again during the night of the 4th/5th of August, and by about 0830 hrs. the 6th Durham Light Infantry were in Catania. The Mayor surrendered the town unconditionally at 0915 hrs. It was much damaged, many main roads were blocked by craters or fallen houses, and the comparatively few remaining inhabitants were very hungry and fought amongst themselves for packets of Army biscuits. Some hundreds were living in conditions of indescribable squalor in catacombs.

The day's advance was again of about six thousand yards, ending up some one thousand yards north of the outskirts of Catania.

On the morning of the 6th of August the enemy was still in the same position. He was found to be holding a ridge of high ground which formed an exceptionally strong position, and his resistance was determined. During the day, however, the 1st London Irish worked round the enemy's right flank, and in the evening a plan was made for them to attack early the next morning supported by the whole of the Divisional artillery. When daylight came, however, the enemy was found to have gone, and the supporting fire was not put down.

On the 7th of August the 151st Brigade on the right were able to advance some seven thousand yards without much opposition, and they finished the day about a mile short of Acireale. On the left the 168th Brigade were operating in more difficult country and were held up after an advance of four thousand yards.

The enemy withdrew only a short distance on the night of the 7th/8th of August, and early in the day the 151st Brigade were held up in the streets of Acireale, whilst the 168th Brigade, still echeloned back behind the 151st Brigade, advanced some four thousand yards and were in touch with the enemy at Acis Antonio. The enemy slipped away completely during the night. On this day No. 40 Royal Marine Commando was placed under the command of the Division, and was available to land from the sea behind the enemy's lines when opportunity offered.

A longer advance of some nine thousand yards was made during the 9th of August, and by the evening both brigades were in touch with the enemy on the Mangano River.

The enemy withdrew again during the night, but the move forward on the 10th was more than usually delayed by demolitions and enemy resistance. The bridges over the two rivers, the Mangano and Leonardello, north of Mangano, had all been blown; the river beds, though dry, had steep sides, and deviations were difficult to make. It was known that the enemy's next stand would be on the line of the River Macchia north of Riposto and Giarre, and there was some evidence that he might attempt to stay some days. The Royal Marine Commando had been warned that it might be required to land on some good beaches about two miles north of Riposto and seize the village on the main road immediately east of Mascali, with a view to cutting off the enemy's retreat, and holding the village until the 69th Brigade, who would attack through the 151st Brigade, joined up with them. The day's advance was, however, only of some three thousand yards, no viewpoint of the country around Riposto was secured, and the proposed operation was postponed for twenty-four hours.

The enemy withdrew during the night to his Riposto position. At about midday on the 11th General Kirkman was able to see the ground over which the infantry would have to attack in order to join up with the Commando, and because it was so unfavourable from our point of view he decided that the Commando would not be used, and instead a plan was made to force the enemy to retire by working forward along the high ground between the left of the 168th Brigade and the right of the 51st Division (who were to relieve the 5th Division), where it was believed the enemy was very weak. An advance there would in due course overlook the enemy machine guns farther down the hill, which were holding us up.

Since there were no roads fit for M.T., measures were taken to obtain mules so that the 168th Brigade could continue and maintain its advance. The country over which the advance would take place was rugged and in places precipitous, but there were ravines which gave covered lines of advance. Generally speaking, any ground selected for an advance would be overlooked by the higher slopes of Etna on the left flank, where the 51st Division were to operate. The advance was likely to take the form of company battles, and in the evening when the Divisional Commander gave the 168th Brigade their orders they were informed that any company could have the support of the whole Divisional artillery. This was, incidentally, the first day during this phase when good observation posts were available.

In the afternoon both Giarre and Riposto were occupied, but observation posts directing enemy shell fire made movement difficult for the 151st Brigade on the northern outskirts of the two towns. The 168th Brigade established one company in Macchia and two companies on Mascarello Ridge.

At daylight on the 12th the enemy was still in position; this was the second and last occasion in which he stayed for more than one night. The 151st Brigade were relieved by the 69th Brigade. A company of the London Scottish who were holding Macchia had an unpleasant night and day. The enemy's resistance here was most determined, and mortaring by both sides was fairly continuous. The advance of the Royal Berkshire Regiment in the hills continued slowly with practically no opposition until evening, when there was an exchange of machine-gun fire.

P

During the day the 231st Brigade (the Malta Brigade) had been placed under command of the Division, and the Division itself was to come under command of the XXX Corps, commanded by Lieutenant-General Sir Oliver Leese, at 0600 hrs. the next day. The Divisional Commander had been told that the 168th Brigade was, at the end of the operations, to return to the 56th (London) Division, and that in its place the 231st Brigade would become an integral part of the Division. The Brigade had served throughout the siege of Malta and had come over to Egypt at about the same time as the Division had reached there from Tunisia. It had landed in Sicily as an independent brigade group under the XXX Corps, and had fought with that Corps during the campaign.

Either according to plan or because of the threat from the 10th Royal Berkshire Regiment on the high ground, the enemy withdrew during the night, and from then onwards the enemy's withdrawal was much more rapid, though owing to the action of our own troops he was more than once pressed for time in carrying out his demolitions.

During the night of the 13th/14th of August the 231st Brigade occupied Piedimonte and patrolled towards Linguaglossa, and the 69th Brigade continued to advance out of contact with the enemy, though delayed again by mines and demolitions. By the evening leading troops had occupied Taormina without opposition. The enemy had made no effort to defend the formidable line of hills which here block all further advance by wheels or tracks except along the narrow coastal strip some few hundred yards in width. Just beyond the fork where the road to Taormina ascends the hills, the road is cut into the side of the cliff, and this part of the road had previously been blown away by shell fire from the Royal Navy. The enemy had made a deviation through the railway tunnel, the rails having been removed, but on leaving he had blown in the tunnel. The tunnel was beyond immediate repair, and it was estimated that it would take a week to bridge the gap in the road.

On the 15th of August the advance along the Messina road was continued by the 7th Green Howards, who walked down a mule track from Taormina to the main road beyond the blown-in railway tunnel. A few landing craft had been brought up to Giardini Bay, just south of Taormina, and essential transport was ferried from a landing place at Cape Schiso, the southern point of the bay, and from now on maintenance had to be by sea from Riposto or Cape Schiso.

At 1530 hrs. the leading company of the 7th Green Howards was approaching Cape San Alessio, north of Taormina. In this area the road is overlooked from the west and north-west by a high, rocky feature on which were several pillboxes. At Cape San Allessio itself, a strongly built medieval castle, which had been turned into a strongpoint, overlooks the road. As the leading troops approached the castle they came under close-range fire from Spandaus and mortars. The enemy fire increased in intensity during the next three hours, causing several casualties. During this time the enemy had worked forward on the high ground on the left flank of the battalion and were in position to snipe the road for some distance in rear of the forward troops. It was difficult for our artillery to support our forward troops, as the latter were very close to the steeply rising ground on which the enemy had his positions.

By 1900 hrs. the battalion was disposed in depth astride the main road, but further advance was not possible. At 1930 hrs. the enemy launched a counter-attack down the main road and part of one forward company was overrun. A company on the left flank was withdrawn to avoid being isolated. During the next hour the road was heavily machine-gunned and shelled, but there were few casualties. The enemy did not attempt to follow up his initial success. Soon after 2100 hrs. the enemy's fire stopped, and several explosions were heard, which were later found to be the blowing of demolitions on the road. The enemy's counter-attack would seem to have been designed to gain time for the completion of these demolitions.

It had been decided by the XXX Corps that an independent force should be landed on the night of the 15th/16th in the rear of the enemy in the Cape d'Ali area, the most northerly point at which the Royal Navy considered it safe to land in view of the coastal-defence guns on the mainland of Italy.

The composition of the force was:

No. 2 Commando.
One squadron, 3rd County of London Yeomanry (tanks).
One troop, 56th Field Battery, R.A. (105-mm. self-propelled).
One troop of 6-pounders.
One troop of 3.7 howitzers.
295th Field Company, R.E., less one platoon.

This force was to be under the command of the 4th Armoured Brigade, initially under command of the XXX Corps. The 50th Division had therefore no responsibility for the force at this stage.

At approximately 0320 hrs. the road at Cape d'Ali, the objective of the expedition, was blown by the enemy. Once ashore, our troops found that demolitions made it impossible to move south to join up with the 69th Brigade, so an attempt was made to advance on Messina, but the road was overlooked and any big-scale movement at once brought down accurate shell fire. A small party was ordered to infiltrate forward to try to save two bridges ahead which were intact, but as our troops approached the first bridge it was blown. It was considered that further forward movement was impracticable by daylight.

It was decided to reinforce the 4th Armoured Brigade expedition during the night of the 16th/17th of August with a force from the Division consisting of:

> 5th East Yorkshire Regiment with pack-mule transport.
> R.A. reconnaissance party.
> Two medium guns.
> One troop of self-propelled guns.
> One troop of light anti-aircraft.
> Remainder of field company.
> Beach brick detachment from "B" Company, 2nd Devonshire Regiment.
> Eight lorries.

As soon as this force landed it was to come under the command of the Brigadier, 4th Armoured Brigade, who at the same time would come under the command of the Division. The 5th East Yorkshire Regiment were to be organized so that they could, if necessary, take to the hills and continue the advance by an indifferent mountain road which joins the Messina—Palermo road about three miles west of Messina, but entire discretion as to how Messina should be captured was left to the commanding officer, Lieutenant-Colonel James, and Brigadier Curry, when the former should have got in touch with him. By last light the leading troops of the 6th Green Howards, delayed as usual by mines and demolitions, were still some five miles short of the rear of the 4th Armoured Brigade at Cape d'Ali.

At 2100 hrs. on the 16th the leading troops of the 4th Armoured Brigade party began to advance. They were subjected to shell and mortar fire until 0430 hrs. and, as it was apparent that the advance was still being opposed, the leading troops, who were marching, were held back so that they should not get too far ahead of their supporting weapons, which were delayed by demolitions. The 5th East Yorkshire Regiment landed before dawn. There was some confusion at sea, as, unknown to the Brigadier of the 4th Armoured Brigade, his maintenance party and the 5th East Yorkshire Regiment had sailed in two separate convoys. The brigadier, in touch with the maintenance party by wireless-telephony, tried to guide them in by wireless-telephony and lights. But, though talking to the maintenance party, he was looking at the four L.C.Ts. which carried the 5th East Yorkshire Regiment party, who were in approximately the right

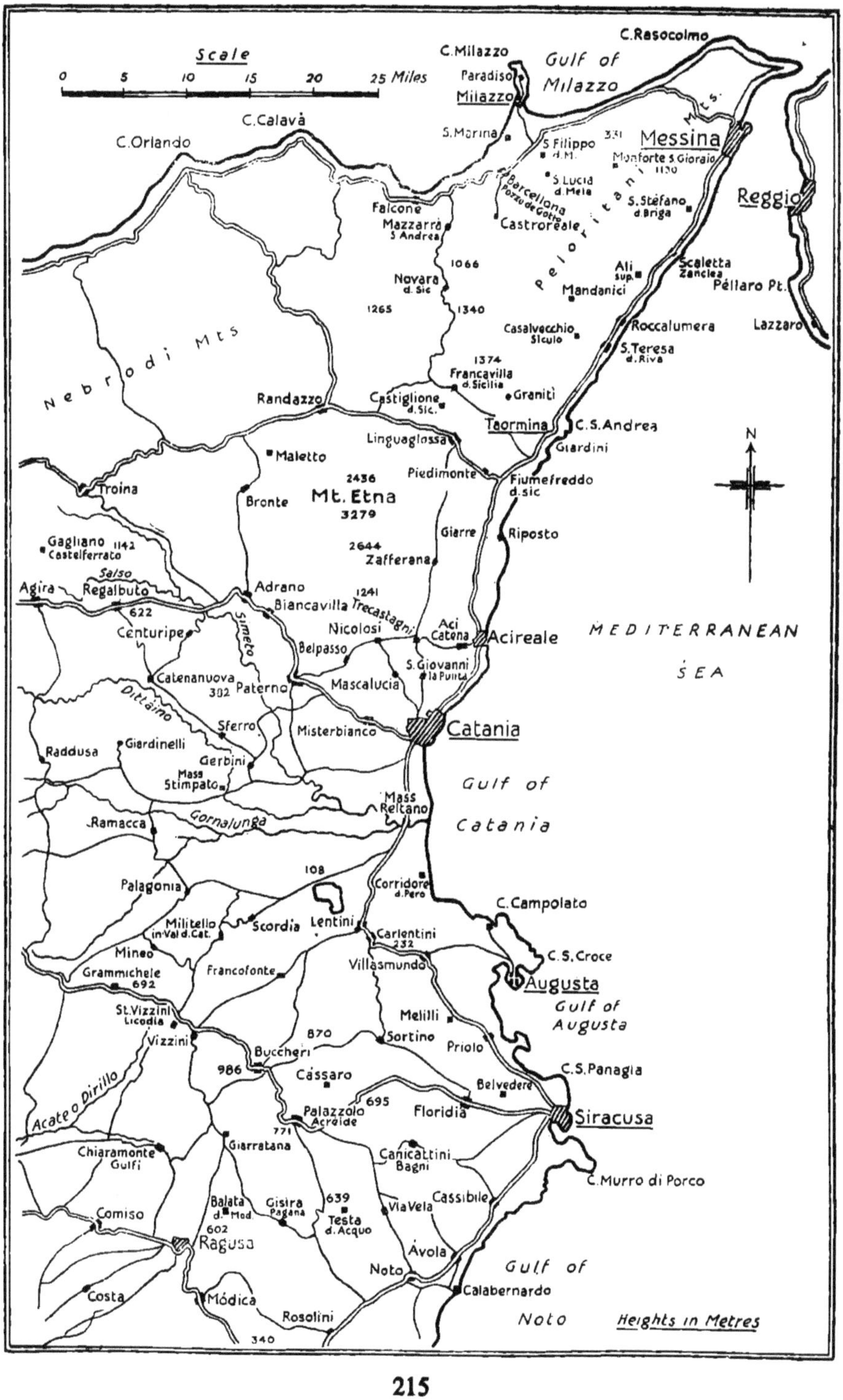

Scale
0 5 10 15 20 25 Miles
C.Rasocolmo
C.Milazzo
Gulf of Milazzo
Paradiso
Milazzo
C.Calavà
C.Orlando
S.Marina
S.Filippo d.M.
331
Messina
Monforte S.Giorgio
1130
S.Lucia d.Mela
Barcellona Pozzo de Gotto
S.Stéfano d.Briga
Reggio
Peloritani Mts
Falcone
Mazzarrà S.Andrea
Castroreale
1066
Alì sup.
Scaletta Zanclea
Novara d. Sic
Mandanici
Péllaro Pt.
1265
1340
Casalvecchio Siculo
Roccalumera
Lazzaro
Nebrodi Mts
1374
Francavilla d.Sicilia
S.Teresa d.Riva
Randazzo
Castiglione d.Sic.
Graniti
Taormina
C.S.Andrea
Linguaglossa
Giardini
N
Maletto
Piedimonte
Fiumefreddo d.sic
Troina
2456
Bronte
Mt. Etna
3279
Gagliano Castelferrato
1142
Giarre
Riposto
2644
Zafferana
Salso
Agira
Regalbuto
Adrano
1241
Biancavilla
Trecastagni
622
Simeto
Aci Catena
Acireale
MEDITERRANEAN SEA
Centuripe
Nicolosi
Belpasso
S.Giovanni la Punta
Catenanuova
302
Paterno
Mascalucia
Dittaino
Sferro
Misterbianco
Catania
Raddusa
Giardinelli
Gerbini
Mass Stimpato
Gulf of Catania
Mass Reitano
Ramacca
Gornalunga
108
Palagonia
Corridore d.Pero
C.Campolato
Militello in Val d.Cat.
Scordia
Lentini
Carlentini
232
Mineo
C.S.Croce
Grammichele
692
Francofonte
Villasmundo
Augusta
Gulf of Augusta
St.Vizzini Licodia
Melilli
Vizzini
870
Sortino
Priolo
Buccheri
986
C.S.Panagia
Cassaro
Belvedere
Acate o Dirillo
695
Palazzolo Acreide
Floridia
Siracusa
771
Giarratana
Chiaramonte Gulfi
Canicattini Bagni
C.Murro di Porco
Balata d. Mod.
Gisira Pagana
639
Via Vela
Cassibile
Comiso
602
Testa d. Acqua
Ragusa
Avola
Noto
Gulf of Noto
Calabernardo
Costa
Módica
Rosolini
340
Heights in Metres

place. The two L.C.Ts. of the maintenance party were too far north and before the mistake was realized they had been fired at unsuccessfully, probably by the enemy, and certainly by the Royal Navy.

As soon as it was light, and mines on the road could be seen, the leading troops were put into M.T. and the advance speeded up. At 1000 hrs. on the 17th of August our leading troops entered Messina. The enemy had gone. At the far end of the town touch was established with American patrols, who claimed to have entered the town at 2000 hrs. the previous evening.

CHAPTER XVII

Out of Action—The Balance Sheet—Homeward Bound

AUGUST TO NOVEMBER, 1943

With the occupation of Messina the Sicilian campaign was over. The Division was the only one in the Eighth Army which had been continuously in action from the initial landing to the end. During the fighting all types of operation had been experienced: the landing on a hostile shore, the rapid advance against ill-organized resistance, the deliberate attack, the active defence, and the pursuit of enemy rearguards in very difficult country.

Generally speaking, except in very minor tactics, troops who had experienced two years of desert warfare and had had little time for specialized training other than for the assault landing, did not find themselves forced to adopt any unexpected technique in a close and mountainous country. The lessons learned during the previous year since the Battle of El Alamein stood all ranks in good stead. The total casualties due to enemy action were four hundred and sixty-two killed, one thousand one hundred and thirty-two wounded and five hundred and forty-five missing. The killed included one hundred and twenty-five lost at sea. Amongst those killed in battle was Lieutenant-Colonel A. B. S. Clarke, D.S.O., commanding officer of the 9th Durham Light Infantry, killed on the 23rd of July. Sickness due to malaria claimed four hundred and thirty, and other causes one thousand seven hundred and eighty. The total number of prisoners who passed through the Divisional cages was four hundred and fifty-three Germans, including ten officers, and eight thousand three hundred and ninety-two Italians.

In the description of the fighting which has been given it is perhaps inevitable that most prominence should have been given to the control of the operations by senior commanders and to the achievements of the infantry.

It must not, however, be forgotten that the other troops played their part with distinction. In the majority of the actions rifle companies were ably supported by machine-gun detachments from the 2nd Cheshire Regiment. The infantry were the first to pay tribute to the excellence of the support given to them by the field artillery, and during the early part of the campaign good work was carried out by the 102nd Anti-Tank Regiment (Northumberland Hussars) and the 25th Light Anti-Aircraft Regiment. In the final pursuit phase the sappers for the first time encountered the regular succession of mines and demolitions which were later to become such a well-known feature of the fighting in Italy and elsewhere in Europe. Without their help the Division would have failed to advance. Throughout the period Signals operated with efficiency. The administrative difficulties of the first few days have already been mentioned. They were considerable and threw a big strain on the services, but at no time was there any form of administrative breakdown. The medical arrangements left nothing to be desired. On the 19th of August the Divisional Commander received the following letter from the Army Commander:

> "MY DEAR KIRKMAN,
> "Now that the campaign in Sicily is over I would like to tell you how well I consider you and your Division have done.
> "One somehow never imagines that 50 Div can do otherwise than well, and in this short campaign it has lived up to its best traditions. The Division has been in the forefront of the battle for the whole 39 days of the campaign, and has had no rest. Please tell all your officers and men how pleased I am with what they have done.
> "Yours sincerely,
> "B. L. MONTGOMERY."

Another tribute came from the pen of the Special Correspondent of *The Times Weekly Edition*. He wrote:

> ". . . But I always had the feeling that the sheet anchor of the army was the veteran 50th Division. They had the hard, dirty work at Lentini and Primosole, and the long slog up-coast from Cantania, past Etna. . . . They got less public mention than some other divisions because theirs was the unspectacular flank of the front. They plugged on, learning the new warfare the hard way, taking their punishment and coming on for more. Tyne and Tees may well be proud of them, for they are a grand division."

As soon as active operations were over the Division concentrated in the most comfortable areas that could be found between Cape d'Ali, about half-way between Messina and Taormina, and Riposto. The 231st Brigade was temporarily removed from the Division to take part in the assault on the Italian mainland. Lieutenant-Colonel Innes was posted to the Staff College, Camberley, as an instructor, being replaced as G.S.O.1 of the Division by Lieutenant-Colonel D. G. Jebb, D.S.O., from commanding the 7th Green Howards. As many units as possible were located near the coast so that they could enjoy to the greatest possible extent the excellent sea bathing. On the 26th of August Divisional Headquarters moved into the San Dominico Hotel, Taormina. This hotel had previously been used as a German headquarters; one wing had been destroyed by bombing, but the remainder was in quite good condition and well furnished.

On the 30th of August the Army Commander toured the Divisional area and saw most units except the gunners, who were away with the XIII Corps to support the assault of the 5th Division and the 1st Canadian Division against the Italian mainland. At one time it had been the intention to employ the Division on this task, but the plan had been changed and the only part taken was in the artillery support, and in controlling the very considerable traffic along the coastal road, through the Divisional area, to the "hards" in and around Messina. The assault was launched at 0430 hrs. on the 3rd of September. It was practically unopposed and made rapid progress.

On the 10th, 11th and 13th of September the Divisional Commander addressed some three thousand officers and men each day in the ancient Greek amphitheatre at Taormina, giving them an outline of the Sicilian campaign, using a large model which had been built just in front of the ancient stage. A peculiarity of this open theatre is its remarkable acoustic qualities, which enable the human voice to be heard from the stage all over the auditorium, which could have accommodated over six thousand people.

On the 14th of September a wire was received from the Army Commander ordering the Divisional Commander and a small tactical headquarters to proceed at once to Italy. Leaving by car in the morning, Major-General Kirkman and Lieutenant-Colonel Jebb, followed later by more of the staff, crossed over from Messina to Reggio and reported to the Army Commander in the evening. The Divisional Commander was ordered temporarily to take control of the 31st Italian Corps, which had recently surrendered. To carry out this task Divisional Tactical Headquarters was established the next day in a pleasant villa at Catanazaro, but this interlude was not to be for long, for on the 19th of September a signal was received that the Division was to return to England, sailing from Sicily on the 25th of September.

The headquarters therefore handed over to a British mission on the 20th of September and returned to Taormina on the 21st, only to be greeted on arrival with the news that the move home had been postponed. The 231st Brigade rejoined the Division on the 24th of September, going into billets in Augusta.

There followed a period of idleness. Nearly all equipment had been handed in, yet the date of sailing was continually postponed. The weather began to get cooler, though bathing was still enjoyable, provided that the sun was shining. Rain became more frequent. At the end of September Brigadier (later Major-General) Urquhart was relieved in command of the 231st Brigade by Brigadier (later Major-General) Ward, but he in turn was shortly relieved by Brigadier Tarlton, from the 5th Division. The 168th Brigade and 140th Field Field Ambulance left the Division early in October, and rejoined the 56th (London) Division in Italy.

On the 17th of October the Divisional Commander unveiled a tablet in the English Church at Taormina to the memory of those who had lost their lives in Sicily. It read:

> "To the glory of God and in memory of those officers and men of the 50th (Northumbrian) Division who gave their lives for their country in the Sicilian Campaign, July and August, 1943. This Tablet is placed in this Church by their comrades, many of whom worshipped here."

Another memorial had been erected to the memory of officers and men of the 151st Brigade who lost their lives in the fighting round the Primosole bridge. It stands at the side of the Catania road, just north of the sunken lane. The tablet on a grey stone cairn bears the following inscription:

> "This memorial has been erected to keep fresh the memory of the soldiers of 151 Durham Infantry Brigade who gave their lives for their country and the cause of freedom during the Sicilian campaign, 10 July—17 August, 1943. It was placed here because it was during the action round the Ponte Primosole, 14 —17 July, 1943, that the Brigade experienced the fiercest fighting in which it took part during the campaign.
>
> "H.Q., 151 Durham Infantry Brigade.
> "151 Durham Brigade Support Company.
> "6th Bn. The Durham Light Infantry.
> "8th Bn. The Durham Light Infantry.
> "9th Bn. The Durham Light Infantry.
>   " 'We will remember them.' "

By the middle of October it was clear that the Division really was to leave. Units gradually moved down to Augusta, and the last vehicles were handed in. Most of the moves were by railway, now repaired and working again as far north as Riposto. Embarkation was more or less completed by the 20th, and the convoy sailed at midday on the 23rd of October. During the afternoon Avola and the Lido d'Avola, where the Division had landed three and a half months before, could clearly be seen. The convoy anchored off Algiers on the 25th, sailing again on the afternoon of the 27th. No leave ashore was allowed. The voyage home was uneventful. Occasionally the escorting destroyers dropped depth charges, but there was no evidence whether or not enemy submarines were definitely identified. North of Ireland the convoy split up, ships going to Glasgow, Liverpool and Bristol, where they arrived on the 5th November, 1943.

APPENDIX TO PART FOUR

ORDER OF BATTLE, 50TH DIVISION
July, 1943

DIVISIONAL HEADQUARTERS

G.O.C.	Major-General S. C. Kirkman, C.B.E., M.C.
G.S.O.1	Lieutenant-Colonel R. G. B. Innes, Seaforth.
A.A. and Q.M.G.	Lieutenant-Colonel R. H. Batten, Hampshire Regt.
C.R.A.S.C.	Lieutenant-Colonel G. W. Fenton, M.B.E.
A.D.M.S.	Colonel J. Melvin, O.B.E., M.C.
A.D.O.S.	Lieutenant-Colonel R. C. Gibb.
C.R.E.M.E.	Lieutenant-Colonel G. D. Pollock, M.B.E., 2nd N.Z.E.F.

R.A.

C.R.A.	Brigadier C. H. Norton, D.S.O., O.B.E.
74th Fd. Regt.	Lieutenant-Colonel G. Marnham.
90th Fd. Regt.	Lieutenant-Colonel I. G. G. S. Hardie.
124th Fd. Regt.	Lieutenant-Colonel C. F. Tod.
102nd A./Tank Regt. (N.H.)	Lieutenant-Colonel A. K. Matthews.
25th L.A.A. Regt.	Lieutenant-Colonel G. G. O. Lyons, M.B.E.

R.E.

C.R.E.	Lieutenant-Colonel E. N. Bickford.

SIGNALS

O.C. Div. Sigs.	Lieutenant-Colonel G. B. Stevenson.

69TH INFANTRY BRIGADE

Commander	Brigadier E. C. Cooke-Collis, D.S.O.
5th E. Yorks	Lieutenant-Colonel R. B. James, D.S.O.
6th Green Howards	Lieut.-Colonel D. J. M. Smith (wounded 13th July, 1943).
7th Green Howards	Lieut.-Colonel D. G. Jebb, D.S.O.

151ST INFANTRY BRIGADE

Commander	Brigadier R. H. Senior, D.S.O., T.D.
6th D.L.I.	Lieutenant-Colonel W. I. Watson.
8th D.L.I.	Lieutenant-Colonel R. B. Lidwell, D.S.O.
9th D.L.I.	Lieutenant-Colonel A. B. S. Clarke, D.S.O. (killed 23rd July, 1943).

168TH INFANTRY BRIGADE

Commander	Brigadier K. C. Davidson, M.C.
10th R. Berks	Lieutenant-Colonel I. R. Baird, M.C.
1st London Scottish	Lieutenant-Colonel H. J. Wilson, O.B.E.
1st London Irish Rifles	Lieutenant-Colonel I. H. Good.

M.G. BATTALION

2nd Cheshire .. Lieutenant-Colonel S. V. Keeling, D.S.O.

ATTACHED

44th R. Tanks	Lieutenant-Colonel E. D. Rash (missing 16th July, 1943).
"A" Sqdn., Royals	
98th Army Fd. Regt., R.A.	Lieutenant-Colonel Hon. C. G. Cubitt, D.S.O.
No. 34 Brick	Colonel J. T. Gibson.

PART FIVE

CHAPTER XVIII

A QUIET HOMECOMING—50TH DIVISION CAST FOR A LEADING ROLE IN THE INVASION OF NORMANDY—A BUSTLE OF TRAINING—PLANNING IN LONDON—THE ENEMY'S DEFENSIVE LAYOUT—ALLIED MILITARY, NAVAL AND AIR PLANS, AND THE 50TH DIVISION'S PART IN THEM—COMPOSITION OF THE DIVISION FOR THE ASSAULT

NOVEMBER, 1943, TO JUNE, 1944

THE ships carrying Divisional Headquarters and the 69th Brigade sailed into the Mersey Estuary in the early morning of the 5th of November and were guided by tugs to their berths in Liverpool.

Mist hung over the river, and at intervals a thin, penetrating rain brought a glisten to the rooftops of the city. As the ships tied up, U.S. military police in spotless white gaiters and helmets patrolled the otherwise deserted docks, and a hidden loud-speaker blared stirring music to welcome home the soldiers. But in general it was a peculiar homecoming. The silent docks and, beyond them, the hum and clang of traffic and trams in the city bespoke a public indifference to the event—which was hardly surprising in view of the stringent security "black-out" on the movement of the Division.

Still, it felt strange. This was the moment the 50th Division had imagined times without number in the burning desert, in the oilfields of Iraq, in Sicily, Cyprus and half a dozen other countries during nearly three years—the moment of arrival in England. And now it had come with rain and mist, with no applause and no relatives, with a battered, busy city spread around us, and American police at the gangways. It was a forcible reminder that the Empire and her Allies were still at war, and that stern tasks still lay ahead of the Division

But the soldiers crowded the bulwarks in their hundreds in high spirits, while the embarkation officers went on board the ships to make arrangements about trains and feeding.

It was for many a moment for a private stock-taking of much that had passed during the years abroad. There was food for thought in the fact that from a dock only three hundred yards from where the returned ships now lay the first brigade of the Division to leave England in 1941 had been borne forth on to the Atlantic. That brigade did not return with us. Its soldiers had either fallen at Gazala or were taken prisoner there.

In less wholesale ways the composition of the Division had gradually changed under the stresses and strains of the Middle Eastern campaigns; and many other good comrades who had sailed down the great river in 1941 had not sailed up it on this misty and memorable morning.

During the next thirty-six hours the troops began to leave the ships *en route* for the special trains which carried them to their new stations in East Anglia. Divisional Headquarters was established at Chadacre Park, near Bury St. Edmunds, the 69th Brigade were in the area of Thetford, the 151st Brigade north-east of Sudbury, and the 231st Brigade south of that area. The remainder of the Division was in that same general area. Within a matter of days the whole Division was at home on disembarkation leave, and the wheels were being kept turning by a skeleton staff provided by the home authorities for that purpose, whose reception and quartering of the returning troops had been admirable.

With the New Year came radical changes. Major-General Kirkman, who had commanded the Division from the closing stages of the North African campaign, was appointed Commander of the XIII Corps and left hurriedly for the Italian front. On the 19th of January, after his departure, Major-General Graham arrived at Divisional Headquarters to take over command. Brigadier E. C. Cooke-Collis, who had commanded the 69th Brigade from the days of the retreat from Gazala, was transferred to command a brigade of the 49th Division, which was at that time earmarked as an assault division for the invasion of the Continent.

The prospect then was that the 50th Division would take part in the assault on the Continent, but that it would not once more be in the first rank; it was to form part of the follow-up force. It was not long, however, before the Division was warned that plans had been changed; that one of the assaulting corps would be the XXX (the old desert corps which had followed the Division home from the Mediterranean), and that in that corps the 50th Division would be the spearhead. This was a compliment to the fighting qualities of the Division in the past two years, but it occasioned no general rejoicing. Experience enabled officers and men to appreciate all it meant, and it was, in general, with a sober and dogged determination that all faced up to what lay ahead.

The tempo of life changed at once. The decision meant a complete and speedy alteration in training and the commencement at once of planning on a divisional level, to be followed by brigade planning in the few months remaining. With regard to the specialized training necessary for an assaulting division, two factors had to be considered. First, the Division had already made a seaborne assault—the invasion of Sicily in July, 1943. For the 231st Brigade it would be their third assault. But since that campaign the Division had undergone very considerable changes, and only about half the officers and men who had taken part now remained. Second, the Division was in a most unsuitable part of the country for combined assault training, with this exception—that the 79th Armoured Division was close at hand at Saxmundham, and they had been studying mechanical means of overcoming the very strong natural and artificial obstacles which the Division would be up against. Each brigade had about fourteen days' training in co-operation with the assault vehicles and crews of the 79th Armoured Division, and then each assault brigade—the 69th and 231st—went for combined operational training at the Combined Training Centre at Inverary. After that brigades moved to the Weymouth—New Forest area, ready for collective training with the Navy and the R.A.F.

That part of the naval force which was to carry the 50th Division across the Channel, protect them, and land them on the beaches of Normandy, was known as Force "G."

Force "G" did not start forming until March, and they had just as much difficulty in getting ready as we had, owing to the non-availability of craft and the lateness in starting the training of the crews. The collective training took place on the South Coast during April and May and consisted of four full-scale brigade exercises. These exercises, together with other exercises for bombarding ships and support craft, took place in Studland Bay and were of the utmost value in integrating the Navy and Army into one assault force. It was unfortunate that the R.A.F. contribution to these exercises was very limited owing to unsuitable flying conditions. The Studland Bay area gave a fair picture of the problem presented by the actual assault beaches. The final rehearsal for the operation took place on the 5th and 6th of May and involved all the British assault forces.

The majority of the exercises took place in fine weather and a calm sea, one exercise only being carried out in conditions approaching those which actually occurred on D Day. No major exercises were held after the 6th of May, as it was considered essential to have a period of final refit and overhaul of ships and craft before the operation. The Army also required a breathing space in order to complete such preparations as waterproofing of vehicles and other specialist tasks.

While all this training had been in progress, planning was going forward simultaneously, and this made heavy demands on both commanders and staffs. Within the Second Army all planning by all formations was done in blocks of flats alongside Westminster Cathedral in London. These flats formed the very nerve centre of the grand invasion project, where the two great secrets of the hour—*where* and *when*—were guarded with every precaution the minds of the security chiefs could devise. Not only that: the doings at the flats had to be kept secret from the public. It would be interesting now to know how many of London's citizens knew what went on, as month succeeded month, in the shadow of the tall cathedral.

All the experience gained in the planning of combined operations against Sicily and Italy was applied in that headquarters, and many of the old campaigners from the Eighth Army were astonished by the ease with which all the relevant information, air photographs, maps and all the rest of the paraphernalia of planning, could be obtained. So far as the 50th Division was concerned, all planning staffs were there down to brigades, with their opposite numbers in the Royal Navy.

To understand fully the magnitude and scope of Operation "Overlord"—the code name by which the invasion was known—the reader must become familiar with some of the facts and the problems which faced these planning staffs in the spring of 1944.

There was the problem of the enemy. How did he propose to defend the Bay of the Seine, the target of the Allied Armies? What troops had he on the beaches and in reserve? How strong were his defences, both natural and artificial? And to what extent would the beaches and the country generally prove to be his ally?

These were questions which demanded answers before our own plans became crystallized. So much had been written in the Press, both Allied and enemy, about the so-called Atlantic Wall along Europe's western coastline that many false impressions were abroad —one of the most notable and mistaken being that the entire coast had been girded with steel and concrete in the shelter of which German armies lived in a sort of Maginot underworld. This was, of course, an opinion expressed with great regularity and frequency in German propaganda. But when the lens of the stereoscope and intelligence reports gave the answer, it was different indeed from this conception.

The German coast defences in Northern France, and particularly in the "Overlord" area, were in the form of a thin crust; and behind them, at points varying from thirty to fifty miles inland, were stationed armoured reserves for counter-attack, backed by the more mobile type of infantry divisions. To defeat any invasion, the Germans relied on the Channel, the difficulties inherent in any combined operation, the blunting power of their coast defences, and a decisive counter-attack by their mobile armoured reserves.

No zones of defence in depth had been prepared, but all ports, even the minor ones like Port-en-Bessin, in the invasion area were strongly held. All good beaches in the area of the ports were defended not only by troops but by ingenious underwater obstacles, of which there was a great variety.

Elsewhere there was a chain of infantry strong-points extending inland to a depth of two or three hundred yards, with plenty of mortars and machine guns, but weakly backed by artillery; in the more inaccessible areas of the coast this chain was not continuous— as was the case in the area in which the 50th Division assaulted.

There the coastline was held by units of the 716th Infantry Division; like the remainder of the German coastal divisions in France, this formation was low category, and included foreigners captured by the Germans and pressed into the service of the Reich. They represented both limits of the military age groups. The 716th Division was static, and had practically no transport. It could therefore fight one battle, and one battle only—the battle of the beaches. And on these beaches it was, in fact, destroyed on the 6th of June, 1944, though its name lived on and was later given to a division which was forming in the South of France.

The 716th Division occupied a series of strong-points at tactically important points, such as villages on the coast, exits from the beaches and so on. The distance between these strong-points varied from five hundred yards upwards. They were usually about one platoon strong (*i.e.*, about forty men), though in small, fortified villages as much as a whole company was encountered. The normal platoon strong-point consisted of about six concrete pillboxes for machine guns, with the sides and roof four to six feet thick. Some pillboxes, however, were mere concrete emplacements with no roof. The defenders of such a strong-point lived within its perimeter either in dug-in huts or dug-outs reinforced with concrete. Mortars, heavy machine guns and anti-tank guns (sometimes non-German) were always sited within an infantry strong-point. Fire from all these weapons was so co-ordinated that any stretch of the coastline suitable for landing could be covered with cross-fire.

Between strong-points ran fences of barbed wire and minefields, to make infiltration as difficult and costly as possible; and, in the case of the Division's assault area, marshy land promised further hindrance.

The beaches themselves were a mass of ramps, stakes, tetrahedra and other obstacles, many of which had mines or shells attached to the top so arranged as to explode on contact. These were Field-Marshal Rommel's special contribution to the defences of the "Overlord" area. His well-advertised spring tour of the coastal defences of Northern France had a special effect on the defences of the "Overlord" area, which at that time were in a condition which (according to the French villagers) aroused his ire. But not all Rommel's anger, nor the flurry of activity which followed his departure in that historic spring, could prevent the penetration of those defences.

Such was to be the 716th Division's role in the defence.

Behind it was the 91st Infantry Division, in the general area of Carentan, and the 352nd Infantry Division, west and south-west of Bayeux. The armoured divisions capable of fairly rapid intervention were the 21st Panzer Division, in the area Caen—Falaise, the 12th S.S. Panzer Division, in the area of Bernay—Verneuil, the 130th Panzer Lehr Division, spread out in the area Le Mans—Laval—Chartres, the 17th S.S. Panzer Grenadier Division, south of the Loire, and the 2nd Panzer Division at Amiens.

In addition to these man-made arrangements for defence there were various natural barriers in our path. It was revealed not long before D Day that there were patches of clay and peat on the beach over which armoured vehicles could not pass—they would just sink in—and this meant last-minute experiments to find an antidote. Special shuttering on tracks was found to be the best answer. Special A.V.R.E. were fitted with this as well as all L.C.Ts. carrying tracked vehicles. This work was completed only a few hours before craft were loaded for the assault.

At both ends of our beach were strongly fortified villages, Le Hamel and Arromanches on the right, La Riviere on the left, with high and strong sea walls. In between, the beach was sandy with very low sand-dunes, and a low, broken-down sea wall, behind which ran a reasonably hard road the whole way. Immediately behind this road there was a wide bog except for a few hundred yards at either end before the villages. All the good exits were at the villages, but there were one or two quite reasonable ones between the villages and the bog. On the right cliffs extended the whole way to the right boundary. There were many trees and gardens in and around the villages. Behind the villages and the bog the ground rose quickly, and the Meuvaines Ridge was a dominating feature. This country was fairly open, with small woods here and there, but farther inland it became very close indeed, and by the time Bayeux was passed it was real bocage country.

The roads were better than had been expected and there were plenty of them. The rivers in the area were mostly low and no real obstacle.

So much for the enemy's plans and resources. Let us now consider our own.

The object of Operation "Overlord" was, in official terms:

"To secure a lodgement on the Continent of Europe from which further operations could be developed."

That sounds simple; behind the formal phrases lay the steadily unfolding plan, which must now be outlined in sufficient detail to show the 50th Division's place in it.

For months beforehand armies of the United States, accompanied by masses of war material, had been moving into England to take station alongside their British comrades. Of the huge force thus assembled and husbanded for this day, the First U.S. Army and the Second British Army were placed under the command of the 21st Army Group, Commander, General Sir B. L. Montgomery, who was with this force entrusted with the task of securing the "lodgement on the Continent."

The general intention was fourfold:

1. To carry out airborne landing during the night[1] D minus 1/D.
2. To assault on a five-divisional front with three British and two United States divisions in landing ships and craft in the Bay of the Seine early on D Day.
3. To land two follow-up divisions, one British and one United States, later on D Day and on D plus 1.
4. Thereafter to build up our force at the average rate of one and one-third divisions per day.

The object of the airborne landings was to protect the flanks of the area in which the first assault divisions were to land. The seaborne assault was carried out by two U.S. divisions on the right (First U.S. Army) and by the 50th, 3rd Canadian and 3rd British on the left (Second British Army). In addition to the landing ships and craft, the naval forces disposed in the Channel for D Day included battleships, cruisers, destroyers, support craft and escort vessels.

The air plan was evolved on the same massive scale. For months before the invasion the R.A.F. and U.S. air fleets had ranged the Continent on strategic bombing missions. As the event approached their tasks were multiplied; they had to provide air defence of the bases in the United Kingdom and protection of coastal convoys, and

---

[1] The day of the invasion was known as D Day, the hour at which craft touched down on the Normandy beaches as H Hour.

of shipping and troop concentrations in the assembly area; they had to protect and support the actual assault, and it was regarded as an essential prerequisite of the operation that the British and American fighter squadrons should attain and maintain an air situation which would ensure that the German Air Force could not interfere with the freedom of action of our sea and land forces.[1]

That, in outline, was the plan for the assault. How were the armies to be maintained once they got there? This, in many ways, presented more difficulties than the operation itself. The plan involved the capture of Cherbourg at an early stage, but this important port was to be used solely for the maintenance of the U.S. forces.

The British Army was to be maintained over the beaches, minor ports, such as Port-en-Bessin, and certain prefabricated ports and havens, the existence of which proved to be one of the best-kept secrets of the war. One prefabricated port (code word "Mulberry") was to be sited at Arromanches in the 50th Division's sector. It was towed over the Channel in sections—surely one of the strangest sights of this or any other generation. Five small havens, called "Gooseberries," were formed prior to the development of the ports, to provide sheltered water. To form them, some fifty Liberty ships were sunk off the coast to act as breakwaters. All this was a naval responsibility; so was the tremendous task of organizing the cross-Channel supply service which had to run at high pressure for months after the landing to bring new forces and maintain those already there. From the military point of view maintenance was effected through Army units known as beach groups (the direct descendants of the beach bricks of Sicily), who handled supplies and material as they came ashore.

Within the framework of this broad plan the 50th Division's task was to penetrate the beach defences between Le Hamel and La Riviere and secure a covering position which would include Bayeux, on the west, and the area of St. Leger, a hill on the main road from Bayeux to Caen, on the east. The 47th (Royal Marine) Commando

---

[1] The following table gives *approximate* figures of the air forces available:

Heavy day bombers	1,400
Heavy night bombers	1,150
Medium and light bombers	830
Day fighters	2,230
Fighter-bombers	560
Night fighters	170
	6,340

was to operate under the command of the Division to capture the small harbour of Port-en-Bessin. They were to land at Le Hamel at approximately H plus 2 hours, march west and assault the port from the south. The 231st Brigade (2nd Devonshire Regiment, 1st Hampshire Regiment and 1st Dorsetshire Regiment) were to assault over the beaches in the area of Le Hamel, and the 69th Brigade (5th East Yorkshire Regiment, 6th Green Howards and 7th Green Howards) were to attack La Riviere.

After capturing the beaches and the immediate hinterland the assault brigades were to carry out the second phase of the operation —the enlargement of the initial bridgeheads. The reserve brigades were to be prepared to land from H plus 2½ hours, on the orders of the Divisional Commander. If the assault of the 231st and 69th Brigades went according to plan, the 56th Infantry Brigade (2nd Gloucestershire Regiment, 2nd Essex Regiment and 2nd South Wales Borderers) was to follow up over the beaches captured by the 231st Brigade, and the 151st Brigade (6th, 8th and 9th Durham Light Infantry) was to land at La Riviere, captured by the 69th Brigade. The two reserve brigades were then to carry out, in conjunction with the 69th Brigade, the final phases of the assault—the capture of Bayeux and the dominating St. Leger feature.

A word should be said here about the composition of the Division for "Overlord."

When the Divisional Commander and his staff began to study the invasion problem early in February, it became apparent that the Division had not sufficient soldiers to make sure of success. A fourth infantry brigade was therefore asked for, and given: *i.e.*, the 56th Brigade. It consisted of three battalions drawn from two different divisions, and a completely new brigade headquarters. No battalion had been overseas, and when they came together at about the 20th of February none had done any training in combined operations. In the short time which remained to them before D Day, therefore, they had to train as a reserve brigade in an assault division, and also to work with the 7th Armoured Division (the follow-up division in the XXX Corps) in subsequent phases of the Corps plan.

In addition to the 56th Brigade, certain other major units and formations were incorporated in the Division for the assault. The principal ones were the 8th Armoured Brigade—an old ally with whom the Division had many times co-operated in the desert war— an American battalion of 155-mm. self-propelled guns, two British self-propelled field artillery regiments and a medium regiment, two self-propelled anti-tank batteries, and units and sub-units with mechanical aids to overcoming natural and artificial obstacles and defences.

Thus the force built around the 50th Division was formidable indeed.

By D Day its strength with all the supporting and administrative units was in the neighbourhood of thirty-eight thousand.

The order of battle and the names of commanders and staffs are given at Appendix I at the end of Part Five.

CHAPTER XIX

D DAY—FIRST GLIMPSES OF NORMANDY—THE BATTLES OF THE 69TH AND 231ST BRIGADES—SIX MILES INLAND—THE CAPTURE OF PORT-EN-BESSIN

JUNE, 1944

SPECIAL D-DAY MESSAGE FROM THE DIVISIONAL COMMANDER TO ALL RANKS OF THE 50th (NORTHUMBRIAN) DIVISION

The time is at hand to strike—to break through the Western Wall and into the Continent of Europe.

To you, officers and men of the 50th (Northumbrian) Division, has been given the great honour of being in the vanguard of this mighty blow for freedom.

It is my unshakable belief that we, together with Force "G" of the Royal Navy, the special regiments of the Royal Armoured Corps, the Royal Artillery and the Royal Engineers attached to us and with the help of the R.A.F. and American Air Force, will deliver such an overpowering punch that the enemy will be unable to recover. Thus shall we be well set to carry through to a glorious and successful end all that is now entrusted to us.

Much has been asked of you in the past and great have been your achievements, but this will be the greatest adventure of all. It will add yet another fine chapter to your already long and distinguished record—the grandest chapter of all.

Very best of luck to every one of you.

D. A. H. GRAHAM, *Major-General,*
Commander, 50th (Northumbrian) Division.

AT the beginning of June, Divisional Headquarters, which had moved from London and Chadacre to the New Forest area, was established on board its headquarter ship at Southampton Docks. Meantime, the various brigade groups had been assembled in separate camps and marshalled into craft loads—a very complicated operation which was performed extremely well by permanent staffs trained for the job.

The whole of the craft of Force "G," with a few exceptions, were loaded at Southampton, and by the evening of the 3rd of June the Division was afloat, part in the West Solent and part in vessels lying alongside at Southampton.

There was a last-minute visit to the troops in their ships by the Prime Minister, Mr. Winston Churchill, Field-Marshal Smuts and the Minister of Labour, Mr. Ernest Bevin—"Shall we get our jobs back when we return, Ernie?" shouted a Durham soldier—and then the stage was set.

There was a postponement due to bad weather; D Day was originally fixed for the 5th of June, but early on the 4th it was altered to the 6th of June. The infantry remained in their craft. Then, at 0730 hrs. on the 5th of June, the first part of the great seaborne force began to move out of the West Solent.

Through the night of the 5th/6th of June the great armada moved steadily across the Channel, led by trawlers sweeping mine-free passages for the ships behind.

Above the enemy coast the metropolitan bomber fleet opened its bomb doors, drenching the defences with high explosive. And the airborne forces were flying out towards the flanks of the target area.

The timing and co-ordination of this supreme effort were intricate. To the shaken defenders of the beaches soon to be assailed by the 50th Division it must have seemed that the R.A.F. was indulging in a mass bombing of the whole coastline, and that the Navy was off shore carrying out a bombardment of a like nature. But in fact the picture was very different. There was not a plane or a ship in the whole of those mighty fleets which had not its pin-point target and its time to the minute.

The assault was to take place in the first hours of daylight—0725 was H hour for the 50th Division—and therefore maximum use had to be made of every available naval, military and air weapon in an attempt to overwhelm the defenders, who would be firing at targets they could see.

Thus at appointed hours each enemy position underwent its ordeal by fire; the bombs of the R.A.F. would be followed a few minutes later by the shells of the Royal Navy; then, perhaps, another air attack; and finally the sudden flare-up from smaller weapons as the infantry division began to fight its way ashore. For example . . .

There was at the western end of the village of La Riviere a strongly defended position, well sited, including an 88-mm. gun, a 50-mm. gun and several machine guns. The 88-mm. was in an extremely heavily constructed casemate. It was so placed as to be invisible from the sea.

[British Official Photograph] [Crown Copyright Reserved]

"The infantry, the humble foot soldiers, now about to fulfil their classic role."
Troops storm ashore near La Riviere.

Face p. 239]

All this we knew before the assault began. On D Day this position was dealt with as follows:

From 0625 to 0700 hrs. it was shelled by four fleet destroyers.

From 0655 to 0710 hrs. four squadrons of heavy bombers dropped their loads on it.

From 0700 to 0725 hrs. three fleet destroyers maintained the attack.

From H minus 35 minutes it was the target for the incoming self-propelled guns of the 86th Field Regiment and rocket-firing assault craft.

Heralded, then, by this huge battering-ram from the air and the sea, the naval force carrying the 50th Division stole in towards the coast of Normandy.

Each man who sailed in the assault convoys will probably carry with him for all time a vivid memory of the first hours of Operation "Overlord." And each man's impression will probably be different from any other. But some memories will surely be common to all.

The night passage across the cold, wintry-like Channel, and the sea-sickness that made life miserable for some; and the curative effect of shell fire at the end of the journey.

The great concourse of shipping of all kinds that was revealed by the dawn. The first glimpse of the Normandy coast, low, sandy, backed by dunes, looking ordinary instead of dramatic and interesting, as befitting the coastline which had been studied for so long from maps and air photographs, and was now the target for the mighty seaborne force that seemed to fill the Channel.

The infantry, the humble foot soldiers, now about to fulfil their classic role as the spearhead of the operation, clambered into their assault craft from the bigger ships which had borne them over the Channel, and strained their eyes towards the hostile shore. Warships were firing steadily at targets still invisible to the infantry, and overhead the fighter squadrons spread their shield.

Many kinds of small craft were moving towards the shore. The infantry, in their comparatively tiny assault craft, bobbed and butted their way through the heavy seas. Bigger, rocket-firing craft flung salvoes of rockets at the defences. Landing craft carrying tanks moved steadily in, with the tank guns firing as they came. Self-propelled guns also fired from their craft.

There was a disappointment when it was realized that the famous but then secret DD tanks, which had been designed to leave their craft some distance off shore and swim their way to the beach just ahead of the infantry, could not be launched owing to the rough weather. A decision was then made to take the craft to the beach and allow the tanks to land in the ordinary way, which they did, providing valuable support to the infantry already landed.

Another disappointment was provided by the Centaur tanks, mounted in pairs in landing craft in such a way that they could fire during the run-in to the beach. Once through they were to provide close support for the battle of the beaches. Sixteen such craft should have reached Normandy, but on the 50th Division front only two, in fact, arrived, the rest being delayed or having to turn back half-way across the Channel owing to the weather.

But the assault went in on time. As always, there were places where the infantry penetrated the enemy defences without undue difficulty and without really heavy fighting; there were others where the assaulting troops soon found themselves locked in battle with determined defenders in well-constructed positions.

But the infantry of the 50th Division, well supported by armour, artillery and the machine guns of the 2nd Cheshire Regiment, did their job. And though some beach defences held out longer than was hoped, and here and there our troops had to fight hard to free the beaches from direct fire, their efforts were of such an order that the build-up of the force as a whole was not interfered with, and while the fighting went on in field and village successive waves of troops and vehicles and equipment were discharged over the beaches and sent to their appointed places in the expeditionary force that was rapidly coming to life on the soil of France.

The main heat and burden of the day was borne by the two assault brigades, the 231st on the right and the 69th on the left, with their supporting arms, though the reserve brigade saw fighting, too.

The story is best told brigade by brigade. Here is an account of the battle fought by the 69th Brigade in the general area of La Riviere:

The battalions leading the assault were the 5th East Yorkshire Regiment and the 6th Green Howards. The former were to land close to the coastal village of La Riviere and the latter a quarter of a mile farther west. The reserve battalion of the brigade, the 7th Green Howards, had the task of landing three-quarters of an hour after the leading troops and advancing immediately through the 6th Green Howards to capture the enemy battery at Ver-sur-Mer, a mile and a half inland.

During the run-in of the L.C.A.[1] from the L.S.I.,[2] which had

---

[1] L.C.A.—Landing Craft Assault.
[2] L.S.I.—Landing Ship Infantry, which carried both troops and L.C.A. across the Channel to the point where the L.C.A. were lowered for the run-in to the shore.

dropped anchor about seven miles off shore, the troops could not see the full effect of the terrific air bombardment which the R.A.F. and U.S.A.A.F. were carrying out on the enemy coastal and inland positions. Even from the frigate H.M.S. *Kingsmill,* on which the brigade commander, Brigadier Knox, was travelling with the S.O.A.G., Captain R. H. Ballance, R.N., the landmarks on the coast soon became obliterated by vast clouds of dust and smoke rising from the coastal belt. The terrific pounding from cruisers, destroyers and smaller supporting craft as well as from aircraft rose to a crescendo immediately before H hour, and very little enemy battery fire was directed at the larger ships now lying off shore.

As the leading L.C.A. approached the shore the beach obstacles, composed of iron stakes with shells or mines tied to the top and sides, could clearly be seen above the water level, and they were to prove a difficult obstacle to later craft, since the tide was rising rapidly.

Shortly after H hour the leading craft touched down and the 6th Green Howards, commanded by Lieutenant-Colonel Hastings, who were landed several hundred yards west of their proper beach, stormed ashore to capture the enemy locality close to the beach which guarded one of the routes inland.

The 5th East Yorkshire Regiment, commanded by Lieutenant-Colonel White, landed on time and in the correct position. The right-hand company crossed the beach in spite of heavy fire directed on them from the western part of La Riviere and advanced inland across a minefield towards the battery of Mont Fleury, some one thousand yards inland. This battery, which had suffered a very heavy and accurate aerial bombardment in the early hours of D Day, was overrun very quickly by our infantry with light casualties. Thirty prisoners were taken, and the battery commander committed suicide as he saw the East Yorkshire Regiment moving towards his position.

The left-hand company of the 5th East Yorkshire Regiment, which landed close to the sea wall fronting La Riviere, met much heavier opposition. Unfortunately the pre-H hour bombardment had missed a fifty-yard strip extending the length of the village, and from there the enemy were firing at them with all the weapons they could muster.

At the western end of the sea wall there was an 88-mm. casemated gun position which had a field of fire straight down the beach, and was supported by machine guns. As the leading craft touched down a murderous fire was directed upon the craft and the troops fighting their way ashore. Craft were also damaged by the beach obstacles during the run-in, and men swimming ashore from them came under fire from the enemy positions on the sea wall and in the houses immediately beyond.

Two A.V.R.E. (tanks specially constructed to deal with fortifications) were hit immediately after landing and, owing to the large amount of explosives they carried, immediately blew up, killing and wounding infantry who were near them, including a company commander, a second-in-command of a company, and three platoon commanders. This was a heavy loss in leaders at the most critical stage of the 69th Brigade's operation.

Under this withering fire the company were forced to seek some protection immediately under the sea wall. They were joined by a reserve company, landing twenty minutes after them. The enemy, on top for the moment, and taking heart of grace, pitched grenades over the sea wall and engaged the troops with mortar fire.

In spite of all this, one platoon, supported by an amphibious tank, forced its way over the wall and through a thick belt of wire on top of it, and began to clean up the enemy Spandau positions in the houses facing the front.

Meanwhile, a platoon of the East Yorkshire Regiment had reached Mont Fleury and turned north-east, and, supported by amphibious tanks and A.V.R.Es., was working its way round the back of La Riviere and, reaching the eastern end, started to clear the houses. These frontal and flank attacks resulted in the clearing of the village by about 0900 hrs. Forty-two prisoners were taken, many Germans were killed, and the attack gained momentum again.

Farther to the west the brigade commander's party had landed at about 0830 hrs., rather delayed by the choppy sea and the beach obstacles, which were not yet cleared on this stretch of the beach. In the craft carrying the brigade commander's party ashore from the frigate were a jeep and a carrier, and the Royal Marine crew manning the boat manœuvred it skilfully through the beach obstacles to land the vehicles and personnel in comparatively shallow water.

The remainder of the brigade headquarters personnel, which included a half-track control vehicle, and was commanded by the brigade major, Major Parker, closed the beach in a tank landing craft an hour after H hour, but the half-track vehicle in which the staff was travelling disembarked from the craft into a bomb crater concealed by the incoming tide, and was later squashed flat by the landing craft, which beached on top of it. The brigade major's party had a near escape from drowning, but managed to get ashore and later joined up with the remainder of the brigade headquarters party, which had commenced to march inland, taking with it the wireless sets of the beach signals unit in handcarts, since these were the only ones available owing to the disaster to the brigade major's equipment.

On the right flank of the brigade front the operation was going

British Official Photograph] [*Crown Copyright Reserved*

"A murderous fire was directed upon the craft and the troops fighting their way ashore . . .".

[*Face p.* 242

well, and before 1000 hrs. the 6th Green Howards had captured the Meuvaines Ridge, over a mile inland, and were continuing the advance south.

The reserve battalion, the 7th Green Howards, commanded by Lieutenant-Colonel Richardson, had landed three-quarters of an hour after H hour, and, after some difficulty in finding a suitable route inland, had captured the Ver-sur-Mer battery position, which was found to be out of action. Fifty prisoners were taken, most of them being found in discreet retirement in the concrete shelters in rear of the gun position. The battalion then continued the advance towards Crepon, followed by the 5th East Yorkshire Regiment, who, in view of their losses in the initial fighting, had reorganized at Ver-sur-Mer into three companies. By 1230 hrs. the 7th Green Howards had reached Crepon and reported that little opposition, except sniping, had been met. An anti-tank gun was firing into the village, but the advance continued, and shortly before 1500 hrs. the battalion had seized the bridge over the River Seulles at Creully.

The 6th Green Howards, on the right flank of the 7th Green Howards, were also continuing the advance, and shortly after 1500 hrs. were on the high ground dominating Villiers-le-Sec, less than a mile to the north-west of Creully. The 5th East Yorkshire Regiment, who had been following up the axis from Ver-sur-Mer, were ordered to advance through the 6th Green Howards, who had the task of holding a firm base on the feature overlooking Villiers-le-Sec and the River Seulles.

On the high ground south of the river and the village there was some opposition, including self-propelled guns, and two of the tanks supporting the leading battalion were knocked out and "brewed up" in the valley before these guns were dealt with. The enemy was found to be dug in in the cornfields on the reverse slope of the ground south of Villiers, and the battalion moved in extended order through the cornfields, beating out the Germans. Enemy mortar fire was heavy, and Lieutenant-Colonel White was seriously wounded by a mortar bomb early in the action. The 5th East Yorkshire Regiment smashed this enemy position and went on without pause towards St. Gabriel. Files of captive Germans began to move down the dusty roads towards the beaches.

The 7th Green Howards, who had met some considerable opposition south of Creully, had by 1800 hrs. fought to a point half a mile south of the town and were now directed on Coulombs, some two miles to the south-east. The 5th East Yorkshire Regiment got to St. Gabriel, but there was no rest for them; they were ordered to occupy Brecy, north-west of Coulombs, but shortly after leaving St. Gabriel

R

they met heavy automatic fire from the woods to the south. The brigade commander decided to attack round the right flank with the 6th Green Howards. The attack, which commenced at 2130 hrs. and was supported by the 86th Field Regiment (S.P.) and "B" Company, 2nd Cheshire Regiment, proved successful, and enabled Brecy to be cleared, and by 2230 hrs. the brigade was established in the area Brecy—Coulombs, with brigade headquarters in St. Gabriel. There the brigade commander decided to call a halt. Thus, by the evening of D Day, the brigade, though a mile short of its planned objective in the St. Leger area, had breached the much-vaunted Atlantic Wall and advanced seven miles inland.

During the day's operations a company sergeant-major of the Green Howards had performed actions for which he later received the Victoria Cross.

During the assault on the beaches and the Mont Fleury Battery, C.S.M. Hollis's company commander noticed that two pillboxes had been bypassed, and went with Hollis to see that they were clear. When they were twenty yards from the pillbox a machine gun opened fire from the slit, but Hollis instantly rushed straight at the pillbox, firing his Sten gun. He jumped on top of the pillbox, recharged his magazine, threw a grenade in through the door and fired his Sten gun into the pillbox, killing two Germans and making the remainder prisoner.

He then cleared several Germans from a neighbouring trench.

Later the same day, in the village of Crepon, the company encountered a field gun and crew armed with Spandaus. Hollis was put in command of a party to cover an attack on the gun, but the movement was held up. Hollis pushed forward to engage the gun with a Piat from a house at fifty yards' range. He was observed by a sniper, whose bullet grazed Hollis's right cheek, and at the same moment the gun swung round and fired into the house. To avoid the fallen masonry, Hollis moved his party to an alternative position. Two of the enmy gun crew had by this time been killed, and the gun was destroyed shortly afterwards.

Hollis later found that two of his men had stayed behind in the house, and he immediately volunteered to get them out. In full view of the enemy, who were continually firing at him, he went forward alone, using a Bren gun to distract attention from the other men. Under cover of his diversion, the two men were able to get back.

"Wherever fighting was heaviest," says the citation, "C.S.M. Hollis appeared, and in the course of a magnificent day's work he displayed the utmost gallantry and on two separate occasions his courage and initiative prevented the enemy from holding up the advance at critical stages.

"It was largely through his heroism and resource that the company's objectives were gained and casualties were not heavier, and by his own bravery he saved the lives of many of his men."

So much for the 69th Brigade's part in the day's operations.

The 231st Brigade's plan was to land on a nine hundred yard beach immediately east of Le Hamel, and to establish itself on high ground to the south and dominating Arromanches, the biggest town in the Divisional sector and site for the Mulberry port which was to play such an important part in sustaining the British armies in Normandy. The brigade was then to capture Ryes, Arromanches and Longues (where the enemy had an important heavy battery), and the 47th Royal Marine Commando, which was under command for the operation, was to capture Port-en-Bessin.

Two outstanding features of the brigade's operation were the Commando's march on Port-en-Bessin and the Hampshire Regiment's stern battle for Le Hamel.

The 1st Hampshire Regiment were on the right of the brigade front. After taking Le Hamel they were to work along the coast, seizing in turn Asnelles-sur-Mer, Arromanches and the defences at Tracy-sur-Mer and Manvieux.

Infantry and tanks stormed ashore at H hour, but, instead of being able to penetrate swiftly into the heart of the enemy's position, were held up at the head of the beach by withering fire from machine guns in pillboxes and 88-mm. guns sited farther inland. This heavy opposition was due in part to the fact that, owing to the uncertain light, R.A.F. bombers, which were to have attacked Le Hamel, missed their mark, and the strong-points in the area therefore missed much of the "softening-up" dealt out to the enemy along the rest of the Norman coast.

The Hampshire Regiment, gathering on the beach under a hurricane of fire, did not of course know this; but they realized that theirs was to be no ordinary battle. Minefields fronting the defences were too deep and too well covered by enemy fire to be gapped, and a way was therefore sought round a flank. At 0900 hrs. two companies made a gap to the east of Le Hamel, and attacked Asnelles from the rear. The position was captured by 1200 hrs. after great work had been done by A.V.R.Es. While the fighting was in progress, civilians continued to walk about the street as if they were watching an exercise.

Not until 1700 hrs. was Le Hamel firmly in the hands of the Hampshire Regiment, and Arromanches was captured at 1830 hrs. This very fine operation, in the face of most determined resistance, cost the battalion dear. The commanding officer was wounded and his second-in-command killed, and all companies had heavy losses.

The 1st Dorsetshire Regiment landed on the left of the Hampshire Regiment. Their principal task was to seize the high ground dominating Arromanches and later to take over the defence of Ryes. By the end of the day they had captured all their objectives almost exactly according to plan, and were established in the area of Ryes. This was not achieved, however, without heavy fighting and casualties. The battalion fought its way ashore quickly, but found that opposition on the high ground was stronger than had been expected. Two strong-points north and west of the feature were also overwhelmed. The final assault of the day was made on the westerly one by "C" and "A" Companies supported by the tanks of "C" Squadron of the Sherwood Rangers with artillery support from the 90th Field Regiment. This was too much for the enemy. He pulled out, abandoning his heavy guns and much of his equipment.

Meanwhile, the 2nd Devonshire Regiment, who had landed behind the 1st Dorsetshire Regiment, had gone through to capture Ryes, over two miles inland, by 2100 hrs. They then swung right towards Longues, on the other side of Arromanches, and its battery of four 155-mm. guns.

Both reserve brigades were ashore by about 1100 hrs. and their day, though not marked by heavy opposition, was not uneventful.

The 56th Brigade advanced to a position just short of Bayeux, and the 2nd Essex Regiment sent patrols into the town.

On the left the 151st Brigade suffered an early setback through the temporary loss of their commander, Brigadier Senior. The brigadier was ambushed in the afternoon near Crepon, wounded in the arm, and forced to lie up to avoid capture. He rejoined his troops the next day, but his wounds necessitated his return to England.

The brigade moved inland, over the green and gentle slopes of the Meuvaines Ridge, and by evening had advanced as far as the railway south-east of Bayeux.

The following description of the 6th Durham Light Infantry's activities, by an officer of the battalion, gives a good example of this brigade's experiences. (On the day of sailing this battalion had the misfortune to lose its commanding officer, Lieutenant-Colonel Green, who was ordered into hospital with an attack of malaria. He rejoined the battalion later. In the meantime, Major G. L. Wood took over command):

> "The ill-effects of the sea crossing were soon shaken off as we advanced to the battalion assembly area near Ver-sur-Mer, and the battalion was assembled and ready to move off by 1400 hrs. A Squadron of 4/7 Dragoon Guards under Major Bell was with us in the assembly area, and took part in the advance during the

next two days. The general plan was for a mobile column, consisting of tanks, carriers, machine guns, mortars and anti-tank guns, with D Company on bicycles, to move ahead and establish three strong-points which would be taken over by the rifle companies as soon as marching personnel reached the objective.

"The mobile column under Major Thomlinson moved off at 1500 hrs., two hours behind the time planned. Movement was slow because of the congestion of troops and material on and near main roads, and the difficulties of driving Shermans through narrow village streets. Some enemy pockets were met near Villers-le-Sec by the mobile column, but quick action by Lieutenant Kirk, in command of the vanguard, drove the enemy from their position.

"During the whole of the move of the mobile column we encountered no enemy artillery fire and were held up only by small pockets of enemy, which were beaten up. The battalion reached its first objective at Esquay-sur-Seulles by 2000 hrs. and, after waiting for some time for permission to advance, was ordered to stop at Esquay and dig in for the night.

"We had our first spoils of war at Esquay in the shape of a 10 h.p. Ford car, proudly driven into the battalion area by Major Kirby, officer commanding C Company. Two days later its German camouflage had disappeared and the emblem TT60 was in bold letters on the body. The car lasted throughout our part in the French campaign. We also took our first prisoners here, mostly foreigners of 642 Ost Battalion, who had no desire to fight and seemed quite content to be marched back under escort."

At last light on D Day most of the infantry of the 50th Division were half a dozen miles inland. Forward elements were reaching out and patrolling into Bayeux. The important St. Leger feature was almost within grasp. And away to the west a small but determined force was threatening Port-en-Bessin in an action which did not end until the 8th of June, but which is described here because it began on D Day.

The 47th Royal Marine Commando landed behind the 231st Brigade at about 1000 hrs. In order to understand the nature of the distinguished action they fought it is necessary to know something about Port-en-Bessin, its situation and its importance to the Allied operations as a whole.

This small fishing port formed the right-hand boundary of the 50th Division sector, and its capture as early as possible was considered vital to the security of the XXX Corps' right flank and to an effective link-up with the 1st U.S. Division, which was our right-hand neighbour. The town is in a hollow between cliffs approximately two hundred feet high. It is fronted by a promenade and backed by closely packed houses with narrow streets. Towards the south-east and southern part of the town the houses are less closely packed and are interspersed with gardens and small fields. Approaches to the town are very open and exposed, particularly the south-east approaches.

Like other ports on the Normandy coast, Port-en-Bessin was well defended by a system of strong-points on the cliffs overlooking the town and including emplaced guns sited to fire seawards, guns and machine guns in open embrasures capable of firing both to sea and inland, trench systems surrounded by minefields and wire at the various strong-points, and fortified houses and pillboxes on the mole and in the town itself.

The garrison was thought to be approximately one company, with some fifty naval personnel in the town and port defences.

In view of the distance from the nearest landing beach at Le Hamel and the already heavy commitments of the 231st Brigade landing there, it was appreciated that a separate force would be required; a force which would be capable of force-marching a distance of approximately eight miles through enemy-held territory, carrying all weapons, with the prospect of a stiff fight at the end of it. A practical knowledge of the technique of combined operations also was required. The plan was divided into four phases:

Phase I.—To land behind the 231st Brigade in the area of Le Hamel.

Phase II.—To proceed by forced march and seize Point 72, a feature approximately one and a half miles south of Port-en-Bessin, at about 1300 hrs., bypassing any enemy localities discovered *en route.*

Phase III.—The capture of the high ground east of the basin at Port-en-Bessin. The timing of this assault would not be before 1400 hrs., and would be governed by the time which would elapse between request for air support and the arrival of the aircraft.

Phase IV.—The capture of the town itself.

The 47th Royal Marine Commando was given call on one cruiser, and also on another for the bombardment of Port-en-Bessin.

Artillery support was to be given by one battery (431st) of the 147th Field Regiment (S.P.). Air support was entirely smoke.

The Commando landed at the correct time, but unfortunately

THE BEACH-HEAD

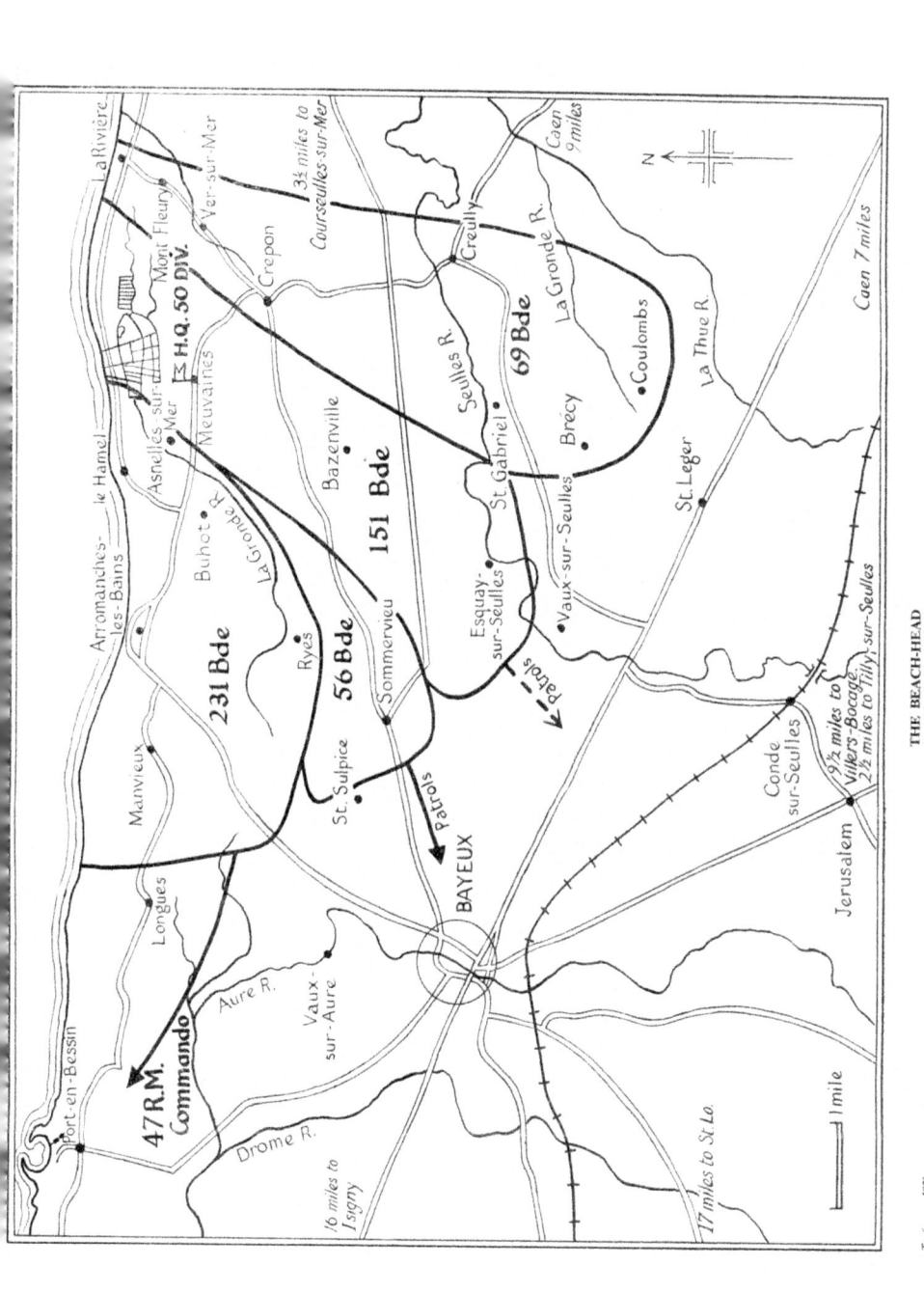

three L.C.As. were sunk in the run-in and seventy men were missing before assembly. Quite a number, however, turned up in time. They equipped themselves with weapons taken from prisoners. Owing to the enemy resistance at Le Hamel where the Hampshire Regiment were fighting, there was some delay in collecting the Commando together, but eventually it was able to fight its way to the prearranged assembly area, which was firmly held by approximately one company of enemy infantry. The Commando had to put in an attack against this position in which they suffered a further forty casualties but captured sixty prisoners. After this action the rather depleted Commando advanced rapidly to Escures, a small village to the south of Port-en-Bessin, which was occupied by last light without opposition.

In view of the delay imposed by the Commando's action at Le Hamel, and the fact that the wireless link with the 231st Brigade had failed to work, it was decided by the commander to abandon temporarily the original plan to attack the high ground east and west of the port under cover of aircraft smoke. The plan decided upon was to leave a small party at Escures and to infiltrate into the town at first light and capture the port. This was done, and shortly after first light the Commando, less fifteen who had been left at Escures, were fighting in the streets of Port-en-Bessin. By last light the town was in their hands, but the cliffs on either side were still held by the enemy. During the following night the Commando attacked these positions and by approximately 0400 hrs. on the 8th of June all resistance had been beaten down. The party left at Escures were attacked and dislodged during the night, but the arrival of troops from the 2nd Devonshire Regiment in the early hours of the 8th of June helped them to restore the situation. By 0830 hrs. the road Port-en-Bessin—Longues—Arromanches was open and supplies and ambulances were sent to the Commando.

Thus ended a remarkably fine action, which, had it gone entirely according to plan, would have been difficult enough. Hampered as the 47th Royal Marine Commando was by loss of men before the operation commenced, the delay and additional fighting in the area of Le Hamel, and by the difficulty of establishing communications and the consequent loss of air support, its work is even more distinguished.

The Commando sustained approximately two hundred casualties all told, and captured over three hundred prisoners, as well as killing a considerable number of the enemy.

CHAPTER XX

The Enemy's problem—The 50th Division's next task—Durham Light Infantry and Dorsetshire Regiment in an armoured thrust—The First Battle for Villers Bocage

JUNE, 1944

The morning of the 7th of June came with the Allied armies firmly established on the Continent. Not all the objectives named for capture on D Day had in fact been taken, but in most instances the Allies had sufficient grip on them to give grounds for satisfaction and great hopes.

The crucial thing about the invasion was the actual landing. A disaster at that stage would have been well-nigh irreparable, and failure to overwhelm the beach defences would have put an end for the time being to all plans for destroying the German armies in Europe; and no one knows how long it would have been before they could reach fruition once more. It was therefore for the act of invasion that our industry and our services had given so largely of their time and energy for so many years. Shipyards, steelworks and factories had been turning out equipment designed just for that one day. Down our roads and railways to the South of England had come long, camouflaged lines of special equipment necessary to the landing of a seaborne force on a hostile shore. In Scotland and on the coastline soldiers had for years scrambled into and out of their assault craft, used their assault vehicles to breach sea walls and concrete ramps, and experimented with secret devices all bearing on the one supreme problem—getting ashore in the face of the enemy.

And now, on this morning of the 7th of June, it all seemed to have come and gone so quickly. One day had sufficed to test and vindicate all that had been done in the time of waiting and preparation. The great trial had come, and the perils were past, and with that behind us, the new phase began at once. The assault was over. The land campaign had begun.

On our right the Americans were recovering from a difficult landing. The infantry had been pinned down on the beaches. One of the German "cushion" divisions had reinforced the coastal defences at the last minute, and the Americans therefore bumped very solid opposition. They had the same experience once before—a year earlier at Gela, in Sicily, when they fought doggedly to retain their grip on a narrow strip of sand in the face of repeated counter-attacks by German armoured reserves. The fight at Gela was repeated on the beaches west of Port-en-Bessin, and with the same result. The Americans stood their ground, reinforced, and then set off for their drive up the Cotentin Peninsula to Cherbourg.

In the centre the 50th Division had completed its D Day tasks with the clearing of Bayeux on the morning of the 7th, and on the left the Canadians and the 3rd British Division were firmly established, though Caen, a D-Day objective, had not been captured and was not, in fact, to fall for many a long day. On the extreme left flank the airborne troops had secured a bridgehead over the Orne, and held a group of hamlets to the east of the river.

From the enemy point of view the situation was critical but by no means hopeless. The best way to defeat an invasion, as the Germans doubtless appreciated, is to prevent the invaders from getting ashore. The Germans failed in this, and there is no doubt that they had reckoned with the possibility of such a failure. The real counter to "Overlord" now lay in an attempt to contain our bridgehead, speedy concentration of armoured reserves and a counter-attack to eliminate the bridgehead. The Allies' problem, on the other hand, was to expand the bridgehead as rapidly as possible and to build up reinforcements and supplies faster than the enemy.

One outside and imponderable factor came to the enemy's assistance—the weather. The seas that rocked the invasion fleet made the work of the Navy and the beach groups always difficult and, from time to time, impossible. Supply ships crossed the Channel on schedule, but unloading was heavily delayed for several days owing to gales. This occasionally caused acute anxiety in Allied quarters, but it did not impede operations in the way the Germans hoped it would. And in the end our build-up across the turbulent Channel was faster and more substantial than the enemy's along his R.A.F.-disrupted interior lines. By the morning of the 7th of June the Germans were getting their armoured reserves on the move. Two of these divisions were already in the battle, or very close to it. In front of Caen the 21st Panzer Division—which was really a "ghost" from Africa, bearing the same number as the Afrika Korps formation the 50th Division had fought so many times—was fighting stubbornly to save the old Norman city. In the cornfields and copses to the north-west their tanks and infantry fought for every yard. The 12th S.S. Panzer Division Hitler Jugend, which was destined to take such a terrible hammering in the later days of the campaign, moved farther west and south of the 50th Division's front. On the other side of the Seine the 2nd Panzer Division prepared to move, and from as far south as the Loire the 17th S.S. Panzer Grenadier Division set off for the battle area. And last, but by no means least, a division called Panzer Lehr, about which little was known by us, prepared for battle. It was, by literal translation, a "demonstration" division, and it was the 50th Division's implacable and skilful enemy until it was ground to bits during protracted and bitter fighting.

The German aim was to contain economically and strike with all the power available in his reserve. The Allies' aim was to operate so aggressively and deeply that the whole of this force would have to be committed piecemeal as it arrived to plug holes in the front.

Our aim was achieved.

The 50th Division's part in this stage of the Allied plan was to contain as many enemy as possible by aggressive action and to allow him no rest. In the Second Army plan for "Overlord" the early capture of Villers Bocage was considered of paramount importance. Villers is a small town nearly twenty miles south of the beaches on which we had landed. It lies on fairly high ground surrounded by hills at the junction of five important roads. As a centre of communications its retention by the enemy was of vital importance to his plans for containing the bridgehead.

Standing sentinel above this little Norman town were hill features which were to become bywords in the 50th Division's campaign—Tracy Bocage to the west, Point 213 on a ridge two thousand yards long to the north-east, and Points 140 and 158 to the east. This country was true bocage. It was closer than any country in which the Division had ever fought before—steep hills, deep valleys, small fields and tall hedges, ditches, and narrow, twisting lanes were its characteristics. It was difficult country for tanks and nerve-racking country for infantry, and called for a battle technique of its own. Before the assault it was envisaged that Villers Bocage would be seized on D Day and accordingly the 50th Division was ordered to make available a strong forward body containing armour to be commanded by Brigadier Cracroft, commander of the 8th Armoured Brigade. This force was to consist of all the 8th Armoured Brigade, the 147th Field Regiment (S.P.), the 1st Dorsetshire Regiment (in vehicles), the 61st Reconnaissance Regiment (armoured cars and carriers), one anti-tank battery, one company of the 2nd Cheshire Regiment, less one platoon, an R.E. reconnaissance party, and a detachment of the 168th Light Field Ambulance.

Neither the 50th Division force nor the complete 7th Armoured Division, which was also used in the attempt, was able to capture the town in the first few days, and instead the 50th Division entered upon a prolonged period of very bitter fighting in which every yard gained had to be fought for and then grimly defended.

["The Times" Photograph]

A typical scene in the Normandy Bocage. Infantry and anti-tank guns moving forward along a "tank track."

Face p. 252]

The original plan to start a 50th Division column on D Day could not be put into effect, as the armour was still fighting for other D-Day objectives, and it was not until 2300 hrs. on the 7th of June that orders were issued for the force to concentrate in the area of Brecy by first light the next day. From this area the column's route lay roughly southwards into the heart of the bocage; over the railway from Bayeux to Caen and along the winding, wooded road leading past Point 103, a dominating feature north-east of Tilly-sur-Seulles; then through the wooded and straggling village of St. Pierre and over the River Seulles to Tilly-sur-Seulles, then due south along a main road to Villers.

The start line for the 8th Armoured Brigade was the railway and the time of starting was 1000 hrs., but the force was delayed by anti-tank fire from a village astride the railway to the east. This opposition was dealt with during the afternoon, and then the column made progress until at last light there were elements of the 1st Dorsetshire Regiment on the bridges between St. Pierre and Tilly and also on Point 103, south of Audrieu. This represented an advance of over six thousand yards through most difficult country, and brought our infantry to the very doorstep of the important road centre of Tilly.

As a result of the experience and information gained during the day's fighting, the 8th Durham Light Infantry from the 151st Brigade was placed under the command of the column and by last light the battalion was north of St. Pierre.

The column had stirred up a hornets' nest. During the night there was strong enemy pressure from the south and east, and the column had to adjust its dispositions to meet the threat. The morning, therefore, found the 1st Dorsetshire Regiment, supported by the 4th/7th Dragoon Guards of the 8th Armoured Brigade, in the area of Audrieu, with the Sherwood Rangers of the 8th Armoured Brigade just east of Point 103 in the area of Le Haut Audrieu.

That which had been done yesterday remained to be done again today, and the story of the action can be told in the following extracts from a record kept by an officer of the 8th Durham Light Infantry:

"By 0845 hours forward elements of 8 Armoured Brigade had moved through Audrieu and had reached Point 103, the high ground overlooking the village of St. Pierre. Enemy was all round this area, in Buceels, in Cristot, and in Tilly-sur-Seulles. The Battalion were now formed up, C, A, and B Companies in that order, riding on the tanks, with D Company bringing up the rear on assault bicycles. The party moved off at 1000 hours, being preceded by a recce troop of 10 Honeys (light tanks).

"As the advance continued reports came in that 915 **Regiment** held a line through Tilly, but prisoner of war information stated that St. Pierre was only lightly held. The forward regiments of 8 Armoured Brigade moved through Audrieu and at 1135 hours the main body halted 1,000 yards from Point 103, with the Dorsets of 231 Brigade behind at Haut Audrieu.

"It was decided to attack St. Pierre with C and D Companies 8 D.L.I. forward, A and B Companies in reserve, the attack to be supported by elements of 8 Armoured Brigade and self-propelled guns. H hour was fixed for 1730.

"The actual attack was delayed slightly, and, after preliminary barrage by self-propelled guns, C and D Companies advanced from Point 103 down the valley towards the village. Enemy resistance, however, proved much stronger than had been anticipated, and the extremely close wooded nature of the country gave added strength to the enemy defence. As one forward Company was still some distance from their objectives B Company was sent in to reinforce the attack. Throughout the action, the start point and the area of attack were heavily shelled from the forward slopes across the valley.

"Sheer weight of three companies eventually proved too much, and about 1900 hours A Company moved down to take up reserve positions. The enemy was still in the area however, and the reserve company came under mortar and Spandau fire on its way down, suffering its first casualties. Major Leybourne, O.C. C Company, and Second Lieutenant Hannah were wounded, and the Company generally had considerable losses.

"By 2100 hours the Battalion was established with C and D Companies forward to the south with A and B Companies in the rear. Tanks of 8 Armoured Brigade moved up in support of night patrols which went west to safeguard the bridge over the Seulles, one main entry to Tilly, heavily held by the enemy.

"The night of 9/10 June was quiet, perhaps deceptively so. The odd Spandau had been forced to withdraw, and throughout the night there was nothing to be heard save shelling and counter-shelling. Stand-to passed without incident, but at 0615 hours the counter-attack came with great suddenness, the brunt being borne by the right forward company—C Company.

"The attack came quickly by infiltration, which could hardly fail to succeed, as the village was overgrown and threaded with narrow wooded lanes and tracks. C Company were heavily shelled and mortared, losing Captain Wheatley, second-in-command, and Lieutenant Mount, who were both killed. The sole remaining officer, Lieutenant Galvin, was wounded.

"C Company were over-run by the enemy, who now threatened the flanks of both A and D Companies. It was then decided to withdraw both companies about 500 yards and to form a defensive ring around Battalion H.Q., as there was no defence now between Battalion H.Q. and the enemy. This was completed almost without incident, except that A Company H.Q. became cut off from the rest of the Company and had to withdraw via Point 103 and then come back to St. Pierre. It was during this withdrawal that Lieutenant Waggott, A Company, was killed.

"The arrival of reinforcements from 8 Armoured Brigade helped to ease the situation, however, and by 1130 hours the crisis had passed, and our own tanks were in the village. Communication between companies was restored, and by 1400 hours the Battalion was reorganized east of St. Pierre, firmly based in the area of Battalion H.Q. St. Pierre itself was 'No Man's Land.'"

The enemy attack had been made by tanks and infantry of the 130th Panzer Lehr and the 12th S.S. Hitler Jugend Divisions—evidence that the enemy's build-up round the bridgehead had begun in earnest. The attacking tanks had come from the direction of Tilly, and back into Tilly they had been driven before midday by the 24th Lancers with casualties estimated at four Mark IV tanks, two Mark VI tanks, three self-propelled guns and many infantry.

Although this fierce action had ended with our troops in command of the battlefield, it had demonstrated that the enemy was in and around Tilly in increased strength; and it was therefore decided that the column would not advance farther, but that it would hold the ground it had already gained. This in itself was no easy task, for the enemy continued to make determined attempts at infiltration with parties of infantry.

As the 50th Division's spearhead stopped moving, so the 7th Armoured Division's got on the move in an attempt to reach Villers Bocage by using roads on our right flank. The Desert Rats had been coming ashore since the afternoon of the 7th of June, and on the morning of the 9th of June they were almost concentrated and had been ordered to advance to a hamlet called Hottot—the scene later of much bitter fighting between the 50th Division and the Panzer Lehr Division—and Tilly-sur-Seulles. Hottot lies to the south-west of Tilly on rising ground on a main road linking Tilly with Caumont, which at the time was one of the German Army's main lateral routes.

This operation was intended to be preparatory to a further attack directed on Villers Bocage, and to help them the 7th Armoured Division were given the 56th Infantry Brigade, hitherto under the command of the 50th Division.

The situation of the 50th Division's armoured column at the time the 7th Armoured Division's attack began has already been described, but the disposition of the remainder of the Division is of interest. The 231st Brigade were deployed on the right flank on the west bank of the River Aune facing west. The 151st Brigade were astride the main road from Bayeux to Tilly, and at their nearest point were some two thousand yards from Tilly. Between the 151st Brigade and the 231st Brigade was a screen of armoured cars and carriers from the 61st Reconnaissance Regiment. East of them the armoured column was deployed around St. Pierre and Point 103, and on their left flank the 69th Brigade were fighting in the area of Audrieu.

The advance of the 7th Armoured Division began at first light on the 10th of June. All through the day their tanks and infantry advanced slowly in the face of constant interference by small parties of enemy armed with anti-tank weapons. Each had to be neutralized in turn by infantry, and the close nature of the bocage set a limit to the speed of the tanks. These small groups of enemy were reinforced by a few armoured fighting vehicles, chiefly half-tracked vehicles, and later by tanks.

Two days of hard fighting had yielded small dividends and on the 12th of June the orders to the 7th Armoured Division were changed. The Division was ordered to move still farther to the right between the 50th Division and the 1st U.S. Division, and to move on Villers Bocage with a right hook, passing north-east of Caumont, and capture the high ground centred on Point 213, which is north-east of Villers.

By the 13th of June all three regiments of the 22nd Armoured Brigade were advancing rapidly against negligible opposition to Villers Bocage. Once in the town, however, the brigade ran into stiffening opposition. Mortar and anti-tank fire was directed against our tanks, and enemy armour appeared in strength.

Later it became known that this armoured encounter in Villers Bocage really represented something like a head-on collision between armoured divisions—on the one hand, the Desert Rats, advancing from the west, and, on the other, the 2nd Panzer Division, making its way from its "peace-time" station east of the Seine to join battle with the Americans.

Extremely bitter fighting ensued in the narrow streets. The headquarters of the 4th County of London Yeomanry was overrun, causing confusion on our side. In an attempt to restore the position in the town the 1st/7th Queen's Regiment of the 131st Infantry Brigade were ordered into Villers to clean up the place and free the 4th County of London Yeomanry to carry on and capture Point 213, but by this time the 2nd Panzer Division was arriving in force.

When reconnaissances were made by us it was discovered that the road leading out of Villers towards Point 213 was crowded with Tiger tanks which were driving towards the town to reinforce the Germans. Efforts to stop them were not successful, and soon the 4th County of London Yeomanry and the infantry of the 1st/7th Queen's Regiment were heavily engaged in the town itself. We suffered severe casualties in tanks and crews.

Our hold on this important objective was rapidly loosening, owing largely to a shortage of infantry, and the 1st/5th Queen's Regiment were called forward in an attempt to save the day. But before they arrived the situation became hopeless, and all British troops in Villers were ordered to withdraw and stand firm on the high ground north-west of the town.

The success of the whole action by the 7th Armoured Division depended on the capture of Villers Bocage and the consequent threat to the supply line of the enemy who were opposing the 50th Division to the north. It was hoped that this threat, combined with pressure by the 50th Division, would cause the forces north of Villers to withdraw, thus allowing a large British salient to be formed with Villers Bocage at its head.

The enemy had evidently appreciated our intentions correctly. Luck may have served him inasmuch as the 2nd Panzer Division happened to be on the scene at the critical moment. However that may be, he had had the better of the first battle of Villers Bocage, and it was decided to withdraw the 7th Armoured Division completely and dispose it in the line on the right of the 50th Division.

It is necessary now to return again to the activities of the 50th Division's armoured column, which on the 11th of June was still holding Point 103 and St. Pierre. On this day the enemy were still hanging on grimly to Tilly, and their artillery was very active. On our side small parties of tanks from the 4th/7th Dragoon Guards succeeded in getting on to the high ground east of St. Pierre.

In the evening the enemy put in another counter-attack in the general area of Point 103. "B" Company of the 8th Durham Light Infantry were attacked by at least three Tiger tanks, which machine-gunned the infantry's slit trenches, killing the company commander, Major Clapton, and seriously wounding Major Dunn, the second-in-command. The battalion was completely surrounded. The commanding officer was at a conference at brigade headquarters and he was unable to return in his jeep, and had to make a hazardous journey back on foot through open fields.

The tanks were shelling battalion headquarters from close range, and eventually the infantry were forced to withdraw and form a close area, with all companies grouped together in a rough square. The attack was not pressed, however, and the infantry's efforts, with those of the tanks and the Northumberland Hussars' anti-tank guns, were sufficient to drive off the enemy.

On Monday, the 12th of June, the battalion reorganized after the evening's excitement and resumed its patrolling of St. Pierre, by this time empty of the enemy. The whole area was shelled constantly during the day. Numbers of enemy were sighted during the afternoon, some of them unarmed, and some prisoners from the 901st Panzer Lehr Regiment were brought in during the day.

During the day the Division was ordered to hold the line from Point 103 to La Belle Epine. This meant the withdrawal of the 8th Durham Light Infantry from St. Pierre. Accordingly, covered by the tanks of the 24th Lancers, the battalion left the straggling little village for which they had fought so fiercely. During their four hectic days in that area there had been very little opportunity for sleep, and for the first thirty-six hours most companies had been without food. The cost to us had been twelve officers (four killed) and one hundred and ninety other ranks.

That brought to an end the first attempts to capture Villers Bocage and Tilly-sur-Seulles. While they were being made, Allied strength within the bridgehead was mounting steadily, despite bad weather at sea, and operations were proceeding on either flank in country more suitable for tanks.

On the whole, the British bridgehead did not expand at the same rate as troops poured into it, and by the 15th of June the small area of Normandy we held presented an amazing scene.

Along the beaches and on their fringes was strewn the wreckage of the German defences and our landing craft and tanks, rusting memorials to the first encounters of the Normandy campaign. Where they needed space the beach groups had bulldozed the debris out of the way and set up their own installations for the handling of supplies and equipment coming in from the sea. And on the roads between the beaches and the British first line there crawled, and stopped, and started again endless streams of lorries, tanks, armoured cars and jeeps.

Although the sea was rough, the sun shone, and the little roads of Normandy, subjected to a strain for which they were never built, began to disintegrate into dust. Every journey became a nightmare compounded of traffic jams, dust, heat and engine fumes. The smallest and most primitive tracks were pressed into service as one-way roads. Suitable leaguer areas for units coming ashore became harder and harder to find as airstrip after airstrip came into commission. Life in the villages became a torment to the French, for throughout the twenty-four hours heavy traffic pounded past their doorsteps in a never-ceasing stream, shaking the little cottages to their foundations and coating them with white dust.

But amid all this seeming confusion and crowded bustle a great British army was being concentrated for the day when it would burst its bonds and flood through France and Belgium to the very frontiers of the Reich. That day, however, was not yet, and there remained for the 50th Division, who had been fighting nearly a fortnight while the main force was coming ashore, a further long and arduous spell in the line without relief.

CHAPTER XXI

STATIC BATTLES IN THE BOCAGE—TOWARDS HOTTOT—FALL OF THE VILLAGE—CASUALTIES TO THE END OF JULY

JUNE TO JULY, 1944

THERE are experienced infantry officers in this Division who say that the phase now entered upon was one of the most unpleasant they have ever known. For now the Division really came to grips with the bocage. The 49th (West Riding) Division came into the line on our left, relieving the 69th Brigade after its hard fighting east of the River Seulles, and this enabled the 50th Division to concentrate its attention on the general area of Tilly-sur-Seulles, Hottot and La Belle Epine. Hereabouts the Division was to fight for a month. The main task was to continue to gain ground at the expense of the 130th Panzer Lehr Division, harass that hard-fighting formation to the maximum extent and at the same time to provide a firm base for the XXX Corps.

It was a most trying time for the ordinary front-line soldier. The enemy harried him unceasingly with artillery and mortars—in the use of the latter Panzer Lehr men were extremely skilled—and there was a great deal of bitter and confused fighting in very difficult country.

Something has already been said about the bocage, but not enough perhaps to give a real idea of the nature of the struggle that now took place in it.

The high, thick hedges, the small fields and deep ditches, and the many orchards were the factors that gave this phase of the campaign its distinctive character.

The country lent itself to concealment while restricting vehicular movement. Often the opposing troops would have merely a small field between them, yet each side would be completely concealed from the other. One day an orchard in the field over the road would be free of the enemy, and the troops would pick the small, green, cider apples of Normandy in a peaceful, sunlit, rural setting. The next day the Germans would have a Spandau there in readiness for the unwary.

Surprise was easy to achieve in small things. You never knew where the enemy were, and this kept nerves taut and minds strained for long periods. A small patrol moving along the side of a hedge might be spotted by German machine gunners. Secure in their concealment, the Germans would hold their fire until our patrol was within, say, ten yards of them, and then open fire. The 50th Division gave as good as they got, learning the new technique quickly.

The French people who lived about this battlefield for the most part made their way elsewhere with a sigh, though some remained obstinately in their farms to tend their livestock. But there were many cows wandering about those deep meadows which were milked one day by the 130th Panzer Lehr Division and the next day by the 50th (Northumbrian) Division. And there were the dead cows—score upon score of them struck down by shell or bullet. It was difficult to burn or bury them. The soldiers grew to loathe them. It was not long before the stench began to affect the health of the forward troops, and some means had to be devised of disposing of the rotting carcasses. It was the bulldozer, that machine of many roles, which came to the rescue.

In this setting, then, of sunshine and orchards and deep meadows, the 50th Division took station for the next round.

It began with a Divisional attack on the 14th of June by the 151st and 231st Brigades. The Durham Brigade launched the 9th Durham Light Infantry towards the village of Lingevres, on the main road three miles west of Tilly, and the 6th Durham Light Infantry's objective was the neighbouring village of Verrieres, north-east of Lingevres. If possible, this battalion was to push on south towards Hottot.

The attack was supported by the Divisional artillery and also by the R.A.F., who strafed the orchards near Verrieres and the main road between Lingevres and Tilly. Companies of the 6th Durham Light Infantry crossed the start line at 1015 hrs. and worked across one of the few areas of open country in the bocage in extended order. "C" and "D" Companies were forward and the battalion was supported by a squadron of tanks from the 4th/7th Dragoon Guards.

The advance went well for about a mile, and then the forward companies were heavily engaged by machine guns in a cornfield just north of Verrieres. The enemy was also well dug in on the forward edges of an orchard, and he held his fire until our leading troops were one hundred and fifty yards away. Then the whole enemy line opened up with machine guns, and our advance was held up. Our artillery shelled the edge of the wood, but did not succeed in knocking out the enemy completely, and the reserve companies had to put in an attack which eventually succeeded, with fairly heavy casualties.

By 1600 hrs., after five hours of heavy fighting, we had a hold on the edge of this orchard. When our troops got there they found that the enemy had been deeply dug-in in a ditch. The quantity of ammunition and equipment lying about these defences indicated that the enemy had had every intention of holding them in strength. The battalion paused to reorganize in the ditch, and enemy guns were turned round to be used against their former owners. "A" and "C" Companies then remained in the enemy defences while "B" and "D" Companies advanced to clear the village of Verrieres and to try to push on to the main road to Tilly. Our troops went through Verrieres without opposition, but then both companies were held up by fire from tanks and infantry.

Eventually the battalion reorganized in the area of Verrieres. The cost had been heavy—three officers, including the commanders of "A" and "D" Companies, had been wounded, twenty-five other ranks had been killed, sixty-two wounded, and fifteen were missing. But the enemy had suffered heavily, too. We captured one half-tracked vehicle in perfect condition, two other half-tracked vehicles carrying 75-mm. guns, and a 75-mm. anti-tank gun.

Meanwhile the 9th Durham Light Infantry, supported by more tanks of the Dragoon Guards, had got to the main road at Lingevres by 1330 hrs. Six Panthers were knocked out by our tanks around the village.

In the evening the Panzer Lehr gathered its strength and launched a heavy counter-attack on the 9th Durham Light Infantry. After very confused fighting the battalion stabilized its positions to include the road just west of Lingevres and extending towards Verrieres.

For its attack on the right the 231st Brigade used all battalions after preliminary air support, and after very heavy fighting managed to force their way on to their objective by nightfall. They pushed through La Belle Epine and made contact with the 9th Durham Light Infantry in the area of Lingevres.

The next day the 69th Brigade moved over from the Seulles sector and leaguered in the general area north of Verrieres preparatory to launching a brigade attack on the 16th of June. Their objective was to be the main road south of the road Lingevres—Tilly-sur-Seulles, the road on which the notorious village of Hottot stands. This meant an advance of nearly four thousand yards. All three battalions were used in the attack, but by the end of the day the brigade were still short of their objective. The forward troops were south of Lingevres, but not in the village, and holding a line south-westwards towards the River Aure at Longraye.

This attack stung the enemy into retaliation, and on the afternoon of the 18th of June the Germans began heavy counter-attacks against the 5th East Yorkshire Regiment and the 7th Green Howards, which forced them to withdraw westwards.

While the enemy were attacking the 69th Brigade the 6th Durham Light Infantry and the 2nd Essex Regiment (of the 56th Brigade) launched an attack on Tilly-sur-Seulles, and by last light the Essex Regiment were established in the north-east corner of Tilly, with the 6th Durham Light Infantry blocking the western and south-western exits.

The 6th Durham Light Infantry had had a most successful battle. They had been given splendid artillery support by three field regiments, which laid down a barrage which moved forward at the rate of a hundred yards in five minutes, and were closely supported by tanks—one troop with each company, and machine guns mounted on carriers performing the function of light tanks.

In the words of an officer who took part:

"Tanks crashed through hedges, shooting into hedge junctions and giving magnificent support. The fire brought down on the enemy was simply terrific, and he was well and truly blasted out of his positions.

"Once the attack started to move there was no stopping it, and the forward companies had a magnificent day; they kept pace with the barrage and D Company had the good fortune to see the Boche get up and run for it.

"Battalion reached its objective by 1700 hours and dug-in; tanks and M.10's stayed with us on the ground, lying in wait for some suspected enemy tanks, and in fact they succeeded in 'brewing-up' two Mark IV Specials.

"This was by far the most successful attack the battalion carried out during six days of heavy and continuous fighting, and the perfect co-operation of artillery, tanks and infantry really showed what could be done. There was no doubt that the enemy had to be blasted out of his positions in that very close country—and after several not-too-successful attempts we seemed to have come upon the best method of doing it. The weary look in the eyes of the men was once again replaced by keenness and eagerness, and even after six days of fighting the defences in our new positions were dug more quickly and better than ever."

The next day the Essex Regiment completed the capture of Tilly, meeting little opposition. This small village had been battered beyond recognition by shells and bombs, and presented a heart-breaking spectacle. It was one of the first of the many towns and villages which were well-nigh obliterated in the process of liberation, and the understanding and fortitude of the French people who returned to their ruined homes both here and elsewhere won the wonder and respect of the British soldiers. Tilly had frequently been shelled by H.M.S. *Warspite*, illustrating how the support of the Navy did not end with the landing of the Division. Spotting for the *Warspite's* guns was done from the air.

Although the enemy's grip on Tilly had thus been prised loose, he was still holding on to Hottot.

During the same afternoon the 231st Brigade attacked towards this village in the face of determined opposition. Eventually the 1st Hampshire Regiment forced their way in, but were pushed out again by a counter-attack by Tiger tanks.

Later, the 2nd Devonshire Regiment fought their way into the village and at last light, after repelling several counter-attacks, still had a precarious hold on it—so precarious that during the night the brigade withdrew slightly to the north, and the enemy occupied Hottot again.

After the failure of this attack on Hottot the Division passed through a period in which there was nothing spectacular to record—nothing to make headlines in the newspapers at home; but it was an unpleasant period of close contact with the enemy, and of continuous attempts to gain ground at his expense. And the Division, it must be remembered, was still in that sniper's paradise constituted by the Norman bocage. We were disposed with, right, the 69th Brigade south of La Belle Epine and La Senaudiere, centre, the 231st Brigade north of Hottot, and, left, the 151st Brigade in the general area of Tilly.

On the 8th of July the 56th Brigade, which had been put under the 50th Division's command again, and which was on the right of the 69th Brigade, attacked with the object of getting across the main road west of Hottot. They crossed the road in face of heavy opposition, and by the afternoon had done all they set out to do. But the counter-attack was not long in coming, and by evening the two leading battalions had been forced to withdraw north of the road again. This counter-attack was the prelude to a more serious affair which started at 0600 hrs. the next day. Three enemy infantry companies and twenty to thirty tanks suddenly appeared in front of the 2nd Essex Regiment, but were thrown back with heavy losses. The enemy lost eight tanks.

The 56th Brigade's attack had brought us nearer to the main road west of Hottot. It now fell to the 231st Brigade to try to conform, and capture Hottot itself.

The attack, which was begun on the 11th of July, was the last which the 50th Division was to make on the village which had caused them so much bitter fighting. Large-scale operations by the First Canadian

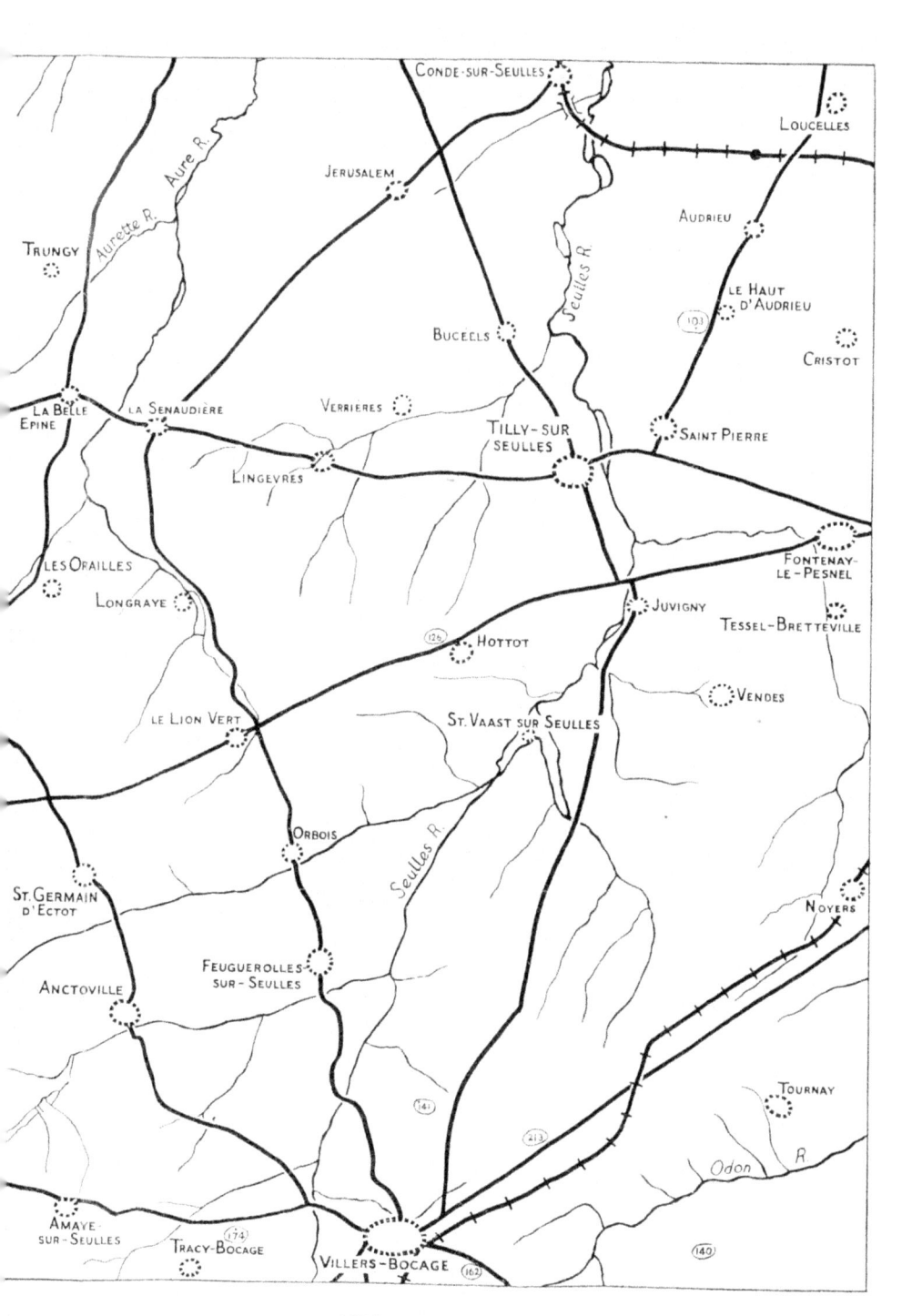

VILLERS-BOCAGE

Army, the Second Army and the Americans were in the making, and preparations were being made to spring the trap which was later to destroy a great German army on the ghastly battlefields south of Falaise.

But the Devonshire, Hampshire and Dorsetshire Regiments of the 231st Brigade, and the tank men of the Sherwood Rangers, did not know this as they began to advance in the early morning towards the frequently disputed village. The leading battalions were the 1st Hampshire Regiment (right) and the 2nd Devonshire Regiment (left). They were preceded by a massive artillery barrage which moved at a pace of fifty yards in two minutes, and was governed in its length of pause on various objectives by the infantry commanders. Flails, A.V.R.Es., mortars and medium machine guns contributed their support.

Opposition was in the Hottot tradition, and a bitter battle was fought throughout the day. The Devonshire Regiment at first got on well, and, with the Sherwood Rangers, knocked out six tanks. They reached their objective, but were so disorganized by the heavy fighting they had had that they were ordered back slightly. The Hampshire Regiment lost two company commanders early in the day, and their commanding officer, Lieutenant-Colonel Howie, later. They took sixty prisoners. At the end of the day the brigade had reached a line just north of Hottot—but the enemy still held the village.

That was on the 11th of July. On the night of the 18th/19th of July the enemy withdrew from Hottot and also on the remainder of the 50th Division's front. He had had enough.

It was the end of a phase, a phase without spectacle or glitter. In weeks of difficult fighting which had yielded no great gains, measured in distance, the 50th Division had slowly ground the enemy into impotence. From becoming incapable of effective counter-attack he passed to the stage where he could no longer hold his line. And back he went, not in rout but carefully and steadily, with the usual array of booby traps and mines in his wake. We followed, pressing him.

Losses as a division up to this time—the end of July—had been sixty-nine officers and six hundred and four other ranks killed, two hundred and eleven officers and two thousand eight hundred and sixty-one other ranks wounded, and thirty officers and one thousand two hundred and six other ranks missing. Of those missing, four officers and five hundred and one other ranks succeeded in rejoining the Division. Total casualties were, therefore, three hundred and six officers and four thousand one hundred and seventy other ranks. The Division had taken about three thousand prisoners.

CHAPTER XXII

On the threshold of the break-through—Fall of Villers Bocage—
Fighting advance to Conde—The trap closed, and the destruction
of an army—On to Antwerp and adventures on the way

JULY TO AUGUST, 1944

THE Allied armies in Normandy now stood on the threshold of the great break-through which was to carry them to the very frontiers of the Reich, and to understand the 50th Division's part in this great triumph it is necessary to outline briefly the main course of events.

On the 18th of July the VIII (British) Armoured Corps made a grand-scale attack south-east from Caen. It was heralded by a massive air assault by Bomber Command and the U.S. Army Air Force which will never be forgotten by those who saw it. It began at 0615 hrs. Rank upon rank of bombers moved in stately procession over Caen, dropped their loads and wheeled for home. Throughout the area of the British bridgehead the ground shook as the bombs crashed home, and the air became thick with dust, as if a desert khamseen was upon us. The smell of explosives was everywhere.

This huge air fleet consisted of one thousand one hundred British heavies, one thousand six hundred American Fortresses and Liberators, six hundred British and U.S. mediums and one thousand two hundred fighter-bombers, and it cascaded eight thousand tons of high explosive on to the enemy positions in two hours.

None the less, this attack did not go well, and it was left to the U.S. First Army, away to the west, to set the ball rolling on the 25th of July. Aided by another great air fleet, they attacked southwards along the west coast of the Cherbourg Peninsula, and in the sunny August days that followed they swept through Le Mans and northwards in a great half-circle to Argentan. The British Second Army pressed south to meet them towards the general line Vire—Conde-sur-Noireau—Falaise, and thus was formed the famous Falaise "pocket" or gap, in which the Germans were slaughtered by the guns, tanks and aeroplanes of the Western Allies.

The Second Army offensive began on the 30th of July. On the right, directed towards Vire, was the VIII Corps, rested and reorganized after its costly attack south-east from Caen. In the centre was the XXX Corps, with the 50th, 43rd and 7th Armoured Divisions; and away to the east stretched the XII Corps, the I Corps and the Canadian Corps.

The 50th Division's share in the drive south to meet the Americans can be divided into two parts: first, the capture of the Amaye feature and the advance to Villers Bocage; second, the advance to Conde-sur-Noireau.

Between the 30th of July and the 1st of August the 56th and 231st Brigades fought their way against slackening opposition on to the high ground in the general area of Anctoville and Feuguerolles-sur-Seulles.

On the 2nd of August the 69th Brigade took over from a brigade of our right-hand neighbours, the 43rd Division, and in the next two days attacked and captured an important hill to the west of Villers Bocage, known to us as the Amaye feature, followed by the village of Tracy Bocage, on high ground just outside the town. The Amaye feature was captured by the 5th East Yorkshire Regiment in the face of small-arms opposition only, but the battalion was shelled at intervals during the night, and the next day shelling continued all the afternoon and evening.

At 1530 hrs. on this day the battalion and the Division lost a fine leader and a well-loved figure. Lieutenant-Colonel R. B. James, D.S.O., the commanding officer, was killed by a shell. He had been brigade major of the 151st Brigade in the days before Alamein, and his name had rung through the Division in the desperate days of Mareth because of his epic defence of the strong-point of Ksiba Ouest. "Jamey" was the name by which he was known; and he is remembered as a modest gentleman with quiet manners and a brave heart.

The advance to Tracy Bocage, and the southward pressure by the 59th Division on our left, tightened the ring round Villers Bocage, and on the 4th of August a patrol from the 1st Dorsetshire Regiment entered the town and found it deserted, and in ruins as a result of a massive R.A.F. attack a few weeks earlier.

Thus the 50th Division had captured Villers Bocage just under two months behind schedule. In its ruined streets was evidence of those earlier attempts in the shape of burned-out tanks, both British and German, twisted lorries and other relics of the head-on collision between the 7th Armoured Division and the 2nd Panzer Division. And the town itself was a grim testimonial to the efficiency of R.A.F. bombing. It was known from air photographs, of course, that it had suffered severely; but few people were prepared for the scenes of stark devastation that met their gaze when they picked their way through the shattered streets on that warm, sunny morning.

The next day brought a strange and welcome experience to the 50th Division—it was relieved from front-line responsibility for the first time since D Day.

The next two or three days were quiet for the 50th Division, but elsewhere the grand attack was in full swing, and the pattern of victory was beginning to appear. The Americans had burst through the Avranches bottleneck and virtually cut off Brittany from the rest of France; their armour had turned eastwards, and the "pocket" was beginning to be formed south of the Second Army. The eastern end of the pocket was still, of course, wide open, and withdrawal to the line of the Seine was still a possibility for the Germans.

But the Corporal overruled the generals once more, and, obsessed by his hatred of giving up a yard of territory, Hitler gave orders for a big counter-attack by the forces in the pocket. The idea was to attack westward from the Mortain area, cut across the American lines of communication, and emerge on the west coast.

On the 7th of August, then, a very strong armoured force struck out towards Avranches. It consisted of the 116th Panzer Division, the 1st S.S. Panzer Division, the 2nd S.S. Panzer Division and the 2nd Panzer Division. The 2nd S.S. Panzer Division recaptured Mortain, and then the counter-offensive was stopped dead in its tracks.

Brilliant use of air power resulted in over a hundred German tanks being knocked out, and any threat there may have been to the U.S. lines of communication disappeared. Yet not until the 12th of August did it appear that the enemy had finally given up his hopes of a miracle at Mortain. By then the U.S. outflanking armour was completing its great wheel, had turned north, captured Alencon and was already north of the town. The British were pressing down towards Falaise to meet them. The jaws of the pocket had thus been closing while the enemy, instead of getting out in good order while the opportunity remained, stayed inside and beat his head against a stone wall.

This was Hitler's personal and direct order, maintained in the face of disagreement with the commanders in the field. The hand that failed to take Hitler's life in July had probably failed also to save the last German hopes of sound conduct of the Normandy campaign.

There is a mountain in Normandy called Pincon, the highest point of which is three hundred and sixty-five metres. It runs from east to west for three thousand yards like a huge hump, and lies between Villers Bocage and Conde, dominating the country west of the Orne in which the greater part of the Second Army had been fighting. Its possession was of great advantage to the enemy, for from its heights he could look northwards for a distance limited only by atmospheric conditions.

"The Pincon" became a byword in the Second Army. French civilians brought in astonishing stories about the great hill—how the Germans were making it into a fortress, manufacturing secret weapons in galleries deep beneath the surface, and so on. These stories were unfounded, but none the less it was one of the bastions of the enemy's Normandy position, and when the 43rd Division captured it on the 6th of August the way lay open for an advance southwards to Conde-sur-Noireau. This little town, which lies at the confluence of two rivers and at a road bottleneck, was one of the vital points along the enemy's northern line of withdrawal from the rapidly forming pocket—the main road Vire—Conde—Falaise. To seize Conde would be to close the trap still further. The 7th Armoured Division was ordered to move at once, with the 50th Division following to mop up. The armour, however, found progress difficult in the enclosed country, and on the 9th of August the 50th Division found itself in the van once more.

The road from Le Plessis Grimoult, on the southern slopes of the Pincon, loses height gradually until it reaches St. Pierre la Vieille, nearly four miles farther on the way to Conde. St. Pierre is a small road centre with a hill on either side, Point 229 on the west and Point 266 on the east. The road then runs over rather higher ground just north of the village of Proussy, before swinging south and downwards into the valley at Conde.

The Divisional plan was for the 151st Brigade to advance half-way to St. Pierre, the 69th Brigade to follow through and capture the village and the high ground, and then for the 151st Brigade to pass into the lead once more. But the operation developed rather differently. Enemy resistance was stubborn—he was, after all, fighting for one of his last links with safety east of the River Orne—and before we had gained our objectives the whole Division had been in action. It was midday on the 9th of August when the 151st Brigade, with, right, the 8th Durham Light Infantry and, left, the 6th Durham Light Infantry, supported by the 13th/18th Hussars, attacked south through Le Plessis. They fought their way in the face of artillery, mortar and machine-gun fire to their objectives astride the road at a point some two and a half miles north of St. Pierre.

By 1400 hrs. it was possible to pass the 69th Brigade through, and the 6th and 7th Green Howards made slow progress in face of stiffening opposition for about another mile, where they were held up. At about 1700 hrs. the position of the 69th Brigade was sufficiently stabilized for a plan to be made for the next day. It was then decided that the 5th East Yorkshire Regiment, the third battalion of the brigade, should continue the attack on the 10th of August with the object of capturing St. Pierre and Point 229.

Throughout the night the battalion were shelled, and the prospect was that when they formed up to attack at first light they would be shelled again, for throughout the previous day the only possible forming-up place had been under heavy and direct fire from 88-mm. guns and artillery of heavier calibre. It seemed that the battalion would at best undergo a searching ordeal immediately before the attack, and at worst would suffer considerable casualties. But as the first light of morning appeared in the sky on the 10th of August the area in which the East Yorkshire Regiment were to form up was blanketed in dense fog, and it was impossible for the enemy to see either infantry or tanks moving forward to the attack.

All went well at first. Enemy outposts on the northern bank of a stream in front of St. Pierre were overrun, thirty prisoners were taken and many more Germans were killed. Then resistance stiffened as the East Yorkshire Regiment came under fire of the enemy established on Point 229 and in St. Pierre itself.

Two companies tried to storm Point 229, but enemy tanks and self-propelled guns appeared on the crest and forced them to withdraw. These tactics were repeated each time the infantry tried to attack. Eventually our attack was halted short of both Point 229 and St. Pierre.

The 231st Brigade now braced themselves for the task of forcing a way on towards the vital town of Conde. A brigade attack was launched at 0830 hrs. on the 11th of August, the 1st Hampshire Regiment being directed on Point 229 and St. Pierre, and the 2nd Devonshire Regiment moving on their left. Again early morning fog hid the battlefield. The enemy fought grimly for both the high ground and the village, and we made only slight progress. The story of that day is of wonderful persistence by our infantry in the face of determined opposition, and as an example of the pluck and stamina displayed one can do no better than quote the fact that at 1900 hrs., after a day of continuous fighting and casualties, the Hampshire Regiment tried to mount a three-company attack. But it was of no avail, and a decision had in fact already been taken to use the third battalion, the 1st Dorsetshire Regiment, on the left flank.

This battalion had passed a trying day also. The weather was hot, and owing to the uncertainty of the situation the infantry had been moved several times to positions from which it was thought they might be used. Owing to mines on the main roads and the poor condition of most of the tracks, the movement of supporting arms had added to their problems. The area in which they had been moving had been under shell fire. But despite all this the Dorsetshire Regiment attacked with great dash at 1845 hrs., in the last hours of the hot summer's day, and by last light were south of the town, in which the Hampshire Regiment were still fighting, and pushing on down the road to Conde.

The attack was now really moving. Orders were given for both the Devonshire and Dorsetshire Regiments to push on at 0600 hrs. on the 12th of August. By 1000 hrs. that day they were nearly two miles south of St. Pierre.

But the situation was far from being comfortable for the forward troops. The brigade had in effect driven a long salient into the enemy position. This penetration had gone into the heart of the German gun area. Thus both flanks were open—and the enemy was still in position behind, in St. Pierre. Self-propelled guns, tanks and 125-mm. guns at one time shelled the forward infantry from east, south-east and west.

Just before last light the enemy gathered his strength and put in a heavy counter-attack on the Dorsetshire Regiment, using a battalion of infantry. The enemy attacked from west and south, and one party made for battalion headquarters, pausing on the way to shoot up one of our tanks. The personnel of headquarters held a "thin red line" on a good reverse slope position, and fought a spirited action for two and a half hours. There was a job for everyone—cooks, batmen, orderly room staff—and a fierce fire fight ensued at ranges between thirty and fifty yards. One of the Dorsetshire Regiment's carriers was set on fire, and this blaze frequently silhouetted the enemy, many of whom were killed. The defenders of battalion headquarters had five casualties.

Eventually the enemy broke off the attack after suffering heavy casualties, many of them caused by the artillery fire put down by the 90th Field Regiment, who were in support of the brigade.

While the Devonshire and Dorsetshire Regiments had been fighting in their long, narrow salient, the 151st Brigade had attacked to the south-east of St. Pierre and the 9th and 6th Durham Light Infantry, admirably supported by tanks of the 13th/18th Hussars and their own carriers, had scored a notable success in seizing Points 249 and 262.

During the next night (the 12th/13th of August) the 7th Green Howards finally threw the Germans out of St. Pierre, and the backbone of enemy resistance north of Conde was virtually broken. On the 16th of August armoured cars were in Conde—a week after the advance had started from Le Plessis Grimoult.

The following message from Lieutenant-General B. G. Horrocks, Commander, XXX Corps, to the Divisional Commander sums up what was gained from the operation:

"I would like all ranks of 50 (N) Division to realise how much their efforts of the last few days have contributed to the general plan for the encirclement and destruction of the German Army.

"The road Vire—Conde and to the east has been one of the main German supply routes and recently the enemy has done his best to use it for the withdrawal of the large forces west of our present area.

"It was vital that this escape route should be closed and the task was given initially to 50 (N) Division.

"During the last week the Division has been fighting down towards Conde from Mont Pincon. Although the country was suited for defence, and although the enemy was fighting stubbornly, all the attacks launched by 50 (N) Division have been successful and many prisoners have been taken.

"Owing to the scarcity of roads deployment was difficult, yet the Division never faltered and we can now say that the escape route through Conde is closed to the Germans.

"I cannot give you higher praise than by saying that the most experienced battle-fighting Division in the British Army has once more lived up to its high reputation.

"Well done, 50 Div."

The advance on Conde had been the 50th Division's contribution to the general effort to trap the German Seventh Army. Operations by the Allied armies as a whole had gone equally well, and by the 19th of August the trap was closed. The Polish Armoured Division, operating southwards from Falaise under the command of the First Canadian Army, met the Americans coming north in the area of Chambois, a road centre some six miles east of the main road from Falaise to Argentan. That closed the Germans' last escape route from the pocket, and the Allies began the systematic destruction of the very considerable forces remaining inside.

Viewed even in the perspective which time has given it, it is not easy now to appreciate the scale of destruction inflicted on the Germans during those sunlit days of August, 1944. At the time few people in England knew how great was the victory in the making in France; and while the Allies actually moved over the ground in the pocket there was no general realization of what had happened. But what the soldiers saw was at once breath-taking and appalling.

The pocket was, in general terms, bounded by the line Falaise—Conde—Flers—Argentan. As it steadily contracted under inexorable Allied pressure, the focal points of interest and effort shifted eastwards to such places as St. Pierre-sur-Dives, Trun and Chambois.

It was in the dusty roads and lanes and fields around these localities and in their streets that a great part of the German Seventh Army died.

Hedged about by British and American armies, the Germans could only try to break out eastwards, and try to break into the pocket from the east with the armoured forces they had managed to extricate before the trap closed. In general, they failed, though odd groups got away.

Inside the pocket German battle groups strove to open the road while the forces not employed in this supreme effort moved eastwards along the crowded roads, ready to take advantage of any bolthole which might be forced open. In the fields and lanes were thousands of administrative and supply vehicles and their crews, who had no part in the battle. They just waited . . . but their task was as unenviable as that of the hotly engaged battle groups.

For the Allies, standing sentinel about this trapped army, divided the ground into zones—one for the air forces; one for the artillery of the XII Corps; one for the guns of an armoured brigade; and so on, until the whole area occupied by the Germans was split up into what became known as "killing grounds."

Into these zones, day and night, poured an increasing torrent of shells, bombs and rockets. Targets of the sort gunners rarely see were continually presented—a column of two hundred motor vehicles jammed bumper to tail and unable to move because the road was blocked by wreckage; a horse-transport column in panic and trapped in a narrow lane.

The Germans moved along the roads until they were choked with dead horses and men and burning wreckage. Then they took to the fields, across which they moved in columns of five and six abreast. At bottlenecks, such as gateways and stream crossing places, the traffic piled up and was then destroyed by shells and rocket-firing planes. Swiftly destruction would be spread across the entire field, until it was impossible for anything on wheels or tracks to move across it. In a day or two many fields became like the roads—simply impassable owing to the carnage and destruction. It was a battlefield that decided the fate of France.

By the last days of August it had become clear that the Germans in the West had not only lost France but were in danger of losing the Reich itself. Crippled by enormous losses, by sheer futility in the higher direction of the war, and by inadequate reserves at the vital points, the remnants made their way eastwards.

Nearly three months of bitter fighting, culminating in a blood-bath big enough even for their extravagant tastes, had produced the turning point of the war in Europe. Paris belonged to France again, and the Allied armies were streaming towards the frontiers of the Reich.

Faced with this bleak outlook, the Germans could in the nature of things have no other aim than to bolt the door on the frontiers of Germany. It meant, of course, abandoning the flying-bomb sites in the coastal area between the Seine and the Dutch frontier; it meant urgent disengagement of the major part of the forces remaining after the Falaise disaster, and an equally urgent regrouping along the Rhine; it meant finding reinforcements from occupied countries or other theatres of war; and it meant a shattering loss of prestige.

But the German High Command, evidently sobered by its discovery that its head and a brick wall could not occupy the same place at the same time, ordered its unfortunate soldiers back towards the Rhine, with the exception of the yet more unfortunate few locked up in the Atlantic and Channel ports.

The British and American armies braced themselves for the great pursuit towards Germany. And within the Second British Army the XXX Corps (including the 50th Division) was in the van. Antwerp was the great prize which fell to the Corps in this phase of the campaign, and an understanding of the broad trend of events leading up to its capture will assist the reader in turn to follow the movements and adventures of the 50th Division.

Between the 25th and the 28th of August the leading troops of the XXX Corps (the 43rd Division) forced a crossing of the Seine at Vernon, and on the 28th of August the Corps ordered an advance over the River Seine to the Amiens area. The Guards Armoured Division was to lead on the right, the 11th Armoured Division on the left. Instructions to both were to press forward at maximum speed regardless of the progress of the troops on the flanks, and to bypass local resistance. The 50th Division was to follow the armour, providing protection for the left flank of the Corps, and mopping up enemy left in the wake of the tanks.

The advance started at first light on the 29th of August. The next day the 11th Armoured Division advanced all day against slight opposition, and continued to move all night, nose to tail at five miles in one hour.

On the 31st of August Amiens was captured (and also General Ederbach, commander of the German Seventh Army). The 11th Armoured Division seized two intact bridges over the Somme at Amiens, and the Guards captured another east of the city in face of considerable opposition, and two more without much trouble. All five bridges had been prepared for demolition, but engineers riding on armoured cars reached the scene in time and withdrew the charges.

On the 1st of September the Guards Armoured Division entered Arras, and on the 3rd they entered Brussels at 2000 hrs., receiving a welcome more fantastically jubilant than any dream. The next day the 11th Armoured Division entered Antwerp, and by evening the great port, with its dock area and vital sluice gates, was firmly in our hands. In five and a half days the tanks had performed the remarkable feat of covering nearly two hundred and fifty miles. Behind them had come the infantry of the 50th Division, steadily clearing up remaining groups of enemy, keeping a grip on towns through which the armour had had to hurry, and generally consolidating the gains won by the dash and speed of the armoured formations. For us, too, it was a triumphal progress, with flowers, kisses, extraordinary welcomes and festivals—and fights with the Germans mixed up with it all.

The story of our progress now to be unfolded is largely an affair of long-distance driving, enthusiastic welcomes, flag-waving and cheers. Of course, there was fighting, but it came on a small scale and at infrequent intervals, and is overshadowed in memory by the more cheerful and colourful events incidental to the liberation of two great European countries.

The 50th Division had travelled a long road towards this moment. Back and forth across the Middle East deserts the "TT" signs had been stuck in the ground to point the way we had come; Tunisia and Sicily had seen them, the same white letters on a red background, painted on a metal plate cut from a petrol tin. Now the same signs streamed across France and Belgium in the wake of the lorry-borne infantry who had returned via Alamein and Sicily to finish the job they had left in 1940. It was a great and triumphant moment; but it was not the sort of war we have described hitherto in this book. There was no real front. Isolated pockets of enemy fell into our hands like overripe fruit—hundreds at a time. Here a bridge had to be fought for, there a wood cleared. This cost lives. There are special sadness and irony in such deaths.

But this narrative now takes on the colour of those days between the 29th of August, 1944, and the early days of September. It deals not with the moves of formations and the formal record of their day-to-day history, for there is little of interest in that save to the student of logistics, but with individual experiences which were typical of the experiences of everyone in those happy days when Hottot and Tilly seemed very far away.

An account of the long journey by an officer of the Divisional machine-gun battalion, the 2nd Cheshire Regiment, gives a good picture of that period. The Cheshire Regiment were one of the oldest

T

components of the Division, and through the long campaigns their companies had faithfully supported the infantry battalions. Often their magnificent efforts and unfailing support went without the publicity that attended the efforts of the others; that is, perhaps, inevitable in the case of a unit which, in the day of battle, splits itself into many parts in order to give support to a brigade of infantry; the brigade as a whole gets the credit. The story of the Cheshire Regiment's officer is as follows:

"Inspiration to success (in the advance to Antwerp) was found in the fact that the operation would involve the clearing of the flying-bomb coast and the relief of Southern England from the pressure of their attack.

"It was hoped to capture Amiens within 48 hours, but when this was revealed to the men there were some cynical grunts from those who recalled the invasion plan for the D day capture of Villers Bocage. 50 Div was again given the task of mopping up after the armour and was responsible also for the flank protection of 30 Corps. 231 Brigade was to move behind the Guards Armoured Division and 151 Brigade behind 11 Armoured Division. 69 Brigade was in reserve behind 8 Armoured Brigade in the centre. Our column, which, including as it did a variety of captured vehicles, had so far presented a picturesque and circus-like appearance, was now reduced both in size and beauty by our having to hand in a number of German trucks and by an order issued at this time forbidding the carrying of flowers on trucks and the long established practice of painting the names of the owner's girl friends on the front of each vehicle.

"During the evening of the 29 Aug, in pouring rain, Battalion Headquarters left their comfortable chateau and, moving through Vernon in artificial moonlight,[1] crossed the river to leaguer in a muddy orchard at La Chappelle St. Ouen where, inevitably, half the trucks became bogged. They were preceded by A Company who spent the night at a village somewhat distressingly called 'Tilly.'

"On 31 Aug C Company despatched one section under Sergeant Abbott to round up a party of enemy reported to them by the F.F.I. They captured one officer, two sergeants and 22 other ranks. Their move this time brought them via Beaugrenier and Chaumont-en-Vixen to Jouy-sous-Thelles. A Company, after a brief pause at Conty, a town which they found beflagged but

---

[1] Artificial moonlight—lighting provided by searchlights.

deserted and where 3 Platoon took some prisoners, went to Saloued and 3 and 5 Platoons took up positions at Pont St. Metz covering two small bridges over the Somme.

"4 Platoon with the 6 D.L.I. had driven straight to Amiens, in the wake of 11 Armoured Division, where they mounted guard over the main road bridge. At first the people of Amiens were restrained in their welcome, not quite sure whether it was not a little premature to start rejoicing, but by the evening, cheering, singing, laughing crowds overflowed the streets and left us in no doubt that they were glad to see us. C.S.M. Wilde of A Company, entering the school at Saloued to enquire about billets, found three German soldiers there drinking champagne with the civilians, who handed them over to him. The same night an S.S. trooper who had tried to swim the Somme gave himself up, soaking wet and minus most of his clothes.

"Battalion Headquarters meanwhile went through Egremont-en-Vexin to Chantoiseau, where D Company again succeeded in finding a large empty chateau, and B Company a short distance only, through Chaumont to Auneuil.

"Major Mellor (B Company) obtained the permission of the brigadier to try and get through to visit friends at Bois Robin, some distance forward, and set off with Corporal Evans and Private Cotterill in his jeep. On the way he passed the greater part of 11 Armoured Division's column and on reaching Fouilloy found himself among the foremost troops. The leading tank had halted short of the railway bridge and its commander informed him that what appeared to be a camouflaged enemy tank was covering the bridge from the far side; he could not engage it without first exposing himself to the enemy's guns. The advance was being held up on this account.

"Major Mellor, who knew this part of the country well, decided to try and outflank the tank on foot and capture its crew. He therefore enlisted the aid of three F.F.I. men who were standing by, one of whom would act as guide across the surrounding fields, and, arranging with the tank commander to cover his movement with the tank Browning and open fire if he should see any movement round the enemy tank, set off with Corporal Evans on his self-imposed mission. Corporal Evans was armed with a rifle, one of the F.F.I. men with a woman's pistol, another with a last-war Mauser which, lacking a magazine, had to be single loaded.

"The party crawled along the hedgerows and ditches parallel to the road until, peering through a gap in the hedge, they found themselves within a few yards of the enemy. The vehicle proved to be a half-track and not a tank, and around it a group of five or six Germans stood gazing up the road towards the bridge, oblivious of the stalkers' approach. By this time two of the F.F.I. men had fallen out of the party, and the third had been left some way back to cover the advance along the ditches. Major Mellor therefore ordered Corporal Evans to cover the Germans through the gap in the hedge while he himself went through it and on to the top of them. The plan was entirely successful and the enemy put up their hands.

"Scarcely had they done so when another German car drove by, and, not seeing the group around the half-track, went on up to the bridge. The tank commander opened up with his Browning, the car swerved into the ditch and its occupants came running back towards Major Mellor, who fired at them with his pistol. Unfortunately the tank commander, seeing movement around the half-track and remembering his promise, chose this moment to open up on it, setting the half-track on fire and bullets flying all around it. The whole party, captives and captors, beat a hasty retreat through the hedge, the group from the car taking cover in a nearby field. Once clear of the road, the astonished Germans were easily disarmed. The F.F.I. man was left to guard them while Major Mellor and Corporal Evans set off after the car party. Corporal Evans wounded one with his rifle and covered the remainder while Major Mellor got round and came up on them from behind, whereupon they too surrendered. The prisoners, who included a C.S.M. of the Afrika Korps, were then marched back to the tank.

"The armour was now able to push forward along the road again, and Major Mellor went on into the village to the house of the local resistance leader. Here he learnt that the enemy was coming up from the opposite side of the village while the armour continued to roll straight through. He therefore organised ambushes, manned by F.F.I., at each entrance to the village and had soon 30 or 40 prisoners in the bag. The arms taken from them were used to equip the F.F.I. recruits, who now included almost the whole village, man, woman and child; since no recruit would accept a firearm without first ensuring that it would fire, the pandemonium may be imagined.

"The Germans soon realised that there were English troops in the village and contented themselves with digging-in on the west side and Spandauing the road. When the armour had passed through, however, they became bolder and moved up to Spandau the village itself. A party of about 30 were reported to be advancing down the road and Major Mellor drove out in his jeep to meet them; he engaged them with a Browning and they withdrew, leaving two Spandaus behind. The F.F.I. continued to bring in prisoners and by dark the total had reached a century.

"A further visit to the half-track resulted in the capture of another group of Germans, including three officers who had been engaged in conversation by the French civilians until Major Mellor could get up to them. An infantry company had now arrived to take over the railway bridge, and all prisoners were handed to them. The total armament captured so far consisted of eight anti-tank and two field guns, some bazookas, six Spandaus, a selection of automatic rifles and tommy-guns and numerous rifles and grenades.

"As darkness fell, contact was made with Eccles, a nearby village, where five enemy tanks and two hundred men were reported. A small fighting patrol of F.F.Is. was laid on to stop them from escaping to the east, but owing to bright moonlight it was not possible to get into the village. At daybreak, however, the village was surrounded, shots were exchanged and the enemy sent one of their number to offer surrender of the whole force; it consisted of two officers, a C.S.M. and approximately 200 other ranks. Allied casualties were two F.F.I. wounded. These new prisoners were marched back to Fouleroy, where it was found that the infantry company had also returned the original ones handed over to them.

"With the numerous additional prisoners brought in by the F.F.I. during the night the grand total now exceeded 500. Many of them begged Major Mellor not to leave them with the F.F.I. and as a large number of them had surrendered to him personally, he determined to see them into a British prisoner of war cage, preferably one organised by 50 Div. Accordingly the prisoners were formed up in column, and with 10 F.F.I. acting as guards and Corporal Evans in the jeep presiding, were marched back along the road. Major Mellor went ahead and arranged with the Town Major at Beauvais for their reception. On his reporting back to brigade headquarters, however, the Brigade Major ordered that they should be brought back to the divisional cage. Brigade had now reached Cachy, where B Company headquarters was established. 8 Platoon, who were with them, spent the day helping the infantry to search the area for more stray Germans.

"Early on 1 Sep 5 Platoon of A Company, leaving 3 Platoon

at Point St Metz, went with the 8 D.L.I. to try and seize the bridge at Pintigny, a few miles down the river from Amiens. The Germans blew the bridge however and prevented all attempts to cross. 5 Platoon therefore came into positions on commanding ground overlooking the far bank of the Somme. At about 1700 hours the enemy decided to pull out, and, forming up in orderly fashion under cover of some woods by the water, moved off in file across our front, a staff car leading the way, followed by horses and carts, followed by the infantry. It was a machine-gunner's dream, an opportunity that comes seldom, and 5 Platoon proceeded to make the most of it. For 30 minutes their guns swept the column; the staff car went up in flames, the horses died in the shafts, and the men crumpled and fell; one man who tried to pretend that he was part of a telegraph pole was, in the words of the number one, 'tied in a knot round it'; claims as to the numbers killed varied between 40 and 60.

"While 5 Platoon was thus occupied, 3 Platoon crossed the Somme and helped the 9 D.L.I. to form another bridgehead across one of the smaller bridges.

"4 Platoon and Company Headquarters remained in Amiens, where the population, now wildly enthusiastic, celebrated their first day of freedom with a general holiday and dealt in the usual manner with the collaborators.

"C Company moved from Jouy-sous-Thelles through St Aubin-en-Bray and Croissey to Le Bosquel, south of Amiens, in the morning, and on again in the afternoon to five miles north-east of the town on the Albert road. Later in the evening 9 Platoon went with 14 Heavy Mortar Platoon and the 2 Devons to take over Arras from the Guards Armoured Division, where the remainder of the company joined them the next day, the platoons being now under command of the three battalions of the brigade. On 2 September, too, A Company moved to Doullens where 3 and 5 Platoons went into positions on the high ground to the north while 4 Platoon occupied the citadel, covering the western approaches.

"During the afternoon the local F.F.I. reported that two of their number had been shot in a small village to the south. As 4 Platoon was not very busy, Major Martin took them off to deal with the matter and, searching the surrounding countryside, rounded up 53 prisoners. One Frenchman, who had acted as guide in the search, spoke excellent English, and when asked where he had learned it, explained that in the last war he had been the mascot of the 10th Battalion The Cheshire Regiment for four years and produced photographs of himself as a boy of 14, dressed in British uniform with the Cheshire badge in his cap.

"On the way back from the search the platoon met the local F.F.I. leader wearing a smart, if motley uniform; on being told of 53 prisoners he took a pace backwards, clicked his heels, saluted smartly and exclaimed in English 'I have to report that we are now completely liberated. Good egg!'

"The move up from Amiens into Belgium which began on 3 September comprised the final phase of the advance.

"The welcome we had received on our way through France had been tremendous, but now we were in Belgium even this was exceeded, and our advance became almost a triumphal progress. In every town and village we were greeted by cheering crowds lining the road and swarming round the vehicles if the column halted for a moment. Each town, it seemed, had a special offering of its own. In Tournai it was plums, Renaix had beer, Ninove presented us with local-manufactured matches, other places tomatoes, cakes or nuts, everywhere flowers and fruit were flung into the trucks as we passed. In exchange, the girls everywhere demanded kisses from 'Tommy.' The hospitality and generosity of the Belgian people were almost overpowering and certainly unforgettable—Brussels, Antwerp, Alost, Ninove, Malines, names such as these will always revive pleasant memories for many of us after the war.

"A special pleasure for several who had been with the battalion in 1940 was the renewal of old friendships; 5 September, which was a static day for all companies, provided a good opportunity for this and the villages in which the battalion had been billeted four years previously were close at hand. Major Martin revisited Templeuve where B Company had then been; C.S.M. Wilde went to Wattines Farm, old A Company headquarters, and Sergeant Lamb and Corporal Chatham to Le Bas, one time Battalion Headquarters. Everywhere they received a great welcome, photographs of men of the battalion of 1940 were produced with many queries as to their present whereabouts—one on the wall of old B Company Headquarters depicted Major Mellor staring morosely at some 1940 line fortifications. At Le Bas Sergeant Lamb discovered and brought back with him the Battalion side drums which had been left behind in the retreat to Dunkirk.

"At one time 8 Platoon lost touch with the infantry, and, crossing the river Schelde, went forward to liberate the town of

Lokeren, engaging parties of enemy by carrier action. Lieutenant Watson, the platoon commander, received a written address from the burgomaster thanking him for liberation, an event which occurred some weeks before others officially claimed to have liberated the town."

So much, then, for the machine gunners' experience in the great advance. There were many other units which had similar adventures. Notable among them was the Divisional reconnaissance unit, the 61st Reconnaissance Regiment, who really came into their own during this phase of operations. The confined country of the bocage had been no place for their armoured cars and carriers, but the long chase gave them opportunity to use their speed and mobility. To them fell in a large measure the task which had been given to the 50th Division of protecting the left flank of the XXX Corps. In doing this job the unit covered about three hundred and fifty miles, took approximately three thousand prisoners, and inflicted a considerable amount of damage on the enemy at a cost to themselves of twenty casualties.

Much of their work was accomplished against weakening enemy resistance, but there were none the less occasions when these light armoured fighting vehicles took on opponents of much heavier metal —and won. On the 1st of September, for instance, a troop of three armoured cars was moving along a road north-west of Amiens. It had met and dealt with small groups of infantry, but had not encountered serious opposition.

Suddenly the leading car was fired on by a Panther tank which was in a copse on the left of the road. This car at once wheeled off the road to the right into the nearest cover, while the other two cars engaged the enemy with all their weapons. Although the 37-mm. guns of the armoured cars could not inflict serious damage on such a tank at anything but the shortest range, the Panther withdrew—a remarkable illustration of the moral of offensive action.

Three days later, a carrier troop under a sergeant with one 6-pounder anti-tank gun fought and won an engagement with about two hundred and fifty enemy infantry, a Mark IV Special tank and three half-track vehicles. The sergeant and his men were covering a bridge at Oudenarde when, at 0600 hrs., an enemy column was heard approaching.

Shortly afterwards the leading vehicle reached the bridge, and an officer got out to make sure that the structure was still intact. Meanwhile, the other vehicles closed up, followed by about two companies of infantry. The reconnaissance men held their fire until the leading enemy troops were about seventy yards from them. The anti-tank gun then opened fire and "brewed-up" the three half-tracks and the tank with four rounds in as many seconds. At the same time the carrier troop opened fire with their small arms. The one anti-tank gun fired high explosive at a wall behind the infantry, causing havoc and consternation, and the enemy withdrew in confusion. But they were not yet finally beaten. They established themselves in a factory dominating the bridge, and also worked snipers through the houses down to the canal.

The carrier troop continued to engage the enemy until 1330 hrs., when the enemy commander, an S.S. officer, came out under a Red Cross flag to remove the dead and wounded. Sixty casualties were collected, most of the wounded being taken over by our own troops.

The battle then continued, but the enemy showed little further fight. Most of his forces dispersed northwards, where they were captured by a troop of "C" Squadron which was astride their main escape route. Our troops suffered no casualties in this action.

During the advance the flexibility of the Division had been tested. Brigades were often sent off on tasks which took them far from the Divisional Headquarters axis of advance. The 231st Brigade was suddenly taken away from the 50th Division, and joined first the Guards Armoured Division and later the 11th Armoured Division, with whom they helped to hold Antwerp. The 151st Brigade were for a time under the command of the Second Army and garrisoned Brussels. On the other side of the balance sheet was the 1st Belgian Brigade, which joined the Division temporarily and was able to take part in the liberation of Brussels. In addition, the speed of the advance and the consequent rapid changes in situation led to many variations of plan.

It became vital that order and counter-order should not deteriorate into disorder, and that orders should get through over those long distances. Communications were stretched to the limit, but on the whole control was well maintained by means of wireless, hard-motoring liaison officers, and personal contacts between commanders and their staffs.

It is on occasions such as these, when an army suddenly breaks loose and its component parts speed outwards and onwards towards situations which change from hour to hour, that a commander has to content himself with an instruction saying where to make for and what to do on arrival, and leave it at that. This is in some respects the supreme test of a division's war-worthiness, when initiative, comprehension of what is required, dash and common sense, good services and smooth staff work are the keys to success.

The 50th Division had done this sort of thing before. With

memories of past pursuits in Africa and Sicily to cheer them, they drove in their dusty vehicles across France and Belgium without trouble and with much enjoyment to themselves. And at the end of the first week in September which rang down the curtain on this phase of the campaign the Division had a "balance sheet" which can be summarized as follows:

Casualties for August.[1]—64 officers; 1,162 other ranks.

Prisoners of war captured at
    9th June: 2,300 (actually counted; the real figure was much higher, but is not known precisely).
    30th August: 4,838.
    4th September: 8,901.

---

[1] Compare with total casualties since D Day: 488 officers; 6,932 other ranks.

CONDE

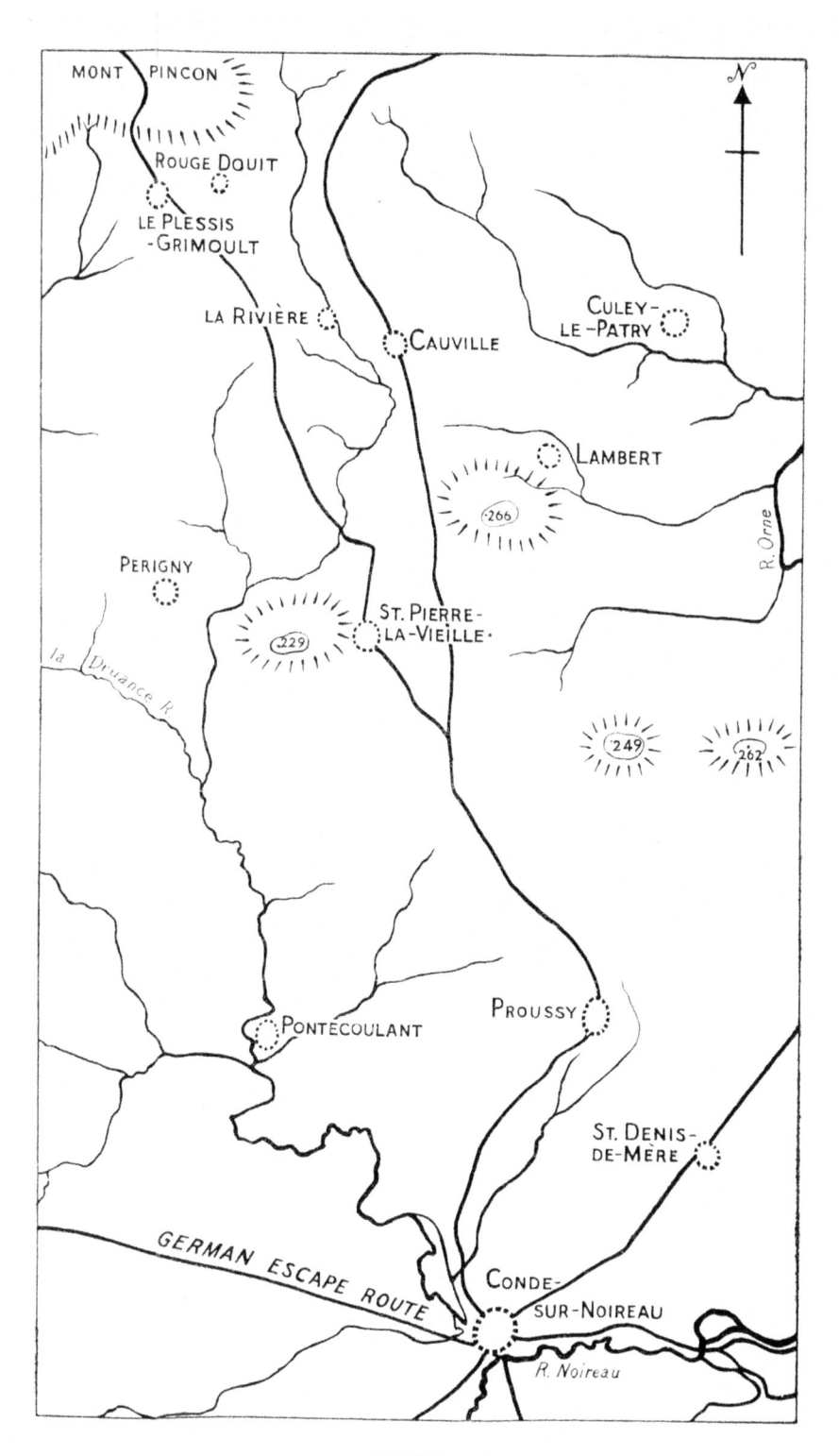

CHAPTER XXIII

The 50th Division's last battles in Europe—The 69th Brigade force the Albert Canal—The 151st Brigade's bitter struggle at Gheel—The operation that culminated at Arnhem—First infantry into Holland—Endurance at Nijmegen—"The Island"—And the End of the Road

SEPTEMBER, 1944, TO MAY, 1945

Thus the pursuit ended, and the 50th Division entered upon the last phase of its campaign with the Second Army in Europe. We now faced the battle for the Albert Canal, which for our part was fought with great bitterness in the area of Gheel. There followed the great airborne land operation known as "Market Garden," which was designed to carry the Second Army across Holland and its water barriers to the North Sea, thus cutting off the enemy forces remaining in the Low Countries. And when "Market Garden" fell short of full success the 50th Division found themselves in the Nijmegen bridgehead—which we came to call "The Island"—until, in the last days of a grey and watery November, it became known that the Division had fought its last battle in Europe and was to return to England.

On the 7th of September the 50th Division was warned that it would be required to cross the Albert Canal, one of the last water barriers before the Dutch frontier, either at Beeringen, behind the 11th Armoured Division, or farther west near Gheel. The wandering children began to return to their parents. The 69th Brigade, which was already under command, moved to Hersselt in readiness to cross the canal. The 151st Brigade, who had been in Brussels, moved to Hersselt on the 8th of September, and on the same day the 231st Brigade reverted to the command of the 50th Division and began to move up from Antwerp.

While the other brigades were on the move the 69th Brigade struck swiftly. Two battalions—the 6th and 7th Green Howards—were at Alost on the 7th of September, fifty miles from the canal. All battalions were ordered to concentrate at Hersselt, and while his battalion was moving up the commanding officer of the 6th Green Howards, Lieutenant-Colonel Hutchinson, was given orders to reconnoitre the canal and to be prepared to make an assault crossing south of Gheel. The intention was to secure a bridgehead to cover the construction of a bridge by the side of the original road bridge, the site of which was near a hamlet called Het Punt. The plan provided for an assault crossing by the 6th Green Howards, with the 7th Green Howards crossing at the same place afterwards.

Speed was the vital factor. There was not time before dark for a close and detailed reconnaissance of the canal, but Lieutenant-Colonel Hutchinson none the less discovered that the bridge was blown, that the canal had a steep bank that would make the launching of assault boats difficult though not impossible, and that the enemy had posts at likely crossing places with patrols between these points.

At the end of their day's journeyings, then, the battalion were faced with the prospect of forcing without delay one of Belgium's great water obstacles. H hour was fixed for 0130 hrs. the following morning. The battalion were to cross about a thousand yards east of the road at Het Punt and to move north-west to seize a bridgehead covering the site of the original bridge. The 7th Green Howards were to cross immediately afterwards and secure the right of the bridgehead. For the whole operation only two assault boats and twelve reconnaissance boats were available. In the whole battalion only the commanding officer and the company commanders had had time to see the crossing places.

In sum, it was a swift operation to be carried out with slender resources. Surprise would be vital, and therefore the first crossing was to be made in silence, with no artillery support.

Heavy rain fell during the evening. Unfortunately it stopped just before the crossing took place and was succeeded by bright moonlight. "A" and "B" Companies had one assault boat each. The infantry bore them up the steep bank to the canal with no little apprehension as to what would greet the sudden appearance of this target in the moonlight. They carried them over the top and pushed them into the water—and nothing happened. The enemy's suspicions had not been aroused, and the Green Howards crossed the canal and reached their objectives on the other side without a shot being fired.

A cable was laid across the canal to guide the assault boats. Ropes were attached to the reconnaissance boats so that they could be pulled back and forth across the canal to supplement the work of the assault boats. But it was a slow and laborious business.

One pair of men in a reconnaissance boat got about half-way across and then began to go round helplessly in circles. Eventually the crew landed with great caution and prepared to deal with the enemy—on the bank from which they had set off.

The shortage of boats made the crossing extremely slow, and the assault troops reached the far bank only a section at a time. Nevertheless, all four companies were across by 0445 hrs. Thus far, the operation had been virtually unopposed. But with morning came a changed situation.

It soon became apparent that "D" Company, who had advanced straight to their objective, had in the darkness moved undetected through several enemy positions. When it grew light both sides understood what had happened, with the immediate result that all the approaches to "D" Company were covered by enemy fire, and our troops were isolated.

At the same time there were signs of activity in the houses at Het Punt. The enemy had been there all the time, but by now was waking up and realizing what had happened. They reacted with light machine-gun and mortar fire on "A" Company. An unpleasant situation was not eased by the wounding of the commanding officer during the morning.

However, the bridgehead was strengthened early in the day by the 7th Green Howards, who began to cross the canal at 0600 hrs. Their first troops had arrived in the area just before midnight, after a long journey over unknown routes, most of it in darkness.

When their turn came to cross, the hard-worked boats were beginning to fail. One was leaking so badly that it was practically unserviceable. However, all four companies had completed their hazardous "voyage" by 0800 hrs. and the 7th Green Howards were on their objective by 0930 hrs.

The bridgehead held firm during the 8th of September, and by 0700 hrs. the next day the 5th East Yorkshire Regiment had arrived and had concentrated just south of the canal, in readiness to cross—either behind the two battalions already in the bridgehead or on their flank.

At 1000 hrs. Brigadier Knox gave orders that they were to make an assault crossing just west of the main crossing place at Het Punt, where enemy resistance was still determined. This would have the effect of squeezing the Germans from the other flank.

In the area where the crossing was to be made a high bank ran parallel to the canal and about four hundred yards away from it. Between this bank and the water was a stretch of flat, sandy country with little cover, and owing to enemy observation it was quite impossible to move on to it. Therefore those responsible for the preliminary reconnaissances were unable to look at the banks of the canal and choose their launching points on the ground. They were helped, however, by the battery captain of the 288th Field Battery (of the 124th Field Regiment), whose guns had already been in action in that area and who therefore had some knowledge of the ground. He also registered two field regiments for a fire plan (at call) and subsequent defensive tasks, while Captain Wood, of the same battery, registered the 124th Field Regiment. A medium regiment also made ready to shoot in support of the East Yorkshire Regiment.

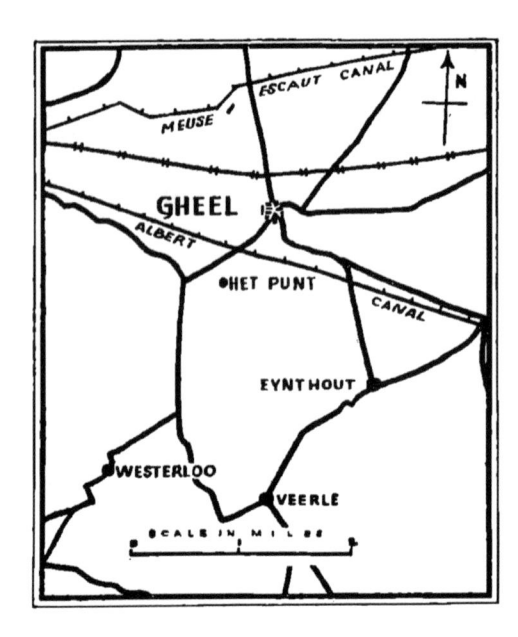

The infantry plan was to attack with, right, "D" Company and, left, "B" Company. The crossing was to be made in silence, but should the enemy offer resistance the fire plan already outlined, in addition to a mortar and machine-gun programme, was to be put into operation to induce a change of heart.

At nine o'clock on the night of the 9th of September the assaulting companies, each with three assault boats, moved forward and formed up under cover of the big bank south of the canal. Darkness was at hand; it was bitterly cold, and rain had begun to fall. Half an hour later the infantry, wet and cold and none too fresh after their travels, dragged the boats up the bank and set out on their dangerous journey across the bare, sandy ground towards the canal bank.

It was dark by now, and the only sound was the hiss of the rain. Yet both the assault companies reached the bank of the canal without having been observed by the enemy. They crossed unopposed. When the reserve companies began to cross, however, the enemy in Het

Punt came to life quite suddenly, and these companies made their landing under a hail of small-arms fire. Battalion headquarters crossed safely, accompanied by a party of the faithful gunners of the 288th Battery. When they reached the north bank they learned that "D" Company was held up by fire from houses in the general area of Het Punt.

At 0100 hrs. it was decided to assault the buildings, using "A" Company supported by fire from "D" Company. Four Piats, three 2-inch mortars, Brens and rifles poured a considerable volume of fire into the buildings, which were set ablaze; and an assault party of ten, under Lieutenant Smith, attacked, cleared the enemy out after capturing two officers and twenty other ranks, and reported that about eight men of the Green Howards, of whom five were wounded, were said to be in a cellar.

Opposition along the entire battalion front then faded away, and by 0400 hrs. matters were sufficiently in hand for prisoners to be ferried back to the other side of the canal.

The 69th Brigade were now all across, and the bridgehead was a solid fact.

That was the 69th Brigade's contribution to the forcing of the Albert Canal. A remarkable action was fought by the 151st Brigade to enlarge the gains won so hardly by the East Yorkshire Regiment and the Green Howards.

During the period from the 8th to the 12th of September the 151st Brigade made and held a bridgehead on the right flank of the original one. They did so in the face of most determined opposition, and at the cost of bitter fighting which led to severe casualties for the Germans. In this battle of the Gheel bridgehead our opponents were, in the first instance, men from two German Air Force regiments who fought as infantry. Such troops had always had a reputation for good fighting qualities, and at Gheel they maintained their traditions until the Durham Light Infantry wore them down and finally disposed of them as fighting units. Then the Germans brought up the 2nd Parachute Division to try to contain the bridgehead. This was a coincidence, for in one of the bloodiest bridgehead battles fought in this or any other war—at Primosole bridge in Sicily—the Durham Brigade had encountered and crippled this same enemy formation. At Gheel the result of the action was the same—defeat of the enemy followed by his withdrawal—but it was no easy victory.

It was on the afternoon of the 8th of September that Brigadier Gordon, who had arrived with his brigade at Hersselt, received orders to make a crossing of the canal to the east of the existing bridgehead, in order to cover the construction of a folding-boat bridge. The brigadier decided that it was a task for a battalion, and in the later afternoon the 8th Durham Light Infantry crossed in face of opposition. No. 5 Platoon and No. 12 Heavy Mortar Platoon (2nd Cheshire Regiment) were ordered to support the infantry. The machine gunners established a section on either flank of the crossing point, but kept their guns hidden below the level of the canal embankment. The enemy were evidently suspicious, for an odd shot or two snapped overhead, and the inhabitants of the neighbouring village hastily took in their flags again.

As the first boats went over the top and down into the water the machine-gun sections slid their guns the last yard to the top of the bank and got into action while the mortar observation-post party crossed the canal with the assaulting wave.

The enemy reaction was immediate. A single Spandau sank three boats almost at once, but was then spotted and silenced by Sergeant Woods's machine-gun section. "Spandau Joe" (the Division's name for any German with a machine gun) had revetted his weapon pit with 75-mm. ammunition boxes without taking the trouble to remove the shells from the inside; after a long burst from our Vickers the whole lot was blown skyward with a gratifying crash, and "Spandau Joe" himself, with his gun, toppled down the embankment in which the position had been concealed.

But there were other enemy still active. Mortar bombs continued to fall among the infantry, and a self-propelled gun on the right shelled them continuously, firing down the line of the canal. Nevertheless, by 2000 hrs. the whole battalion was firmly established on the north bank of the canal, and work was in progress on the bridge.

The enemy reacted quickly to this second bridgehead with a counter-attack at 2250 hrs. on the right flank, which was beaten back without difficulty. That was the prelude to the bitter struggle which lay ahead. For the 50th Division the paramount task was to strengthen and expand the bridgehead; for the enemy, to muster from his jaded troops a force strong enough to drive it in.

At 0410 hrs. the enemy was ready. He attacked the right-hand company of the 8th Durham Light Infantry—"A" Company—and infiltrated to within grenade range. "C" Company, who were in rear of "A" Company, became involved, but after fierce fighting the situation was restored. The two companies lost seven officers, including both company commanders.

By 0700 hrs. "C" Squadron, 61st Reconnaissance Regiment, crossed the folding-boat bridge and, passing through the 8th Durham Light Infantry, patrolled vigorously, especially to the right, the open flank. They were quickly in contact with the enemy, notably in the area of the village of Doornboom, and were prevented from making any further advance.

The 6th Durham Light Infantry were to cross the bridge after the armoured cars and carriers of the Reconnaissance Regiment, but before they could do so the bridge collapsed, possibly owing to one of the boats being struck by shell splinters. This meant that the infantry had to cross in assault boats, and that their anti-tank guns and carriers had to stay behind. Meanwhile, the 8th Durham Light Infantry (in the words of an official account) "continued to engage the enemy."

Just what that means in terms of determination and steadfast application to the job in hand is not easy to describe. The action was like so many others in the long story of war—it had no salient and spectacular feature. It was just a matter of hanging on grimly and under continuous bombardment until someone relieved a thoroughly uncomfortable situation. And it requires great faith to crouch in a forward slit trench, accepting the chastisement of the enemy and giving back what is possible under the circumstances, and hoping that eventually friends will arrive to ease the pressure.

So the 8th Durham Light Infantry, under long-range machine-gun fire from the right flank, mortared and shelled by self-propelled guns, stood their ground. They were helped, as always, by the machine guns and mortars of the Cheshire Regiment. No. 3 Platoon went into position by themselves on the canal bank south-east of the bridgehead in an attempt to draw off the machine-gun fire and keep the enemy on that flank occupied. For thirty-six hours this platoon waged a lonely and most successful war against the enemy infantry dug in only forty yards away across the canal. At first the enemy were most aggressive, but after Lieutenant Dupre's guns had knocked out two Spandau teams and the crew of a 20-mm. gun, the Germans became much quieter, and kept their heads down. A 2-inch mortar was therefore borrowed from the infantry, and with the aid of this little weapon the Germans were forced from their defences on the canal bank. As they ran for cover in the woods the machine gunners shot them down.

Civilians later told our troops that eleven of the enemy had been killed and twenty-three wounded, and that the remainder wished to surrender, but were unable to do so because they were shot at every time they showed themselves.

Meanwhile, in the bridgehead itself, the fighting increased in scale and intensity as the 6th Durham Light Infantry continued to cross the canal. By 1100 hrs. the bridge was in use again, and the carriers and anti-tank guns began to cross. But the advance of the 6th Durham Light Infantry through the 8th Durham Light Infantry was hotly

U

contested. This cost the enemy dear, for by the end of the day there were sixty enemy dead in the battalion areas alone, and casualties as a whole were conservatively estimated at a hundred killed, with wounded in proportion. Prisoners taken during the day came from two Luftwaffe regiments and one or two *ad hoc* units. The Luftwaffe troops were between eighteen and twenty years of age, and this had been their first—and last—battle in the Second World War. Most of them had been called up during the last three or four months.

It was obvious from what these youths said that the enemy was trying frantically to organize some sort of mixed force to hold the 50th Division on the line of the Albert Canal. The familiar German formula for seemingly hopeless situations was being applied again. The remains of what had been the best formations had been withdrawn either into reserve or to refit. To the front had gone improvised units and formations hastily raked together from training depots, garrisons and even hospitals. Their fate was, of course, sealed from the moment they set off for the front. They were really a buffer between us and the seasoned enemy forces in process of recovery, and the cold German intention was to gain time while we were destroying these hapless units—who fought extremely well and bravely—before being forced to commit their best troops again.

But the enemy's intentions did not materialize in quite that way in the Gheel bridgehead battle, for, by the 10th of September, all battalions of the 151st Brigade were in the bridgehead and pressing the enemy so hard that the "buffer" showed signs of premature collapse, and a few of the remaining precious German tanks appeared on the scene to try to restore a situation which, for the enemy, was becoming serious. The 6th Durham Light Infantry had forced their way into Gheel, and the 9th Durham Light Infantry had advanced on the right, while a tank squadron of the Sherwood Rangers had crossed the canal and joined the battle.

By early evening on the 10th of September the first enemy tanks had appeared, and were at once engaged by the Rangers. This did not prevent the enemy from marshalling his forces for two counter-attacks at 2000 hrs.

One was delivered against the 9th Durham Light Infantry and was by infantry supported by tanks, and the other was against "A" and "C" Companies of the 8th Durham Light Infantry, who were moving up to protect the left flank of the 6th Battalion. This process had not been completed at the time of the counter-attack, and as a result there was a gap between the two battalions, through which the Germans, prompt as ever to seek out the weak spot and exploit it, began to infiltrate. Through the gap lay the road from Gheel to the canal, and of course the enemy used it. At this unpropitious moment Headquarters, 151st Brigade, was moving into position in the bridgehead, having crossed the canal. They were moving along a narrow track, near the Gheel road, when the battle suddenly swayed towards them. The track was too narrow for the long column of vehicles to do anything but continue their slow progress, and the defenceless, cumbersome command vehicles, with their wireless masts swaying and jolting, moved on across the fringe of the battlefield towards their new location.

By 2300 hrs. brigade headquarters was established two hundred yards from a cross-roads on the main Gheel road, round which a furious battle was raging. The brigade intelligence officer, Captain W. W. Teggin, sitting in his unarmed office lorry with the wireless earphones on, looked out of the window and saw a German tank a few hundred yards away. He reported this fact over the air to his opposite number at Divisional Headquarters, who received the report with suitable expressions of commiseration. Then the tank fired—but not at the brigade headquarters. It fired often after that, but always at other targets. None the less, bullets and shells whistled between the vehicles on several occasions, and the darkness was lighted by the glare of burning houses and vehicles. The German infantry fired flares continuously, and with the aid of their light the enemy tanks were selecting targets and engaging them with disconcerting accuracy.

The battle in the bridgehead now developed into a series of small, fierce actions at close quarters.

Lieutenant Wood, for instance, who commanded No. 4 Platoon of the 2nd Cheshire Regiment, reported over the wireless that there was a Tiger tank a hundred yards from his position, and that he was exchanging hand grenades with German infantry occupying the same hedgerow as his guns. None of our own infantry were in the immediate neighbourhood, and the situation of his platoon seemed critical. An attempt was made, amid the darkness and confusion, to disengage the platoon and move it to a flank, but finally Lieutenant Wood was ordered to stay firm until daylight. This he did, forming a strong-point with the aid of various stragglers.

Much of the fighting in other parts of the bridgehead that night was of the same order.

The situation of all three battalions was most confused, with both the 8th and 9th Durham Light Infantry dealing with enemy who were infiltrating through their positions, and with the 6th Durham Light Infantry in Gheel, free from counter-attacks but completely cut off from the rest of the brigade.

The situation took a turn for the better when the Sherwood

Rangers and a battery of the Northumberland Hussars knocked out two tanks which had been causing confusion, and when the 9th Durham Light Infantry finally beat off their enemies and restored the position on their front. The 8th Durham Light Infantry were ordered by the brigade commander to push forward at all costs and link up with the 6th Durham Light Infantry.

Just before 0100 hrs. it was decided within brigade headquarters to sink all pride and move back over the canal to the south bank. In the existing situation, with enemy infantry and tanks operating in rear of our forward troops, dawn would have spelt destruction of the soft-skinned vehicles of the headquarters.

A heavy mist arose before first light on the 11th of September, and the brigadier gave orders that everyone should "stay put" until it cleared and enabled co-ordinated action to be taken to wipe out the enemy. As it lifted, however, enemy tanks, cunningly concealed around the houses and defiladed from our anti-tank guns, took toll of our own tanks and transport. Each time one of our Shermans attempted to move up to engage them it was promptly knocked out. One German tank commander, however, who was standing up in his turret shouting orders to the infantry and occasionally (in English) proclaiming his determination to "die for Hitler," had his wish gratified by Corporal Owen's section of No. 4 Platoon of the Cheshire Regiment. As the morning light grew stronger the enemy, surveying the scene of damage and confusion, evidently decided that he could achieve no more, and discreetly tried to withdraw.

This, not unnaturally, proved completely impossible. The enemy was virtually imprisoned in the heart of the bridgehead in broad daylight. And now, as his tanks came out of their hiding places to move back down the road, it was the turn of our own armour to cause havoc. The German infantry, withdrawing in the same manner, fell victims to the machine guns. No. 3 Platoon of the Cheshire Regiment saw a party of about a hundred Germans moving back behind a Mark IV tank and engaged them. The infantry went to ground and the tank turned round and waddled back along the road to cover their withdrawal. Sergeant Cleator, of No. 3 Platoon, laid the gun of a Sherman on to his target, and the tank was "brewed up" with the first shot. The machine gunners then advanced in their carriers and engaged the enemy at point-blank range as they lay in the open. Fifteen Germans were killed, over twenty were wounded and sixty surrendered. In the words of the Cheshire Regiment's own account of this action: "The ground looked like a ploughed field, so scored was it with our bullets."

But in most parts of the bridgehead bitter fighting—infantry versus infantry and tank versus tank—continued throughout the day. Losses were heavy among the enemy, but the 50th Division, too, had not got off lightly.

A total of one hundred and eighteen prisoners were captured on this day, including men from nearly every company of the two regiments opposing us. One officer, who had been adjutant in his battalion, said that as a result of counter-attacks it had been ordered to make it had virtually ceased to exist. The commanding officer had been killed. There is good reason to believe that the other enemy battalions had known a similar experience and fate, and that their fighting quality had declined sharply, for it was during the evening of this day that the Durham Brigade captured a paratroop prisoner who gave the information that the 2nd Parachute Division had arrived in the sector in lorries from Germany. The Germans were still evidently intent on stopping the hole at all costs.

But, as we shall see, matters had already gone too far. On the 12th of September the Germans resumed their desperate attempts to break into the bridgehead, but met with no better success. More prisoners were taken from the 2nd Parachute Division, showing that this formation was lending its weight to these counter-attacks.

In the evening the 151st Brigade were relieved of the burden they had borne for so long in the bridgehead. Their tasks were taken over by the 15th (Scottish) Division, and the brigade moved back over the Albert Canal and concentrated near Pael, about three miles west of the Beeringen bridgehead, and still on the "home" side of the canal.

To set the seal on their feat of arms came a message the next morning from the 15th Division that the enemy had voluntarily pulled back from Gheel and retired over the Escaut Canal, leaving a very considerable number of German dead on the battlefield. The Germans, in fact, had had enough, and the 50th Division's battle for the Gheel bridgehead had been fought and won. Both the 69th and 151st Brigades had been relieved and withdrawn into reserve, to make ready for the next phase of the campaign.

* * *

At this point it is necessary once more to look at the wider picture in order to understand the 50th Division's place in it.

The operations of the Western Allies had reached a stage which seemed to have in it the elements of decision. The forces which the Germans could bring to bear against us were, in the main, those we had smashed in France and whose remnants we had pursued back to their own frontiers, and the thin trickle of units coming from Germany itself. German garrisons far from the Reich had ceased to be a protection and had become instead an anxiety. The evacuation from South and West France and from Rumania had already proved immensely costly, and those from Finland, Greece and Yugoslavia —even longer and more difficult—had still to be faced. In the words of a S.H.A.E.F. intelligence summary published at this time:

"Good German bodies and souls are dropping in thousands by the wayside, and will be missing in the hour of the defence of the Fatherland. Even those that get back will get back too late. The whole wreck of the Balkans and Finland may yield up perhaps half a dozen divisions.

"These will go no way to meet the crying need for more divisions to man the West Wall; moreover, a line in Transylvania will need to be manned. Where, then, are more divisions to be found? Not in Norway, withdrawal would take too long, and the troops are of too low category to be worth much; they pay more dividends where they are. Denmark might still supply one division, and a dozen or more may yet be found in Germany, given time, from training units, remnants and so forth. The Italian and Russian fronts risk collapse if anything more is withdrawn from them. In Italy, in particular, any form of withdrawal to the Alps would probably cost as many men in casualties as it saves by improving the line, even if complete disaster is not incurred in the process. In short, C-in-C West may expect not more than a dozen divisions within the next two months to come from outside to the rescue.

"C-in-C West himself salvaged rather over 200,000 fighting troops from the second battle of France. Since then he has had a further 70,000 trapped in Belgium, of which many no doubt will escape, but he has gained some 50,000 additional troops from Germany, and perhaps 30,000 replacements may be acquired by degrees (a generous estimate). If 50,000 fighting troops escape from the south of France, the total troops available for manning the West Wall should eventually be around 300,000 or the equivalent of about 15 divisions, to which the speculative dozen from other quarters have to be added. It is most unlikely that more than the true equivalent of four panzer/panzer grenadier divisions, with 600 tanks, will ever be found.

"To sum up, C-in-C West will soon have available the true equivalent of about 15 divisions, including four panzer, for the defence of the West Wall. A further five or six may struggle up in the course of the month, making a total of about 20.

"The West Wall cannot be held with this amount, even when supplemented by many oddments and large amounts of flak."

It was therefore appreciated that on the 21st Army Group front the enemy forces were inadequate to offer prolonged resistance along any line. And in the light of this situation there was conceived and launched the daring operation known to those who fought in it as "Market Garden," and to the world at large as the battle that culminated in the grim contest at Arnhem.

"Market Garden" was an attempt to make a rapid thrust due northward to the shores of the Zuyder Zee with the intention of splitting Holland in two and cutting off the many thousands of Germans in the western part from all chance of retreat to Germany. This involved the crossing of several water obstacles, including three major rivers—the Maas, the Waal and the Neder Rijn (Lower Rhine). To facilitate the passage of the land troops over these barriers the largest airborne landings ever attempted were to be made along the line of the advance to seize the various main crossing places.

Three airborne divisions were to be used—1st British, 82nd U.S. and 101st U.S. Airborne Divisions. The 101st Division was to seize canal and stream crossings in the area of Eindhoven, Zon and Veghel; the 82nd Division was ordered to capture the bridges over the Maas at Grave and over the Waal at Nijmegen; and to the 1st British Division was given the task of capturing the bridges over the Neder Rijn at Arnhem.

So far as the ground troops were concerned, the main effort was to made by the XXX Corps, with the VIII and XII Corps protecting the flanks of advance. The XXX Corps' orders were to advance at maximum speed and secure the area from Arnhem to Nunspeet, on the shores of the Zuyder Zee. The Corps was to operate on a one-divisional front in the following order:

Guards Armoured Division.

43rd Division.

50th (Northumbrian) Division.

The 50th Division's tasks were to follow in the wake of the leading formations as Corps reserve; send a detachment to secure a crossing over the River Ijssel at Duesburg, about twelve miles north-east of Arnhem; and to secure the high ground north of Arnhem.

As the day for "Market Garden" drew near, the Corps Commander, Lieutenant-General Horrocks, addressed senior officers of the Division and told them that this daringly conceived operation would go down in military history as a masterpiece of planning, and would form the subject of special study by experts long after the war was over.

At 1330 hrs. on the 17th of September it began. Troops of the 231st and 151st Brigades, holding bridgehead positions over the Escaut Canal through which the armoured spearhead was to pass, looked up from their slit trenches to gaze on the astonishing procession of aircraft passing in thunderous array above their heads. The airborne army was rushing towards its objectives.

At 1430 hrs. the Guards Armoured Division began to move out of the Escaut bridgehead. Guns of the 50th Division and mortars of the Cheshire Regiment joined in the barrage which launched the British armour into Holland.

Although initial resistance was flattened, the Guards soon ran up against more determined opposition, and lost nine tanks before they had advanced far. The 2nd Devonshire Regiment and the 1st Dorsetshire Regiment of the 231st Brigade were then called upon to follow up immediately behind the Guards to clear the woods on the left of the main road, from which most of the opposition was coming. These two battalions entered Holland that evening.

At first light on the 18th of September, with the armour moving on ahead with greater freedom, the Dorsetshire Regiment took over the township of Valkenswaard. The commanding officer virtually became military governor, and liaison was promptly established with the famous Dutch Resistance organization, the P.A.N.

On the whole, this day passed quietly on the Divisional front, except for a counter-attack on the 9th Durham Light Infantry, who were still holding the Escaut bridgehead. The Guards, leading the advance, were making slow progress, and by midday had got through Eindhoven. But not until the 19th of September did the advance really begin to make significant headway.

On that day British forces advanced north through the American bridgeheads at Zon, Veghel and Grave, and came into contact with the enemy at the southern ends of the Nijmegen bridges and also between the Rivers Maas and Waal in an area just west of the Reichswald, the great forest that was later to become a household word wherever newspapers were read.

Up to this point—Nijmegen—the American airborne troops had met with great success. Immediately after their jump on the 17th of September they had wiped out the 1st and 2nd Battalions of the Para Training Regiment Hermann Goering at St. Oedenrode and Zon, and elsewhere they had gained their objectives without opposition.

But at Nijmegen there was a different story to tell. The enemy was entrenched in pre-war concrete emplacements sited to protect the southern ends of both road and rail bridges, and not until the 20th of September were the bridges captured by the Americans, aided by the

Guards Armoured Division. There remained the last and most important bridge—that over the Neder Rijn at Arnhem, where the British Airborne Division was still fighting tenaciously in face of ferocious counter-attacks.

The success at Nijmegen brought the 50th Division into the picture and was the cue for the 69th Brigade to move forward towards Nijmegen.

From the moment that "Market Garden" began the principal route forward had been jammed with vehicles, and indeed the whole operation presented a nice problem in traffic control. When the 69th Brigade were ordered to move, five days later, the road was still choked with traffic, and the brigade did not get under way until about 2000 hrs.

As the long column of travel-stained vehicles rumbled northwards towards Nijmegen, the Germans were putting the finishing touches to preparations for an operation designed to assist their S.S. troops who were locked in battle with the British at Arnhem. The plan was to cut the main route forward used by the troops of the XXX Corps who were hastening to relieve the situation at Arnhem.

On the 22nd of September, the day after the 69th Brigade began their move, the enemy struck with about two battalions of infantry and a regiment of tanks. This force got astride the main road in the area of Uden, some eight miles south of the bridge over the Maas at Grave. North of the cut in the road were the 5th East Yorkshire Regiment, and south of it the remaining battalions of the 69th Brigade.

The 124th Field Regiment, R.A., who had been moving up with the 69th Brigade, found itself in a similar predicament. The main body was cut off from its commanding officer, second-in-command, C.P.Os. and Survey. After investigating the position, the battery captain of the 288th Battery, Captain Dowdeswell, put the regiment into action in support of the 101st U.S. Airborne Division, who were holding the crossings in the area of St. Oedenrode. Batteries were "tied on" to the 86th Field Regiment. Two groups of mixed artillery were eventually collected, and the commanding officer of the 86th Field Regiment acted as an extra C.R.A. to the American divisional commander.

Matters were now so arranged that when, the next day, the Germans attempted to strengthen their grip on the road by attacking Veghel, farther south, they were accorded a remarkably warm reception, and American infantry and British tanks and artillery, working in improvised but close co-operation, drove them off with heavy losses—a fine example of Anglo-U.S. co-operation in the field.

As a result of this action (in which the Guards Armoured Division played a prominent part) the road northwards was temporarily reopened and the 69th Brigade, united once more, drove onward to Nijmegen, there to take their place alongside the defenders of the bridgehead over the Waal.

But the threat to the main road was by no means ended. The Germans had scraped together tanks and infantry from resources that had become strained to the uttermost, and they clearly meant to use them at what they considered to be the decisive points—Arnhem and the road in the area Uden—Veghel.

The 50th Division's main task thus became the protection of part of this road, which was in fact the lifeline of the Army. On the 23rd of September the Division was ordered to move north and west of Eindhoven to look after the right flank. Only two brigades were left to the Division now, in view of the 69th Brigade's departure, but in addition to the Reconnaissance Regiment it was given under command two other reconnaissance units—the Royals and the 52nd Reconnaissance Regiment. This force moved forward on the 23rd of September, and the next day found itself faced with a further German attempt to cut the road, this time a few miles south of Veghel. The 52nd Reconnaissance Regiment at once moved off to gain contact and try to drive the enemy off in conjunction with the 101st U.S. Airborne Division, while at Divisional Headquarters plans were made to put in a heavier blow at first light the next day should the immediate counter-attack fail.

For this purpose the 131st Infantry Brigade of the 7th Armoured Division, and a regiment of tanks from the same formation, were put under the command of the 50th Division; and, the preliminary probing by the 52nd Reconnaissance Regiment and the Americans on the evening of the 24th of September having failed to clear the road, this additional armour and infantry was committed to battle on the morning of the 25th of September. The 5th Dragoon Guards and the 1st/7th Queen's Regiment assembled on the road Oedenrode—Veghel, and the 8th Hussars and the 1st/5th Queen's Regiment on the road Oedenrode—Schindel. (Schindel, a village four miles north-north-west of Oedenrode, was apparently the assembly area from which the Germans had sallied forth to cut the road, and where a force of the enemy was suspected still to remain.)

These armoured battle groups attacked a few hours after the 101st U.S. Airborne Division had launched a thrust towards the road from the west. The enemy resisted stiffly on both flanks, and not until the next day was it possible to consider the road finally clear.

That marked the end of the enemy's real effort to cut the road, and for the next few days the 50th Division, though occupied with patrols, picquets and moves, were not engaged in any major action.

Not so with the 69th Brigade, however. When they arrived at Nijmegen they came under the command of the Guards Armoured Division. Their first job was to capture Bemmel, north of the river and east of the main road. This the 5th East Yorkshire Regiment achieved on the 25th of September, but the Germans were not reconciled to the loss of this tactically important little village, and kept our troops under heavy artillery fire by day and night.

On the 26th of September the 6th Green Howards were ordered to occupy Halderen, a village just east of Bemmel, containing a number of factories with tall chimneys, which were, of course, being used as enemy observation posts. Nos. 6 and 8 Platoons of "B" Company, 2nd Cheshire Regiment, were used in support, but the infantry ran into severe opposition, and failed to reach the village. The 7th Green Howards, who advanced on their left, gained all their objectives.

The brigade attacks in the direction of Halderen continued throughout the 27th of September. It was not easy country in which to fight, for it is very enclosed—not unlike that around Hottot, only flatter and intersected with many wide and deep ditches—and enemy resistance was unwavering.

The East Yorkshire Regiment gained some ground during the day. They were supported by a quick barrage which was planned by the battery captain of the 288th Battery, registered with the battery by Captain Ramsden, and in due course fired, after one check round, by the 55th Field Regiment (of another division) with good effect. At this time the 124th Field Regiment were supporting the Green Howards.

The airborne troops farther north at Arnhem had by now been withdrawn. The attempt to reach them by land had clearly failed, and attempts to supply them by air had been only partially successful. Thus the final objective of Operation "Market Garden"—the splitting of Holland and the turning of the Rhine defences—had not been achieved.

The immediate effect on the 69th Brigade of this failure was to transform a stiffly resisting enemy at Nijmegen into an aggressive one. Tanks and infantry which had been engaged at Arnhem were freed for action against the Waal bridgehead. On the 28th of September the 69th Brigade were warned that the enemy was preparing for a counter-attack on a relatively big scale, and so our operations against Halderen were abandoned for the time being, and the infantry were regrouped to meet the threat.

At 0800 hrs. the next morning there occurred an event which suggested that the Germans had aggressive intentions. The German Air Force, which was now taking the air again with more frequency than during the preceding two or three months, tore a forty-foot gap in the Nijmegen railway bridge with a well-aimed parachute bomb; and on the same day the other link with the south bank of the Waal, the road bridge, was damaged by "human torpedoes."

To the infantry and their supporting arms, fighting from a "toehold" on the north bank of the river, with the bridges in their rear temporarily gone, the lines of communication threatened at intervals, and only a small part of the Second Army forward, the outlook cannot have been cheerful.

The brigade, and also the 5th Guards Brigade, now came under the command of the 43rd Division, which at this time was the only complete division north of the river.

The first of the blows for which everyone had been waiting came on the 30th of September. After heavy shelling, the enemy tried to counter-attack the 5th East Yorkshire Regiment on a narrow front. German infantry advanced, but were beaten off by light machine-gun and artillery fire. The East Yorkshire Regiment and other troops in the line stated afterwards that no attack could have materialized through such withering fire.

The next day the enemy launched a much stronger attack on a broad front, with the intention of driving through to Nijmegen and eliminating the bridgehead. It was estimated at the time that the Germans had available for this operation the equivalent of an infantry division and approximately seventy tanks. The battle is well described by the historian of the 124th Field Regiment, Royal Artillery, gunners who had a prominent and successful part in the action.

"Movement of tracked vehicles was heard during the night all along the 69 Brigade and 5 Guards Brigade fronts, and at 0400 hours on 1 October attacks began. These were probably feints, and at 0550 hours, preceded by heavy mortar and shell fire, the real attack began against 7 Green Howards and Irish Guards from the north.

"An attack was also put in against 43 Division across the Neder Rijn. It was soon apparent that the main attack was directed on the 69 Brigade front, but in the early stages 43 Division artillery was employed solely on their own front, and 55 and 124 Field Regiments alone had to support 5 Guards Brigade and 69 Brigade. The regiment (124) was continuously firing D.Fs., and when not engaged on 69 Brigade front answered calls from 43 Division.

"12 enemy tanks were sent in against 7 Green Howards, and

although two were knocked out the remainder succeeded in infiltrating between B and C Companies. This forced C Company to give ground, and exposed A Company, who were soon isolated.

"It was in this position that 7 Green Howards held on from 0700 hours (when the attack developed in earnest) to 2300 hours (when the 5 East Yorks relieved them) against continuous pressure from the enemy on all sides.

"During this period our O.Ps. continually engaged enemy tanks and infantry, causing heavy damage and casualties to the enemy. A favourite concentration area of the enemy was an orchard; this became a Regimental target, and the directing staff lost count of the number of times this target was engaged both by the Regiment and also by 43 Division artillery.

"43 Division provided very quickly the additional fire which was so badly needed on our Brigade front at this critical time.

"The Brigade Commander decided to use 5 East Yorks to relieve 7 Green Howards, and in addition a further troop of tanks was sent to support them. At 1800 hrs 5 East Yorks with a squadron of 13/18 Hussars advanced to the relief of 7 Green Howards, supported by 124 Field Regiment. The East Yorks received information that the 7 Green Howards were unlikely to hold out long enough for them to arrive in time, and began to dig in short of the Green Howards' positions. Then, as a result of the weight of fire put down by 124 Field Regiment and 43 Division, the position eased, and the Green Howards reported that the position could be held provided the 5 East Yorks came up immediately.

"At 2300 hrs A Company was relieved, and the enemy attack was a complete failure.

"5 East Yorks, after the relief, were again subjected to a most severe pounding from numerous enemy batteries. Whenever not engaging other targets, these hostile batteries were engaged by the 124 Field Regiment and when possible the fire from 43 Division artillery was employed.

"124 Field Regiment was firing continuously from 0400 hrs to 2300 hrs, and fired a total of 12,500 rounds during this action. This was more than the regiment fired at Alamein.

"B Company of the Cheshires also had a tremendous day, and later both 6 and 7 Green Howards congratulated them on their shooting. It was generally agreed in the company itself that they had never put in a more effective day's work. Two platoons alone fired 95,500 rounds."

This was indeed support on a magnificent scale. But perhaps the last word of praise should go, after all, to the infantrymen of the 7th Green Howards, who endured in their positions, from 0550 to 2300 hrs., the worst that the enemy could do to them. Infantry and tank attacks succeeded one another, and all the time the enemy artillery, which was present in considerable strength, maintained a high rate of fire.

Through it all the Green Howards hung on, and they had their reward when the day was saved by the arrival of the East Yorkshire Regiment.

The 69th Brigade was now joined by the remainder of the 50th Division, which was ordered to take over the eastern sector of the bridgehead. The 151st and 231st Brigades moved into position, relieving the 69th Brigade, and on the 4th of October these two brigades attacked with the limited object of improving the line and capturing Halderen. Opposition was stiff, but the objectives had been captured by the 6th of October.

There ensued a period of static warfare, the last operations undertaken by the 50th Division in the Second World War. The Division was switched to another sector of the bridgehead, and settled down to a comparatively quiet period on "The Island." This was the nickname given to the country between the Neder Rijn and the Waal, and the 50th Division came to know it well.

"The Island" was an area of low-lying fields, rich apple and pear country, and criss-crossed with dykes. It was divided roughly into two halves by the road running between Arnhem and Nijmegen. The 50th Division spent the whole of October and most of November there, and it was we who first gave the area its name; true enough, we were certainly surrounded by water most of the time, and our link with the "mainland," the splendid bridge at Nijmegen—threatened as it was by the enemy gunners, who had a fair degree of observation over its approaches, and the exploits of the enemy web-footed swimmers—could not entirely remove our feelings of insularity.

A smoke screen was maintained over the river east of the bridge and at night searchlights shone across the surface of the water; a strange combination which made the gaunt curves of the bridge seem shrouded in a luminous fog. With typical understatement, large notices invited you not to loiter.

Yet, apart from the physical discomfort, which for the forward troops was extreme, life on "The Island" was by no means intolerable. The battalions, all of them under strength, particularly in officers and non-commissioned officers, would certainly have welcomed a rest. Yet spirits were kept up; one remembers vividly three games of Rugby played at Slijk-Ewick (we called it "Slicky-Wick"), where Divisional Headquarters was; the teams came from the 151st Brigade, the 2nd Cheshire Regiment, Divisional Headquarters Staff and Divisional Signals. In one game the American liaison officer, from the 508th Regimental combat team (under command of the 50th Division at that time), finding his boots uncomfortable, took them off and played the rest of the game in his bare feet, which was not bad for a front-row forward.

The high-light, however, of "The Island's" social season was a dance held in Nijmegen and attended by over two hundred people; for the Dutch girls it was the first time they had been to a dance since the enemy had invaded and occupied their country. Good friends at Headquarters, XXX Corps, winked an eye at certain infringements of the curfew regulations, and even signed and lighted the route to and from the dance hall.

We could see sometimes at night in the sky away to the north-east points of light that might have been shooting stars except that they were moving upwards. They were V2 rockets leaving their platforms on the first stage of their journey to England, and if we felt inclined to grumble at the mud and rain and the bitter wind, it was a reminder that people at home were facing the same enemy and the same dangers.

October and November wore on, with the weather deteriorating and the 50th Division still on "The Island," and no major operations. In Nijmegen troops resting from their spell in watery front-line trenches could have baths and visit the theatre and cinema. Leave was opened to Brussels and Antwerp.

On the 29th of November the Division was relieved in "The Island" and moved back to concentrate in Belgium. That was the end of the fighting career of the 50th Division. To solve the urgent problems of reinforcement, the 21st Army Group had to be reduced by one division. The 50th Division was selected as that division. Field-Marshal Montgomery explained the situation to the Divisional Commander, Major-General Lyne, who was temporarily commanding in the brief absence through a leg injury of Major-General Graham, who had brought the Division from the Normandy beaches to Holland. In a letter the Field-Marshal said it was unthinkable that a division with so fine a record should lose its identity, and therefore it would become for the time being a training division, stationed at home.

Some units and personnel stayed on in the 21st Army Group, and the skeleton Division returned to its parent North Country and settled down in Yorkshire to train men of other arms as infantrymen.

* * *

Shortly after VE Day the 50th Division marched to York Minster to give thanks for victory, and to remember those in its ranks who had died to make it possible. This book is dedicated to them.

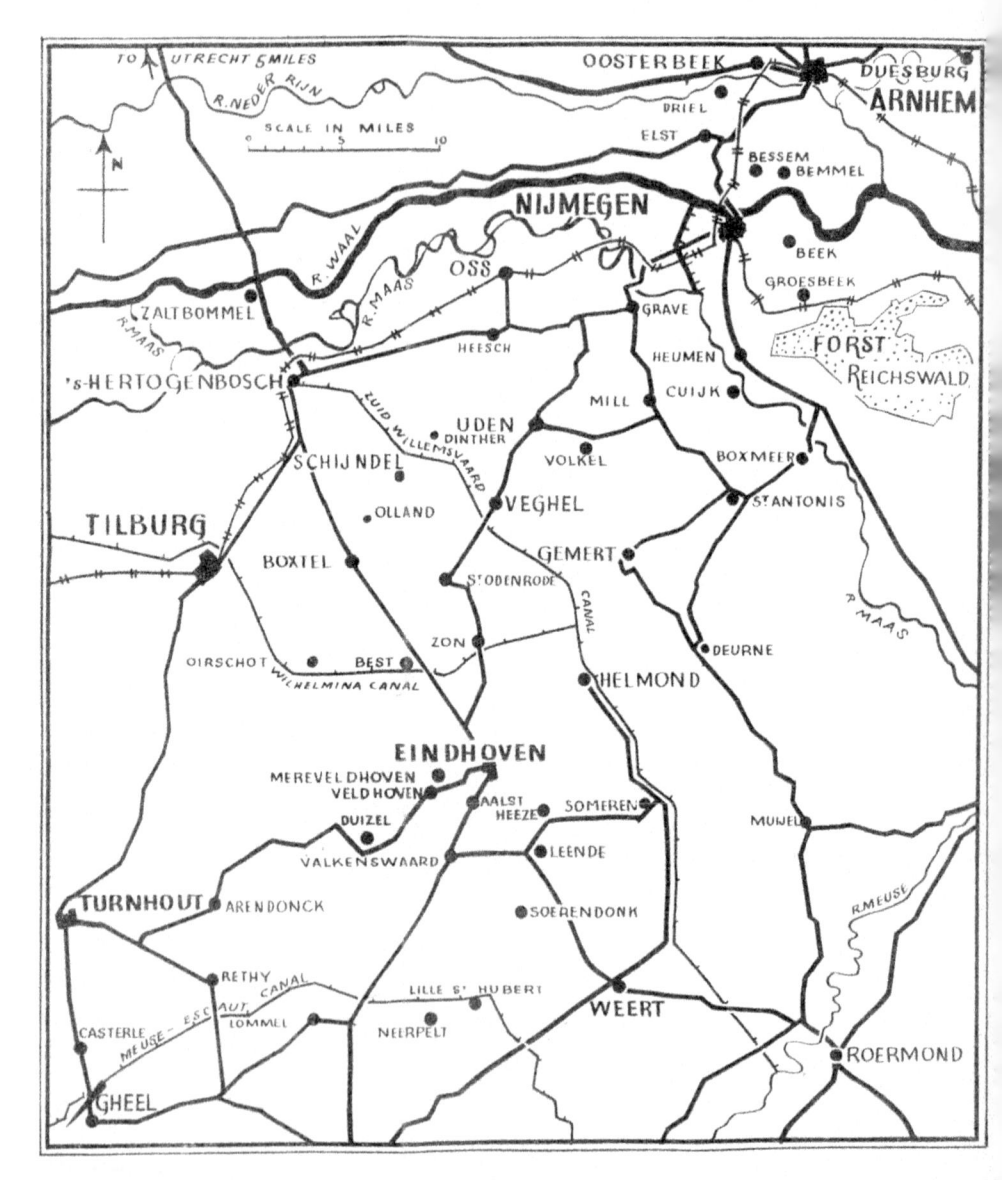

ARNHEM—NIJMEGEN

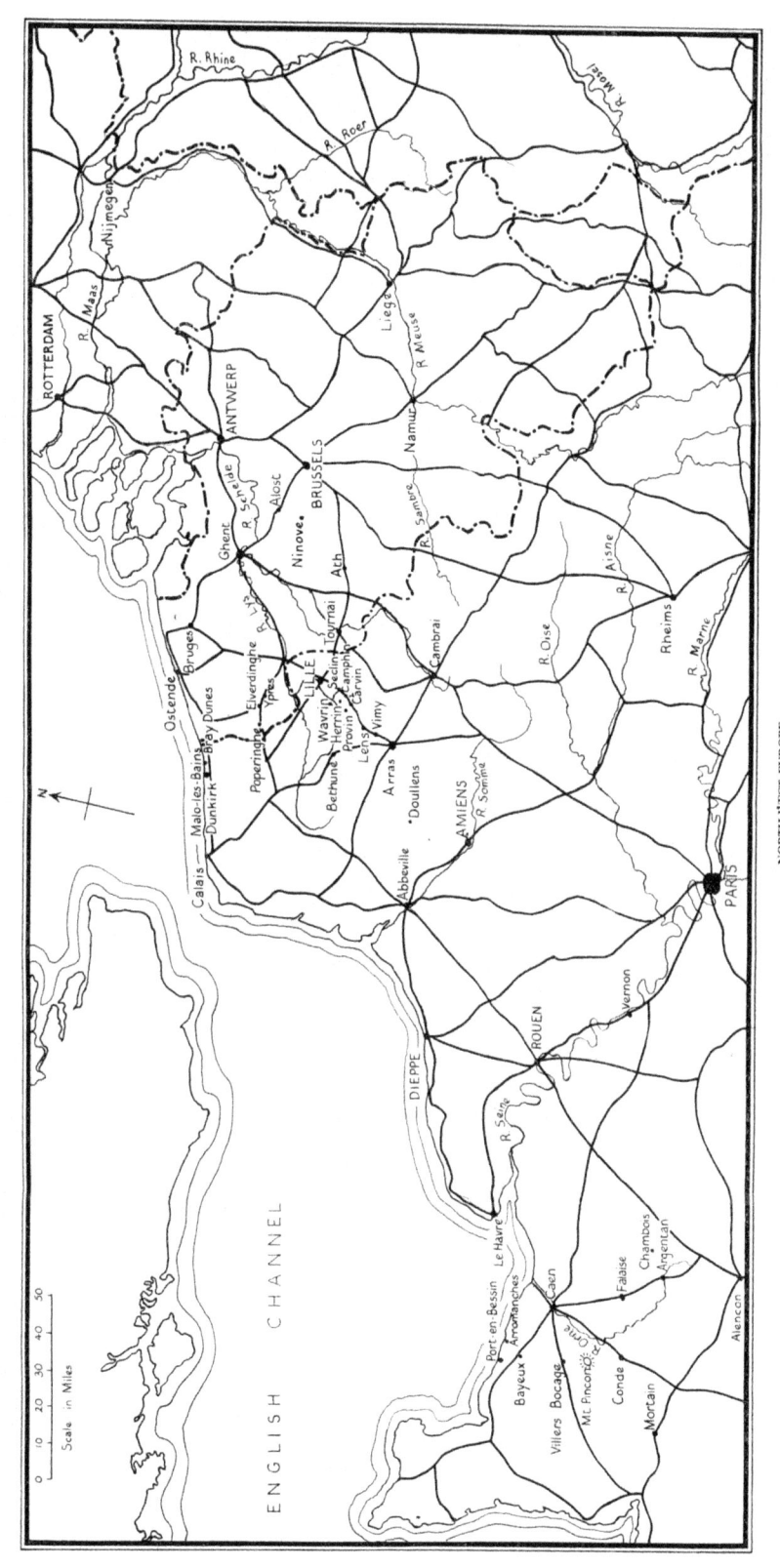

NORTH-WEST EUROPE

APPENDIX I TO PART FIVE

ORDER OF BATTLE, 50TH (NORTHUMBRIAN) DIVISION

COMMANDS AND STAFF, 22ND MAY, 1944

G.O.C.	Major-General D. A. H. Graham, C.B.E., D.S.O., M.C.
A.D.C.	Lieutenant B. Henderson.
G.S.O.1	Lieutenant-Colonel R. L. G. Charles.
G.S.O.2	Major J. M. Dickenson.
G.S.O.3 (O.)	Captain N. H. Golding.
G.S.O.3 (I.)	Captain G. Mansell.
G.S.O.3 (C.W.)	Captain G. R. Aspin.
G.S.O.3 (L.)	Captain R. J. Somerville.
Intelligence Officer	Captain P. D. Crichton-Stuart.
A.A. & Q.M.G.	Lieutenant-Colonel T. J. Black.
D.A.A.G.	Major W. H. L. Urton, M.B.E.
D.A.Q.M.G.	Major I. McLeod.
Staff Captain, "Q"	Captain J. G. Wood.
A.D.M.S.	Colonel J. Melvin, O.B.E., M.C.
D.A.D.M.S.	Major R. L. Macpherson.
A.D.O.S.	Lieutenant-Colonel R. C. Gibb, O.B.E.
Orderly Officer	Captain H. L. Thomson.
A.P.M.	Major C. F. Dunn.
S.C.F.	Reverend J. W. Warner (C.F., 3rd Class).
Camp Commandant	Captain A. A. Standley.
Provost Company	Captain W. R. Hunter.
Catering Adviser	Captain R. H. Nott.
Liaison Officer	Lieutenant J. C. B. Mant.
Liaison Officer	Lieutenant H. N. Meek.
Liaison Officer	Lieutenant A. R. B. Ellis.
D./E. Platoon	Lieutenant R. S. Ball.
F.S.S.	Lieutenant Hockliffe.
Postal	Second-Lieutenant F. Calip.
Field Cashier	Captain S. W. Beattie.
Education Officer	Captain R. D. N. Tamblyn.
Transport Officer	Lieutenant D. C. Russell.

56TH INFANTRY BRIGADE

Commander	Brigadier E. C. Pepper, O.B.E.
Brigade Major	Major L. B. B. Beuttler.
G.S.O.3	Captain J. C. Riley.
Staff Captain	Captain A. G. L. King.
Intelligence Officer	Captain R. T. Gilchrist.

2ND BN. THE ESSEX REGIMENT

Commanding Officer	Lieutenant-Colonel J. F. Higson, M.C.
Second-in-Command	Major C. G. Elliott.
Adjutant	Captain J. Townrow.

2ND BN. THE GLOUCESTERSHIRE REGIMENT

Commanding Officer	Lieutenant-Colonel D. W. Biddle.
Second-in-Command	Major J. O. Hopper.
Adjutant	Captain R. C. Nash.

2ND BN. THE SOUTH WALES BORDERERS

Commanding Officer	Lieutenant-Colonel R. W. Craddock, M.B.E.
Second-in-Command	Major F. F. S. Barlow.
Adjutant	Captain K. V. Coles.

69TH INFANTRY BRIGADE

Commander	Brigadier F. Y. C. Knox, D.S.O.
Brigade Major	Major C. P. N. Parker.
G.S.O.3	Captain C. W. Mallinson.
Staff Captain	Captain N. H. Nicholson.
Intelligence Officer	Captain J. M. B. Isaac.

5TH BN. THE EAST YORKSHIRE REGIMENT

Commanding Officer	Lieutenant-Colonel G. W. White, M.B.E.
Second-in-Command	Major J. H. F. Dixon.
Adjutant	Captain T. G. Fenwick.

6TH BN. THE GREEN HOWARDS

Commanding Officer	Lieutenant-Colonel R. H. W. S. Hastings, M.C.
Second-in-Command	Major C. M. Hull.
Adjutant	Captain G. S. Piper.

7TH BN. THE GREEN HOWARDS

Commanding Officer	Lieutenant-Colonel P. H. Richardson.
Second-in-Command	Major H. R. D. Oldman, M.C.
Adjutant	Captain F. W. M. Underhay.

151ST INFANTRY BRIGADE

Commander	Brigadier R. H. Senior, D.S.O., T.D.
Brigade Major	Major The Viscount Long.
G.S.O.3	Captain J. W. Thompson.
Staff Captain	Captain R. R. Coddin.
Intelligence Officer	Captain W. W. Teggin.

6TH BN. THE DURHAM LIGHT INFANTRY

Commanding Officer	Lieutenant-Colonel A. E. Green.
Second-in-Command	Major G. L. Wood, M.C.
Adjutant	Captain R. S. Loveridge, M.C.

APPENDIX I TO PART FIVE

8TH BN. THE DURHAM LIGHT INFANTRY
Commanding Officer .. .. Lieutenant-Colonel R. P. Lidwell, D.S.O.
Second-in-Command .. .. Major A. H. Dunn.
Adjutant .. .. Captain J. C. Walker.

9TH BN. THE DURHAM LIGHT INFANTRY
Commanding Officer .. .. Lieutenant-Colonel H. R. Woods, D.S.O., M.C.
Second-in-Command .. .. Major H. J. Mogg.
Adjutant .. .. Captain R. C. Rickett.

231ST INFANTRY BRIGADE
Commander .. .. Brigadier Sir A. B. G. Stanier, Bt., D.S.O., M.C.
Brigade Major .. .. .. Major I. A. Robertson.
G.S.O.3 .. .. Captain D. Montgomery.
Staff Captain .. .. .. Captain H. M. Johnson.
Intelligence Officer .. .. Captain K. S. Hollebone.

1ST BN. THE HAMPSHIRE REGIMENT
Commanding Officer .. .. Lieutenant-Colonel H. D. N. Smith, M.C.
Second-in-Command .. .. Major A. C. W. Martin, D.S.O.
Adjutant .. .. Captain F. H. Waters.

1ST BN. THE DORSETSHIRE REGIMENT
Commanding Officer .. .. Lieutenant-Colonel E. H. M. Norie, O.B.E.
Second-in-Command .. .. Major A. E. C. Bredin.
Adjutant .. .. Captain L. Browne, M.C.

2ND BN. THE DEVONSHIRE REGIMENT
Commanding Officer .. .. Lieutenant-Colonel C. A. R. Nevill, O.B.E.
Second-in-Command .. .. Major G. B. Brown.
Adjutant .. .. Captain T. A. Holdsworth.

61ST RECONNAISSANCE REGIMENT
Commanding Officer .. .. Lieutenant-Colonel Sir W. M. Mount, Bt., T.D.
Second-in-Command .. .. Major P. H. A. Brownrigg.
Adjutant .. .. Captain E. E. Mocatta.

2ND BN. THE CHESHIRE REGIMENT
Commanding Officer .. .. Lieutenant-Colonel S. V. Keeling, D.S.O.
Second-in-Command .. .. Major H. R. Moon.
Adjutant .. .. Captain L. J. Cutler.

ROYAL ARTILLERY
Commander .. .. Brigadier C. H. Norton, D.S.O., O.B.E.
Brigade Major .. .. Major H. A. C. Dundas.
Staff Captain .. .. Captain E. N. Briscomb.
Intelligence Officer .. Captain N. S. Harrison.

74TH FIELD REGIMENT

Commanding Officer	Lieutenant-Colonel H. W. W. Harris, D.S.O.
Second-in-Command	Major E. N. Dawson.
Adjutant	Captain R. B. Hutt.

86TH FIELD REGIMENT

Commanding Officer	Lieutenant-Colonel G. D. Fanshawe, O.B.E.
Second-in-Command	Major J. B. M. Smith.
Adjutant	Captain R. R. Thornton.

90TH FIELD REGIMENT

Commanding Officer	Lieutenant-Colonel I. G. S. Hardie.
Second-in-Command	Major J. F. Murphy.
Adjutant	Captain M. H. Shepheard.

124TH FIELD REGIMENT

Commanding Officer	Lieutenant-Colonel P. H. Gough.
Second-in-Command	Major E. H. Colville.
Adjutant	Captain L. G. Heptinstall.

147TH FIELD REGIMENT

Commanding Officer	Lieutenant-Colonel R. A. Phayre.
Second-in-Command	Major C. V. Broke.
Adjutant	Captain P. W. Gee.

102ND ANTI-TANK REGIMENT

Commanding Officer	Lieutenant-Colonel A. K. Matthews.
Second-in-Command	Major D. J. Cowen.
Adjutant	Captain G. S. Spence.

25TH LIGHT ANTI-AIRCRAFT REGIMENT

Commanding Officer	Lieutenant-Colonel G. G. O. Lyons, M.B.E.
Second-in-Command	Major C. D. B. Campling.
Adjutant	Captain J. D. Johnson.

ROYAL ENGINEERS

C.R.E.	Lieutenant-Colonel R. L. Willott, D.S.O.
Adjutant	Captain R. G. Bishop.
Intelligence Officer	Lieutenant R. L. Rolt.

233RD FIELD COMPANY

Officer Commanding	Major J. R. Cave-Browne.
Second-in-Command	Captain A. D. Campbell.

295TH FIELD COMPANY

Officer Commanding	Major C. W. Wood.
Second-in-Command	Captain R. E. Sperling.

505TH FIELD COMPANY

Officer Commanding	Major C. A. O. B. Compton, M.C.
Second-in-Command	Captain W. L. Kent.

235TH FIELD PARK COMPANY

Officer Commanding	Major I. L. Smith.
Second-in-Command	Captain E. G. Richards, M.C.

15TH BRIDGING PLATOON
Officer Commanding .. .. Lieutenant G. Sumner.

ROYAL CORPS OF SIGNALS
Commanding Officer .. .. Lieutenant-Colonel G. B. Stevenson.
Second-in-Command .. .. Major G. St. L. King.
Adjutant .. .. Captain J. E. Sergeant.

ROYAL ARMY SERVICE CORPS
C.R.A.S.C. .. .. .. Lieutenant-Colonel G. W. Fenton, M.B.E.
Second-in-Command .. .. Major D. Dalton, M.B.E.
Adjutant .. .. Captain L. Panton.

346 COMPANY
Officer Commanding .. .. Major A. B. Belcher.
Second-in-Command .. .. Captain J. B. Adams.

508 COMPANY
Officer Commanding .. .. Major V. H. J. Carpenter.
Second-in-Command .. .. Captain J. E. Osborne.

522 COMPANY
Officer Commanding ..   Major H. S. Butterworth, M.C.
Second-in-Command ..

524 COMPANY
Officer Commanding ..   Major L. Carrick.
Second-in-Command ..   Captain J. V. Marlow.

ROYAL ARMY MEDICAL CORPS

149TH FIELD AMBULANCE
Commanding Officer .. .. Lieutenant-Colonel S. R. Trick.
Second-in-Command .. .. Major O. G. Prosser.

186TH FIELD AMBULANCE
Commanding Officer .. .. Lieutenant-Colonel C. W. Arnot, O.B.E., M.C.
Second-in-Command .. .. Major W. S. Gale.

200TH FIELD AMBULANCE
Commanding Officer .. .. Lieutenant-Colonel W. A. Robinson, O.B.E.
Second-in-Command .. .. Major M. N. S. Duncan.

22ND FIELD HYGIENE SECTION
Officer Commanding .. .. Major R. W. Elliott.

47TH FIELD DRESSING STATION
Officer Commanding .. .. Major H. S. H. Gilmer.

48TH FIELD DRESSING STATION
Officer Commanding ..   Major J. M. C. Almond.

ROYAL ARMY ORDNANCE CORPS

50th Division Ordnance Field Park
Officer Commanding .. .. Major D. C. H. Merrill.

69th Brigade Workshops Section
Officer Commanding .. .. Captain W. Kirkby.

151st Brigade Workshops Section
Officer Commanding .. .. Captain H. L. Smith.

231st Brigade Workshops Section
Officer Commanding .. .. Captain P. A. W. Turner.

ROYAL CORPS OF ELECTRICAL AND MECHANICAL ENGINEERS

C.R.E.M.E. .. .. .. Lieutenant-Colonel E. H. Rundle.
Second-in-Command .. .. Major R. E. Thornton.
Adjutant .. .. Captain N. R. Earnshaw.

69th Brigade Workshops Company
Officer Commanding .. .. Major S. F. Coaten.

151st Brigade Workshops Company
Officer Commanding .. .. Major C. Whitehead.

231st Brigade Workshops Company
Officer Commanding .. .. Major T. J. A. Hunter.

APPENDIX II TO PART FIVE

CASUALTIES, REINFORCEMENTS AND PRISONERS OF WAR OF 50TH (NORTHUMBRIAN) DIVISION IN B.L.A., 6TH JUNE TO 1ST DECEMBER, 1944

	KILLED		WOUNDED		MISSING		MISSING Rejoined		TOTAL CASUALTIES		REINFORCEMENTS	
	Officers	O.Rs.	Officers	O.Rs.	Officers	O.Rs.	Officers	O.Rs.	Officers	O.Rs.	Officers	O.Rs.
June	52	436	157	2,012	28	1,104	4	439	233	3,113	173	3,102
July	17	168	54	849	2	102	—	62	73	1,057	29	924
August	16	159	46	940	2	190	—	127	64	1,162	56	1,360
September	15	150	44	470	6	233	3	112	62	741	35	712
October	12	111	30	611	7	107	3	89	46	740	38	1,204
November	1	21	8	85	1	16	—	3	10	119	27	717
Total	113	1,045	339	4,967	46	1,752	10	832	488	6,932	358	8,019

TOTAL P.O.W. taken, 17,202

TOTAL P.O.W. at : June 9 2,300
August 30 4,838
September 4 8,901
September 5 13,766
September 12 16,034
October 22 16,998
December 1 17,202

P.O.W. taken on September 5, 4,865

NOTE:—Figures for total casualties exclude normal wastage. e.g., cases of sickness, etc.

EPILOGUE

THERE are now memorials to men of the 50th Division in many of the countries in which they fought: in Sicily, near the Primosole Bridge, where the Durham Light Infantry fought their great battle against German paratroops; and in the church at peaceful Taormina, in the neighbourhood of which the Division rested after the Sicilian campaign; and in several places on the mainland of Europe.

The two principal memorials at the time of writing are at Vimy, where a new inscription has been added to the memorial of the First World War, and at Bayeux, in the heart of the bridgehead which the Division helped to capture in the Second World War.

This last memorial is a tablet set in the wall which bounds the building which houses the famous Bayeux Tapestry. It was unveiled on the fourth anniversary of D Day (the 6th of June, 1948) by Major-General D. A. H. Graham—who commanded the 50th Division on D Day and afterwards led them through France, Belgium and Holland—in the presence of representatives of nearly every unit of the war-time Division, and a great gathering of French people.

The representatives of the 50th Division, some thirty strong, had journeyed to France in the flotilla leader *Zephyr*. They travelled by motor-coach from Ouistreham along the coast to Bayeux, passing the beaches which the Division had assaulted four years earlier. Those beaches were still strewn with a tangle of rusting war material. Village walls still bore fading TT signs marking the way the Division had come. Ammunition boxes cast away by Green Howards and East Yorkshires at La Riviere had been painted bright green and turned into window-boxes. Some street names had been changed to honour the troops of the 50th Division.

The scars of war still lay across the French countryside. There were houses patched with corrugated iron, and one mayor, who did the honours for his small community with a touching dignity, was wearing socks darned with coarse string.

But everywhere the representatives of the 50th Division were given a warm welcome. Flags fluttered bravely. In village halls wine glasses were mustered on snowy linen.

The French people joined in services of remembrance with the men of the 50th Division. At Asnelles and at Hottot, which the party visited in the afternoon when they toured some of the battlefields farther inland, memorials to the 231st Brigade were unveiled.

And at Hottot, scene of such bitter fighting against the Panzer Lehr Division, representatives of the Englishmen who fought there handed over £100 to the mayor to speed the work of reconstruction.

INDEX

Abbeville, 11.
Abbott, Sgt., 276.
Achicourt, 16, 17, 18.
Acireale, 210.
Acis Antonio, 210.
Adam, Lt.-Gen. Sir Ronald, 22, 24.
Adinkerke, 24.
Adrano, 202, 205.
Afrika Korps, 90, 94, 109, 114, 251, 278.
Agedabia, 110.
Ageila Pass, 67.
Agnone, 184.
Akaba, Gulf of, 145, 146.
Akhdar Hills, 47.
Alam Nayil, 92.
Albert Canal, 10, 285, 289, 292, 295.
Alem Hamza, 51, 54.
Alencon, 268.
Alexander, F.-M., 26, 89, 90, 137.
Alexandria, 75, 80, 88, 89, 92, 104, 140, 144, 145, 146, 147, 152.
Alexandria Garrison, 88.
Algiers, 221.
Almaza, 85, 89.
Alost, 281, 285.
Amaye, 267.
American Army, 142.
Amiens, 7, 11, 232, 274, 276, 277, 280, 281.
Amiriya, 85, 89.
Anctoville, 267.
Anderson, Pte. E., V.C., 130.
Antwerp, 274, 275, 276, 281, 283, 285, 305.
Argentan, 266, 272.
Armies:
    Second, 229, 233, 252, 264, 266, 268, 269, 274, 283, 285, 302.
    Eighth, 43, 48, 49, 50, 51, 52, 56, 61, 65, 74, 75, 80, 88, 89, 90, 93, 94, 97, 105, 109, 111, 112, 124, 137, 217, 230.
Army Groups:
    18th, 137.
    21st, 233, 297, 305.
Army Tank Brigade, 1st, 12, 13, 19, 20, 54, 56, 57.
Arnhem, 297, 299, 300, 301, 304.
Arram, 113.

Arras, 11, 12, 13, 14, 19, 28, 275, 280.
Arromanches, 232, 234, 245, 246, 249.
Asnelles-sur-Mer, 245.
Ataka, 146.
Ath, 10.
Auchinleck, F.-M. Sir C. J. E., 42, 43, 90.
Audrieu, 253, 254, 256.
Augusta, 172, 180, 220, 221.
Aune, River, 256.
Auneuil, 277.
Aure, River, 262.
Australian Division, 9th, 95, 103.
Avola, 143, 145, 148, 149, 150, 154, 155, 156, 158, 159, 160, 164, 166, 221.
Avola, Lido d', 148, 149, 156, 157.
Avola, Marina d', 148, 149, 154, 160.
Avranches, 268.

B.E.F., 9, 10, 11, 12, 20.
Baalbek, 45.
Bab el Qattara, 104.
Baggush, 49.
Baghdad, 44.
Bahariya, 99.
Bailleul, 22, 23.
Balkans, 147.
Ballance, Capt. R. H., R.N., 241.
Banks, Maj.-Gen. Sir Donald, 8, 30.
Bapaume, 13.
Batten, Col. R. H., 111.
Bayeux, 232, 234, 235, 246, 247, 251, 253, 256.
Beach Brick, No. 34, 144, 145, 150, 151, 159, 162.
Beake, Brig., 108, 124.
Beart, Lt.-Col., 16, 19.
Beaugrenier, 276.
Beaurains, 17, 18.
Beauvais, 279.
Beeringen, 285, 295.
Belgian Brigade, 1st, 283.
Belgium, 9, 10, 259, 275, 281, 284, 286, 305.
Bell, Maj., 246.
Bemmel, 301.

317

Benghazi, 47, 110, 111, 112, 144, 146.
Bendy, Lt.-Col., 8, 30.
Bergues, 24.
Bernay, 232.
Bethune, 11.
Bevin, Mr. Ernest, 238.
Bickford, Lt.-Col. P., 42.
Billy Montigny, 7.
Bir Aslagh, 57, 58.
Bir Hacheim, 48, 50, 51, 54, 55, 56, 64, 65, 70, 72.
Bir Harmat, 49, 56, 57.
Bir Naghia, 50.
Bir Tengeder, 50.
Bir Temrad, 53, 54.
Bir Thalata, 48, 49, 74.
Birch, Lt.-Col. Gentry, 52.
Bitter Lake, 145.
Black, Lt., 41.
Blandford, 29.
Bois Robin, 277.
Bottaceto Ditch, 182, 196, 202, 203, 205.
Bransom, Maj. I., 57.
Bray Dunes, 25.
Brecy, 243, 244, 253.
Brewer, Maj. J., 60.
Brigades:
  Airborne, 178, 179.
  1st Armoured, 88.
  4th Armoured, 97, 178, 179, 180, 196, 200, 213, 214.
  8th Armoured, 235, 252, 253, 254, 255, 276.
  9th Armoured, 102.
  22nd Armoured, 256.
  5th Guards, 302.
  13th Infantry, 13.
  25th Infantry, 8, 10, 11, 22, 26, 28.
  56th Infantry, 235, 246, 256, 263, 264, 267.
  69th Infantry, 29, 41, 43, 44, 45, 54, 55, 56, 60, 63, 64, 66, 71, 73, 75, 85, 86, 87, 88, 90, 93, 94, 96, 97, 98, 99, 103, 104, 105, 106, 114, 115, 119, 122, 123, 124, 125, 127, 139, 145, 146, 147, 150, 159, 160, 161, 162, 164, 165, 166, 167, 168, 171, 172, 174, 178, 179, 180, 184, 185, 192, 193, 196, 199, 200, 205, 207, 211, 212, 213, 227, 228, 229, 235, 240, 242, 245, 256, 260, 262, 263, 264, 267, 269, 276, 285, 289, 295, 299, 300, 301, 302, 304.
  131st Infantry, 257, 300.
  150th Infantry, 8, 10, 11, 12, 13, 22, 23, 24, 25, 26, 28, 40, 41, 43, 44, 45, 48, 49, 50, 54, 55, 56, 57, 58, 59, 60, 61, 63, 85.
  151st Infantry, 8, 10, 11, 13, 22, 23, 24, 25, 26, 28, 41, 43, 44, 45, 54, 55, 56, 60, 63, 64, 66, 76, 85, 90, 92, 93, 94, 96, 98, 99, 106, 108, 109, 111, 114, 115, 116, 119, 121, 122, 124, 138, 139, 144, 145, 147, 149, 150, 156, 159, 164, 165, 167, 171, 172, 178, 179, 180, 183, 184, 187, 191, 195, 196, 203, 205, 210, 211, 220, 228, 235, 246, 253, 256, 261, 264, 267, 269, 271, 276, 283, 285, 289, 292, 293, 295, 298, 304, 305.
  168th Infantry, 139, 144, 145, 147, 151, 172, 180, 183, 193, 196, 198, 199, 200, 203, 205, 210, 211, 220.
  231st Infantry, 212, 218, 220, 228, 229, 235, 240, 245, 247, 248, 249, 254, 256, 261, 262, 264, 265, 267, 270, 276, 283, 285, 298, 304.
Brittany, 267.
Brooke, F.-M. Sir Alan, 23.
Brownrigg, Lt.-Col. C., 111.
Brussels, 9, 14, 275, 281, 283, 285, 305.
Buceels, 253.
Buerat, 110.
Bulscamp, 24.
Buq Buq, 75.
Burgh el Arab, 86.

Cachy, 279.
Caen, 232, 234, 251, 253, 266.
Cairns, Lt.-Col., 121.
Cairo, 75, 88, 89, 140, 141, 142, 143, 145, 151.
Calabernardo, 154, 155.
Calais, 19.
Caldwell, Lt.-Col., 49.
Cambrai, 13.
Cameron, Maj., 127.
Camphin, 22.
Canadian First Army, 264, 265, 272.
Canadian Corps, 267.
Canadian 1st Division, 219.
Canadian 3rd Division, 233.
Canicattini Bagni, 164, 165.
Capetown, 41.
Carlentini, 168, 172, 174, 178, 179, 180, 184.
Carvin, 22, 23.
Casey, Mr., 90.

INDEX

Cassibile, 143, 149, 159, 160, 161, 167.
Cassibile, River, 159.
Catanazaro, 219.
Catania, 143, 165, 167, 171, 182, 183, 190, 191, 194, 195, 197, 199, 202, 204, 205, 207, 208, 209, 210, 218, 220.
Catania, Plain of, 167, 171, 180, 193.
Caumont, 255, 256.
Centuripe, 205.
Chadacre, 228, 237.
Chambois, 272.
Chance, Lt.-Col. P. K., 111.
Chantoiseau, 277.
Chartres, 232.
Chatham, Cpl., 281.
Chaumont-en-Vixen, 276, 277.
Cherbourg, 7, 234, 251.
Cherbourg Peninsula, 266.
Cheshire Regt., 2nd Bn., 52, 57, 63, 85, 90, 112, 118, 127, 138, 150, 151, 175, 180, 187, 192, 200, 217, 240, 244, 252, 275, 280, 290, 291, 293, 294, 298, 301, 303, 305.
Chet Meskine, 114, 116, 117.
Christchurch, 30.
Churchill, Brig., 13, 17, 22, 23.
Churchill, Mr. Winston, 238.
Clapton, Maj., 257.
Clarke, Lt.-Col. A. B. S., 217.
Clay, Maj. E. W., 52.
Cleator, Sgt. 294.
Cojeul, River, 13.
Cole, Capt. F. L., 63.
Commandos:
  No. 2, 213.
  No. 3, 164, 172, 178, 185.
  No. 40 (Royal Marine), 210, 211.
  No. 47 (Royal Marine), 234, 245, 247, 248, 249.
Concert party, 45, 111.
Conde-sur-Noireau, 266, 267, 268, 269, 270, 271, 272.
Conty, 276.
Cooke-Collis, Brig. E. C., 24, 57, 59, 75, 86, 87, 88, 98, 105, 127, 139, 159, 169, 172, 174, 228.
Cooper, Lt.-Col. L., 52.
Corps:
  I, 9, 10, 11, 24, 25, 266.
  II, 8, 9, 10, 11, 23, 24.
  III, 22.
  VIII, 39, 266, 297.
  X, 78, 89, 90, 95, 99, 103, 106, 109, 110, 111, 125, 127, 137, 139.
  XII, 267, 273, 297.
  XIII, 57, 89, 90, 93, 95, 96, 97, 103, 104, 105, 109, 139, 142, 143, 145, 146, 147, 172, 174, 198, 219, 228.
  XXX, 80, 90, 95, 99, 109, 124, 142, 143, 161, 164, 167, 202, 205, 212, 213, 228, 235, 247, 260, 266, 271, 274, 276, 282, 297, 299, 305.
Cotentin Peninsula, 251.
Cotswolds, 6, 7.
Cotterill, Pte., 277.
Coulombs, 243, 244.
County of London Yeomanry:
  3rd, 127, 213.
  4th, 256, 257.
Cracruft, Brig., 252.
Crepon, 243, 244, 246.
Crete, 147, 195.
Creully, 243.
Cristot, 253.
Croissey, 280.
Cruewell, Gen., 59.
Cubitt, Lt.-Col. Hon. C. G., 144.
Cunningham, Gen. Sir A. G., 51.
Curry, Brig., 196, 214.
Cyprus, 41, 42, 43, 227.
Cyprus Regt., 42.
Cyrenaica, 47, 76.

Daba, 103.
Dainville, 16.
Davidson, Brig., 172, 184, 196, 197, 199.
Davis, Lt. S., 45, 111.
"Dead Horse Corner," 184.
Deir el Shein, 104.
Dempsey, Lt.-Gen. Sir M., 143, 160, 164, 172, 183, 191, 195, 202.
Dendre, River, 10, 11.
Dennis, Capt. B., 61.
Devonshire Regt., 2nd Bn., 214, 235, 246, 249, 264, 265, 270, 271, 280, 298.
Disputed Ridge, 58, 59.
Divers, Brig. S. T., 29, 62.
Divisions:
  3rd, 24, 25, 233, 251.
  5th, 10, 12, 13, 23, 24, 25, 143, 147, 150, 152, 154, 156, 158, 159, 160, 161, 164, 165, 167, 172, 174, 178, 180, 183, 184, 187, 200, 202, 206, 211, 219, 220.
  15th, 295.
  43rd, 266, 267, 269, 274, 297, 302, 303.

44th, 92, 93, 94, 95, 96, 97, 103, 104, 109, 139.
49th, 228, 260.
51st, 11, 95, 99, 115, 119, 123, 125, 126, 127, 143, 164, 173, 185, 206, 211.
56th, 139, 212, 220.
78th, 202.
1st Airborne, 297, 299.
1st Armoured, 54, 57.
7th Armoured, 54, 75, 86, 95, 96, 97, 98, 103, 124, 125, 137, 235, 252, 255, 256, 257, 266, 267, 269, 300.
11th Armoured, 274, 275, 276, 277, 283, 285.
79th Armoured, 229.
Guards Armoured, 274, 275, 280, 283, 297, 298, 299, 300, 301.
Divisional Headquarters, 7, 8, 10, 11, 16, 22, 23, 24, 40, 41, 55, 56, 59, 60, 61, 62, 69, 75, 78, 80, 85, 86, 106, 116, 118, 120, 121, 143, 144, 145, 146, 147, 150, 151, 153, 156, 157, 159, 160, 161, 164, 174, 183, 190, 195, 196, 198, 202, 219, 227, 228, 237, 283, 293, 300, 305.
Djerba, Isle of, 113.
Donking, Capt. I., 52.
Doornboom, 291.
Dorsetshire Regt., 1st Bn., 235, 246, 252, 253, 254, 265, 267, 270, 271, 298.
Doullens, 280.
Dowdeswell, Capt., 299.
Dragoon Guards:
4th/7th, 246, 253, 257, 261, 262.
5th, 300.
Duesburg, 297.
Duff, Lt., 197.
Duisans, 17, 18.
Dunkirk, 19, 24, 26.
Dunn, Maj., 257.
Dunn, Sgt., 102.
Dupre, Lt., 291.
Durban, 41.
Durham Light Infantry, 5, 53, 64, 195, 208, 289.
6th Bn., 16, 18, 19, 22, 23, 68, 100, 101, 102, 119, 122, 149, 154, 156, 159, 166, 167, 172, 173, 179, 190, 192, 193, 195, 196, 209, 220, 235, 246, 261, 263, 269, 271, 277, 291, 292, 293, 294.
8th Bn., 16, 17, 19, 22, 23, 66, 67, 100, 101, 117, 118, 122, 150, 156, 158, 159, 164, 168, 174, 179, 187, 188, 190, 191, 196, 220, 235, 253, 254, 257, 258, 269, 280, 290, 291, 292, 293, 294.
9th Bn., 9, 22, 23, 63, 67, 77, 97, 100, 101, 117, 118, 119, 122, 149, 155, 156, 158, 159, 178, 179, 182, 192, 193, 194, 195, 217, 220, 235, 261, 262, 271, 280, 292, 293, 294, 298.
Dyle, River, 9, 10.

East Anglia, 228.
East Yorkshire Regiment, 5.
4th Bn., 40, 49, 50, 53, 58, 59, 60.
5th Bn., 29, 66, 77, 86, 87, 88, 96, 98, 111, 114, 115, 119, 121, 122, 123, 126, 127, 130, 145, 160, 166, 167, 168, 170, 174, 178, 179, 184, 185, 214, 235, 240, 241, 242, 243, 262, 267, 269, 270, 287, 288, 289, 299, 301, 302, 303, 304.
Eastman, Brig. C., 111.
Eccles, 279.
Ederbach, Gen., 274.
Edgar, Maj., 98.
Egremont-en-Vexin, 277.
Egypt, 46, 89, 109, 139, 140, 142, 145, 162, 163, 212.
Eindhoven, 297, 298, 300.
El Adem, 109.
El Agheila, 49, 109, 110.
El Alamein, 41, 76, 80, 85, 89, 94, 99, 104, 106, 109, 111, 137, 139, 217, 267, 275, 303.
El Aqqaqir, 103.
Elverdinghe, 24.
Enfidaville, 137, 138, 139, 140, 146.
Errington, Col., 29.
Escaut Canal, 295, 298.
Escaut, River, 10, 11.
Escures, 249.
Esquay-sur-Seulles, 247.
Essex Regt., 2nd Bn., 235, 246, 263, 264.
Etna, Mount, 153, 167, 202, 205, 206, 211, 218.
Evans, Cpl., 277, 278, 279.
Everbecq, 10.
Everett, Col. M., 8, 30.
Evron, 7.
Exmoor, 39.

Fachri, 54.
Falaise, 232, 265, 266, 268, 269, 272, 274.

Index

Farmiloe, 2/Lt., 60.
Fatnassa Hills, 125.
Ferens, Maj. M., 68.
Feuguerolles-sur-Seulles, 267.
ffrench-Kinde, Lt. D. A., 155.
Field, Capt. D. E., 53.
FitzMaurice, Lt.-Col., 16.
Flers, 272.
Fleury, Mont, 241, 242, 244.
Floridia, 160, 161, 164, 165, 166, 167, 168, 171, 172.
Force "G," 229, 237, 238.
Forrester, Maj., 18.
Fort Maddalena, 65, 66, 72, 73.
Fouilloy, 277.
Fournes, 24.
Fowler, Brig., 89.
Fox, Maj. P., 59.
France, 6, 7, 259, 275, 281, 284.
Franklyn, Gen. Sir H. E., 12, 13, 14, 18, 19, 23, 39.
Free French, 50, 51, 54, 55, 56, 64, 95, 113.
Free French, 2nd Brigade, 88, 89, 90, 99, 103, 104, 105.
Freeman-Attwood, Maj.-Gen. H. A., 5, 8.
Freetown, 40.
French, 1st Light Mechanized Division, 12, 13.
Fuka, 78, 80.

Gabes, 114, 120, 124.
Gabr el Aleima, 53.
Galloway, Lt., 93.
Galloway, Maj., 154.
Galvin, Lt., 255.
Garet el Auda, 50.
Garet el Himeimat, 87.
Gaza, 145.
Gazala, 47, 48, 50, 51, 54, 61, 62, 67, 74, 78, 80, 111, 227, 228.
Gebel, 47.
Gela, 250.
German Seventh Army, 272, 273, 274.
German Divisions:
  164th, 100, 114.
  91st Infantry, 232.
  352nd Infantry, 232.
  716th Infantry, 231.
  Hermann Goering, 184, 204.
  90th Light, 56, 95, 100, 140.
  1st (S.S.) Panzer, 268.
  2nd Panzer, 232, 251, 256, 257, 267, 268.
  2nd (S.S.) Panzer, 268.
  12th (S.S.) Panzer, 232, 251, 255.
  15th Panzer, 56, 95.
  21st Panzer, 56, 95, 232, 251.
  115th Panzer, 174.
  268th Panzer, 268.
  17th (S.S.) Panzer Grenadier, 232, 251.
  130th Panzer Lehr, 232, 252, 255, 260, 261, 262.
  901st Panzer Lehr, 258.
  2nd Parachute, 289, 295.
German Regiments:
  904th Fortress, 195.
  3rd Parachute, 195.
  4th Parachute, 204.
Gheel, 285, 289, 292, 293, 295.
Giardini, 212.
Giarre, 210, 211.
Gibson, Col. J. T., 144.
Gibson, Capt., 28.
Gilmour, Lt. R. J., 161.
Gloucestershire Regt., 2nd Bn., 235.
Good, Capt. C., 60.
"Gooseberries," 234.
Gordon, Brig. D. S., 289, 290, 294.
Gordon Highlanders, 25.
Gornalunga, River, 193.
Gort, Lord, 10, 12, 23, 26.
Gott, Lt.-Gen., 57, 64.
Graham, Maj.-Gen. D. A. H., 228, 235, 237, 271, 305.
Graham, Col. R. M., 28.
Grave, 297, 298, 299.
Greek 1st Brigade, 88, 89, 93, 94, 95, 96, 97, 99, 103, 104, 105.
Green, Lt.-Col., 246.
Green Howards, 5, 209.
  4th Bn., 23, 40, 50, 51, 52, 58, 59, 60.
  5th Bn., 40, 50, 58, 59, 60, 61.
  6th Bn., 29, 57, 59, 86, 87, 88, 96, 98, 114, 115, 117, 127, 171, 174, 175, 176, 177, 179, 193, 214, 235, 240, 241, 243, 244, 269, 285, 286, 289, 301, 303.
  7th Bn., 29, 63, 86, 99, 114, 115, 116, 117, 126, 127, 128, 174, 175, 177, 178, 179, 185, 199, 200, 212, 213, 219, 235, 240, 243, 262, 269, 271, 285, 286, 287, 289, 301, 302, 303, 304.
Grigg, Sir James, 146.
Guards:
  201st Brigade, 50, 54, 61, 86, 138, 139.
  Grenadier, 24.
  Irish, 302.
  Welsh, 12.
Guides Cavalry, 88.

Hachana Ridge, 125.
Haifa, 44.
Halderen, 301, 304.
Halfaya Pass, 47.
Halfway House, 88, 89.
Hall, Brig. R., 111, 124.
Hampshire Regt., 1st Bn., 235, 245, 246, 249, 264, 265, 270, 271.
Hannah, 2/Lt., 254.
Harlow, Rev., 80.
Harrison, Maj. K. C., 170.
Hassett, Brig., 75.
Hastings, Lt.-Col., 241.
Hay, Capt. I., 200.
Haut Audrieu, 254.
Haydon, Brig. C. W., 8, 23, 24, 53, 54, 60, 61.
Herbert, Maj.-Gen. W. N., 6.
Herceaux, 10.
Herrin, 22.
Hersselt, 285, 289.
Het Punt, 286, 287, 288.
Heyland, Lt.-Col., 16, 17.
Hill, Brig., 124, 146.
Himeimat, 95.
H.M. The King, 6, 39.
Holland, 10, 285, 297, 298, 301, 305.
Hollis, C.S.M., V.C., 244, 245.
Holmes, Lt.-Col. L. G., 51.
Hopkins, Lt. 59.
Horrocks, Lt.-Gen. Sir B. G., 109, 271, 297.
Hottot, 255, 260, 261, 262, 264, 265, 275, 301.
Howell, 2/Lt. P. J., 52.
Howie, Lt.-Col., 265.
Hudson, Capt., 194.
Hussars:
  3rd, 42.
  8th, 300.
  13th/18th, 269, 271, 303.
Hutchinson, Lt.-Col., 285, 286.

Ierna, River, 164.
Ijssel, River, 297.
Indian Divisions:
  4th, 51, 95, 104, 123, 125, 126, 127, 137.
  5th, 44, 86.
  10th, 75, 76.
Indian Brigades:
  7th Infantry, 49, 88.
  21st Infantry, 86.
  26th Infantry, 88.
Innes, Lt.-Col. R. G. B., 91, 140, 144, 219.
Inverary, 229.
Iraq, 44, 45, 227.

Italian 31st Corps, 219.
Italian Divisions:
  Ariete, 56.
  Brescia, 106.
  Folgore, 92.
  Littoria, 100.
  Livorno, 181.
  Napoli, 164, 171, 172, 173.
  Trento, 100.
  Young Fascists, 114.
Italy, 219, 230.

Jackson, Maj. B., 59.
Jackson, Lt.-Col. M. L. P., 66, 118.
James, Lt.-Col. R. B., 111, 126, 167, 169, 170, 214, 267.
Jebb, Lt.-Col. D. G., 219.
Jebel Kalakh, 86, 87.
Jebel Meide, 125, 127.
Jebel Romana, 125, 127.
Jeffreys, Maj., 18.
Jouy-sous-Thelles, 276, 280.

Kabrit, 139, 144, 145, 146, 152.
Katsotos, Col., 93.
Keeling, Lt.-Col. S. V., 52.
Kendrick, Cpl., 176.
Kennard, Charles, 197.
Kennedy, Lt.-Col., 30, 42, 69.
King's Own Yorkshire Light Infantry, 154.
Kingsmill, H.M.S., 241.
Kirby, Maj., 247.
Kirk, Lt., 247.
Kirkby, Capt. P., 50.
Kirkman, Gen. Sir S. C., 128, 137, 139, 140, 142, 144, 147, 150, 152, 158, 159, 160, 162, 164, 165, 172, 174, 180, 183, 184, 190, 191, 196, 199, 211, 212, 218, 219, 220, 228.
Kirkuk, 44, 45.
Knightsbridge, 49, 54, 56, 57, 58, 61.
Knox, Brig. F. Y. L., 241, 244, 287, 303.
Knutsford, 27.
Kreyer, Brig., 8.
Ksiba Est, 114, 119.
Ksiba Ouest, 114, 116, 117, 118, 119, 122, 267.

La Belle Epine, 258, 260, 262, 264.
La Chappelle St. Ouen, 276.
La Panne, 25.
La Riviere, 232, 234, 235, 238, 240, 241, 242.
Lamb, Sgt., 281.
Lance, Lt.-Col., 98.

Index

Lancers:
  12th, 12.
  24th, 255, 258.
Laval, 232.
Lawrence, Lt., 93.
Le Bas, 281.
Le Bosquel, 280.
Le Hamel, 232, 234, 235, 245, 248, 249.
Le Mans, 7, 232, 266.
Le Plessis Grimoult. 269, 271.
Le Senaudiere, 264.
Leese, Lt.-Gen. Sir Oliver, 212.
Lens, 7.
Lentini, 165, 167, 168, 172, 174, 175, 178, 179, 180, 183, 184, 185, 192, 193, 218.
Leonardello, 210.
Leonardo Bridge, 175, 178, 179.
Leonardo River, 167, 172, 184.
Leybourne, Maj., 254.
Libya, 46.
Lidwell, Lt.-Col. R. B., 118, 156, 189.
Lille, 9.
Lindrea, Capt., 92.
Lindsay, Maj., 66.
Lingevres, 261, 262.
Linguaglossa, 212.
Littleboy, Lt.-Col. C. N., 23, 52.
Liverpool, 40.
Loire, 232, 251.
Lokeren, 282.
London Irish Rifles, 1st Bn., 193, 198, 199, 210.
London Scottish, 1st Bn., 193, 195, 197, 198, 211.
Longraye, 262.
Longues, 245, 246, 249.
Loos, 8, 11, 22.
Lowe, Lt., 171.
Lyme Regis, 30.
Lyne, Maj.-Gen., 305.

Maas, River, 297, 298, 299.
Macchia, 211.
Macchia, River, 210.
McCracken, Maj., 29.
Maison Triolet, 114.
Malines, 281.
Malo Les Baines, 26.
Malta, 52, 80, 212.
Mammeledi, River, 149, 154, 155, 159.
Mangano, River, 210.
Manvieux, 245.
Marble Arch, 110.
Mareopolis, 80, 85.

Mareth, 110, 111, 112, 113, 114, 118, 123, 124, 128, 267.
"Market Garden," 285, 297, 299, 301.
Martel, Lt.-Gen. Sir G. Le Q., 6, 7, 9, 10, 12, 13, 14, 16, 17, 18, 20. 22, 23, 27, 30.
Martin, Maj., 280, 281.
Martuba, 53.
Mascali, 210.
Mascarello Ridge, 211.
Massy, Brig., 9, 10, 27, 28.
Matmata Hills, 112, 122, 123.
Mattock, C.S.M. T., 67.
Medenine, 112, 113, 114, 124.
Melilli, 172, 180, 183.
Mellor, Maj., 277, 278, 279, 281.
Melvin, Col., 111.
Mena, 41.
Mersa Matruh, 48, 74, 75, 76, 78, 106, 109.
Messina, 143, 145, 205, 212, 214, 216, 217, 218, 219.
Meuvaines Ridge, 232, 243, 246.
Mezan, Capt. P., 113.
Miller, Lt.-Col., 16.
Mitchell, Maj., 30.
Mitchell, Capt. A. P., 58.
Montgomery, F.-M. Viscount, 90, 94, 95, 123, 137, 138, 142, 146, 172, 174, 191, 202, 218, 219, 233, 305.
Morrison, Col., 111.
Mortain, 268.
Moss, Lt. E. H. St. G., 70.
Mount, Lt., 255.
M'Rassus, 68.
Msus, 110.
"Mulberry," 234, 245.
Munassib Depression, 92, 93, 95, 96, 97.

Naqb el Khadin, 87.
Newcombe, Rev. R. T., 8.
New Forest, 229, 237.
New Zealand Division, 49, 90, 92, 95, 99, 100, 112, 122, 123, 124, 125, 137, 138, 139.
Nichols, Maj.-Gen. J. S., 53, 85, 86, 88, 89, 90, 98, 104, 105, 118, 122, 124, 125, 127, 128, 137.
Nicosia, 42.
Nijmegen, 285, 297, 298, 299, 300, 301, 302, 304, 305.
Ninuve, 10, 281.
Norman, Lt.-Col., 49, 53.
Normandy, 229, 239, 245, 248, 258, 260, 266, 268, 269, 305.

Northumberland Hussars (102 Anti-Tank Regt.), 90, 93, 99, 109, 112, 150, 151, 157, 200, 218, 258, 294.
Norton, Brig. C. H., 146, 151, 183, 197, 207.
Noto, 143, 149, 155, 159, 160, 161, 164.
Noto, River, 154.
Nunspeet, 297.

O'Carroll, Brig., 57.
Olivier, Lt.-Col. C., 85, 91.
Orne, River, 251, 268, 269.
Osborne, Maj. M. A. C., 144.
Oudenarde, 282.
Ouerzi, 114, 116, 118, 121.
Ouerzi Est, 114, 119, 121.
Ouerzi Ouest, 114, 116, 119, 121.
Ouidane el Hachana, 127.
"Overlord," 230, 232, 233, 235, 239, 251, 252.
Owen, Capt., 168.
Owen, Cpl., 294.

Pachino, 143.
Pael, 295.
Page, R.S.M., 101.
Palazzolo Acreide, 149, 164, 165, 166, 167, 173.
Palestine, 44.
Palermo, 214.
Pancali, Mount, 174, 175, 193.
Parbury, Maj. P., 66.
Paris, 274.
Parker, Maj., 89, 242.
Pearson, Lt.-Col., 187, 188.
Pecq, 10.
Penwell, Capt., 168.
Percy, Brig., 67, 68, 69, 108.
Petre, Maj.-Gen., 12.
Piedimonte, 212.
Pincon, Mont, 268, 269, 272.
Pintigny, 280.
Plan "D," 9.
Point 103, 253, 254, 255, 256, 257, 258.
Point 140, 252.
Point 158, 252.
Point 213, 252, 256, 257.
Point 229, 269, 270.
Point 249, 271.
Point 262, 271.
Point 266, 269.
Pont St. Metz, 277, 280.
Poperinghe, 23, 24.
Porgini, Gen., 172, 173.

Port-en-Bessin, 231, 234, 235, 245, 247, 248, 249, 251.
Port Said, 147, 152.
Port Tewfik, 41.
Pratt, Brig., 16.
Priestman, Maj., 28.
Primosole Bridge, 167, 172, 178, 179, 180, 182, 184, 193, 202, 203, 204, 218, 220, 289.
Priolo, 165.
Proussy, 269.
Provin, 22, 23.
Punta Giorgi, 154.

Qattara Depression, 89, 95.
Queen's Regt.:
  1st/5th Bn., 257, 300.
  1st/7th Bn., 257, 300.
Que-vau-Villiers, 7.

Raches, 11.
Rahman Track, 99, 102, 104, 105.
Ramsden, Capt., 301.
Ramsden, Maj.-Gen. W. H. C., 28, 39, 40, 42, 49, 64, 70, 77, 78, 79, 80.
Ras el Eleba, 53.
Rash, Lt.-Col. E. D., 144.
Reconnaissance Regt.:
  44th Bn., 109.
  52nd Bn., 300.
  61st Bn., 252, 256, 282, 290, 291, 300.
Red Sea, 41.
Reggio, 219.
Regina, 110.
Reichswald, 298.
Renaix, 281.
Renton, Maj.-Gen., 88.
Rhine, River, 274, 297, 299, 301, 302, 304.
Rhodes, 147.
Richardson, Lt.-Col., 243.
Riposto, 205, 210, 211, 212, 218, 221.
Ritchie, Brig., 25.
Robinson, Pte. A., 66.
Rommel, Gen., 19, 41, 49, 55, 56, 61, 89, 90, 92, 112, 230.
Rotunda Segnali, 54.
Royal Air Force, 204, 229, 233, 238, 241, 245, 251, 261, 266, 267.
Royal Army Medical Corps, 29, 218.
  140th Fd. Amb., 139, 151, 220.
  149th Fd. Amb., 29, 61, 99, 150.
  150th Fd. Amb., 23, 29, 40, 61.

Index

168th Fd. Amb., 252.
186th Fd. Amb., 29, 61, 151.
Royal Army Service Corps, 5, 25, 29, 61, 165.
Royal Artillery, 5, 25, 28, 85, 89, 100, 125, 138, 200, 210, 211, 214, 219, 266.
  7th Med. Regt., 54.
  24th Fd. Regt., 180, 182, 183.
  55th Fd. Regt., 301, 302.
  65th Fd. Regt., 109, 139.
  72nd Fd. Regt., 23, 28, 40, 49, 50, 60.
  74th Fd. Regt., 42, 116, 151, 183.
  86th Fd. Regt., 239, 244, 299.
  90th Fd. Regt., 139, 151, 177, 183, 246, 271.
  92nd Fd. Regt., 183.
  98th Fd. Regt., 144, 150, 155, 172, 173, 175, 180, 182, 183.
  124th Fd. Regt., 57, 93, 150, 172, 175, 180, 181, 183, 184, 287, 288, 299, 301, 302, 303.
  147th Fd. Regt., 248, 252.
  102nd A/Tk. Regt.—*see Northumberland Hussars.*
  107th A/Tk. Regt., 150.
  25th L.A.A. Regt., 60, 90, 93, 109, 111, 151, 162, 218.
  3rd Survey Regt., 150.
Royal Berkshire Regt., 10th Bn., 193, 211, 212.
Royal Corps of Signals, 9, 29, 69, 218, 305.
Royal Electrical and Mechanical Engineers, 161, 166.
Royal Engineers, 11, 28, 30, 50, 86, 100, 102, 103, 111, 114, 116, 118, 189, 206, 218, 252.
  232nd Fd. Coy., 23, 40, 58, 59, 75.
  233rd Fd. Coy., 86, 93, 150.
  295th Fd. Coy., 139, 213.
  501st Fd. Coy., 151.
  505th Fd. Coy., 90, 99, 150.
  235th Fd. Pk. Coy., 151.
Royal Navy, 141, 162, 212, 213, 216, 229, 230, 238, 251, 264.
Royal Northumberland Fusiliers:
  2nd Bn., 24.
  4th Bn., 5, 9, 10, 49.
Royal Tank Regt.:
  4th Bn., 14, 16, 18.
  7th Bn., 14, 16, 17.
  8th Bn., 100.
  42nd Bn., 57.
  44th Bn., 57, 58, 144, 151, 173.
  50th Bn., 114, 118, 120, 121, 122.
Royals, 50, 144, 151, 193, 196, 300.
Russia, 195.

Ruweisat Ridge, 80, 85, 86, 92, 93, 95, 104.
Ryes, 245, 246.

St. Aubin-en-Bray, 280.
St. Gabriel, 243, 244.
St. Leger, 234, 235, 244, 247.
St. Oedenrode, 298, 299, 300.
St. Pierre la Vieille, 269, 270, 271, 258.
St. Pierre la Vielle, 269, 270, 271.
St Pierre-sur-Dives, 272.
St. Pol, 14.
Saloued, 277.
San Alessio, Cape, 212.
Sardinia, 147.
Saxmundham, 229.
Scarpe, River, 12, 13.
Schelde, 281.
Schindel, 300.
Schiso, Cape, 212.
Scordia, 184.
Scriven, Lt.-Col., 61.
Seagrim, Lt.-Col., V.C., 99, 115, 116, 126, 128.
Sebket el Hamma, 124.
Seclin, 8.
Seine, River, 230, 251, 256, 268, 274.
Senior, Brig. R., 124, 139, 153, 159, 179, 183, 190, 191, 192, 195, 200, 246.
Sensee, River, 13, 18.
Seulles, River, 243, 253, 254, 260, 262.
Sheferzen, 72.
Sheffield, Lt.-Col., 29.
Sherwood Foresters, 1st Bn., 42.
Sherwood Rangers, 246, 253, 265, 292, 293.
Sicily, 139, 141, 142, 145, 146, 147, 148, 152, 179, 212, 217, 219, 220, 227, 229, 230, 250, 275, 284, 289.
Sidi Barrani, 74, 76.
Sidi Bregisc, 52, 54.
Sidi el Rahman, 99.
Simeto Bridgehead, 200.
Simeto River, 167, 172, 179, 182, 190, 193, 201, 203.
Sirte, 110, 111.
Siwa, 106.
Slight, Maj. J. C., 67, 68, 69.
Sliuk-Ewick, 305.
Smith, Lt., 289.
Smith, Capt. P. S., R.N., 144, 152.
Smuts, F.-M., 238.
Solarino, 165, 166, 167, 168, 171, 172, 173.
Solent, 238.

Sollum, 47.
Somerset, 39.
Somme, 11, 274, 277, 280.
Sortino, 165, 166, 167, 168, 169, 171, 172, 174, 175, 178.
Sousse, 128, 137.
South African Armoured Cars, 57.
South African Divisions:
　1st, 51, 54, 56, 64, 65, 95.
　2nd, 54, 55.
South Wales Borderers, 2nd Bn., 235.
Southampton, 237, 238.
Spiers, Lt.-Col., 29.
Stansfield, Lt.-Col. G., 77.
Steele, Lt.-Col., 80.
"Stink Alley," 182.
Studland Bay, 229.
Sudbury, 228.
Suez, 41, 144, 145, 146, 147, 152.
Suez Canal, 75, 139, 147.
Syracuse, 143, 153, 159, 161, 164, 167, 172, 183.
Syria, 45, 145.

Takruna, 139.
Taormina, 205, 212, 218, 219, 220.
Taqa Plateau, 86, 87.
Tarlton, Brig., 220.
Tebaga Fatnassa, 126, 127.
Teggin, Capt. W. W., 293.
Tel el Eisa, 99, 100.
Templeuve, 281.
"The Bastion," 114, 116, 117, 119, 128.
"The Cape," 96, 97, 98.
"The Cauldron," 56, 59, 63.
"The Island," 285, 304, 305.
"The Kennels," 74.
"The Moor," 96, 97, 98.
"The Pimple," 126, 127.
"The Thugs," 114, 116.
Thetford, 228.
Thomlinson, Maj., 247.
Thompson, Lt.-Col., 29.
Tilly-sur-Seulles, 253, 254, 255, 256, 257, 258, 260, 261, 262, 263, 264, 275.
Tmimi, 51, 53.
Tobruk, 48, 55, 56, 58, 62, 64, 68, 69, 75, 109, 110.
Tournai, 281.
Tracy Bocage, 252, 267.
Tracy-sur-Mer, 245.
Transjordan, 44.
Trigh Capuzzo, 54, 55, 56, 58, 59.
Trigh el Abo, 58.
Tripoli, 110, 111, 144, 145, 146, 152.
Tripolitania, 112.

Trun, 272.
TT Sign, 5, 275.
Tunisia, 110, 111, 112, 113, 125, 127, 137, 140, 145, 163, 212, 275.
Turton, Lt.-Col. R. H., 30, 62.
Two Rivers, 45.

Ualeb, 54, 55.
Uden, 299, 300.
Urquhart, Maj.-Gen., 220.
Urton, Lt.-Col. W. H. L., 79.
U.S. First Army, 233, 264, 266.
U.S. Army Air Force, 241, 266.
U.S. Divisions:
　82nd Airborne, 297.
　101st Airborne, 297, 299, 300.
　1st Infantry, 248, 256.

V.Cs., 76, 77, 128, 130, 244, 245.
Valkenswaard, 298.
Veghel, 297, 298, 299, 300.
Ver-sur-Mer, 240, 243, 246.
Verneuil, 232.
Vernon, 274, 276.
Verrieres, 261, 262.
Villers Bocage, 252, 253, 255, 256, 257, 258, 267, 268, 276.
Villiers-le-Sec, 243, 247.
Vimy, 12, 16.
Vire, 266, 269, 272.

Waal, River, 297, 298, 300, 301, 302, 304.
Wadi Akarit, 116, 124, 125, 126, 128, 130.
Wadi Zigzaou, 112, 113, 115, 116, 118, 119, 122, 123.
Waggutt, Lt., 255.
Wakenshaw, Pte. Adam, V.C., 76, 77.
Walton, Capt. H. E., 155.
Ward, Maj.-Gen., 220.
Warlus, 17, 18.
Warspite, 264.
Watney, Lt., 115.
Watson, Lt., 282.
Watson, Capt. P. B., 60.
Watson, Lt.-Col. W. I., 156.
Wattines Farm, 281.
Wavrin, 8.
Welch Regt., 1st Bn., 144.
Western Desert, 41, 45.
Western Desert Force, 43.
Westminster, 230.
Weymouth, 229.
Wheatley, Capt., 254.
Wheeler, Col. R. H. L., 51, 80.
White, Lt.-Col., 241, 243.
Wigram, Maj., 189.

Wilde, C.S.M., 277, 281.
Wiltshire Regt., 2nd Bn., 166, 167.
Wood, Capt., 288.
Wood, Lt., 293.
Wood, Lt.-Col. G. L., 155, 246.
Woods, Sergt., 290.
Worrall, Maj. E. W. H., 101, 117, 155.

York Minster, 306.
Yorkshire, 306.
Ypres, 23, 24.

Zarat, 114, 119, 120, 121, 124, 127.
Zarat Sudest, 114.
Zon, 297, 298.
Zuyder Zee, 297.